Rites of Passage

RITES
OF
PASSAGE

Adolescence in America

1790 to the Present

JOSEPH F. KETT

Basic Books, Inc., Publishers   *New York*

Library of Congress Cataloging in Publication Data

Kett, Joseph F
    Rites of passage

    Includes bibliographical references and index.
    1. Youth—United States—History. 2. Adoles-
cence. 3. United States—Social conditions. I. Ti-
tle.
HQ796.K397   301.43'15'0973   76-43465
ISBN: 0-465-07043-4 (cloth)
ISBN: 0-465-07044-2 (paper)

TO ELEANOR

CONTENTS

Contents

PART TWO

Toward the Age of Adolescence, 1840–1900

PART THREE

The Era of Adolescence, 1900–Present

Contents

ACKNOWLEDGMENTS

I WELCOME this opportunity to thank several people and organizations for assistance on this book. John R. Gillis and H. C. Erik Midelfort provided both extremely valuable criticisms of the first draft and provocative insights in conversation. Discussions with John Demos and Tamara K. Hareven helped me to clarify my objectives during the early stages of preparing this book. I am also indebted to Robert D. Cross, John Israel, and Peter R. Knights for criticism of later drafts. Michael G. Kammen vacuumed the penultimate version for pieces of chipped logic and dusty prose. At a critical juncture, Paul D. Neuthaler of Basic Books gave me good advice. In addition, financial support from the National Endowment for the Humanities and from Harvard University's Charles Warren Center enabled me to spend a year at the latter institution, where I benefited from the continued friendship and scholarly criticism of Donald Fleming. The University of Virginia provided more summer faculty fellowships than I had a reasonable right to expect. Finally, several graduate students at the University of Virginia, including Joan I. Brumberg, George Curtis, John Kneebone, Suzanne D. Lebsock, John Schlotterbeck, Charles J. Young, and Jamil Zainaldin, contributed insights that I have not been able to acknowledge adequately in the footnotes.

Rites of Passage

Introduction

THOSE who measure the success of revolutions by their completeness will judge the revolution which has overtaken American young people in recent decades to be one of the most successful. Compared to their predecessors in 1800 or 1900, young people in the 1970s spend much more time in school, much less at work. They are essentially consumers rather than producers. Their contacts with adults are likely to occur in highly controlled environments such as the classroom, and the adults encountered are usually conveyors of specialized services such as education and guidance. For the most part, young people in the 1970s spend their time in the company of other young people. This pattern of age segregation frequently prevails even when the young people hold jobs. Only in television commercials are the employees of short-order food chains likely to be over 21; in the real world, they are usually teenagers.

To observe that youth today are primarily consumers rather than producers is not to deny their economic importance. Indirectly, young people sustain a wide range of service occupations: teachers, guidance counselors, adolescent psychologists, market research analysts, printers, clothiers, disc jockeys, even policemen and judges. But the economic and social relationship between youth and adults has clearly changed. Further, the change has been abrupt as well as profound. Its roots can be traced back to the late 19th century, when industrialization began to displace young workers, but only since 1945 have vast

3

Introduction

numbers of American youth experienced the mixture of leisure, affluence, and education that now distinguishes their social position.

Why, then, begin a history of American youth in 1790? Why begin
in the late 18th century if the process that displaced young people from
most occupations did not start until the late 19th century and has only
culminated in recent decades? There are several reasons. First, the distinctive position of youth in our society inevitably spurs judgments and
evaluations, which require historical perspective. It is valuable to recognize, for example, that youth has long been viewed as a problematic
time of life, and that innumerable precedents exist for the process, familiar to us, by which small groups of influential adults single out the
experiences of small groups of young people and pronounce those experiences as archetypical, uniquely important, and harbingers of all future
tendencies. At any period, these judgments have tended to say more
about adults than about young people, yet often such judgments have
become the basis for the ideas and institutions that subsequently govern the relations between youth and adults. Put differently, the social
perception of youth—the way in which adults publicly define and debate the rising generation—has never encompassed the polymorphism
that usually has characterized the social experience of young people.
Further, those who engage in public debates and discussions about
youth have usually had their own distinctive characteristics and preoc-
cupations. In many ways, these are as untypical as the traits of the
young people on whom they focus. My aim, then, is to provide historical perspective on the biases and distortions that inevitably enter into
society's response to youth.

Second, taking the long view will help us to sort out and assess the
various factors that have shaped both the social experience and society's perception of young people. For example, it became fashionable
during the 1960s for conservatives to blame campus upheavals on the
decay of family discipline. During the same decade, liberals were inclined to argue that the "accelerated pace of social change" and "growing complexity of life" accounted for the problematic nature of youth in
our time. To my mind, neither judgment survives close examination.
What strikes most historians about the family in the past is less its
strength than its fragility, its vulnerability to disruption by depression,
disease, and mortality. Family discipline in our society may be weak,
but it is not obviously decaying. With respect to the liberal explanation,
it is worth remembering that every generation of intellectuals since 1820
has been convinced that an acceleration of the velocity of social change
has disrupted traditional harmony and has had a calamitous effect on
youth.

While discrediting some interpretations, historical perspective underscores others. It sensitizes us, for example, to the role of demographic changes, which often move with glacial slowness and whose implications become clear only over the long course. Demographic factors establish the perimeters of the field on which the generations meet. For example, the aging of society, signified by the doubling of the median age of the American population during the last two centuries, has altered the relationships between young people and adults in sundry ways. In the 1970s the age structure of society roughly resembles a rectangle; in the past it was more like a pyramid because of the sharp contractions in successive age layers. For a young person verging on adulthood, it makes a crucial difference whether young people represent a small majority or the vast majority of society as a whole. Some of the most significant changes in families, schools, and youth institutions have also been demographic in origin. Not only are families smaller than in the past, but the age range between siblings is narrower. Similarly, during the 19th century, loosely structured academies containing young people between the ages of 10 and 25 gave way to educational institutions that exclusively served teenagers; during the same period, voluntary associations for youth between the ages of 10 and 25 were replaced by adult-sponsored institutions for teenagers. One reason why psychologists in the early 1900s equated adolescence with the teen years rather than with the much broader age range traditionally signified by the term "youth" was the growing age segregation of teenagers.

The third reason for beginning at the end of the 18th century is that, from the perspective of 1790, changes since 1945 constitute only one of a number of critical transitions for young people in America. The first of these, between 1790 and 1840, was reflected in the uprooting of young people from agriculture, their migration to cities, a dramatic rise in the degree of occupational and intellectual choice available to youth, and the increasing disorderliness and violence that marked their educational and social institutions. In one form or another, this revolution occupies a central position in the first four chapters of this study. Inasmuch as these chapters also seek to convey my impression of the direction of change between 1650 and 1790, they are transitional as well as introductory. A second critical period, best dated 1880 to 1900, witnessed a radical differentiation of the economic opportunities available to middle-class and lower-class young people. During these decades middle-class parents were forced to adopt new strategies to guarantee the satisfactory placement of their children in occupations, strategies which emphasized the young people's passivity and acquiescence. These strategies, their antecedents, and their institutional implications form the subject of Chapters 6 and 7.

Between 1890 and 1920 a host of psychologists, urban reformers,

Introduction

educators, youth workers, and parent counselors gave shape to the concept of adolescence, leading to the massive reclassification of young people as adolescents. During these critical decades young people, particularly teenage boys, ceased to be viewed as troublesome, rash, and heedless, the qualities traditionally associated with youth; instead, they increasingly were viewed as vulnerable, passive, and awkward, qualities that previously had been associated only with girls. A consensus developed among small but influential groups that young people stood less in need of earnest advice than of the artful manipulation of their environment.

The pioneering book of adolescent psychology was G. Stanley Hall's two-volume *Adolescence*, published in 1904. *Adolescence* was a feverish, recondite, and at times incomprehensible book, the flawed achievement of eccentric genius. Yet in its day it had an undeniable impact on educators and social workers, men and women who responded enthusiastically to Hall's conception of adolescence as a stage of life distinctive for aesthetic sensibility and inner turmoil, and who used Hall's viewpoint to justify the establishment of adult-sponsored institutions which segregated young people from casual contacts with adults. If Hall enunciated adolescence, they constructed it.

The eager response of these educators and social workers to Hall's work was anomalous, for *Adolescence* was filled with rhapsodic passages and sesquipedalian words which gave it the aspect of a forbidden temple, while the architects of adolescence themselves were usually unimposing people with prudish morals and flat imaginations. They did not even contain in their number an astonishing curiosity like General Robert Baden-Powell, the founder of the British Boy Scouts, whose outlandish intellectual eccentricities partly compensated for his bleary social vision. One of the most discouraging aspects of working in the field of adolescence, I found, was the fact, significant in itself, that the answers to the most basic questions lie in the compost heap of American cultural life in the 1890s and early 1900s rather than in the mature fruits of creativity. Yet, despite the limitations of the architects of adolescence, both their ideas and the institutions they built played a major role in defining American society's official posture toward youth during the next fifty years.

Chapter 8 not only describes and assesses the significance of the concept of adolescence but also seeks to explore its cultural constituents. Along with most historians of the family, I believe that the concept of adolescence was conditioned by social forces, that it reflected the demographic and industrial conditions of the late 19th and early 20th centuries. I depart from others, however, by insisting that moral values which often masqueraded as psychological laws were at the root of the

6

concept, and that these moral values grew out of a particular cultural heritage. The concept of adolescence did not develop as a mere by-product of the later stages of industrialization but was an expression of distinctive values relating to children and the family that originated in America as early as the 1830s.

In this and other chapters readers will note some chronological overlap. In truth, the degree of overlap in the text understates the degree of overlap in social experience. In the final chapter I note that age groupings pervasive in America two centuries ago survive in parts of the nation today. A more serious heuristic difficulty is the fact that everyone was young once. About whom does one write? I have derived some aid from the fact that at any given period Americans who have written about youth have worn blinders. Whether in 1800 or 1850 or 1900 or 1975 they have focused on certain types of young people whose experiences they thought were especially significant. I have fastened on a similar pair of blinders in this study by seeking to trace the connection between past discussions of youth and past experiences of youth. In effect, I have sought to locate the kind of young person about whom people were talking and to understand the relationship between perception and experience at different points in time. This principle of selection has created some inevitable biases in the attention accorded to different social groups. At most periods, for example, and particularly in the three decades after 1890, social comment focused more on young men than on young women. In subordinating the experiences of female youth, and for that matter of black and immigrant youth of both sexes, to that of native-born white male youth, my intention is not to slight the significance of these others' experiences. Rather, I am merely reflecting the direction of social commentators in different periods who usually focused on white male young people living in settled areas. For this bias, then, I will accept responsibility rather than blame. For other biases or deficiencies, I accept both responsibility and censure.

PART ONE

———

Youth in the Early Republic, 1790–1840

CHAPTER 1

The Stages of Life

The Language of Age

IN preindustrial America the language of age had a nebulous quality. The term "infancy," for example, did not refer to suckling babes but to the years of maternal control over the child. Infant schools, popular in the 1820s and 1830s, accepted those from 18 months to 6 years of age. "Childhood" also had a broad connotation, often applying to anyone under 18 or even 21. A revivalist in the 1790s remarked that "young children" aged 7 to 16 had shown signs of religious change. An educator declared in 1819 that the Pestalozzian system of education was best suited to "young children" between the ages of 6 and 16. Isaac Ray, the psychologist, described the period between 6 and 13 as "the first few years of childhood." Words like "youth," "young people," and "young men" had a similarly broad extension. Alvan Hyde still described himself as a youth at the age of 24. William Gilmore Simms, in his biography of Nathanael Greene, extended his subject's wild and heady youth up to Greene's marriage at the age of 32, although Greene had been elected to the Rhode Island general assembly while still in his 20s. Cotton Mather distinguished only three age groups: children, young men, and old men.[1]

Expressions of age were not only broad but also interchangeable. In some of his sermons Cotton Mather equated "young people" with "children," in others with "young men." John Comly related that during the winter of 1780 he had often been carried to school "by a large boy, or young man, who lived with my father." Perhaps Comly's indifference to more precise terminology reflected his own education, for his approved reading prior to his 11th birthday was a magazine called *The Young Man's Companion*. Confusion about age and levels of psychological development also applied to the content of children's literature. An issue of *Every Youth's Gazette* in 1842 contained a pedantic lecture on the role of the affections in learning followed by the story of Little Red Riding Hood.[2]

This nebulous language of age might suggest that contemporaries, while able to distinguish a 7-year-old and a 17-year-old, viewed such differences as unimportant and, as a corollary, were unfamiliar with any distinctive experiences that would mark youth as an intermediate stage of development between childhood and adulthood. In this view, "youth" was merely a word, interchangeable with other words, to describe the growing child. Yet such a conclusion would be misleading for several reasons.

Although contemporaries did not consistently assign a specific age range to youth, they often made distinctions between age groups. In 17th-century Massachusetts, for example, boys aged 7 and over were separated from those younger by a variety of methods, including a prohibition against sleeping with their sisters and female servants, while special provisions existed for the military instruction of boys aged 10 to 16. In these cases, consistent verbal distinctions between childhood and youth did not accompany practical distinctions between age groups. In other cases, those who made clear verbal and conceptual distinctions between childhood and youth did not specify the age range appropriate to each. Without mentioning chronological age, David Barnes devoted part of his 1796 address to the trustees of Derby Academy to the importance of adjusting subject matter and instructional methods to the different needs of children and youth.[3] In still other cases, verbal distinctions harmonized with distinctions between age groups. Describing the age and sex distribution of converts in the religious revivals of the 1790s and early 1800s, ministers consistently distinguished between children and "young people," usually equating the latter with the age group between 12 and 22 or 23.[4] Moralists, in addition, often spoke of a "critical" period of youth between the ages of 14 and 21 (or, at times, 25).[5] Just as distinctions between children and youth were drawn, so too were they made between youth and adults. For penal purposes Roman law distinguished not only *infantia* (birth to 6) and *pueritia* (7 to 13) but also *pubertas* (14 to 20) and adulthood. In addition, the common law principle *malitia supplet aetatem* (in effect, malicious intent is more important than age) gave juries both in Britain and America an element of discretion in dealing with teenage offenders.[6]

Inasmuch as distinctions between children, youths, and adults were made, what did the often slack quality of the language of age signify? In part, it reflected the fact that many people in preindustrial society did not know their own exact age, much less those of acquaintances, friends, and relatives. In agricultural communities physical size, and hence capacity for work, was more important than chronological age, a fact which explains the popularity of terms like "large boy" or "great boy." During the Revolutionary War a committee declined to administer an oath of allegiance to William Akerly, "being a Lad of about fifteen years of age." Increase Mather, as well educated as any Puritan minister, precisely stated his brother's age at death, but his statement was off by three years.[7] In part, a loose vocabulary of age underscored the broad range of ages in most peer groups and institutions. Late 18th-century colleges, for example, often included young men of 25 as well as boys of 14, a fact which discouraged precision in the language of age without altering the status of the college as an institution for "youth." Finally, the vocabulary of age reflected an underlying indefiniteness in the timing of life experiences. In the absence of set ages for leaving home or going to school or starting out in a profession or vocation, terms designated different statuses which individuals passed into and out of at varying times. "Young people," for example, signified a village cohort. In the 1740s, Ebenezer Parkman, a Massachusetts minister, recorded in his diary that he "warmly inveighed against the Libertys allowed to Young People." [8] As late as the 1890s the same term appeared in the titles of various adult-sponsored institutions for youth, such as the Young People's Society for Christian Endeavor. In the early 19th century "youth" increasingly connoted independent status away from home. A 17-year-old who still followed the plow was a "large boy" at work and a "young person" at play, but a 14-year-old who had gone off to an urban countinghouse was a "youth" or "young man" (terms often used interchangeably).

The overlap of terms is revealing and important in itself, but also frustrating for the historian who seeks to describe patterns of experience among young people in the past. Any attempt to get beyond an enumeration of curious happenings runs into the problem of radical divergence between and among individuals. What "patterns" were there in the life of a John Levy, born in the West Indies in 1797, who was bound out as a carpenter's apprentice, became a sailor, was robbed by pirates, was impressed into the British Navy, and then deserted, went into business for himself selling crockery on the Isle of Man, and finally made his way to Boston, all before the age of 20? Where does one fit William Otter, born in Yorkshire in 1789, who by age 16 had run away from home after a brutal beating by his father, signed onto a merchant ship going to Greenland, been shipwrecked, been impressed into the British Navy, deserted, returned home to find that his parents had gone to America, and smuggled himself to New York on an American merchant ship, finally becoming an apprentice? [9]

Perhaps such instances were exceptions, but exceptions to what? And why need they have been so exceptional? Shipwrecks were not unusual, and impressment was a time-honored practice of the British Navy. Boys often ran away from home after quarrels with their parents; those who did would have little way of knowing whether their parents would still be there on return. Early 19th-century society could exert about as much control over the comings and goings of young people as over epidemics or business cycles—which is to say, not much. Just as the age grading of the experiences of young people in our society makes it possible to apply horizontal concepts such as adolescence to, say, all 14-year-olds, radical differences among youth in the past render numerical age a poor guide to stages of development. Rather, it is preferable to begin with the types of status—dependency, semidependency, and independence—which different individuals passed through at varying ages. These terms did not correspond to our own stages of development, such as childhood, adolescence, and adulthood. Dependency in the early 19th century was briefer than our own period of childhood, while semidependency lasted longer than does present-day adolescence and possessed fundamentally different characteristics.

From Dependence to Semidependence

Total dependence, or complete reliance on parents for financial support without the compensatory performance of serious labor, began at birth and usually ended before puberty. Until he or she was big enough, a child could scarcely perform useful labor on a farm. More hindrance than help, children were placed under the care of females, their mother or older sisters. Not only were families in the early 1800s larger than now, but the age range within families was greater. A child of 5 was likely to have older siblings, often much older siblings. Female influence extended to educational experiences as well, for in rural areas district schools had summer sessions, taught by women and attended by boys and girls under 7 and by girls over 7 during the busy months of planting, haying, and harvesting.[10]

While female influence was the norm during the years of "infancy," exceptions occurred, especially in the case of orphans. To be orphaned by the death of either or both parents was a much more common experience then than now, not only because of primitive medical care but also because of the way in which births were spaced. Today, parents usually have their children within the span of a few years, but in 1800 a father who began to have children at 25 might not cease until he was 45 or older. As a matter of statistical probability, the father would be dead before the youngest children reached maturity. The same applied to mothers. What the 20th century has considered to be the "typical" life cycle of a woman—survival at least until her youngest children reach maturity—was untypical in the first half of the 19th century, occurring in only about 20 percent of the cases. Institutional care for orphans, although becoming more available after 1820, was still the exception. Orphaned children were more often sent to live with relatives, older siblings or uncles and aunts. This was true even when one parent remained alive; a mother with three or four children could not always carry on by herself.[11]

Shocks caused by the sudden death of a parent differed in degree but not in kind from the other dislocations of families which were so common as to be almost normal in the early 19th century. Dependence on female influence did not mean that the experience of "infancy" was secure or stable. The need to find work or cheaper housing often propelled whole families into move after move. Alongside the well-documented westward migrations of the period, historians have more recently pointed to the constant swirling of population around settled areas in the East, with even large cities often little more than funnels for people heading in new and different directions.[12] Contemporaries were well aware of their peripatetic habits. As a biographer of the Universalist clergyman and author E. H. Chapin wrote: "The youthful days of Chapin were spent in various towns, wherever his father could gain employment in his profession [medicine]. He knew not the full worth of homestead, but only of the boarding and tenement house."[13] The childhood diary of Emily Chubbock is replete with instances of sudden and desperate moves by her family, as she and her parents sought to stave off pauperism in rural New York during the 1820s.[14] As a young diarist wrote in 1820:

> The time has come when I must leave this place where I have been residing, for a time to pursue my studies, under the tuition of Mr. M. Hallock. This is just according to the course of the world. We reside in one place a short time, and then leave it—*then* in another a while, and then leave *that*.[15]

For many children infancy was the last as well as the first stage of life. In Bedford, Massachusetts, between 1808 and 1822 more deaths occurred among those 4 and under than among those 5 through 29; as many died 4 and under as from 40 through 69. In Edgartown, Massachusetts, between 1780 and 1793 almost as many died aged 4 and under as from 30 through 69.[16]

If we define infancy as the period in which feminine control was paramount, its end would have come when a child began to perform serious farm labor during the summer months. Thereafter a child was likely to attend school, if at all, only in the winter months. Just as summer sessions were taught by women and attended by small boys and by girls of varying ages, winter sessions of district schools were taught by men and attended by girls and older boys. This transition usually took place between ages 6 and 12, with the timing conditioned by a host of factors, including size of the farm, the presence or absence of older siblings to help with work, and the health of one's father. Verbal references suggest that the change often occurred between 10 and 12, at least among children of landowners. Elias Smith said that in late 18th-century Connecticut, boys were kept at home for farm work in the summer after age 11 or 12; Samuel A. Foot began to work on his father's farm when he was 10 years old, but added that this was earlier than most of the boys in his neighborhood and attributable to his father's failing health.[17] Maternal associations, organized in a number of eastern cities and towns in the 1820s and 1830s for the exchange of child-rearing advice and mutual encouragement, explicitly defined their scope as the first 10 years of life and assumed that older children would be principally under male control.[18] A few communities characterized by tight control over their members and by more or less rigid age groupings among dependents used 12 as a critical age in determining work assignments. In North Carolina the Moravians had separate categories for small and large boys, with those aged 12 to 18 classed as large boys and expected to perform heavy labor.[19] At John Humphrey Noyes's Oneida Community, children between 2 and 10 or 11 lived in a separate building, while boys aged 12 to 17 and girls 10 and over were "considered as having graduated from the Children's Department" and were organized separately for purposes of work and religious instruction.[20]

Drawn from various times and places, evidence of this sort is suggestive rather than conclusive and, in any event, says little about the amount of labor performed by a working child. In his influential study of French family life, Philippe Ariès claims that children in medieval France were incorporated fully into the work force at around the age of 7, an assertion that some historians have greeted skeptically. Our evidence indicates that in early 19th-century America, entrance into the labor force occurred as a rule after the age of 7 but before puberty.

"Full" incorporation, moreover, probably occurred around the time of puberty—that is, at 15 or 16, when a boy was judged physically able to carry a man's work load. Prior to the middle of the 19th century, contemporaries associated puberty with rising power and energy rather than with the onset of an awkward and vulnerable stage of life which would later become known as adolescence. Census classifications also underscored the importance attached to the age of 15 or 16, for after 1740 censuses generally distinguished those under 16, the "dependent" ages, from those between 16 and 60, the "productive" ages.[21]

Since children entered the work force in stages, it is not surprising that contemporaries customarily distinguished infancy, boyhood, and young manhood. A second measure of passage out of infancy, the commencement of departures from home, points toward a similar conclusion. Nineteenth-century lithographs depicted the act of leaving home as a single and irrevocable event, with the young man disappearing into the mist and out of range of the muffled cries of grieving parents. Yet sporadic home leaving, a pattern of departures for brief periods followed by returns to home, antedated the final departure by several years. As far back as the 17th century, colonial parents had placed children in the homes of neighbors, relatives, and even strangers.[22]

Various reasons lay behind the practice. Sometimes a child might be sent for tutorial purposes to live as a boarder in the house of a minister or lawyer. Ezra Stiles Gannett, a grandson of the Yale president, was sent to live and to study with a minister at age 8.[23] Educated people often took in a number of boys and conducted "family boarding schools."[24] But education was not always or even principally the motive, for educated people such as ministers placed their own children out in families. The diary of Ebenezer Parkman provides a running commentary on the difficulties an attentive father might encounter in trying to place out an incorrigible son. In April 1747, Parkman sent his son Thomas to live with a Mr. Emms of Boston; but by June, Parkman was forced to relate that "my hopes [are] all blasted representing his living with Mr. Emms, who is discouraged and throws up."[25] Whatever the exact nature of Emms's discomfiture, this was not the end of Parkman's woes, for a year later he again confided in his diary that another master had sent Thomas back home in disgust.

Although placing a child out might have educational advantages, the motives often lay in another direction. The older and larger a child, the more space and food he took up, and the greater the economic incentive to send him to live elsewhere. This was especially true where there were younger children who, in effect, pushed the older ones out. James R. Newhall, whose father was a widower with six children, was sent at 11 to live with an uncle in Marblehead, Massachusetts, as a "boy of all work," a common expression which connoted running errands, chopping wood, drawing water, and, in the country, leading cows to pasturage. Children placed out in this way were servants rather than apprentices, for they were not yet learning a particular trade. Their work involved making themselves generally useful, but not learning the intricacies of a craft. Of course, the time of apprentices was often taken up by the same sort of busywork, but the usual age of apprenticeship was 14, with variations as likely to be up as down the age ladder, while the boy of all work was likely to be between 7 and 14.[26]

A second form of home leaving was for a young person to go out on a seasonal basis in search of work or perhaps advanced education. In the case of landowning farmers, winter was the preferred season to allow a boy to leave. "Farmers spared their boys in the winter," Octavius B. Frothingham wrote, "reckoning that their labor was about equivalent to their board; but in the summer, if they went away from home while under age, they must pay the labor of a substitute."[27] At times this arrangement endured even after the attainment of majority. When Theodore Parker left home for the final time at 23, he hired a cousin to work for his father.[28] The winter occupations of young people who left home on a seasonal basis were varied, ranging from lumbering and construction to schoolteaching and school attendance. Edgar J. Sherman, in a pattern duplicated by countless New England and Southern boys in the early 19th century, attended district school in his hometown in the winter, went to an academy in Vermont in the spring, and worked on his father's farm in the summer.[29]

The fact that this seasonal pattern of home leaving and homecoming extended to education as well as work can be grasped more firmly by an examination of the academies, the distinctive educational innovation of late 18th-century America. Academies ranged from established, incorporated academies such as Andover, Exeter, Leicester, and Worcester to unincorporated and often ephemeral institutions whose "appointments" amounted to a room over a shoe store. One feature common to virtually all academies, however, was a broad range of ages. At Exeter in 1812, for example, the age range was 10 to 28; at an academy in Hampton, New Hampshire, in 1811 it was 8 to 22. The spread at New Ipswich, in New Hampshire, was almost as broad, as the following table shows.[30]

Ages of Students at New Ipswich Academy, 1831

AGE	12	13	14	15	16	17	18	19	20	21	22	23	24	25
Number	1	1	1	1	2	3	1	1	2	2	3	1	0	1

The broad age span common to most academies was not the result of prolonged education but of a combination of late starts and random attendance stretched out over a number of years, with sizable gaps between sessions attended and with attendance in a given year rarely embracing more than a month or two. Although some academies published graded curriculum sequences covering three or four years, few students appear to have remained long enough in a given academy to have benefited from whatever advantages such sequences offered. The low level of persistence from term to term is indicated by the records of Pinkerton Academy for the academic year 1850/51. Of thirty male students enrolled in the winter term, only ten were still in attendance in the spring term, while thirteen of the original thirty re-enrolled in the fall of 1851. In 1862/63 at Leicester Academy, seventeen of the thirty-five students enrolled originally in the fall term re-enrolled in the winter.[31]

All other considerations aside, the ease with which seasonal labor patterns could be combined with academy attendance contributed to the latter's popularity. The academy provided, in other words, a form of seasonal education to complement seasonal labor patterns in preindustrial American society. Not surprisingly, academies were popular, although their evanescent and protean character prevents precise statements about enrollment. Bernard Bailyn has suggested that Henry Barnard's estimate—6,085 academies served by 12,260 teachers and enrolling over a quarter of a million students in 1850—was probably an understatement. Bailyn's suggestion is reinforced by the fact that Alexander Inglis counted 640 academies in Massachusetts in 1860, only a decade after Barnard had put the total at 400.[32]

The expenses connected with education at academies were modest. For an incorporated academy, tuition rarely ran to more than $4.50 for an eleven-week term. The charges at Leicester Academy in 1838 were $4.50 per term for the classical course and $3.50 for the English course. The same institution estimated board at $1.17 a week and room at $1 to $3 a week, depending on quality. Taking the higher of each optional figure, but excluding travel and entertainment, the cost per term was a little under $50. At unincorporated academies the costs were probably even lower. Furthermore, the seasonal quality of education at academies made it possible for students to earn money to defray expenses. Students could also easily find employment while in attendance. Academies were not boarding schools; rather, students lived in licensed dwellings in the town and could earn money in their free time. Young George Moore, for example, worked as a court clerk and took an active part in town affairs while studying at Concord Academy in the 1820s.[33]

Nevertheless, there were limits to the academies' appeal. The very looseness of structure which made academies accessible led many young men to despair of ever obtaining a thorough education at institutions that simultaneously embraced remedial, preparatory, and terminal education. Further, modest as they were, the costs of academy education were enough to deter unskilled laborers or poor farmers from sending their children. Academies were truly "colleges of the middling classes," but "middling" here means not the dead center of the income spectrum in antebellum America but the children of substantial farmers, professional men, and artisans.[34]

Analogies existed, however, between the seasonal quality of academy attendance and the educational experiences of boys and girls who, for one reason or another, never went beyond primary school. Although attendance at academies fluctuated from term to term, in district schools it fluctuated from day to day and hour to hour. George Moore's diary indicates why schoolmasters in rural areas did not complain heatedly about truancy. The idea of truancy presupposes an anterior concept of normal attendance, and the latter could not exist as long as students drifted in and out of school at random, at virtually any hour of the morning or afternoon. Moore had only the haziest idea of which scholars "belonged" to his school until several weeks into the term. The age range of students in district schools was also broad. Contemporaries said that it ran from infancy to manhood. One day in 1828, Moore recorded the ages of all of his pupils at Acton, Massachusetts, so that "I may see what will become of them hereafter." [35]

Age Range of Pupils at Acton District School, March 28, 1828

Boys

AGE	6	7	8	9	10	11	12	13	14	15	16	17	18	19	20
Number	2	2	1	4	3	3	0	2	2	5	1	4	5	1	1

Girls

AGE	4	5	6	7	8	9	10	11	12	13	14	15	16	17	18
Number	1	1	1	8	2	3	2	4	1	1	2	4	0	3	1

In Moore's school, girls were as likely as boys to attend between ages 7 and 12; girls began younger but were less likely to be found in school in their late teens. Nearly half the boys were 15 or over, but less than a quarter of the girls. Contemporary accounts of district school life suggest that Moore's snapshot of his school was representative of conditions elsewhere in the 1820s and 1830s. Complaints about the tendency of girls to conclude their schooling at 15 or 16 were as common as laments about the number of "large boys" of 16 or 17 and young men of 18 or 20 in district schools.[36] But for either sex, education in district schools beyond age 12 was an extensive rather than intensive experience, with school taking up a few weeks or perhaps months each winter, for winter after winter. Further, students still attending district schools at 18 or 20 were not the ones with advantages of birth or wealth. The duration of seasonal schooling varied from youth to youth, but was almost negatively correlated with social class. The son of a merchant was likely to have finished his "literary" education in an academy or family boarding school at 14 or 15, but the plowboy with few prospects might stay around the district school till 18 or 19.[37] In a general way, the same was true of college students, among whom the age range was likely to run from the middle teens to the middle 20s; those graduated from college at 25 rather than at 18 were likely to be young men who did not begin any serious literary or classical education until the approach of majority because their teen years were taken up by farming. Broadly speaking, the higher a young man's social status, the faster he would move through his preparatory period and the sooner he would "get out into life" (see pp. 32–33).

To talk about getting out into life or starting in life made sense only for young men who were going somewhere, who had aspirations beyond farm service. But what about children of poor families? In the late 19th century it became fashionable to portray preindustrial American society as a time when wealth and luxury had not yet raised up classes. In industrial and urban America in the 1880s and 1890s, class distinctions were highly visible and were reinforced by residential segregation and strife between capital and labor. In preindustrial America class gradations were probably less visible, but they were no less sharp. Because mortality was higher among the poor, the disruption of families by the death of parents was more common. Because poor fathers owned no land or very little land, they were unable to utilize directly the labor of their children. Thus, while poor children remained dependent, parents had little incentive to keep them at home. As soon as these children were able to work, they had to leave home to find it.[38]

The autobiography of Asa Sheldon casts light on the nature of dependency in poor agricultural families in the early part of the 19th century. Born in 1788, Sheldon was a farmer who spent his life in the area of Wilmington, Massachusetts. At the age of 7 he began to hire himself out for short periods:

> When 7 years of age, I made a contract with Clark and Epps, of Lyndboro, N. H., and Col. Flint of North Reading, drovers, to drive their cattle and sheep from our house to Jerre Upton's tavern, two miles distant, that they might ride ahead and take breakfast while I drove them on, for four coppers each trip, which occurred weekly.[39]

The same pattern continued for the next few years. In the spring of 1796, Asa was employed by local farmers to drive oxen to plow at a shilling a day. A year later a Mr. David Parker came to Sheldon's house "to get a boy to live with him" and selected Asa, "because he is the youngest." [40] Sheldon called this his first home leaving, "an important event in the history of a youth." Sheldon also suggested by implication the reason for his parents' consent to Parker's request:

> My father owning but a few acres of land, worked much of his time stoning wells and cellars, and consequently was with his family but little. Generally working in Salem, we saw but little of him, except on the Sabbath.[41]

If this laconic comment suggests that rural families might not have been such tightly knit units as some historians have claimed, it also underscores the earlier suggestion that departures from home at early ages, under 12 or 13, were often responses to economic necessity; by 8 or 9 years of age Asa would be of little use to his father but a burden on his mother.

After working from his 9th to 13th year as a servant to Parker, Sheldon was formally bound to Parker by his father. Sheldon's father was to receive $20 from Parker, and Asa was to receive $100 at age 21. As an apprentice, Asa had an element of freedom hitherto missing in his working arrangements. Following the common practice not only of farm servants but also of sons living at home, Asa often performed "stints" or extra work in return for cash rewards or free time. More complete freedom came at 15 when Asa, increasingly at odds with the domineering Parker, walked out on his indenture, citing as his justification the recent death of his father. Now it was Parker's turn to bargain, for if Asa is to be believed, Parker soon missed the boy's strong back and willing spirit. Parker journeyed to Sheldon's home, now managed by Asa's mother, and persuaded Asa to return, but only after agreeing to sign a contract raising the latter's cash reward at attainment of majority to $200, while adding the promise of a new suit of clothes and a month's education each winter. Asa's troubles with Parker were not at an end, however, for the latter soon reverted to his despotic ways. In protest, Asa hired himself out part-time to another farmer. Technically still bound to Parker and in fact forced to return the agreed-on suit of clothes each Sunday night after meeting, Sheldon now had attained a further measure of freedom within the general context of semidependency. Shortly thereafter, now with Asa in his late teens, he walked out on all obligations to Parker and passed the remainder of his minority in a variety of service jobs.[42]

After his 8th birthday, Sheldon had little family life in the sense of warm and intimate bonds with parents. His father had been a remote and distant figure even before his death; his mother could not keep Asa at home, for that would have entailed feeding and lodging him without deriving any wages in return. So Asa left at an early age and became a "youth" in semidependent service. He described his parents with respect but not emotion, and in this respect followed the custom of his day. Where the simplest kinds of security were absent, affection lavished was likely to be affection frustrated. Parents and children were not unfeeling toward one another, but as long as children lived, affection had to be kept in check. The same emotional restraint governed relationships between siblings. Emily Chubbock's diary contains the following subdued description of a brother's homecoming: "March, 1830. Benjamin came home (he had been for five years in the employ of a farmer), and he and father commenced building fences and other spring work." [43]

Behind this emotional restraint lay family priorities and values very different from our own. Children provided parents in preindustrial society with a form of social security, unemployment insurance, and yearly support. As soon as children were able to work, in or out of the home, they were expected to contribute to the support of their parents; when parents were no longer able to work, children could look after them. A parent's first obligation was to have children sufficiently numerous to ensure that enough would survive. The second obligation was to supervise the placement of children between their 7th and 21st birthdays. Parents of means had a third obligation, to give children a "start in life," a stake in the form of capital or land that would enable the children to achieve economic independence. These three obligations are listed not only in chronological sequence but also in order of importance, for many parents, because of death or poverty, were in no position to discharge the third obligation. [44]

Social class conditioned childhood experiences in various ways, but certain common elements united the experiences of children of wealthy, comfortable, and poor parents. The ravages of mortality fell heaviest on the poor but struck all social classes. Leaving home was also an experience common to youth of different classes, although its nature differed from class to class. Landowning farmers sanctioned seasonal departures of sons from home, but wanted their children back in the spring and summer. Wealthy merchants often sent their sons out as cabin boys at 8 or 9 or as supercargo at 15 or 16 as part of a process of grooming that was to lead to a junior partnership at 21. Differences between rich and poor were often those of motive rather than deed; children of the wealthy left home because of parental preference rather than stark necessity. [45]

A source which throws light on the elements of similarity in the ex-

23

periences of youth of different classes is a collection of biographies of New England manufacturers compiled in 1876 by J. D. Van Slyck, an enterprising journalist.[46] Van Slyck's collection was largely free of the fulsome ornamentation that often pervaded late 19th-century biographies, and it has the added merit of being based on autobiographical data submitted by the subjects, data which provides unusually precise information about the sequence of jobs during youth. Obviously, at the end of their careers Van Slyck's subjects had risen far above the average level of attainment, and even at birth they were not a cross section of the society from which they sprang. Although only about 1 percent attended college, all of them had some formal education, and many were able to benefit from parental assistance at key points in their careers. In view of this class bias, it is interesting to note the similarities between their occupations during their teens and those of Asa Sheldon.

A majority of Van Slyck's manufacturers were sons of farmers (86 out of 145 on whom data was available), but a sizable minority came from the artisan or petty manufacturing class (44 of 145). The proportion from other backgrounds was negligible; only seven were sons of professional men, while eight were sons of merchants. Those who came from farming families fell into two general classes. The larger proportion passed their early and middle teens as plowboys, going out first as farm servants but returning home frequently. Philip Corbin, born in Connecticut in 1824, worked seasonally at farm labor away from home between ages 15 and 19, when, tiring of the agricultural routine, he went to New Britain and entered a factory as a "boy," doing menial jobs for a locksmith who paid him according to the value of his labor. This lasted for a year, at which point Corbin had learned enough of locksmithing to begin as an independent contractor.[47] Jared Beebe, born in Wilbraham, Massachusetts, in 1815, similarly worked on a farm and attended district school until he was 20, when he entered a woolen mill as a spinner. Beebe's rise thereafter was slow, and it was not until 1852 that he had amassed enough capital to enter a partnership.[48] It is, indeed, a little ironic that late 19th-century business leaders romanticized rural boyhood, for the evidence indicates that a farm boyhood was essentially a drag on careers. Half the manufacturers who were sons of farmers did not follow any nonagricultural occupation until they were 18 or over. Even then, many of them merely became store clerks and were several steps away from a small manufacturing partnership.

A smaller proportion of the manufacturers from agricultural backgrounds were sons of farmers who also had some other identifiable trade, often blacksmithing, which was carried on as a way to increase a family's earnings during slack seasons. Many of Van Slyck's subjects picked up their initial experience with tools in small shops attached to the farmhouse or located in an outlying shed. Such experiences might have prompted them to try their luck in manufacturing establishments, a conclusion which is supported by the fact that manufacturers whose fathers had some occupation ancillary to agriculture were more likely than the average to move into artisan or manufacturing jobs before age 18.

Although delays of various sorts marked the movement of sons of farmers into industry, they usually began to work at early ages at agricultural tasks, attending school only in the winter and only for a few weeks at a time. Even those of Van Slyck's subjects who had some advanced education usually spent no more than a term or two at an academy in their late teens. Similarly, artisans and petty manufacturers, including ones who could have provided advanced education for their sons, placed little premium on schooling beyond the rudiments. Of forty-four individuals from artisan or manufacturing families, fourteen had taken some form of steady employment before they reached age 14, while an additional thirteen began to work at 15 and 16.

The difference lay, of course, in the kind of work performed, for the sons of artisans proceeded directly into learning the routine of mills and shops. Compared to Philip Corbin, caught in the routine of farm labor until he was 19, Baxter D. Whitney moved down a well-greased track. Whitney was born in Winchendon, Massachusetts, in 1817; his father owned a small woolen mill. At the age of 6, Whitney began to work at piecing rolls in his father's mill, a task which occupied him full-time until he was 11, except for two weeks spent each summer and winter in school. At 11 he was sent to work at carding, at 12 on repairs. A year later his father sent him to Worcester to assist a firm of machinists in constructing looms for the senior Whitney's mill. Four years later Whitney, now 17, entered Fitchburg Academy for a term before returning to Winchendon as a repair foreman for a company which had bought his father's mill.[49]

The same shifting of situations every few years marked the youth of Moses Pierce, born in Pawtucket in 1808. After attending school until age 11, Pierce was placed in the spinning room of a mill. A year later he entered the yarning room and stayed there until 1822, when he took employment in a succession of factory stores in Pawtucket and Valley Falls. After six years in various stores, Pierce was given charge of a small cotton factory in Willimantic, Connecticut, where he rewarded his employer's confidence by introducing a new system of bookkeeping at a time when any system of bookkeeping was a novelty. Finally, at 21, he entered into a partnership to manufacture bleach.[50]

Pierce and Whitney were typical of the New England manufacturers in that both managed to pack an impressive number of experiences into their first twenty years and neither served a seven-year apprenticeship. Those who maintain that apprenticeship fixed the status of youth before the dramatic expansion of school enrollment at the end of the 19th century ignore the fluid quality of youthful experience in the early Republic. Indeed, long apprenticeships were never common, either in America or Britain, except for a few highly skilled crafts and for the binding out of pauper children.[51]

More interesting is the fact that, despite all their shifting around and apparent independence as teenagers, Pierce, Whitney, and the others continued to be caught up in a curious form of dependence. Perhaps they went into a variety of situations, but, more accurately, they were *sent* into various positions. The ties which held them were often stretched to the limit, but they were still there. In some cases, the bonds were plainly visible, for while seven-year apprenticeships were rare, three-year apprenticeships were common. Albert Curtis abandoned farm work at age 17 to become an apprentice in a machine shop in Worcester. His contract ran for three years, stipulating that he was to receive board plus $40, $60, and $80 in each successive year. Then, at 21, he became a journeyman in the same shop at $1.25 a day.[52] At times, apprenticeship survived in an invisible form even after it had ceased to be visible. The father of Estus Lamb sent him at age 13 to live with a cousin to learn the millwright trade (although the senior Lamb was also a millwright). There was no formal apprenticeship here, although Lamb was obviously an apprentice for all practical purposes. After learning the trade, Lamb left his cousin at age 18 to work as a millwright at Oxford Plains, Massachusetts, agreeing to a contract of $200 in pay for two years' work. This was not a formal apprenticeship, but the level of remuneration suggests that Lamb was still in a semidependent and subordinate position, as does the fact that Lamb's father claimed the entire $200, "relinquishing, however, his claim for the remaining year of his son's minority."[53]

Dependency at times took horizontal rather than vertical forms, with younger brothers dependent on older brothers. Samuel Walker, an orphan, was "given away" to an older brother at 7. The brother kept him until age 11, and then placed him out on a neighboring farm. The older brother assumed many of the functions of a father, not the least being that he claimed Samuel's labor in return for board and oversight until Samuel reached majority. In practice, it did not work out quite that way. After returning to live with his brother for a short period, Samuel decided to strike out on his own. The brother agreed, but only on condition that Samuel pay him cash in lieu of time. Since Samuel did not have any money, the brother's condition presented obvious difficulties, which were resolved by an agreement that Samuel would leave, pick up whatever work he could, and then at 19 pay off the stipulated sum. Strangely, Samuel's relations with his brother, if not exactly characterized by warmth, were not freighted with antagonism either. Samuel lived up to his part of the deal, and after he turned 21, his brother helped him out in business by endorsing small notes.[54]

Whatever forms dependency took, it did not necessarily involve prolonged residence under the parental roof. The factory apprentice who lived at home was an exception, although those who spent their teens moving around from mill to mill were often placed with relatives, particularly with older brothers and uncles. The father of Phinehas Adams, for example, combined the occupations of farmer, mechanic, and petty mill owner, and was sufficiently well off to give Phinehas a private education up to age 13. Then, Phinehas was placed as a bobbin boy in a mill for which his father acted as agent. A short time later, Phinehas entered another mill for which his uncle was agent. Then, at 19, he linked up with his father in yet another mill.[55]

This kind of movement under the supervision of relatives or parents was not always possible and was much less likely to occur in the case of young plowboys like Philip Corbin, who stumbled into factory work without benefit of connections. Even the petty manufacturers often sent their children away from home for various reasons without requiring that they be placed with relatives and without granting them independence. Oliver Chace was not a poor man, but he seems to have thought nothing of placing his son Harvey in a mill as a bobbin boy at age 9, and then sending him around Rhode Island as a teenager to supervise the installation of machinery in whatever factories the elder Chace had acquired a financial interest. Dependency and residence at home were not interchangeable concepts before the middle of the 19th century.[56]

Relatives not only provided supervision for young men during their minority, but they also supplied capital to help the young people start on their own. Prior to the middle of the 19th century the partnership rather than the corporation was the preferred form of business enterprise, and relatives (especially brothers and cousins) were the preferred partners in many cases. An example of the manner in which close ties between brothers provided a crude form of family continuity and economic security is the case of John and Salmon Putnam, born in New Hampshire in 1812 and 1815, respectively. Their father was a scythe maker who, lacking capital, worked on contract for merchants and hence was forced to shift the family repeatedly around New Hampshire. The eldest of the two brothers, John, became an apprentice at 14 to Loammi Chamberlain, a machinist in Mason Village. It is not clear whether anything was actually written down, but John was to receive board and clothing for five years, with permission to attend school one month a year. The apprenticeship ended when John turned 19, and he continued as a journeyman in Chamberlain's service for a dollar a day. Saving his money, John hired part of Chamberlain's shop in 1835 and began to make cotton machinery on contract. Meanwhile, the failure of a contractor for whom the senior Putnam was working had reduced the family to penury and forced it to dispose of Salmon, the younger brother, by sending him off at 8 years of age to work in a New Ipswich mill where a relative was overseer. Later, Salmon went to Lowell, Massachusetts, and obtained employment with one of the larger cotton factories, rising by age 17 to become overseer of the spinning room. Two or three years later, he linked up with John, who was just beginning business as a contractor. In 1836 the brothers went to Trenton, New Jersey, and started a machine shop. Caught short by the Panic of 1837, they left Trenton, stored their tools in Mason Village, and took separate jobs in different parts of New Hampshire until better times permitted them to establish a machine shop in Fitchburg, Massachusetts. There they continued in partnership until 1858, when they converted the business to a stock company ultimately capitalized at over a quarter of a million dollars.[57] The careers of the Putnam brothers primarily illustrate the importance of sibling relationships in early 19th-century business enterprise, but they also underscore the importance of work in machine shops, which required a high degree of technical skill but a relatively small amount of capital, in facilitating the movement of artisans' sons into manufacturing enterprises.

The early career of Milton Morse offers an apt summary of the oscillation between independence and dependence, between home leaving and homecoming, in the early 19th century. Morse was the son of a sometime carpenter and farmer, Oliver Morse, and Waitstill Stratton, a woman whose Puritan surname was scarcely descriptive of her later mobility. Milton was born in 1799 in Foxboro, his mother's hometown, but soon moved with his family to Wrentham, Massachusetts, where Milton was put to work in a small cotton factory, picking cotton by hand and putting it on the cards. After doing this for two years, Milton was apprenticed to a blacksmith, with the stipulated term to run until his 21st birthday. Milton was still under 13 at the binding; we know this because at 13 he walked out on his apprenticeship and returned to his parents. The family then moved to Attleboro, where the senior Morse engaged as a woodworker in nearby Pawtucket, while Milton continued to work at his single skill of picking cotton. Still in his teens, Milton took a job as a handyman in a mill at Seekonk, learning various phases of the routine until age 21. On coming of age, Milton left Seekonk to join his father, who had rented a farm at East Providence, and

worked for him a year before hiring himself out as a farmhand to his
uncle at Foxboro. For the next six or seven years Milton returned periodically to farm labor, probably for no more than a few months at a
time, certainly not often enough to keep him from working as a journeyman mechanic and overseer on a seasonal basis. All the while he
amassed capital without the risks of ownership, and when a business
slump in the late 1820s forced a number of failures, Morse and an acquaintance formed a partnership to manufacture cotton goods.[58] He
went on to become a celebrated manufacturer and a pillar of New
England industrial society, until he died in 1877 from injuries caused by
a falling derrick.

"Semidependence" has been used at a number of points to describe the status of youth aged 10 to 21 in the early part of the 19th century. The word is intended to signify two aspects of the economic experience of young people. First, as young people grew older, they
customarily experienced greater freedom and acquired new responsibilities. They left home, took different jobs, and moved again in search
of still more jobs. But "semidependence" also signifies a different view
of growth, not as a gradual removal of restraints but as a jarring mixture
of complete freedom and total subordination. Autobiographers who
lapsed routinely into the passive voice when describing the events of
their youth were unconsciously conveying an important aspect of 19th-
century family life, for in the quasi-contractual relationship between fathers and sons, the obligation to work lay heavily on the son.[59]
    As noted earlier, the conditions of semidependence were affected
by social class. Poor farm children were forced out of the home early;
children of prosperous, landowning farmers left home at a somewhat
later age and returned home more frequently; children of wealthy manufacturers and merchants left early, but because of parental preference
rather than necessity. The degree of freedom also depended on social
class. To the extent that poor households were more frequently
disrupted than wealthy ones, poor children often had more de facto
freedom (unless bound as paupers), although, it must be added, there
was little that they could do with their freedom.
    Social class is one variable; another is historical periodization. To
what extent have we described timeless components of preindustrial
society and to what extent have we identified patterns unique to the
period from 1790 to 1840?
    The tendency to send children away from home before puberty was
well established in early 19th-century America for the same reason it
had been well established in England during the 16th and 17th centuries. High birthrates in both cases made the labor of children redun-

dant in the home and forced their removal. Moreover, the element of patriarchalism so evident in labor contracts between sons and fathers was a characteristic feature of American society in the period between 1650 and 1790, just as it was after 1790.[60] Some of the basic features of semidependence in 1800 or 1820 were rooted in the preindustrial nature of society.

Yet the period 1790–1840 departed in important ways from earlier times. By the late 18th century, American social structure had become notably more complex and differentiated than in the 17th and early 18th centuries. Whether the social structure was also becoming more stratified remains an open question, but by 1800 one could identify in most regions large numbers of commercial as well as subsistence farmers, several gradations of wealth among commercial farmers, a growing class of artisans and shopkeepers in towns and cities, and a fluid body of nondependent, propertyless urban workers. Asa Sheldon's occupational career, the early parts of which have already been sketched, illustrates the direction of change. Late in life Sheldon described himself as a farmer, and indeed he did engage in farming, but he was primarily an enterprising Yankee jobber who supported himself in his mature years by working on contract to provide farmers and tradesmen with lumber and to develop real estate.[61]

The growth of urbanization during the first half of the 19th century did not have a revolutionary effect on young people, mainly because class differences around 1800 were not reflected as sharply in the teen years as in mature life. On farms and in shops and stores young people of different classes mingled in an atmosphere of informality, although their ultimate destinations would be different. Moreover, urban tradesmen and industrialists often operated farms on which their sons supplied the labor.[62] Nor was the nature of the early factories such as to transform the time and work rhythms of agricultural society; an alternation of seasonal labor and seasonal education marked the lives of factory youth as well as farm youth. Eleven-year-old Emily Chubbock recorded this laconic comment in her diary: "December, 1828. The ice stopped the water wheel and the factory was closed for a few months. January, 1829. Entered district school."[63]

Yet economic change altered the experiences of young people in important ways. The transportation revolution between 1815 and 1840 stimulated large numbers of young men to abandon agriculture for commercial and industrial occupations in towns and cities and for construction jobs both in rural and in urban areas. In the 17th and early 18th centuries young men had usually remained dependent until marriage or their father's death; by 1820, however, increasing numbers of young men were pushing out on their own in their late teens and early

20s.[64] Large towns and cities could sustain a range of political, educational, and social institutions which small towns and rural areas could not, so that the corporate life of youth shifted from involuntary associations (family and village) to voluntary associations such as academies, young men's societies, and political clubs. In the curious balance between dependence and independence which together made up semidependence, the weight was increasingly on the side of independence.

From Semidependence to Independence

No clear and distinct barrier divided semidependence from independence; no consensus existed as to the moment when a boy became a man. Few institutions marked the passage from one stage of life to the next, and in any event, young people passed less time in 1800 than now in institutional settings. Various criteria for the attainment of full manhood can be advanced, each with some justification: the age of marriage, the age at which a young man left home for the final time, perhaps even the age at which one joined a church.

For the moment, without dismissing any of these, we will examine a different criterion, the age at which an upwardly mobile youth entered one of the learned professions. The unimposing quality of professional and preprofessional requirements in the early 19th century lends plausibility to the idea that early entry into the professions was normal. With the exception of the ministry of a few orthodox denominations, a college degree was not a prerequisite for professional practice, while professional education itself was normally shortened for college graduates. Since legal and medical apprenticeships could be entered at 16 (and sometimes earlier), a nongraduate could have been ready to practice at 21, the legal minimum. Some individuals did begin to practice law or medicine at 21; indeed, some began at 17 or 18, either ignoring the law or benefiting from legislative dispensations. But the more pronounced tendency was toward late entrance, "late" in this context meaning from 25 to the early 30s. In 1894 a New Hampshire lawyer and antiquarian, Charles Bell, published a collection of biographies of nearly every lawyer known to have practiced in the state.[65] The great majority of Bell's lawyers were born between 1780 and 1830. Fully two-thirds were 25 or over at the start of legal practice; a quarter were 28 or over. A few individuals were not admitted to the bar until their 40s or 50s; in their case, law was less a career than an avocation, taken up in

Youth in the Early Republic, 1790–1840

middle life and ancillary to their main occupation. But for most of the New Hampshire lawyers, entrance to legal practice was the result of a more or less permanent vocational choice made in young manhood, but toward the end rather than the beginning of young manhood.

What took them so long? Considering the relatively low barriers guarding access to professions in antebellum America, why all the foot dragging? A high proportion of Bell's 780 lawyers (63 percent) were college graduates. But this fact does not explain the frequency of delays into the late 20s, and in any event, the nongraduates among his lawyers were actually slightly older on average than the graduates at entry to practice. The fact that fully 75 percent of the college graduates among Bell's lawyers began to practice within four years of graduation provides a valuable clue. Many of those who began to practice late left college late, not at 18 or 19 but at 23 or 24. Such late graduations were very common at colleges outside the South in the first half of the 19th century; 23- and 24-year old graduates formed a procession of which Bell's lawyers were merely the tail end.[66] The likeliest explanation for late graduations, in turn, lies in late decisions to prepare for college, for preparation itself was not time consuming. Logically, such late decisions would be more frequent where the young men's families lacked ties to professions or to merchant houses where advanced education was valuable. In other words, these young men were originally destined for some other line. In fact, only a tiny fraction of Bell's lawyers (40 of 780) were themselves sons of lawyers. An equally small fraction (36 of 780) had close relatives in the law. But if most did not come from legal backgrounds, what kind of families did they come from? Here the limitations of evidence are severe, but we might take a clue from Bell, who said that New Hampshire lawyers were very often raised on farms. If so—and prior to 1830 alternatives to agriculture were meager in New Hampshire—it is likely that many of Bell's lawyers experienced the drag force of a farm boyhood in their early years. Mired in obligations to their parents, they must have also suffered from their lack of personal connections to the state's professional life, and from their inability to find patrons to smooth their path. The difference between the age at entrance to practice of those of Bell's subjects who were sons of lawyers and those known to have been raised on farms is striking, all the more so because the sons of lawyers were almost without exception college graduates.

Bell's collection happens to be unparalleled for completeness, but collections of biographies do exist for other states and other professions. Data on Massachusetts and New Hampshire Congregationalist and Presbyterian clergymen born before 1830 point to a similar pattern of late access, with ordination usually delayed until the late 20s or early

32

New Hampshire Lawyers: Ages at Entry to Practice

AGE RANGE	18–24	25–27	28 AND OVER
Total: N = 500	37.0%	34.2%	28.8%
Sons of lawyers	68.8	25.0	6.2
Had relatives other than father in legal profession	45.5	39.4	15.1
Sons of farmers	14.9	25.9	59.2

30s.[67] Perhaps date of ordination is misleading as an indicator, since ordination coincided with installation rather than with the completion of preparation for the ministry. But even if we take the other possible indicator, date of licensing to preach, or "approbation," the picture does not change significantly. More than three-quarters of the candidates of the Essex North Massachusetts ministerial association, for example, were 25 or over at licensing; a third were 28 or over.

That orthodox clergymen experienced delays before licensing is not surprising in view of the value placed in New England on an educated clergy. But allowing three years for professional education and assuming college graduation at 21, approbation should not have been postponed much beyond age 24. In fact, the traditional assumption was that only five years should elapse between the commencement of Latin grammar and the first sermon.[68] But much longer delays were clearly common, delays caused less by time spent in professional education than by late graduation from college. Nearly a third of the Essex North ministers were 25 or over at college graduation; more than two-thirds were 23 or over. Two points can be made about this tendency toward late graduation and late approbation. First, only 13 percent of the Essex North ministers were themselves sons of ministers. Predictably, sons of ministers were younger at graduation than the average. Secondly, in early 19th-century New England, periodic waves of religious enthusiasm, supplemented by the benevolent work of various educational societies, were pulling numbers of young men from the plow and workbench and propelling them in the direction of college and ministerial education.[69] It is likely that in the ministry as in law, track switching, with all its concomitant effects, was inducing marked delays in the ages at which young men entered professions in the early 19th century.[70]

The life of one Alfred Poore, born in 1818 in West Haverhill, Massachusetts, provides an illustration of these forces and, incidentally, suggests how an individual with meager preprofessional and professional training might not reach the level of formal qualification for a profession before age 28. Poore was the son of a farmer and cordwainer; in his youth he learned the latter trade, practicing it except for interim periods of farm labor and district schooling. Like many farm boys, he was nearly 20 when he stopped attending district school. In the winter of 1837–1838 he spent one term at Atkinson Academy, deriving in the words of a laconic memorialist "an increased desire for knowledge." [71] He then entered the Bradford Teachers' Seminary, but never actually taught school. Instead, he conceived the desire to study medicine and, after a brief apprenticeship, he spent one term in the medical department of Dartmouth College, receiving a preceptor's certificate in 1846. One could end the story there, with Poore finally entering a profession, but for the fact that he never did practice medicine. Rather, he spent the next ten years clerking in a country store and farming before finally turning to antiquarianism, a field in which he won sufficient notice to merit a brief obituary in 1908 in the *New England Historical and Genealogical Register*.

To what extent did these particular groups or individuals represent the nation? Was delayed entry into professions normal or aberrant? Part of the answer lies in the fact that, even in New England, the tendency toward late access concealed a less conspicuous but equally important trend, the wide distribution of ages at entry, since there were individual cases of lawyers practicing at 18 or ministers preaching at 21. We are really confronted, then, by two distinct tendencies, late entry as a probability and early entry as a possibility. Significant deviations from the model of late access, moreover, did exist in other professions and other sections of the country. Physicians, for example, usually began to practice at earlier ages than either Bell's lawyers or the New England clergymen. Analysis of a sample of 500 doctors drawn from William B. Atkinson's directory *Physicians and Surgeons of the United States* provides some illuminating comparisons. [72] Only about half of Atkinson's physicians, most of whom were born between 1810 and 1850, were 25 or over at entrance to practice; the proportion of very late entries, 28 or over, was much lower than among Bell's lawyers.

Several explanations help to account for the lower age of entry into medicine. Prior to 1870 the medical profession was probably the least prestigious of the professions, and certainly the most accessible. A medical degree was not a prerequisite to practice, and by 1845 most states had abandoned licensing efforts, in effect throwing medical practice open to all comers. [73] But there were important regional differences in the ages at which Atkinson's doctors began to practice. Physicians born in New England were older at entrance to practice than those born in the Middle Atlantic states, and much older then those born in the South. New England doctors, in fact, were almost as old at the start of

practice as Bell's lawyers. Southerners, in contrast, often began to pre-
scribe drugs and to treat patients when scarcely out of adolescence.

Ages at Entry: Doctors by Region of Origin

AGE RANGE	18–24	25–27	28 AND OVER
Total: N = 500	59.0%	29.2%	11.8%
New England	36.0	43.7	20.3
Middle Atlantic	69.9	18.8	11.3
Midwest	52.5	31.5	16.0
South (incl. Md. and Ky.)	72.0	19.2	8.8

The pattern of early access in the South was not confined to medicine. In sharp contrast to the New Hampshire pattern, Southern lawyers generally started to practice in their early 20s. Variations were as
often downward into the late teens as upward, despite the fact that professional standards in many parts of the South where early entry predominated were comparable to those of New England.[74] Why, then, did
southerners move so much more rapidly than northerners? Part of the
answer probably lies in the survival of so many elements of prescriptive
status and hierarchy in the antebellum South at a time of their erosion
in the North. Among southern aristocrats, family name acted as a
guarantor of maturity and responsibility almost without regard to chronological age. This helps to explain why in South Carolina some of the
leading judges in the state were only in their mid-20s. The antebellum
South, especially states like Virginia and South Carolina, carried over
the tradition which decreed that status rather than age determined a
man's position. This tradition accounted for many of those astonishing
instances of precocity which, like that of William Pitt, the 24-year-old
prime minister of Great Britain, can so easily be ripped out of context to
"prove" that youth in the past routinely achieved eminence at much
earlier ages than now.

Just as the accelerated development of privileged southern youth
reflected the continued vitality of such traditions in the South, delays
among northern youth in entering professions reflected the withering
of traditions of status and hierarchy in the North. Pointing to a variety
of youth movements spawned by modernization, a recent student has
described European youth between 1770 and 1870 as "troubled." There
are good reasons to apply the same adjective to American youth between 1790 and 1840, but a more comprehensive description of northern youth in the latter period would be "restless." To a greater extent
than in the South, urbanization in the North was bringing into exis-

tence a kind of town life that had few antecedents before the Revolution. After 1820 the growth of metropolises had a dramatic effect on all age groups, but for a young man around 1800 the town was the key development. The presence of an increasing number of towns of about 5,000 people, combined with pressure on available land, tempted young men to abandon agriculture without, at the same time, providing new beacons to guide them.[75]

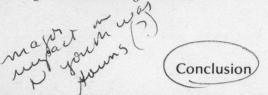

Conclusion

A model which divided early 19th-century life experiences into childhood, adolescence, and adulthood, corresponding to age groups of 1–13, 14–20, and 21 and upward, would fail to convey the real complexity of the situation. Few apprenticeships began at 14 and ended at 21; some began at 12, some at 16 or 18. Moreover, young people often had more than one apprenticeship, whether formal or informal. Apprenticeship did not necessarily mark the first leaving of home; many left at 8 or 9 as servants. Those who left home in boyhood often returned for longer or shorter periods, a fact which prompted the distinction between sporadic (in, out, and in again) home leaving and the final departure, or "start in life," which might come at 14 but usually came later.

If childhood is defined as a period of protected dependency within the home, then its extent was much shorter then than now. If adolescence is defined as the period after puberty during which a young person is institutionally segregated from casual contacts with a broad range of adults, then it can scarcely be said to have existed at all, even for those young people who attended school beyond age 14. Nevertheless, it is possible to speak of youth in the early 19th century, either as an often lengthy period of semidependence between ages 10 and 21 or as a time of indecision between ages 15 and 25. Of course, there were still young men who plunged into the business of life like comets. A few months after his arrival in America, the German-born scholar Francis Lieber, recorded the following in his diary:

> Story from real life. I arrived here in October, 1835. In January, 1836, W——— and another student were expelled [from college] on account of a duel. Since that time W——— has:
> First. Shot at his antagonist in the streets of Charleston.
> Second. Studied(?) law with Mr. De Saussure in Charleston.
> Third. Married.

Fourth. Been admitted to the Bar.
Fifth. Imprisoned for two months in the above shooting.
Sixth. Become father of a fine girl.
Seventh. Practised law for some time.
Eighth. Been elected a member of the legislature.
Now he is only twenty-two years old. What a state of society this requires and must produce! [76]

But such prodigies, always rare, were becoming even rarer. In the ensuing decades, the idea of youth as a period of prolonged indecision would rise to prominence.

There seems to be that there
was loosening of structured
paternal control of earlier
(ie regaining following
paternal occup'/ or withholding
land until son's marr.
or father's death).
Paternal controls meant
placing out, establishing
a career, letting school/
career training blend
together for a while. Some
indecision allowed esp
life career, schooling +
marit. ladders not
yet solidified + choices
meaning wider
of forms. These placed
sporadic learnings usu.
them in Mod. households - often
of Kin

37

CHAPTER 2

Order and Disorder

The Social Experience of Youth

To a much greater extent than now, American society between 1790 and 1840 was composed of children and youth. The median age of the population was 30.8 in 1950 but only 16 in 1800. As a corollary, there were relatively few middle-aged people in the early 19th century. Those aged 45 to 64 comprised only 9 percent of the population, a proportion which had nearly doubled by 1930.[1] In itself, the pyramidal age structure conditioned rather than determined the relations between age groups. But combined with other social factors—the gradual undermining of traditions of status and hierarchy, rapid shifts of population, and an increase in the number of towns large enough to sustain the organized activities of youth—this demographic fact led to a succession of discontinuities in the experience of young people and nurtured a kind of relationship between adults and youth which bears little resemblance to the rules which have governed such relationships in the 20th century.

In general, the social life of young people followed the contours of semidependence described earlier. As young people pushed into their teens, they customarily experienced greater personal liberty. One aspect of such liberty was the joining of social institutions for youth. Voluntary associations for youth in the early decades of the 19th century were extraordinarily diverse. Churches often had young people's socie-

38

ties or special hours set aside for prayer meetings for young people.[2] But the organized activities of youth did not have to take a pious direction. For example, in the early 19th century most towns contained volunteer military companies which functioned simultaneously as militia, welcoming parties for visiting dignitaries, and social clubs for young men who attired themselves in the uniforms of hussars or dragoons, hired saber instructors from the Continent, and paraded before the ladies on holidays.[3] By all accounts, companies like the Richmond Light Infantry Blues or Philadelphia Lancer Guard or Brattleborough Light Infantry were high-spirited in more ways than one. When the captain of the Brattleborough Light Infantry ordered all cold water men to march three paces forward during an 1830 muster, no one moved a muscle.[4] An observer described a typical muster in Ohio as "a holyday for the lower classes, and the occasion of much intoxication and many brutal fights."[5]

The minimum age for membership in volunteer military companies was usually set at 18, but exceptions were common. John W. Geary, later governor of Kansas, was a lieutenant in the militia at 16.[6] At times, boys formed their own auxiliary companies. In Alexandria, Virginia, in 1860 the "Young Riflemen," boys aged 10 to 15, paraded with neat uniforms and knapsacks.[7] Being under age presented few real problems in the early 1800s. Since the military companies were voluntary, age requirements could be dispensed with whenever the members felt disposed to do so. Even during wartime, underage soldiers had little trouble joining the army. Random references to 14- and 15-year old soldiers during the Revolutionary War probably reveal no more than the tip of an iceberg.[8] Susan R. Hull was able to write a factual and meaty volume based entirely on the exploits of teenagers in the Confederate Army, some of them as young as 13.[9]

Somewhere between the piety of the church youth societies and the rowdy military companies were self-improvement societies, which at times contained specific references to young men or young people in their titles but which, even if they did not, were usually composed of youth. A "Young People's Total Abstinence Society" was formed in Dublin, New Hampshire, in 1842.[10] Few towns in antebellum America were without their young men's debating or mechanics' societies, where books, ideas, and fellowship circulated freely.[11] Lyceums, the quintessential expression of the idea of self-culture, were often outgrowths of young men's societies. In its original form the lyceum was little more than a young men's society for mutual instruction; only gradually did lyceums evolve into forums for outside lecturers, and even then young men's societies continued to play a role as sponsoring agents.[12]

By mid-century, young men's societies in the larger cities had become well-organized, prominent civic institutions with handsome budgets, well-stocked libraries, and a membership drawn mainly from young businessmen in their 20s. The constitution of the Young Men's Association of the City of Milwaukee, organized in 1847, entitled those between 18 and 35 to become members, while limiting those under 18 to use of the library.[13] The association's age range thus approximated that of a modern Junior Chamber of Commerce. Prior to 1840, however, young men's societies were less well organized and probably embraced a more youthful age group. Apprentice associations had long carried on many of the same functions as young men's societies, and the former certainly included teenagers. In towns, moreover, self-improvement societies were likely to contain a mixture of boys, girls, young men, and young ladies, even after 1840.[14] A literary club in Surry, New Hampshire, begun in 1853 with the purpose of staging debates and theatricals, provides a good illustration of the persistence of promiscuous age groupings outside of large cities.[15]

Members' Ages: Literary Club, Surry, N.H.:, 1853–1854

Males

AGE	11	12	13	14	15	16	17	18	19	20	21	22	23	24	30
Number	0	0	2	2	3	3	2	3	3	1	0	1	2	1	1

Females

AGE	11	12	13	14	15	16	17	18	19	20	21	22	23	24	30
Number	1	0	2	2	1	2	2	2	1	3	0	0	0	0	0

Loose age groupings like this one survived longer in towns than in cities, but even in cities teenagers under 18 often formed junior appendages of organizations in which the majority of members were between 18 and 30. Young men in their early to middle teens served urban volunteer fire companies in various ways, although they were too young for full membership (see Chapter 4). The Sons of Temperance had a junior branch called the Cadets of Temperance. Most of the members of the Young Men's Christian Association were over 18, but the minimum age was usually as low as 15.[16]

Alongside structured and organized activities a host of less formal pursuits engaged the spare time of young people, pursuits which ranged from firing off guns all night on the Fourth of July to dating and dancing. When Silas Felton, who grew up in a small Massachusetts town toward the end of the 18th century, related that he spent most of his evenings either reading or "roving about . . . which is generally the case with boys 10 to 21 years old," he expressed an important aspect of youthful life experience.[17]

Two broad impulses underpinned the innumerable specific forms taken by youthful pranks before 1840: ritualized insubordination and parody. Ritualized insubordination would be a fair description of the acts of "Knotts of Riotous Young Men" who nightly serenaded Cotton Mather during the early 1700s with "profane and filthy" songs, and of the schoolboys who engaged during the 18th and early 19th centuries in the custom of "turning out" schoolmasters who refused their demands for holidays. In contrast, parody was the dominant impulse behind the mock commencements often staged by college freshmen. At times the two impulses merged. At a Pennsylvania industrial village a troop of thirty to fifty "jovial young fellows" joined in a band each New Year's Eve, equipped themselves with powder, guns, and wadding in joking imitation of militiamen, and marched from farm to farm, firing off salutes and demanding hospitality and "all manner of good cheer." This particular custom had died out by 1843, after careless shooting resulted in injuries and death to a few luckless inhabitants.[18]

Contemporary accounts of New England and southern society also abound with references to sleigh rides, chitchat, and dances among young people. Brantley York, born in 1805 in Randolph County, North Carolina, related how the youth held "disorderly and demoralizing" dances in the vicinity of his home every Wednesday and Saturday night.[19] The diary of Hezekiah Prince, a young man living in Templeton, Maine, in the 1820s, related an almost continuous round of parties and sleigh rides among the youth of Templeton and adjoining towns, with no adult chaperonage.[20] Parents, especially pious ones, often objected to youthful socializing, but there was always the recourse outlined by Amos Kendall in his autobiography.

> The family government was strict, and so far as it bore upon their eldest children, severe. They were not only prohibited from dancing, playing cards, and all like amusements, but from going to places where they were practiced. The consequence was that the elder sons deceived their parents and indulged in those forbidden recreations clandestinely.[21]

The degree of freedom rose with age. Sixteen was the usual age at which young ladies began to keep company with young men, although there were variations down to 14 and up to 18. As an example of the latter, in 1781 the 22-year-old Erkuries Beatty, an officer in the Continental Army, sent his brother Reading a kind of Baedeker to the charms of young (and some old) maidens in the vicinity of Yorktown, Virginia, where Reading was about to be sent. The list included Bekky Miller, who "rather got a sourness in her looks, but is very good Natured," and "her father will give her a very good fortune if he pleases," and fifteen other maidens, plus

> one buxom Rich widow, two old maids, three or four young girls that have got married, with a number of married ladies in the town—I could enumerate a great many more young ones to you between ages 18 and 15, but as we were never admitted into the company of those above mentioned, being too young, it is not worth while.[22]

Whether the girls between 15 and 18 were deemed too young for dating or just too young for a bounder like Erkuries Beatty is open to question. The evidence is somewhat conflicting, but Erkuries's lack of success with girls 15 to 18 was probably atypical, especially in view of the amount of dating that went on between cousins. As Erkuries related to Reading a year earlier, "that night Cousin Polly and me set off a Slaying with a number more young People and had a pretty Clever kick-up." [23] The extent to which the social life of young people went on within the kin group or as an offshoot of kin relations probably softened prohibitions against youthful socializing.

If "dating" is defined as social meetings between young people of opposite sex who have no intention to marry, then it is a more accurate term than "courtship" to describe social engagements in the early 19th century. The presence of so many unescorted young people at social gatherings probably reduced pressures to establish formal courtship but at the same time distinguished such meetings from our own style of dating, which places a premium on physical intimacy in public and exclusive pairing.[24] The presence of adults, more as spectators than as chaperones, had the same effect. Logging bees, quilting bees, and apple bees included all ages and often ended up with "a nice supper or refreshment and the usual play or dance, kept until midnight or after." [25]

As one would expect, greater freedom marked the passage from dependence to semidependence in the social as well as economic relations of youth. But semidependence also contained a more complex element of alternation between precocious, adultlike independence and demands for childlike subordination. Young people at times experienced a halfway blend of freedom and restraint, with elements of freedom becoming more pronounced over time. But at other points they were exposed to temporally alternating opportunities for independence and adult responsibility on one side and demands for submission on the other. They grew up on a series of separate timetables, with certain elements of social maturity coming much earlier than now, and others much later.[26]

If we label one side of the ledger "precocity," the list of experiences would stretch far down the page. In the churches, for example, the pres-

ence of catechetical classes for young people did not release them from
the obligation to attend regular services, nor did it exclude them from
religious revivals. In the revivals of the early 1800s, teenagers usually
played a more prominent role than adults, and even small children of 7
or 8 were not exempt from the religious injunction that "early piety"
begin early (see Chapter 3). The fact that young people had their own
self-improvement societies did not exclude them from joining societies
which had no minimum or maximum age requirements. A Delaware
abolition society formed in 1800 included one teenager, a 14-year-old
clock and cabinet maker, three men in their 20s, one in his 30s, two in
their 40s, and one in his 50s.[27] As a variation, a society originally
formed by and for young men might change itself into a society without
age specification. The Young Men's New York Bible Society, established in 1823 and open to youth under 30, dropped the name
"young men" in 1839 and removed its outer age limit.[28] Further, auxiliary and regular organizations could exist side by side. The presence of
the Cadets of Temperance for those aged 16 to 21 did not stop the Sons
of Temperance from admitting anyone 14 and over to membership,
while restricting voting rights to those 18 and over.[29] Finally, in contrast to adult-sponsored youth organizations in the 20th century, the
great majority of young people's societies in the early 1800s were voluntary, organized and conducted by young people themselves. Young
people occasionally called in adults for assistance, but only for ceremonial or legal purposes. Apprentice associations, for example, customarily sought adult sponsorship, but simply as an expedient; adults
could sign legal contracts pertaining to the use of halls and meeting
places. Associations were not only of youth and for youth but by youth
as well (see pp. 199–204).

Political education also began at an early age. Public political gatherings were likely to attract children and youth as well as adults. The
ubiquitous village debating societies were not substitutes for political
involvement. Sixteen-year-old Merrill Ober of Monkton, Vermont,
passed hour after hour in the village store, talking politics with adults.[30]
Charles Turner Torrey attended town meetings with his grandfather
when 5 or 6. Samuel Rodman, a New Bedford merchant, took his 13-
year-old son to hear Wendell Phillips speak in 1837, just as he allowed
his sons to accompany him on his daily business rounds.[31]

Children and young people witnessed the events surrounding
death as well as life. Samuel J. May, born in Boston in 1797, related the
death of his brother, when Samuel was 4 years old.

> Then they put grave-clothes upon him, and laid him upon the mattress in
> the best chamber, and straightened out his limbs, and folded his beautiful
> hands upon his breasts, and covered him only with a clear, cold, white
> sheet. I saw it all,—for they could not keep me away.[32]

More accurately, "they" did not want to keep him away. Responding to Samuel's desire to see where they put his brother, his uncle took him to the family vault and showed him where his brother and ancestors were entombed. Then "my kind uncle opened one of the coffins, and let me see how decayed the body had become, told me that [my brother] Edward's body was going to decay in like manner, and at last become like the dust of the earth." [33]

Necrophilia? Perhaps, but more likely Samuel's uncle was merely applying an approved psychological principle of the day, that the durability of any impression depended on the force and distinctness of the original perception. According to facultative psychology, the development of memory preceded reason, and childhood was the time to implant both strong impressions and regular habits. Death was as real as life. Everyone died, children included, and the sooner children learned about death the better. A few years later May's father was to justify a severe and probably unjust whipping that Samuel had received in school with the observation that the world was filled with injustice and that Samuel had to be inured to it.

Although evidence is difficult to recover, it seems that even in the early 19th century some parents had scruples against letting children see too many of the events surrounding a death in the family or neighborhood.[34] But even if many parents of that era had been reluctant to expose children to scenes of death, they could hardly have succeeded with any regularity, for people did not usually die in hospitals but at home, right in front of the family. Nor could parents have controlled the content of sermons aimed at youth, which were characterized by the pervasive theme of *memento mori*.

Thus, convention dictated that young people quickly be exposed to the religious, political, and emotional concerns of adults. Yet in other ways the process of maturation was slow. If we return to our ledger and label the other side "delayed development," a fairly long list of experiences can justifiably be included. For one thing, puberty came later than now. Allowing for variations between social classes and acknowledging that generalizations are no more than educated guesses based on the impressions of contemporary physicians, a reasonable estimate would put male puberty at around 16, with female puberty coming a year earlier. (Corresponding ages now would be 14 and 12, again with some qualifications.) Not only did puberty come later, but physical growth was a much more gradual process than now, with final height not attained by young men until around age 25. (Today, young people grow little beyond age 18.) The gradual nature of growth helps to explain why contemporaries used terms like "youth" and "young man" to describe those in their 20s. William Gilmore Simms's description of the fictional Ralph Colleton bears comparison with Francis Lieber's description, cited earlier, of "W___." Simms wrote: "Our traveller, on the present occasion, was a mere youth. He had probably seen twenty summers—scarcely more. Yet his person was tall and well developed; symmetrical and manly; rather slight, perhaps, as was proper to his immaturity." [35]

Delayed development was not just a matter of the timing of physical growth. We have seen how various factors, such as dependence on agriculture, the absence of graded and lubricated educational tracks, and the need to establish personal connections, all conspired to delay young men seeking to enter professions. It seems likely, too, that behind some of the foot-dragging noted earlier was a lack of intense social pressure on young men to decide on vocations. It was one thing to warn against idleness, quite another to exhort young men to break out of familiar molds, leave behind familiar scenes, and push ahead in the scramble for position. After 1840, rising in the world increasingly became a kind of moral injunction on youth; indeed, it was the major conclusion of the success philosophy. But the mandate of success philosophy was only dimly perceived in agricultural communities in the early 1800s.

A no less important feature of early 19th-century society was the emphasis on the subordination of young people. Subordination had many antecedents. It was part of a tradition that decreed that sons and daughters were inferior members of the family hierarchy. It was this tradition which led young men to recall the dignified reserve which their fathers presented to them on so many occasions, and which led boys and girls to send their "duty" rather than their love to parents. [36] The same tradition led fathers to sound like commanding officers when they addressed even mature sons. Although he was 25 years old and living in Boston, Aaron Dennison received the following advice from his father in Maine in 1837:

> I am afraid that you do not have exercise enough to keep you in good health and spirits and to remedy that difficulty as much as possible I should like to have you retire to rest by 9 and rise certainly by 5 in the morning and take a long walk in the morning air at least one hour every morning when it is suitable weather. Don't neglect this for I think it is important. [37]

Finally, the same tradition of hierarchical deference prompted the father of James Duncan to write in his will: "I also *order* my son James to live with his mother until he arrive to twenty-one years of age and to be dutiful to his mother." [38]

Hierarchical deference prevailed within families not only between parents and children but between brothers. Older brothers addressed

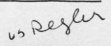

young ones in letters with the same combination of formality and tutorial attentiveness that characterized addresses from fathers to sons. "You are now in a critical state of life," 24-year-old William Beaumont wrote to his 18-year-old brother in 1809. "Errors and improprieties will beset you on every side in spite of your precautionary efforts to evade them. . . . The strongest and most effectual barrier against these deviations is to cultivate your mind and procure a stock of familiar ideas and useful information." [39]

In the 18th century these attitudes had been rooted in the land base of society and had found their most forceful expression in the intricate provisions of wills by which fathers sought to tie sons to the land. Common in the 18th century, such provisions are less frequently encountered after 1800. But as one traditional technique to establish the subordination of youth declined, others survived, revealing themselves nowhere better than in the widespread use of humiliation and disgrace in schools. [40]

In his essay "Education," Ralph W. Emerson wrote that while many teachers of his day entered the classroom filled with idealism, the size of classes and diversity in age and preparation among students quickly put to flight the nascent aspirations of pedagogues to control their charges by moral influence alone. "Something must be done, and done speedily," Emerson continued, "and in their distress the wisest are tempted to adopt violent means, to proclaim martial law, corporal punishment, mechanical arrangements, bribes, spies, wrath, main strength and ignorance, in place of that wise and genial providential influence they had hoped, and yet hope in some future day to adopt." [41] Perhaps this is what Geroge Moore, the Acton schoolmaster, had in mind when he told his pupils on his first day in class that he intended to " 'conquer or die.' " [42]

Although "main strength" was a popular technique of school discipline, humiliation was usually the favorite weapon of the schoolmaster's arsenal. Joseph Lancaster, originator of the Lancasterian system of education, in which the older boys taught the younger ones, spent pages denouncing corporal punishment before outlining the substitutes dear to his own heart—suspending miscreants from the ceiling in a kind of birdcage, forcing them to march backward around the room with their necks yoked, or pinning signs on their backs naming their transgressions. The birdcage does not appear to have been used in America, but most American children in district schools of the early 19th century knew that "sitting on the wall" meant sitting on thin air (squatting with only the back against the wall for balance), and that "holding nails into the floor" meant to stoop for hours. They also knew what it was like to serve as the master's footstool or to shave publicly with a wooden razor. None of this was new in the 19th century. Puri-

vs
Degler

46

tans in earlier times had been simultaneously skeptical of corporal punishment and great believers in the value of humiliation. Lancaster himself, raised as a Scottish Presbyterian, absorbed a religious tradition distinctive both for its avid belief in the importance of education and in its unshakable commitment to humiliation as a technique of discipline.[43]

Despite the persistence of certain similarities, there was a basic change in the practice of humiliation between the 17th and 19th centuries, for in the earlier period humiliation was part of a larger pattern of social control. If boys held nails into the floor, adults sat in the stocks. By 1830, in contrast, public shaming was no longer a primary method for maintaining social order among adults, but it continued to flourish in the schools—a good example of the tendency, noted by Philippe Ariès, whereby practices once generally accepted survive only among youth.[44] Perhaps because public humiliation prevailed in schools long after its disappearance elsewhere, its application after 1800 resulted increasingly in student mutinies and disruptions.

The school disruption, also called a "breaking-up," a "carrying-out" (of the master), a "turn-out," and a "barring-out," was often little more than a community ritual. This tradition, which gradually declined in the 19th century but which flourished in the small towns and villages of 150 years ago, provided a healthy outlet for pent-up energies in the dreary winter months. Spiced as it is with the flavor of the humorist, Augustus Longstreet's recounting of a fictional turn-out in *Georgia Scenes* is worth recounting. Visiting a Captain Griffen, the author learns that the local schoolboys plan to turn out the master the next day. Griffen urges that they witness the struggle, "for though the master is always upon such occasions, glad to be turned out, and only struggles long enough to present his patrons a fair apology for giving the children a holyday," the boys still will try to prove their valor, "and, in their zeal to distinguish themselves upon such memorable occasions, they sometimes become too rough, and provoke the master to wrath, and a very serious conflict ensues."

On the appointed day of the struggle, the boys arrive first and barricade themselves in the school, called an "academy" but just a long pen with a roof on top. The master, feigning ignorance of the motives of the boys, attacks with a fence rail, punctures a hole in the side of the school, and storms in, over the protests of the "largest boys," the recognized champions of the pupils. Seating himself on the desk, he leans back and puts his feet on a nearby table, thus making himself a perfect target for the next contrivance. The boys grab the master by the leg, carry him out, and wrestle with him in the yard until he finally yields to their pleas for a "holyday." [45]

Sometimes the turn-out had nothing to do with a petition for a holiday but was a forceful response to brutal and self-important masters. R. C. Stone related a local quarrel over school discipline in Rhode Island. His son, aged 15 or 16, was teaching school in Easton when "a few large scholars" grew insubordinate. Their ringleader was expelled, whereupon he appealed to his friends outside the school, young village toughs willing to take matters into their own hands. Breaking into the school, they forced young Stone out. Since it took a court decision to return Stone to his desk, we can label this as more than a community ritual. Similar turn-outs were widespread in the early 19th century, despite sustained criticism of the practice by authorities on school discipline. Horace Mann described the evil as "enormous" and blamed it on the older boys and young men aged 15 to 20, a point on which his contemporaries agreed.[46]

Even in the absence of turn-outs, disorder born of large numbers, disparate ages, late arrivers, and early leavers was routine in district schools. Confronted by a phalanx of indifferent or disgruntled plowboys in school or by their cronies outside, masters often resorted to violence in anticipation of violence, thrashing the ringleader before the trouble began.

Problems inherent to the teacher's position, moreover, exacerbated difficulties caused by the students. In theory, the authority of teachers to keep order was absolute, or nearly so, but in practice authority was conditioned by all sorts of limitations. Many of the teachers were collége or academy students on vacation between terms. Often they were younger than their students. Had R. C. Stone's 16-year-old son been teaching in George Moore's Acton school, he would have been younger than more than a third of the students. Schoolmasters were often outsiders who "boarded around" in the community, living by night with the parents of students whom they taught by day. When disputes arose between pupils and teachers, townspeople were likely to remember that they were neighbors and parishioners of the students' families, forgetting their obligations to the teachers. Schoolmasters could not point consistently to any source of authority beyond themselves to sustain their actions. Law courts might help in individual cases, but in the absence of a bureaucracy to administer discipline, pressure fell mainly on the teachers. The school was theirs, to be "kept." [47]

Taken collectively, these factors exerted a number of conflicting pulls and tugs. The physical proximity of teacher and student could facilitate a friendly relationship, but it could also produce a redoubling of efforts to maintain tutorial dignity, Edward Magill, referring to his experience at a country school in 1841, aptly summarized the problem:

> From the opening of the school I was engaged with my pupils in games of ball, snow-balling, etc., during the recess, just as one of them, but was

careful to put on the serious and resolute schoolmaster's face when I rang the bell for them to reassemble. This acting a double part as master and student, was made all the more difficult, because my pupils were my own personal friends, relatives, and near neighbors, and a number of them, both boys and girls, were my seniors by several years.[48]

The experiences of Silas Felton of Marlborough, Massachusetts, illustrate the connection between the proximity of age groups, insecurity of status, and the administration of discipline. Felton's early life was typical of New England farm boys of the period. He attended school periodically, returning to his father whenever called, and enjoyed the usual rounds of social visiting among the town's young people. Although at 19 he had no advanced education and was "almost ignorant of the English grammar," Felton was called upon to teach school in 1795. Meeting with some success in his first engagement, Felton decided to try his luck again as a teacher. But he concluded that he needed additional formal education, and thus sought and received permission from his father to attend a term at Leicester Academy, then conducted by Theodore Dehon, in later life Episcopal bishop of South Carolina but at that time on winter vacation from Harvard. Dehon and Felton were the same age, 20, but there the resemblance ceased, for Dehon was a polished college man, a banker's son, ignorant, according to Felton, of both human nature and the manners of country people, and overbearing toward his students.[49]

Felton "took" a number of schools after his term at Leicester, but he was involved in only one notable controversy, brought on by a severe whipping which he administered to a 10- or 12-year-old boy. The occasion was a lie told by the boy, but the severity of the beating was actually the result of the boy's refusal to admit the lie:

> I took my ruler, it was a large round ruler made of Cherry tree Wood, this I applied to his hand, quite moderately at first, but he insisted he was innocent, and they [his accusers] as strongly that he was guilty; I repeated the operation of the ruler again to his hand till I made him confess the crime and say he was sorry.[50]

After various threats and counterthreats, Felton apologized to the boy's father. In his reminiscences, Felton justified himself on grounds that he had administered much more severe beatings in the past. Yet he was not a martinet by nature, nor an unthinking traditionalist, but a free thinker of sorts who had never quite gotten over his reading of Thomas Paine's *Age of Reason* at 16. But, as was likely true of Dehon, his mentor, Felton found that the application of main strength was one of the few ways in which a teacher without clear and recognized authority could force students to take him seriously. Interestingly, Felton related one additional instance of his whipping a boy, his own brother Aaron, who had boasted that "he wasn't going to mind Silas," until "I whipt him once or twice more and he afterwoods behaved well." [51]

School discipline fell on children and youth alike. Some masters tried to separate younger and older children in seating arrangements, but they had to be in the same room, regardless of age. A teacher who looked across his desk to see a mixture of infants, boys, girls, young men, and young ladies was unlikely to grade his discipline according to the specific age or level of development of the pupil. If anything, he was likely to note that the older boys, the 15- to 20-year-olds, usually made the most trouble and hence had to be brought into line first.

Differences in social class altered the nature but not the fact of subordination. Wealthy and well-educated parents usually held district school education in low esteem; private "select" schools, "family boarding schools," and academies flourished to suit the needs of parents who could pay for a better product. But the difference between education for ordinary people and education for the children of the rich was not that of a hard and severe regimen versus a soft and malleable one, but of the spasmodic discipline of the district school versus the more consistent but still severe discipline of a private institution. James Russell Lowell was the son of a minister who could have educated him at home but who chose instead to send young James to a preparatory boarding school characterized by harsh discipline. [52] Similarly, Samuel J. May was taken from a dame school for young children at 8 years of age and placed in a strict preparatory school, in accordance with his father's desire that he be toughened. [53] As a corollary, wealthy fathers often preferred to send their children away from home for education, just as wealthy merchants elected to send their children out as cabin boys or supercargo. [54]

Before the professionalization of teaching, a process only beginning in the 1820s and without significant effect until much later, there was little to cushion head-to-head collisions between teachers and pupils. The teacher was not the agent of some clearly recognized higher authority; he was not clothed in the panoply of certification, nor even, necessarily, of learning. With their own roles ill-defined, teachers had difficulty finding the right tone to adopt toward students. The anomalies in the teacher's position promoted the disposition to be stiff, formal, and strict, while simultaneously making the exercise of authority appear incongruous and inconsistent to the pupils. Sanctioned as they were by long-standing practice, hierarchical distance and humiliation were also nourished by the very proximity of age groups in the early Republic. [55]

Deference and Disorder in American Colleges

The inconsistent administration of discipline and the alternation of freedom and submission were factors which connected the experience of students in district schools and academies with those of college students. Although they comprised only a small and declining proportion of the population, college students came from a fairly broad range of backgrounds. A few were sons of the very rich, sometimes delinquent sons shipped off to college for the same reasons that their descendants in the 20th century have been packed off to military boarding schools. But many antebellum college students were raw rubes from the villages who had abandoned farming to their less ambitious brothers in order to seek out advanced education. Others were indigents subsidized by the various evangelical benevolent societies to prepare for ministerial careers.[56] The colleges themselves were underfinanced, top-heavy with clergymen, and often intellectually sterile. Yet nowhere else in antebellum America were youth gathered in such a controlled environment, so that the 19th-century college is valuable as a kind of test tube in which to study contemporary assumptions about the behavior of young people.

Any student of antebellum college life has to confront the incongruous mixture of deference, discipline, and authority on one side and "great rout, riot, and disorder" on the other. College discipline revealed a near obsession with order at every turn. The concept of *in loco parentis* does not do justice to the traditional philosophy of college discipline, for with few exceptions those who wrote about college discipline assumed that parental discipline was too mild for the management of large groups of young men. Even Philip Lindsley, generally a humane spokesman for progressive ideals of college government, emphasized that "the government of a family is but an epitome or remote resemblance to that which obtains in a college." [57] *In loco parentis* was at most an ideal worth pursuing, at worst a corrupt philosophy, but on no count a description of the norm.[58]

Two reasons were usually given for the inadequacy of the concept of parentalism. First, in America parental discipline was too mild; it was not even good enough at home.[59] Second—and this argument had deep roots in the history of educational institutions—whatever might be said about young men as individuals, in groups they were a menace to themselves and to society. Pedagogues had associated for centuries "congregate" or "public" education, the education of youth in groups, with moral danger and had agreed on the need for strict supervision.

Few administrators seriously believed that young people could be managed in colleges along parental lines, but at the same time few were willing to abandon the promotional value of advertising a mild system of discipline. The blurb of the College of East Tennessee was both a vivid expression of this dilemma and, incidentally, a classic of double-talk:

> The administration of the government of the College shall ever be mild and equitable, and as nearly parental as the nature of the establishment will admit. The reformation of the offender shall be steadily and judiciously aimed at, as far as practicable; and no severe or disgraceful penalty shall be awarded, except when the paramount interests of the Institution shall demand it, or when the flagitious character of the offence shall render it indispensable.[60]

Or, as the latitudinarian minister told his parishioners, if one sins, as it were, and does not repent, so to speak, one shall be damned, to a certain extent.

To supplement parental discipline, American colleges had issued lists of rules and regulations from their earliest days, modeled first on the statutes of English universities and later on each other. By 1800 the rule books which students were expected to sign left little to the imagination. Not content with outlining acceptable behavior, some even prescribed the curriculum. The Hamilton College laws of 1802 consisted of eleven chapters of seven to twenty-three sections each.[61] An element of exquisite detail marked some of the manuals. At Yale in the 18th century, students were forbidden to wear hats within five rods of tutors and eight rods of professors.[62] In general, the regulations had four aims. First, they prescribed behavior in chapel and classroom, often requiring daily attendance at both. Second, they limited freedom of movement from the environs of the college, prohibiting students from leaving town without the permission of the president or from going to the village during study hours. Third, they sought to safeguard students from each other by outlawing knives and guns. Finally, they forbade loud noises, the playing of musical instruments during study hours, idle conversation around doors and gates, gambling, and drinking.[63]

To ensure that the rules were obeyed, colleges provided a wide range of graduated penalties. At the bottom of the scale were private admonitions and fines, leading up to public admonition, forced public confession, suspension, rustication, and expulsion. Practices varied from college to college and between the 18th and 19th centuries. Public whippings, permissible in 17th-century and early 18th-century colleges, passed out of use in the latter part of the 18th century. At times, degradation to a lower class was added to other penalties. But at any period the college functioned in theory more like a petty despotism than like a family. The system of penalties was parental only in the sense that admonition was to precede the application of more severe penalties.

If a preoccupation with deference and authority formed one pole of antebellum college life, the other was marked by a mixture of pranks, violence, and rebellion by students. There had always been some petty harassment of college officials in the form of ringing the college bell all night, sticking dead ducks in the chapel, and snowball fights leading to broken windows. Pranks like this continued in the late 18th and early 19th centuries, with some refinements of the art. A Princeton president who commenced chapel by opening his Bible to the appropriate passage found a pack of cards staring up at him. South Carolina College students often "defiled" the pulpit, presumably with urine. At Dickinson College, Moncure Conway got even with an overbearing president by informing authorities at Staunton, Virginia, where the president was attending a church meeting, that a harmless lunatic who fancied himself the president of Dickinson College had escaped from custody, was thought to be in the Staunton area, and should be confined at once to the local asylum. A Providence farmer one morning found his horse and wood transported to the top of University Hall at Brown; later, President Asa Messer's horse made an overnight stand at the same elevation, courtesy of young Samuel Gridley Howe.[64]

The difference after 1750, however, lay less in the perfection of traditional twitting than in an increase of violence to persons and the emergence of organized student rebellions. At Yale, when President Thomas Clap—"a Tirant and a sovraign," the students said—over-reacted to tormentors who wrecked his sleep by ringing the college bell, the result was continuous rebellion between 1760 and 1766, when Clap finally resigned.[65] At Brown, students stoned Messer's house almost nightly in the 1820s.[66] Harvard had a riot over bad bread in the commons in 1766, a "bread and butter riot" in 1805 over the same thing, and a "great Rebellion" in 1823.[67] During a riot at Princeton in 1807 the faculty lost control and had to call in the townspeople for help. At Virginia, Thomas Jefferson, who originally had hoped that the university would be run more or less without rules, lived long enough to see a number of students expelled for "vicious irregularities." Had he lived longer, he would have seen much worse: repeated insurrection, culminating in the murder of Professor Nathaniel Davis by a student in 1840.[68]

Student violence was not exclusively directed against people in authority. Beatings of blacks and servants and fights between students were frequent. At South Carolina College in 1833, two students fought a duel; one was killed, the other maimed for life. Two of the leading politicians in the state served as seconds, a curious example of young and old mingling in a common cause.[69] Fist and knife fights were more common than formal duels. In 1799 a North Carolina student was publicly whipped for stabbing another student, but the whipping did not deter others from similar offenses in subsequent years.[70] The long war between the rival literary societies at Chapel Hill was not always a war of words.[71] Nor were fights between students confined to the South. The rebellion of 1823 at Harvard, which ended in a confrontation between students and faculty, began as a struggle between rival student factions.

The faculty, however, being the nearest authority, received more than its share of abuse. Davis's case at Virginia was exceptional only in its outcome. Eight years before Davis was murdered, a proctor at Virginia had investigated a loud noise on the lawn, only to encounter a crowd of students parading in disguise. His remonstrances were met first by threats, then by a barrage of rocks. Professor Harrison was beaten by a student in 1830, and horsewhipped by two students in the presence of a hundred bystanders in 1839. A year earlier, Professor Blaetterman had been attacked by a student in his classroom.[72] No wonder Henry Barnard called Virginia students a "set of pretty wild fellows." At the University of North Carolina in 1850 a number of drunken students stoned two professors who presumed to interfere in their revels, forcing the teachers to take refuge in a barricaded room.[73] At Davidson in the 1850s students rioted over a difficult assignment and showered professors with stones. Amos Kendall related how Dartmouth students in the 1820s attacked professors' homes, blasting out the windows with shotguns.[74] Philip Lindsley summed up the situation crisply:

> They [students] form a party by themselves—a distinct interest of their own—view with suspicion every measure or movement of the faculty—and resolve to contravene and thwart their plans as far as it may be in their power.[75]

What was behind antebellum student disorders? Why was the period between 1790 and 1840 (or, more broadly, between 1750 and 1850) filled with such extraordinary turmoil? In the late 19th century, college officials who were familiar with past disorders often claimed that antebellum student riots were the result of attempts to apply an absurdly severe system of discipline on young men. This "argument from repression" held that antebellum students led such monkish lives and groaned under the weight of such an elaborate pyramid of rules that their human instincts drove them into periodic and desperate spasms of violence before they sank back, exhausted and defeated, into apathy.

This interpretation helps to explain some aspects of antebellum student life. The petty enforcement of petty rules *was* galling, not only at pioneer universities like Indiana, where professors were determined to turn half-literate backwoodsmen into polished gentlemen, but at Harvard and Yale too. Our knowledge of the agents of discipline—professors, presidents, and tutors—lends further support to the argument from repression, for these men were often unsuited by temperament to their tasks. Too many of them were overbearing and officious, inordinately fond of the prerogatives of petty power. Probably more pious than the average person and certainly more likely to be a minister, the old-time college president often had trouble keeping perspective on student mischief. He was scandalized when others might have been indifferent or tolerantly amused. Professors and tutors often lacked the self-assurance to stay calm before taunts and indignities; indeed, they viewed themselves as islands of cultivation in a sea of barbarism. Moreover, many of those charged with the administration of discipline were young themselves, scarcely older than the students. Tutors were usually recent graduates, often younger than many of the students. To a lesser extent, the same was true of professors and presidents. Joseph Caldwell, who presided over the chaos at Chapel Hill, was only 24 when he became president. In itself, the youthfulness of the authorities could have cut either way. It might have induced tutors and professors to adopt a chummy stance toward the students, but more often it had the opposite effect, leading officials to assume the air of stiff-necked martinets.

Although the argument from repression does fit some features of antebellum student life, its defects are manifold. The argument ignores the role played in antebellum student upheavals by the changing composition of student bodies. Most of the students in 17th- and early 18th-century colleges had been teenagers, and most were preparing to become ministers. The latter part of the 18th century, in contrast, witnessed the beginning of an influx of older and poorer students, many of whom did not intend to become ministers. The presence of an abundance of young men in their 20s in colleges was the result of the same social forces that were delaying the entrance of young men into professions. The growth of towns and the pressure on available land in northern states were transforming the expectations of young men and propelling many from the plow and workbench into colleges. Changes in the student population put new kinds of stress on the traditional system of tutorial watchfulness, for economic necessity forced poor students to seek work outside the college walls. Meanwhile, the enforcement of petty rules infuriated older students, who resented the imposition of a kind of authority more suited to schoolboys than to young adults.[76]

The argument from repression also ignores the amount of real freedom experienced by the students. Because professors and presidents were much more concerned with the moral than with the intellectual development of students, for example, they usually were indifferent to the intellectual subculture that emerged at most colleges in the form of literary societies, such as the Linonian at Yale, the Jefferson at the University of Virginia, and the Philogian at Williams. Literary societies provided students with the very things that they could not find in class or commons: privacy, conviviality, and intellectual stimulation. In the literary societies, students gave speeches in the style of Webster and Choate, debated slavery and antislavery, and read romantic poets like Byron. The unofficial *Vernunft* of the literary societies flourished without really challenging the official *Verstand* which reigned in the classroom. The narrowness of the official curriculum was actually an advantage, for all the students were obliged to do was to prepare for recitation in class, an enterprise less time-consuming than working through the reading lists found in many 20th-century colleges. While colleges in theory sought to become totally regulated environments, they were in practice willing to allow a significant role to self-cultivation. Throughout the antebellum period a lively extracurriculum thrived alongside a stuffy curriculum in American colleges.[77]

Antebellum students also enjoyed a respectable degree of social freedom. Unchaperoned dating was the norm, whether in the form of the parlor visit, the moonlight walk, or the sleigh ride.[78] The increasing tendency of students to board not in commons but in the town provided an added degree of social freedom. For financial reasons newer colleges often lacked residential facilities; so did some of the older colleges, such as the University of Pennsylvania.[79] Even at institutions with commons—Harvard and South Carolina, for example—students won the right to board out.[80] Like other aspects of student freedom, residential freedom lacked a theoretical justification. It just happened.

In addition, even the enforcement of moral rules was often fitful. Rule books embodying Puritan assumptions about ideal behavior also betrayed the pragmatic side of the Puritan mentality, the candid if usually unspoken recognition that gaps between real and ideal behavior were rarely bridged in this world. Puritans and pietists had always been inclined to announce a set of elevated ideals and then to assume that most individuals would miss the mark. Even President Clap of Yale, probably the most autocratic college president in 18th-century America, routinely ignored a range of petty offenses.[81] The best illustration of the dualism, however, was the rigid and detailed system of fines which prevailed in colonial colleges and survived into the early 19th century, for such a mechanical system assumed that students would go right on committing petty misdemeanors.

Dualistic assumptions about behavior were not the only mitigating factors in college discipline. Although their paper authority was nearly limitless, college officials in the early 1800s often had little practical power to respond to offenses. There were too many colleges, and they needed students more than students needed them.[82] The system of fines, whatever might be asserted in its defense, was best suited to minor infractions by individuals, not to violent felonies by student mobs. As violent disruptions increased, administrators resorted to suspensions, which students were usually willing to risk, and expulsions, which could be more costly to the college than to students. Even well-established colleges like Harvard, which responded to mass disorders with mass expulsions, found themselves on the brink of disaster.[83]

If this result was occasionally missed by professors, it did not escape trustees, who often reinstated students expelled by the faculty. Because they needed students, moreover, college officials tempered the application of authority not only by reinstating miscreants but also by widespread resort to the notorious dismission-readmission or "out-in" loophole. That is, students expelled from one university were admitted somewhere else, usually with little more than a statement of repentance or evidence, almost any sort of evidence, that they had been victimized by arbitrary authority.[84]

Merely to note that antebellum students had various types of practical freedom does not invalidate the idea that the application of rules caused disruptions, for authority administered fitfully can be more contemptible than the mailed fist. But recognition of the real limits of authority in antebellum colleges does put matters into a new perspective, and underscores similarities between the maintenance of authority in colleges and in district schools or academies. In each case discipline was inconsistent and the experience of it discontinuous.

In one respect, however, colleges were unique, for their students were more conscious of their own status as students than were their counterparts in other institutions, perhaps because colleges had virtually the only students in America for whom studentship was a chronologically continuous experience. This growing self-consciousness among college students affected the morphology of student rebellion. Usually there was an original spark, often a confrontation between students and professors over some trivial matter, but the uprisings which afflicted institutions as different as Harvard and the University of Virginia really began not with the unruly incident but with a threat by the students to leave the institution if a penalty applied to one of the original malefactors was not rescinded. The threat to quit was, in turn, usually contained in a remonstrance or petition drawn up by students and marked by lengthy declarations of their rights both as men and as students. Although not ideological in the sense that they sought to change the larger society, student remonstrants did seek to ground their case in the accepted political rhetoric of the day. An official at the University of North Carolina aptly summarized the content of the petitions and the faculty's reply to them when he complained in 1805 that

> nothing can be more ridiculous than *Boys at school* talking of "sacred regard for their rights," "the high and imposing duty of resistance," and of "denouncing laws," etc., etc., the genuine slang of the times, culled from the columns of newspapers.[85]

Student rebellions in the form of mass threats to leave posed a serious challenge to college authority, both in practice and in theory: in practice, because a successful rebellion could wreck an institution; in theory, because rebels, in effect, placed their horizontal allegiance to peers above their vertical allegiance to authorities. As such, the issue created by student rebellion bore on a second issue, whether a student could be held accountable for refusing to inform on another student. Few issues so well illustrated the dilemma faced by antebellum college government. College authorities had long insisted that loyalty to peers could never take precedence over loyalty to college government. Although college officials had traditionally promoted hazing and fagging, they had done so merely to develop a young man's loyalty to his class as the first step in introducing him to the hierarchical society of the college. Before freshmen could recognize the prerogatives of seniors and seniors those of professors, each group in the traditional view had to discover itself as a group.[86] Promotion of hazing had never involved acceptance of the idea that colleges should become self-governing junior republics, or tolerance for peer loyalty as such. Accordingly, officials dismissed student insistence on the absolute value of peer loyalty as no more than a "low principle of school boy ethics," while acknowledging with chagrin that students viewed it as "the depth of dishonour to testify when called upon by college authorities against the grossest violator not only of collegiate but municipal law." [87]

The intrinsic weakness of tutorial espionage in detecting infractions, coupled with the increasing number of infractions after 1800, brought the issue to a head. Tutors and professors cut preposterous figures when they went snooping. "The Old Brick resounds very frequently," a Brown student wrote, "with the breaking of glass bottles against Tudor T.'s door, if he can be called a tutor. We have given him the epithet of Weazle. He is frequently peeking through the knotholes and cracks to watch his prey." [88] If it was night, or if the student was wearing a mask or his hat over his brow, professors who gave chase to fleeting shadows might be left at the end out of breath and without a shred of evidence. Hence, the administration often told students to surrender offenders, and students often said that it was dishonorable to do so.

Both in their rebellions and in their refusal to inform on their peers, antebellum students were expressing a level of self-consciousness that had no precedent before 1750. Antebellum students continued to accept the hierarchical nature of college government, but at the same time they sought to delineate a sphere of independence for themselves. They accepted many petty rules, and even when they broke petty rules, they accepted punishment. The routine administration of discipline produced major rebellions only when the faculty tried to force students to testify against each other or when the faculty intruded in an area of student life that the students viewed as private. The rebellions at the University of Virginia, for example, grew out of the following incidents: (1) in 1833 the faculty passed an antiriot law which provided that during any disturbance students must return to their rooms on signal from their professors and that absence from one's rooms after the signal would be proof of participation in the disturbance; (2) in 1836 the faculty sought to establish control over a student volunteer military company organized several years previously; and (3) in the spring of 1845 the faculty attempted to suppress an organization known as the Calathumpian Band, a group of students who paraded and serenaded at night. In each of these cases students perceived the intrusion of arbitrary authority. The antiriot law was ex post facto; it had not been part of the rules students signed at matriculation. In forming a volunteer military company, students were doing what young men anywhere in the country were able to do. The Calathumpian Band had been allowed by the faculty to flourish for nearly six months before action was taken.[89]

Lewis S. Feuer and others have argued that antebellum student disorders were not politically motivated.[90] This observation is correct in the sense that disputes over political issues of the day rarely occasioned student uprisings. But antebellum students often used the political ideology of human rights to establish that studentship was a limited status, or that faculty rules could go just so far and no further. A considerable distance separates the ideology of antebellum students from that of student radicals in the 1960s, but an equally great distance demarcates students between 1790 and 1840 from their predecessors in the 17th and 18th centuries.

¯ Conclusion

Regardless of the type of school they attended—district school, academy, or college—young people frequently encountered alternating currents of oppression and freedom. These two poles were related in a symbiotic way. David Rothman has observed that the Draconian quality of colonial criminal law actually reflected the feebleness of police authority in the 18th century rather than the inhumanity of the lawmakers.[91] In a similar way, the practical limits of school authority reinforced the stiffness of pedagogues and contributed to the verbal despotism of the college rule books.

These observations about discipline apply directly only to schools and colleges, institutions which many young people either never attended at all or attended only sporadically. Yet there were similarities between school discipline and the sort of discipline encountered in occupations or families. The tendency of young people to shift from apprenticeship to apprenticeship, the sporadic home leavings and returns, the loose routine of the district schools, the disposition of students to shift academies every few years, and the ability of college students to defy authority were all part of a pattern of slack control over youth tempered only by occasional obtrusions of overbearing authority. Uncompromising in expression, authority was often compromised in application.

Some aspects of the social experience of youth in the early Republic were present long before 1800. The emphasis on humiliation, for example, was a feature of Puritan social discipline in the 17th century. Moreover, the necessity to leave home had long given young people certain types of practical freedom. But in the balance between freedom and oppression, the elements added after 1790 were increasingly on the side of freedom. The growing self-consciousness and radicalism of college students was as much a sign of the direction of change as was the tendency of young men after 1790 to leave home and to "start in life" at earlier ages.

After the middle of the 19th century, Americans shaped an image of the rural past as a time when young people were firmly in their place, subordinated to the wise exercise of authority and bound tightly by affective relationships to family and community. This image of the rural past became a powerful motive force behind the construction of adult-sponsored institutions for youth in the 1890s and early 1900s. So compelling was this image that the architects of institutions for city youth returned to the countryside after 1910 and sought to provide village and farm youth with surrogate experiences of the rural past. Ironically, most of the architects of adult-sponsored youth organizations at the end of the 19th century were born after 1850 and possessed little understanding of the past whose qualities they sought to recreate. Convinced that communal warmth and subordination had been characteristics of the past, they missed all the elements of tension and conflict between age groups and ignored the footloose ways of antebellum youth. Yet these misperceptions were themselves significant, for they legitimized the efforts of youth workers around 1900 to define the peripatetic habits and expressions of independence among the youth of their own day as deviant and pathological.

CHAPTER 3

Youth and
Religious Conversion

Adolescent Conversion in Perspective

MOST OBSERVERS today are familiar with periodic upsurges of religious "enthusiasm" among young people. The forms taken by religious revivals vary with social class and level of education, ranging from avant-garde explorations of Zen Buddhism to "Jesus freaks" and boy evangelists. Despite its myriad forms, religious enthusiasm has probably had a more pervasive effect on American youth since the end of World War II than have more widely reported episodes of political radicalism.

The association between youth and revivalism did not begin in 1945. In fact, the correlation of adolescence with religious conversion was an important part of the exploration of adolescent psychodynamics by such American psychologists as G. Stanley Hall and Edwin D. Starbuck at the turn of the 20th century. "This much we may say with certainty," Starbuck wrote, "that spontaneous awakenings are distinctly adolescent phenomena." [1] To prove their point, psychologists amassed statistics drawn from questionnaires sent to evangelical Protestants. Since most of the replies pointed to conversion in the teen years, they concluded that religious enthusiasm was in some way intrinsic to adolescence.[2] In retrospect, their research had more functional than scientific value. By tying adolescence to idealism and moral heroism, Hall and Starbuck helped to define and upgrade adolescence as a stage of life. But awareness of the methodological sloppiness of the original field work and a growing recognition of the cultural determinants of adolescent behavior led later psychologists quietly to inter the adolescent-conversion syndrome.

While no longer of much scientific interest, the correlation of adolescence and religious conversion has historical significance, for in attempting to describe a universal phenomenon, Hall and Starbuck struck instead on the tail end of a dragon whose head lay far back in the early history of Puritanism and whose body straddled the turn of the 19th century. In America between 1790 and 1840, evangelical Protestantism was the context in which the moral and intellectual conflicts of young people often received their primary expression.

In breaking with Catholic and Lutheran sacramental theology, Calvinists had placed the heaviest burdens on the individual conscience. At the core of Calvinism lay a profound paradox which derived from its dual insistence on unconditional election and individual responsibility. Man was culpable for his unregenerate condition, and yet the moving force behind regeneration was God. Conversion, or the turning toward God, might involve strenuous spiritual exertion, but, strictly speaking, its outcome was foreordained. This paradoxical character of Calvinism accounted for the raised temperature of so many Puritan conversion narratives. Many Puritans, moreover, were prone to compound the difficulty of conversion by piling onto it elaborate rules and rituals of humiliation and self-analysis. Thomas Hooker, for example, "deliberately fostered an attitude of doubt so that no man could claim to be regenerate without close self-examination."[3] Despite this, scorching conversion experiences affected only a minority of individuals throughout the history of Puritanism. Those who were spiritually less intense contented themselves with the pursuit of propriety and morality, and for much of the 18th century in America outward behavior was taken as sufficient evidence of inner worthiness.[4]

Exceptions to this equation of behavior and inner worthiness developed during periods of religious revivalism, most notably during the Great Awakening of the 1740s and 1750s and again during the Second Great Awakening, that massive outpouring of religious enthusiasm which swept one section of the nation after another between 1790 and 1840. Revivals did not automatically replace morality with deeper piety, but they did place new pressures on people to exhibit visible and even obtrusive piety. In practice, moreover, revivals usually led to a view of the operation of divine grace which deemphasized gradual spiritual growth in favor of immediate regeneration. That is, revivalists were likely to play down the elements of self-analysis and antecedent convic- tion, at least in comparison with a Thomas Hooker, and to dwell instead on the nature of radical change wrought by the sudden infusion of grace.[5]

Partly for this reason, conversions during periods of religious en- thusiasm not only became more common but also occurred at relatively earlier ages. Contrary to the common assumption, Puritans did not en- courage early conversion as a normal experience. Rather, they were convinced that conversion in childhood or early youth would occur only among a few precocious saints, with most conversions coming in matu- rity.[6] Such evidence as exists for the colonial period indicates that peo- ple usually joined churches shortly after conversions or public profes- sions of faith in young adulthood.[7] Even the tendency toward earlier conversions during the Great Awakening was reversed in the latter part of the 18th century.[8]

During the revivals of the early 1800s, in contrast, a tendency to- ward teenage conversions began to emerge, a tendency which hard- ened into a mold by mid-century. Time and again, evangelicals in- volved in these revivals noted the prominent role of youth, at first with curiosity, then with expectancy, and ultimately with resignation. The comment of a North Haven, Connecticut, minister in 1819 was typical: "this work like most awakenings was principally among the youth." [9] The *Congregationalist* observed of a later revival that the majority of con- verts, "as is usual, are young people." [10] Revivals not only attracted youth but often began among young people. In a compilation of de- scriptions of New England revivals between 1797 and 1814, Bennet Tyler concluded that fifteen of the twenty-four began among youth, with the remainder making no mention of the age structure of the re- vival.[11] Charles G. Finney and others noted that on some occasions older people rebuked the revival because of the lopsided involvement of youth.[12] A critic of revivals, Menzies Rayner, made the same point in a different way when he complained that it was common for the young "to rise up in the assembly and undertake to teach and exhort the con- gregation." Then, "from teaching and exhorting they proceed to dictate the prayers, and offer up the devotions of the congregation, in extem- pore effusions, with such an air of assurance, such extravagant and in- coherent expressions, and such enthusiastic fervor, as puts common sense and common modesty to the blush." [13]

Most of the converts in revivals during the early 19th century were in their teens or early 20s. True, some descriptions referred to conver- sions among children aged 7 to 13, but narrators usually adopted a guarded tone when confronted by such early manifestations of "saving change," and preferred to categorize these juvenile experiences as "hopeful conversions," indications of future prospects rather than the thing itself.[14] "Young people," a category referring to those between 12 or 13 and 22 or 23, accounted for the largest number of conversions.[15] Further, books proffering advice to recent converts on the principles of Christian duty usually aimed at a youthful audience and at times explicitly stated the intended age range. Jacob Abbott's *The Young Christian*, designed for the newly converted, noted that such persons "are generally among the young, that is, from fifteen to twenty-five years of age." [16] Abbott was a Congregationalist and ignored differences among denominations in the timing of religious experiences, but the effect of revivals was to minimize such differences. Thus, while Methodists had long promoted conversions in early adolescence and while Congregationalist and Presbyterian youth were not expected to become religious until 18 or 20, in practice the enthusiasm of the revival caught up boys and girls as well as men and women, regardless of sectarian allegiances.[17]

Accounts of revivals not only dwelled on youthful conversions but also pointed to a predominance of female conversions. Throughout the 19th century, women outnumbered men in the churches by about two-to-one, which also seems to have been the ratio in the Second Awakening. In the 1850s, Ebenezer Porter systematically studied accounts of revivals and concluded that female converts outnumbered males by two-to-one. Critics of revivals often cited the dominance of young women to prove that religious enthusiasm appealed only to the weak-minded portion of the community, and while proponents of revivals rejected this conclusion, they did not dispute assertions about the sex ratio.[18]

If we were to accept the viewpoint of critics who claimed that revivals thrived on the sensibilities of the immature, especially females, we would have no problem in explaining either the spread of revivals or their composition. In the critics' view it was just a matter of "sympathetic enthusiasm" or peer emulation, with hysterical girls and cocky lads throwing decorum to the winds.[19] Young Albert G. Dow of western New York state made the same point less philosophically in the 1830s when he observed that he and his chums were wont to visit revivals "for the fun of seeing the girls have 'the power.' " [20] In fact, ministers often did hold special prayer meetings for boys and girls, designed to whip up group conversions. John Q. A. Edgell left a vivid portrait of social pressures on teenagers around 1815:

> At the age of twelve years my father moved his family to Lyndon, Vt., where there was no Congregational church, and preaching rarely by Congregationalists: Methodists and Free Will Baptists being prevalent, held

many meetings in the neighborhood, and often of an exciting character.
When about fourteen years old, I attended a preparatory lecture preached in a neighborhood schoolhouse, by a Congregational missionary, Rev. M. Goddard. Many boys of my age and acquaintance were present, and we boys did not enter the house till the meeting commenced. And then they devolved it on me to lead the way. As we entered there were no seats but a slab-bench, stretching from the minister's knees toward the door. I was crowded along on the seat till I was near the minister, and the long bench was full of boys. In the conclusion of his sermon, the preacher addressed the long row of boys.[21]

The pressures on Edgell were informal compared with the veritable institutionalization of juvenile piety in the Sunday school and college revivals of the early 1800s. By the 1830s evangelical Sunday schools were deemphasizing mere memorization of biblical verses in favor of direct efforts to promote conversions, while college revivals, rare in the 18th century, were becoming virtually annual rituals, as predictable as spring's first warbler.[22]

Not only did evangelical ministers seek to induce conversions by whipping up peer pressure, but they also seized relentlessly on the deaths of young people to drive home a connection between *memento mori* and *sic transit gloria mundi*. A morbid crowd by any standard, evangelicals customarily used the funerals of young people to point out the need for immediate repentance and saving change. In his *Sermons to Young People*, widely circulated in America, the English evangelical Philip Doddridge asked his readers:

> How many of you have attended the funerals of youth like yourselves, of children much younger than yourselves! They have given up the ghost, and where are they? What a change hath death made!—where are they?
> . . . Could your eye penetrate a few feet of earth, you would see them; but oh, what spectacles of horror would you discover! Yet perhaps a year ago they were in the number of the most amiable objects of your sight.[23]

Evangelicals also took pleasure in circulating ghastly biographies of pious children for whom "early piety" seemed to be as much a cause of death as a symptom of holiness. Small wonder that the death of a sibling or friend often initiated the conversion cycle, or that youthful diarists of the period made their birthdays the occasions for sobering entries to the effect that the end was drawing closer. In the 20th century, youth has symbolized vitality and energy; in the early 1800s it often symbolized death as well. Put together, all these factors lend credence to the viewpoint of contemporary liberals that conversions were manufactured like pieces of cloth.[24]

Nevertheless, such partial and patronizing explanations of youthful conversions are ultimately as reductive as Hall's idea, daring and controversial when first advanced, that conversion was a by-product of sexual maturation. The defects of either view are numerous. First, not all conversions came during revivals. Often the revival, or a fit of depression born of homesickness or the death of a friend, were only the occasions of juvenile religious anxiety, sparks which set in motion a train of religious experiences whose terminus lay far beyond the initial event.[25] Second, narratives of converts in the early 1800s display a serious antagonism between a yearning for the experience of grace and a more or less scrupulous respect for passing through the traditional "steps" of conversion—sin, despair, conviction, conversion, regeneration, sanctification—as outlined in popular works such as Doddridge's *Rise and Progress of Religion in the Soul* or Matthew Mead's *The Almost Christian Discovered.*[26] Religious doctrine, in other words, had a logic of its own. If conversion was to be a radical change, then it had to be a decisive move away from one state of mind and toward another. The gloomier the antecedent conviction, the more plausible the conversion. Converts who routinely emphasized their wickedness as children were acting out their roles as young "almost Christians." Recounting the experiences of his boyhood, Lyman Abbott recalled the expectation that "you must feel very sorry because you are a sinner, and then very glad because you have been forgiven."[27] A biographer of Pliny Fisk found him to be "faithful, dutiful, and affectionate as a child," but Fisk himself considered the "whole course of my life up to my sixteenth year, as having been one continual course of rebellion against God."[28] Simple cheerfulness, Oliver Wendell Holmes, Sr., once observed, was a noble accomplishment for a New Englander with a Calvinist boyhood.

Thus, the religious responses of young converts were often patterned rather than spontaneous. A biographer of Harlan Page underlined key phrases in Page's conversion narrative, as if to remind his readers that Page had gone through all the appropriate motions: *"walking in spiritual darkness . . . exposed to temptations . . . under serious impressions."*[29] Biographers at times described the commencement of the conversion cycle as if it were the onset of a disease. A southern youth, David Morton, "was too well instructed in youth not to know the symptoms when they came. He had *heard of* the call long before he definitely *heard* it."[30] Converts often so internalized expectations that any distinction between spontaneous and patterned behavior becomes idle in the long run. Many writers berated themselves for failing to feel what they were supposed to feel. A 20-year-old woman spoke for them when she confided in her diary in 1833 that "I am often grieved that I have not experienced deeper convictions of sin, and stronger feelings of repentance: but I desire to experience any feeling that is profitable."[31]

Much of the distress experienced by converts, moreover, flowed from the nature of the theology passed down to them, as well as from social expectations about the behavior appropriate to one "under conviction." Catharine E. Beecher described New England household religion of the early 19th century in these terms:

> The child is taught that it has a "nature" or "heart" so dreadfully depraved that, until it is regenerated, all feelings and actions are sinful and offensive to God, so that even prayers to have the heart changed are hypocritical and insulting; next, that all blame for this rests on the child, and not on God; next, that nothing the child can do has any promise of encouragement from God to secure a remedy, but that He regenerates some and does not others, without any reason that man can discover. [32]

As the daughter of Lyman Beecher, Catharine Beecher had encountered a particularly virulent strain of New England Calvinism, one that prejudiced everything she later said about the system. A few lines later she conceded that in some households parents softened the message of Calvinism by making concessions to human nature, so that Calvinist theology rarely oppressed the young as relentlessly as her original description of it might suggest. But none of the concessions changed the fact that in religious households piety was to begin early. Conversion in youth was often the outcome of a process that commenced at 7 or 8, with the symptoms going into remission in ensuing years. [33] A common variation was an alternating cycle of intensity and lapse. "Often between my twelfth and sixteenth years, was my soul deeply awakened to a sense of my sins; often did the pains of hell well-nigh get hold upon me," wrote George Brown. [34]

Conversions, thus, were not necessarily the results of revivalistic frenzy, but often arose out of protracted religious anxiety. Concessions to human feelings might have softened the imperatives, but they were just as likely to compound the confusion by creating inconsistencies along the line. Thus, while signs of "early piety" were encouraged, evangelicals prior to the 1830s remained at best lukewarm to conversions under age 12. In effect, children were ushered into religious anxiety at early ages and then told that they could not escape it until later. They were locked into a kind of moral and religious pressure cooker.

Although conversions developed from acceptance of standard theological tenets, they often led to concrete and specific decisions. Growing theological vindication of human capacity in the early 19th century made the experience of conversion more a matter of choice and self-willed commitment than a passive ascertainment of foreordination. Converts were more prone than ever before to describe their conversions not merely as "the awakening" but as "the crisis and decision." [35] The decision might take the form of a choice of a particular denomination. In the long run, revivalism nurtured a nondenominational "religion of the heart," but in the short run its effects spurred sectarian differences. Successful revivalists were usually men of modest theological attainments, but many of them took their creeds seriously. An untutored circuit rider like the Methodist Peter Cartwright still took pride in his ability to confute Baptists and Universalists. Furthermore, by its nature, revivalism imparted to the churches a dynamic approach toward proselytizing which led inevitably to intellectual collisions between rival sects. By the early 1800s it was no longer possible to isolate dissenters such as Quakers and Baptists in watertight compartments like Rhode Island. Religious pluralism lay just beyond the parental door.[36]

The extravagant claims of each sect accentuated the importance of making a choice. In his autobiography, the Mormon leader Joseph Smith drew a revealing protrait of small-town religious commotion in New York's burnt-over district at a time when Smith was only 15:

> Indeed, the whole district of country seemed affected by it, and great multitudes united themselves to the different religious parties, which created no small stir among the people, some crying "Lo, here!" and others "Lo, there!": some were contending for the Methodist faith, some for the Presbyterian, and some for the Baptist.[37]

Although "called up to serious reflection and great uneasiness" during the excitement, Smith was unable to reach any sure conclusion. He wondered who was right and who wrong, or whether they were "all wrong together." Smith's resolution of his dilemma, his discovery of the Book of Mormon and the launching of a new religion, was untypical, but his antecedent anxieties over religious choice found expression elsewhere.[38]

Evangelical denominations in the early 1800s had an unprecedented outward reach, cutting across church and family lines in an aggressive pursuit of more members. A recent student has concluded that, with only moderate exaggeration, "one may regard all of American theology between Samuel Hopkins and Charles G. Finney as a constant search for the forms in which to express and justify the generation's increasingly unavoidable commitment to evangelical action." [39] Merely with respect to church membership, the growth after 1800 was remarkable. The General Assembly of the Presbyterian Church, for example, reported an increase in communicant membership between 1807 and 1834 from 18,000 to 248,000, although Presbyterians during the same period were actually losing ground to Methodists and Baptists.[40]

The swelling membership of churches was significant in at least two ways. First, it guaranteed that many young people who in earlier generations would never have been exposed to consistent religious pressures would now be caught up in the evangelical sweep. Second, it had a curious multiplier effect, for it also meant that children of converts would grow up in families which expected them to undergo a religious experience at some point. Thus, the originally spontaneous involvement of youth in revivals made it likely that future generations would encounter pressures not only to make religious decisions but also to make them early in life.

Decisions which led converts toward particular denominations were part of a larger pattern, for conversions often took place during times of intense crisis about life plans. For many young men, conversion involved an initial antipathy to whatever they had been doing and a vocational decision to become a minister. Without reading too much between the lines, one can detect in some attestations of despair before conversion a secular frustration with the parochial limitations of village and farm life. The decision to enter the ministry represented an attractive alternative to the cobbler's bench or a life of farm service. The success of the various benevolent societies which subsidized the education of pious indigents for the ministry underscored the presence of large numbers of youth for whom conversion marked a decision not only to become a minister but not to go on being a farmer.[41]

Finally, for a gifted minority of young people in the early 19th century, conversion acted not only as a resolution of religious and vocational anxieties but also as a supercharger, propelling them into religious careers characterized by lofty aims and extraordinary self-sacrifice. In America the home and foreign missions provided important outlets for the restlessness which seized youth in many countries in the early 1800s and which elsewhere was channeled into nationalism and romantic rebellion.

A Christian Crusade

New England towns had long contained moral and religious societies composed of earnest young men between 15 and 25, but such voluntary associations reached their apex of influence in colleges between 1790 and 1850. Some of these societies—principally Adelphoi Theologica (formed at Harvard in 1785), the Yale Moral Society (1797), and the various Philadelphia societies, including Williams (1804), Bowdoin (1806), Middlebury (1808), and Amherst (1826)—existed to promote theological debate and discussion, and thus resembled secular college literary and debating societies. Others, such as the Saturday Evening Society at Harvard and the Praying Societies of Bowdoin and Brown, were basically devotional.[42] Viewed in retrospect, the most influential was the Society of Brethren, formed in 1808 at Williams "to effect in the persons of its members a mission or missions to the heathen." [43] Among its members the Brethren included Luther Rice, Ezra Fisk, Gordon Hall, and Samuel J. Mills. Over the years a variety of myths have grown up around the Brethren, so that reconstruction of their exact activities is difficult. But several of the members did go on to Andover Theological Seminary, recently formed to counter the influence of Unitarianism at Harvard Divinity School, and there they encountered two like-minded spirits, Adoniram Judson, Jr., from Brown and Samuel Nott from Union College. Collectively, they formed another Society of Brethren and, in their most famous act, petitioned a ministerial association meeting at Bradford in 1810 for guidance in becoming missionaries. [44]

The ministerial association's response was the appointment of nine older ministers to an "American Board of Commissioners for Foreign Missions." The specific outcome was the decision of several of the young men, including Judson, to become missionaries to the "heathen in Asia." At about the same time, one of the members of the original brethren at Williams, Samuel J. Mills, consecrated himself to the home missions and embarked on a career of evangelism that was to take him to every state and territory. [45]

The immediate progenitor of missionary enthusiasm in colleges and seminaries was the Second Awakening. But the American awakening was itself part of an essentially transatlantic evangelical movement which began in Britain with William Wilberforce and the Clapham Sect, if not earlier with Wesley and the Methodists. The writings of British evangelicals were factors in stimulating some of the original interest in the home missions in America. In both nations a combination of chiliasm and plain fear of rampant godlessness snapped pious Christians out of lethargy; in both countries evangelicals were increasingly in the grip of a mood of immediatism. As Samuel J. Mills wrote, "though we are very little beings, we must not rest satisfied until we have made our influence extend to the remotest corner of this ruined world." [46] Or, as a British evangelical expressed it in 1842, "it is affecting to think that while we are sitting perhaps in our home, comparatively unmoved, there are, elsewhere, above six hundred millions of our race under the almost undisturbed domination of Satan." [47]

The earnest young men who composed the college moral and inquiry societies of the early 1800s and who went forth as home or foreign missionaries had before them not only the model of British evangelicalism but a distinctive set of ideas about Christianity and the world. At the core of their thinking were the views of Samuel Hopkins, a New England minister who both modified and elaborated the doctrines of Jonathan Edwards. Picking up various millennial strands of New England theology, Hopkins dedicated his *Treatise on the Millennium* to future generations who "will live in that happy era, and enjoy the good of it in a much higher degree than it can now be enjoyed in the prospect of it." [48] Hopkins then enthroned "disinterested benevolence" as the advance agent of the millennium. For Hopkins, all sin was essentially selfishness, all virtue an outgrowth of self-sacrifice. While Hopkins's concept of benevolence did not exclude the practice of philanthropy, its essential element was preaching the Word. The benevolent man, in other words, was one who spent as much time worrying about his neighbor's soul as about his own. [49]

The doctrines of millenarianism and benevolence were potent stimulants to the sort of youthful enthusiasm exemplified by Adoniram Judson, Jr., perhaps the foremost American missionary of the 19th century. Judson was born in Malden, Massachusetts, in 1788, the son of a minister. Like many New Englanders of his day, he grew up in a succession of towns—Malden, Wenham, Braintree, Plymouth. At once precocious and possessed of the usual educational advantages of a minister's son, Judson entered Brown at 16 and soon won the approbation of President Asa Messer for "a uniform propriety of conduct, as well as an intense application to study." Before he was out of his teens, Judson had opened a private academy and published two short textbooks on arithmetic and grammar. He also dabbled in French philosophy until the death of a close friend, who had espoused Deistic views, jarred young Adoniram out of his fashionable skepticism. Although he had the usual bouts with religious anxiety in his teens, Judson traced both his first serious impressions and his religious conversion to the fall and winter of 1808, when he commenced studies at Andover. [50]

Judson's decision to become a missionary was the product of many factors, although lack of domestic opportunities was not one of them, for he had turned down a tutor's appointment at Brown as well as the possibility of a major Boston pulpit. In 1809 he came across a sermon by Claudius Buchanan, quondam chaplain of the British East India Company, which described the progress of Christianity in India and which had "a very powerful effect on my mind." [51] Association at Andover with the Brethren from Williams College confirmed the original direction of his interests. His reading of various travel accounts stirred his curiousity about the Orient, while his fiancée, Ann Hasseltine, supported his ardor for the missionary cause. This was not surprising in view of her own conversion at 16 from a life of secular pleasure toward the cultivation of piety, under the impact of Hannah More's *Strictures on the Modern System of Female Education*. [52] Adoniram's own ardor stemmed from a conversion experience which left him with a scorn for all material seductions. As he wrote to Ann in 1810:

Each day will not only be a witness of our conduct, but will affect our everlasting destiny. No day will lose its share of influence in determining where shall be our seat in heaven. How shall we then wish to see each day marked with usefulness! It will then be too late to mend its appearance. It is too late to mend the days that are past. The future is in our power. Let us, then, each morning resolve to send the day into eternity in such a garb as we shall wish it to wear forever. And at night let us reflect that one more day is irrevocably gone, indelibly marked.[53]

Young missionaries like Judson were expected to relinquish material pleasures; Samuel J. Mills resolved not to marry on grounds that no man was fit to be a missionary who sighed for the delights of a lady's lap.[54] But neither Judson nor Mills had to forsake an active life in becoming missionaries. As the century progressed, American Protestantism became a business of sorts, remarkable for its organization and executive dispatch. The Young Men's Christian Association was the best example of the tendency, but the foreign missions ran a close second. Even in Judson's day, commitment to the life of a missionary was an ascetic but not a monastic decision. It left a youth in the world, more so in fact than if he had never broken with parochial restraints. Samuel J. Mills filled his diary with declarations of his need for complete dependence on God and with equally intense declarations of his desire "to fill up life well." [55] By venturing into the mission field he was able to satisfy both urges.

For some young men, the choice of a life in the missions represented an implied criticism of the materialism and acquisitiveness of American life. More often, however, the choice grew out of dissatisfaction with bleak prospects, a mixture of romance, idealism, and ambition. Missionaries were usually recruited from villages in upper New York state or New England rather than from commercial centers.[56] Moreover, the cycle of conviction and conversion itself played a major role in raising religious temperatures. Missionaries generally came from pious families, and few appear to have had quick, painless conversions. Samuel J. Mills, for example, experienced alternating moods of conviction and indifference from the time of his first religious tremors ("when quite a child") to the time of his conversion at 18. Shortly before his conversion, he told his mother that he had been "to the very bottom of hell," while he saw his conversion as marking a complete transformation, a virtual rebirth.[57] Conversion provided the motive force for Mills, which later took specific outlet in his choice of a career in the missions.

The ties between evangelicalism and youth were manifold. Creation of the evangelical empire of benevolence was not entirely the work of young men, but the original thrust often came from those in their teens or 20s, from individuals who thought of themselves as youth and who were so perceived by their elders. They were youth not merely in the sense that they were not yet old but, according to contemporaries, because they exhibited the putative qualities of youth—vigor, energy, and idealism.[58] The various moral and missionary societies in the colleges were spontaneous organizations of young men; some were secret societies whose existence was unknown to adults. Most of the influential figures in the founding of the various Sunday school, Bible, and tract societies for the spread of Christianity had experienced their original commitment to a life of religious proselytizing in youth.[59] Finally, the deluge of college and village revivals between 1810 and 1840 provided a steady flow of young men to support "the great missionary movements of the age." After four major revivals between 1783 and 1819, for example, Yale had annual revivals between 1820 and 1829, with the exception of 1827, when the establishment of a college temperance society compensated for the absence of a revival.[60]

Some of the constituents of a modern youth movement were present in the activities of evangelical youth in the early 19th century: numbers of young men, possession of a distinctive ideology (millenarianism, Hopkinsianism), a pervasive scorn for "this ruined world," a willingness to sacrifice familiar and parochial attachments in pursuit of a cause, and, especially in the 1830s and 1840s, involvement in moral issues with strong political overtones, namely temperance and abolition. Lane Theological Seminary in Cincinnati was one connecting link between the religious enthusiasm of Andover Seminary and the political enthuasiam of antislavery. Like evangelicals, abolitionists very often experienced their initial commitment to a radical cause in youth. Abolitionists were willing to march to the end of the road under an unpopular banner, just as Judson or Mills were, although some abolitionists (notably William Lloyd Garrison) abandoned their evangelical faith before adopting the antislavery cause.[61]

The one element added by some modern youth movements but absent in the Christian youth movement in early 19th-century America is consistent hostility to adults and a corresponding celebration of the brotherhood of youth as a class. There are some bits of evidence indicating a split between youth and adult groups in the earlier period, but closer inspection reinforces the impression that such a split was unimportant. It is true that young men often formed separate evangelical societies and that the leadership of the major evangelical organizations (the American Board of Commissioners for the Foreign Missions, the American Sunday School Union, the American Bible Society, and the American Tract Society) was in the hands of veteran pietists who were not young by any contemporary definition. But the relationship between adult evangelical societies and young men's societies was parallel rather than antagonistic. At times, young men's societies merged with societies that had no age restrictions. The American Home Mission Society, founded in 1826, was created out of a number of smaller societies, including the Young Men's Missionary Society of New York.[62] In any event, there is little evidence of real hostility between the two types of organizations. Antagonisms between generations were common in antebellum America; agricultural societies routinely give birth to such conflicts. But the belief of evangelicals, young or old, in the primacy of spiritual grace made it unlikely that conflicts between individual young men and old men would be cast within the framework of a general conflict between youth and maturity. As men who took the doctrine of grace seriously, evangelicals could never view a biological process of maturation as self-justifying. "It is confessed by all who know what religion is," a writer for the *Panoplist* stated in 1816, "that no one can indulge in the amusements commonly practised by youth, and at the same time enjoy the comforts of religion." [63] Evangelicals praised the vigor of youth, but only of converted youth—young men who had crossed the line and who could, therefore, play a collective role in church affairs.

Girlhood and Piety

While the conversion narratives of young men were filled with the rhetoric of decision-making, those of young women usually associated the embrace of piety with qualities of submission and humility. On one side stood gay companions, girlish chatter, and vivacity; on the other, self-denial, self-sacrifice, and self-abnegation. "For though I now felt the importance of being strictly religious," Ann Hasseltine wrote, "it appeared to me impossible that I could be so, while in the midst of my gay associates." [64] Perhaps because they were conditioning themselves to make a choice between mutually exclusive absolutes, the world or Jesus, young women often experienced painful and protracted conversions. A neighborhood revival might touch off the initial mood of seriousness, but it often did little more than that, with the remainder of youth taken up by a struggle between pleasure and humility, ambition and submission.[65]

It is tempting to jump from this analysis to the conclusion that conversion reinforced feminine passivity, that it hammered down the nails on the coffin of domesticity. In practice, however, the effect of religious conversion on girls was often far more complex. First of all, for many girls conversion did not place the sort of indelible seal on the religious life which it was supposed to. Rather, it merely elevated existing anxieties to a higher plane. Second, release from religious anxiety often came not in the form of final submission but in the decision to embark on a life of Christian activism. The Second Awakening did more than stimulate conversions among girls; it also indirectly provided an entrée for them into a legitimate form of female activity through the various mission and education societies which appeared in its wake. The difference between the Great Awakening of the 18th century and the Second Awakening lay not only in the latter's stronger emphasis on voluntarism but also in its entrepreneurial character. The rhetoric of conversion narratives was highly individualistic, but the outcome was in the direction of organization and chain of command. Between 1800 and 1850, Protestant benevolence became an industry in itself, differing from secular occupations and professions in that it threw up relatively few barriers to female involvement. Evidence of "saving change" was the sine qua non for a life of religious benevolence. At the moment of conversion, young girls thought that they were rejecting the seductions of active life, but in reality many were merely substituting a life of religious activism for their merry ways.

The life of Harriet Atwood Newell vividly illustrates both the antecedents and outcome of religious experience in youth. Since her life was short, the bare outline of its events takes up little space. She was born in 1793 in Haverhill, the daughter of a prominent merchant. In 1811 she married Samuel Newell, a member of the Brethren at Andover. Along with other members of the society, Newell had resolved to become a missionary, and shortly after their marriage Harriet and Samuel left for Calcutta. Once there, they encountered immediate opposition from the British East India Company, which opposed evangelism within its borders, and from the British governmental authorities who, at a time of war with the United States, naturally viewed American missionaries as potential spies. Seeking to quit British jurisdiction, Newell and his young wife left for the Isle of France. Harriet gave birth to a daughter on the voyage, but the child died five days later. At the same time, Harriet was stricken with consumption and lived only long enough to reach Port Louis, where she died on November 30, 1812, at age 19.[66]

Harriet Newell's decision to leave America for the uncertainties of a missionary life distinguished her from her contemporaries, as did the intensity of her religious anxiety. But although her society could plausibly have written her off as a romantic visionary who met an unfortunate but predictable end, it chose not to. Rather, Harriet became a Christian martyr. A memorial sermon delivered by Leonard Woods of Andover Seminary became the basis of a devotional biography which circulated widely in America and Britain. Partly this was because the essential constituents of Harriet's religious life, an antagonism between self-abnegation and a desire to achieve something of lasting value, reflected the same tension felt by other girls of her generation.[67]

From the commencement of her "deep religious impressions" at age 13 during a revival at Bradford Academy, her letters were taken up with an unrelieved excoriation of all human vanities and pursuits. To a girlhood friend she wrote in 1808:

> But let me tell you, I am still the same careless, inattentive creature. —What in the world can we find capable of satisfying the desires of our immortal souls? Not one of the endowments, which are derived from anything short of God, will avail us in the solemn and important hour of death. All the vanities which the world terms accomplishments, will then appear of little value.[68]

Although a reading of Doddridge's *Sermons to Young People* reinforced her initial seriousness, it took her three years to move from the initial conviction of her unworthiness in 1806 to her conversion in July 1809. All the while she blamed herself for her "awful backslidings." Perhaps she lacked a strong will, but more likely (in view of her later commitment to the missionary field) she was going through the kind of catharsis decreed by the Protestant *Volksgeist* as a prelude to conversion. Further, even her conversion and joining of the church in 1809 did not resolve her religious anxieties. Although the events of August formed themselves into "a precious season long to be remembered," within a year the pages of her diary displayed the same tone of self-accusation.[69] Her problem now lay in her inability to find in her heart sensations of sufficient intensity to match her original expectations about rebirth.

When Samuel Newell arrived on the scene with his earnest plans to convert the heathen, Harriet's initial response was confusion, for she knew that such a scheme meant the abandonment not only of worldly pleasures but also of domestic supports. Yet she agreed to go with him, and made it clear that she did so not merely out of love but because of the opportunities offered her by the mission.[70] Leonard Woods made a similar point in his memorial sermon:

> Had she lived in retirement, or moved in a small circle, her influence, though highly useful, must have been circumscribed. But now her character has by Divine Providence, been exhibited upon the most extensive theatre, and excited the attention and love of Christian nations.[71]

Her decision to enter missionary work did resolve many of Harriet Newell's anxieties. Although her troubles were just beginning, her letters from India were marked by a tone of satisfaction and accomplishment.

It is possible that when Harriet Newell censured the pursuits and distractions of the world, she was really making a judgment about the failure of the world to provide a place for her. Certainly the gap between her education at Bradford Academy, followed by her earnest pursuit of self-culture in a Haverhill literary society, and the actual range of occupations open to her was profound. But it is unlikely that she turned to religion as part of a general rebellion against social conventions which confined women to the domestic arts. The danger here lies in reading attitudes demonstrably widespread later in the century back into earlier decades. So far from exhibiting a tone of rebelliousness, her letters were filled with declarations of respect and admiration for adults, including men. Religion did more to reinforce than to blunt her orientation toward adulthood. Whenever she went through one of her periods of religious intensity, she accompanied it with strictures on youthful rather than adult concerns. Harriet Newell was unquestionably seeking some outlet for her interests which would go beyond an exclusive commitment to domesticity. But she perceived no antagonism between her desire for a life of Christian activism and her desire for a subordinate role to her husband in marriage. In the end, Leonard Woods could hold her up both as a model of the "tender female" and as a model of "decision of character." [72]

The number of women able or willing to follow in Harriet Newell's path was limited, but the benevolent empire provided a broad range of opportunities for young ladies who sought less ambitious evangelical roles. It is easy to adopt a patronizing tone toward the female mission societies of the 1820s and 1830s, and even easier to censure the wretched verse and morbid moral tales which young women contributed to the religious publishing houses. But those who moved from conversions into one or another aspect of benevolence entered a world infused by strong strains of millennialism and perfectionism. By the 1820s, for example, Sunday school teaching was perceived less as a useful adjunct of religious education than as a vehicle for transforming the world by the immediate regeneration of the rising generation.[73]

Religious conversion served functions even for young women who declined to enter benevolence. At the simplest level, a converted girl was ready for marriage. Young men were exhorted to select mates of religious character, and a public profession of faith was the most visible seal of inner worthiness. Although no one ever said so, it seems likely that the same demand did not apply to young men. That is, while a young man was not supposed to be openly hostile to religion, the mere fact that he had passed up opportunities to make a public profession did not render him an unacceptable partner in marriage. Such are the many faces of the double standard.

Conversion was more, however, than a certification of marital suitability; it also served as a passport to the emerging profession of Christian motherhood. After 1820 a cavalcade of tracts and pamphlets on the principles and duties of Christian motherhood issued from the presses. The home did not suddenly become the woman's sphere in the 19th century, but there was something distinctive about the fervor with which people wrote about the home. William L. Burn has noted, in a statement as applicable to America as to Britain, that to hear Victorians talk about the family one would suppose that it had been invented in the 1830s and that previous generations had lived in a kind of nomadic promiscuity.[74] Family ideology in the 19th century was distinctive not just for its fervor but for the preeminent position it gave to motherhood. If fathers figured at all in the literature, it was merely as remote chairmen of the board.[75] In practice, the Second Awakening gave rise to a number of associations of mothers whose meetings were marked by earnest discussions of ways to apply evangelical principles to child rearing.[76]

The fact that religious conversion opened a number of avenues to women helps explain why young ladies were much more prone than young men to undergo conversion experiences. Contemporary liberals who used the lopsided involvement of girls in revivals to discredit religious enthusiasm not only underestimated the intelligence of the girls but also missed the important spiritual and practical functions that enthusiasm served for them.

Whether reference is to males or females, however, conversion in youth was usually an experience that pushed converts in the direction of adulthood. Peer rivalry was a factor in some conversions, but there was nothing juvenile about the outcome of conversion. Many of the more articulate converts went from conversion directly into preaching, but even the inarticulate ones were expected to make public professions of faith before adult church members.[77]

Conversion and Identity

In the early 20th century, Hall and Starbuck postulated that conversion was an outgrowth of adolescence, arising spontaneously from the interaction of biological maturation and social imperatives. "New powers" that had no legitimate outlet forced expression for themselves in one form or another, often in religious conversion.[78] Both Hall and Starbuck were moral conservatives, but like many moral conservatives of their day they were seeking to break with the Victorian reign of silence about sexuality and to open up the field to a more candid and scientific discussion. The price they paid for their boldness was exorbitant, for in order to render discussion of sexuality acceptable to their contemporaries and indeed to themselves, they had to equate it with vital force, romantic love, and high idealism, an equation which allowed them to talk about sex and God in the same breath but which also gave their writings an overwrought and fulsome quality.

At points in their analysis, however, both Hall and Starbuck sought to develop a psychology as well as a biology of conversion. Starbuck insisted that behind all the epiphenomena of adolescence a new personality was taking shape.[79] Adolescent personality, he conceded, was often enshrouded by the mist created by the multiplicity of demands on youth, but in religious awakening a young person was stumbling from confusion to certitude and from a diffuse to a precise conception of himself. Take away the gibberish of the first generation of religious psychologists, the statistical tables "proving" that 16 was the age of conversion, and there emerges a psychological viewpoint in some way similar to Erik H. Erikson's concept of identity formation as an essential task of adolescence.

According to Erikson, identity formation in youth is the culmination of a process which stretches back to infancy and which involves first a realization by the child of its separateness from its parents, then a need for self-trust and self-satisfaction, and ultimately, in youth, a need for persons and ideas to have faith in, "which also means men and ideas in whose service it would seem worthwhile to prove oneself trustworthy." [80] Finally, Erikson views identity formation not merely as an act of self-recognition but as an interchange between the individual and his community, a process by which a community recognizes a young person as distinct from other youth, as having a style of his own.[81]

Some striking analogies exist between Erikson's concept of identity formation and the effects of religious conversions on young people in the past. Conversion often marked a transition from boyhood or girlhood to Christian adulthood. The community often bestowed visible marks of approval on a convert—for example, by admitting him or her to full church membership—while a convert who delivered an experiential narrative before church members spoke to them as an adult, perhaps for the first time.[82] Further, conversion often involved a selection of some aspects of one's personality at the expense of others. That is, to be converted meant that one had decided to lay aside childhood associations and to embrace the new associations appropriate to adulthood.

Finally, although converts usually could point to a single moment of conversion, a more or less protracted process of intensity and lapse from age 7 onward often preceded conversion.[83] Interestingly, both Hall and Starbuck noted this, but then downgraded its importance in their attempts to accentuate the significance of puberty. Erikson is more helpful here, for, as noted, he views identity formation as a process rather than an event. It is possible that alternating currents of religious anxiety were related to the often jagged contours of physical and mental growth in the early Republic. The emphasis on shame and humiliation encountered by boys in school, the frequent home leavings and home-comings, and the presence of poles of submission and assertion in youthful experience may have complemented the effects of disjunctive religious practices which sanctioned an early entry into religious anxiety but not an early exit.

If this point has value for historical analysis, it also implies that youth was a difficult period for some individuals for exactly the opposite reasons that render it a troubled time for some today. Erikson has argued that, in our own day, adolescence is an especially difficult period for those who find that the standardization of experience in youth makes it impossible for them to satisfy their quest for identity. Our society provides a ladder of age-graded experiences for young people—sports, clubs, schools—which in theory conforms to their needs but which in practice often does not.[84] At least part of the trouble now arises because a young person's status as an adolescent is *too* well defined, whereas in the past the diffuseness of role conceptions created anomalies at every turn. On the other hand, these anomalies may actually have propelled the young people toward adulthood, if only to rid themselves of the incongruities of semidependence. It is significant that religious enthusiasm among youth in the early 1800s led them toward maturity, while today the comparable enthusiasm of the "Jesus freaks" seems only to reinforce the latter's status as adolescents—that is, as cultural outsiders who assume a detached stance toward conventional institutions and beliefs.

In a study of the age of converts in 18th-century Andover, Philip J. Greven, Jr., demonstrated that a declining age for making public professions of faith accompanied a declining age of marriage and earlier acquisition of property. Between 1711 and 1729, men in Andover usually married late, inherited property late, and rarely became full church members before they were 30; in the succeeding period, 1729 to 1749, all of these indicators dropped, with public professions of faith now coming most frequently among the eldest of the 15-to-24 age group.[85] It is also likely that the frequency of conversion during the teen years in the first few decades of the 19th century reflected contemporaneous economic and social changes, such as the accelerated movement of population and the earlier age of final home leaving. Young people were becoming independent and experiencing conversion at earlier ages than in the 18th century, even earlier than during Greven's 1729–1749 period. But the exact relationship between earlier conversions and social change is difficult to define. Were conversions most common among young people who were in the best position to capitalize on economic change? Or were they more frequent among youth less well situated? Any generalization is risky, for time has drawn its veil over much of the story, but searing conversion experiences appear to have been more common in the towns and villages of western New York, New England, and the Ohio Valley than among city youth, and more frequent before than after 1840.[86] The type of young person deeply affected by religion in the early 19th century was likely to be restless and confused, isolated from the main centers of economic change, and still vaguely ambitious.

For such a young person, religious conversion was to be the choice to end all choice, the final definition of life purpose. In practice, however, conversion often did little more than usher in a new phase of uncertainty and confusion. The problem was that the explosion of revivalism and the institutionalization of juvenile piety in Sunday schools, factors which contributed to the rising frequency of conversions in youth, paradoxically accounted for the transient quality of many of the same conversions. As social pressures for early conversion multiplied, many individuals found themselves being converted more than once.

False conversion was not an altogether new syndrome. Puritans, Daniel B. Shea, Jr., has observed, "suffered chronically from an adolescent disease that masqueraded as true conviction until it disappeared and left good health and a heart more depraved than ever."[87] But the false-conversion syndrome underwent a subtle change in the early 19th century. Puritans had agonized over whether they had really been converted; their descendants agonized over the failure of their postconversion experience to conform to the model of rebirth. As theology moved in the direction of voluntarism and as the disposition developed to proclaim that emotional experience was proof of saving change, those converted in late childhood or in their early teens were commonly left with the sense that their initial conversions had been shallow and premature, like vaccinations which did not take. Adin Ballou recalled his dismay when he recognized the abortive character of his initial conversion in a revival at age 11:

> As time went on and the enthusiasm began to wane, I was gradually brought to realize that I had undertaken a more difficult task than at first appeared obvious. I had pledged myself to the Christian life without counting the cost.[88]

Ballou put the blame partly on himself and partly on his mentors:

> This arose partly from my own ignorance and partly from the extravagant representations of the older professors and of my religious teachers generally. The notion that "experiencing religion" was a miraculously radical change led me, as it has led others, to conclude that if the conversion was genuine, the natural propensities and passions would either be eradicated or so neutralized as to be harmless.[89]

Gradually, he perceived the truth that his "animal nature" had remained unchanged by conversion in youth. At the age of 19, Ballou went through another conversion and settled upon the ministry, only to find his orthodoxy now slipping away as quickly as his adolescent enthusiasm.

Ballou's experience resembled those of two famous contemporaries, John Humphrey Noyes and Orestes Brownson. Noyes was converted first at 8, then at 16, and again in his 20s.[90] Brownson, born like Ballou in 1803, had his initial conversion at 14, but like Ballou's it proved to be less a final commitment than the first of a prolonged series of religious tremors.[91] The impact of false or multiple conversion on all three men differed fundamentally from the effect on Harriet Newell of her inability to make postconversion sensations conform to anterior expectations, for the combination of religious intensity and uncertainty led her into a life of activism as a therapeutic release, while the others drifted from premature conversion into prolonged periods of religious seeking.

Unhappy experiences with premature and multiple conversions were not the only causes of the growing disenchantment with the revival as a method of molding character. A few scrupulous individuals who more or less resisted intense parental and community pressure to undergo conversion in their teens were left with a similar hostility, partly because they saw others around them giving in to such pressures and partly because they resented the pressures put on them. Catharine Beecher, for example, repeatedly and explicitly connected her advocacy of preserving spontaneity in children with her own unsuccessful quest for a model conversion experience, a quest that led her from minister to minister like an invalid passing from spa to spa seeking a cure.[92] When her sister, Harriet Beecher Stowe, depicted Esther Avery in *Oldtown Folks* as a morbid introspectionist who, at 19, had learned only how to dissolve every hopeful emotion in a fit of self-analysis, she was giving expression to an aspect of the experience of her generation.[93] The abolitionist and pacifist Henry Clarke Wright finally submitted to overwhelming community pressure and underwent conversion during an intense depression at age 20. Later on, however, he sensed that his conversion had been a forced experience, the product of social convention rather than healthy growth. He recollected feigning cheerfulness as a child lest pious neighbors think that he was "under conviction," the prelude to conversion. He wrote of his conversion: "bitterly now did I suffer the consequences of having imbibed, in childhood, a theology at variance with the facts relating to my physical and moral being." [94] This was a retrospective view; at the time, conversion led Wright into the ministry. The doubts came later, and he began his autobiography with the flat assertion that "the history of a church or government is but the history of the fagot, the gallows, the sword, the bayonet and the bombshell; of fraud, speculation, hypocrisy, wrath, and revenge." [95]

The most articulate critique of the character-building potential of revivals came not from Wright, Beecher, or Brownson but from Horace Bushnell, another contemporary who learned in later years to repent a premature religious decision. As H. Shelton Smith observed, Bushnell's religious life "did not come easily, nor did it evolve smoothly." [96] Converted at 19, Bushnell soon lapsed. Then, as a student and tutor at Yale, he went through a number of religious experiences that left him emotionally drained and increasingly skeptical of many standard theological tenets. In his influential book *Christian Nurture*, Bushnell upgraded the role of family influence and downgraded that of the revival in shaping character, but more fundamentally, he substituted an ideal of gradual, evenly paced development for that of radical change. [97]

It can plausibly be argued that *Christian Nurture* was a utopian treatise, for it presented the family not as a collection of self-contained individuals bound together by duty and property, but as an all-encompassing environment which, rightly conducted, would virtually guarantee the proper moral and religious development of the young. At a time when others were building utopian experiments in the country, Bushnell attempted to turn the urban family into a utopia in its own right. Catharine E. Beecher similarly became a leading advocate both of the cult of domesticity and of Christian nurture. Other gifted young people for whom conversion had been a disorienting rather than directing force also took refuge in absolute and secure ideologies in later life. Noyes gravitated to the Wesleyan doctrine of perfectionism and constructed utopian communities, first at Putney in Vermont and later at Oneida in New York. Brownson, after passing through several denominations, attempted to start his own religion and then flirted with radical social movements; finally he became a Roman Catholic in the 1840s. Others moved into reform movements, usually as radicals. For example, Henry Clarke Wright became an advocate of Garrisonian abolitionism and of a peculiarly militant form of pacifism. If absolutist expectations went into the conversion experience, absolutist conclusions often emerged.

Conclusion

Evangelical households in early 19th-century America were often nurseries of neurotic disorientation in young people, a fact which should temper easy acceptance of the claims, made frequently in the 20th century, that youth has become a time of distinctive "storm and stress" only in our own day. Along with disorientation, however, evangelical households also nurtured idealism. Between 1840 and 1860 the idealism spurred by revivals leaped beyond the boundaries of religious denominations into reform movements such as abolitionism, which likewise sought to purge society of sins. After 1860 the evangelical temper, distinguished as ever by absolutism, physical energy, and organizational genius, sought and found new forms of expression, as confidence in the efficacy of revivals waned. Shorn of its former faith in revivals, evangelicalism survived as a coherent force in American society. Wherever it survived, it was to retain its deep interest in the moral and spiritual welfare of young people. Throughout the 19th century, no group surpassed evangelical Protestants in their institutional and intellectual concern with youth.

CHAPTER 4

"Doubling the Cape":
Young Men in the Cities

THROUGH the agency of the revival, the religious enthusiasm
which had begun in the villages and open country was invading the cities by the 1820s and 1830s. Religious enthusiasm, however, was just
one of a number of points of contact between the life-styles of village
and urban youth. The rough scrimmaging between boys and young
men, the loose age groupings which threw together boys of 13 and
young men of 30, and chronic trouble-making at all ages had precedents
in village and small-town life and ample scope in cities. At some point in
the 19th century, urban life began to force discontinuities between age
groups and to deprive teenagers of social roles and economic functions,
but that point had not been reached by 1850. The major difference between country and city was one of scale. The city magnified whatever it
touched. Amateur thespians and street minstrels no longer performed
in front of select audiences of friends, sweethearts, and parents, but in
front of whoever wandered by. Urban military companies did not have
to wait around for the annual encampment or for a muster to have their
fling. Political excitement did not depend on the arrival of the Fourth of
July or on the itinerary of some great man.

Yet by mid-century these differences in scale were creating qualita-
tive differences in the life-styles of urban youth of rival social classes.

The novel element lay not in class differences as such but in the self-conscious efforts of moralists of the propertied classes to demarcate the life-style of middle-class youth from that of children of the laboring poor. These efforts, in turn, were stimulated by the combination of immigration, crowded living conditions, and plain economic misery in cities, a combination which facilitated the emergence of a lower-class youth culture that was perceived by the propertied classes as threatening and uncontrollable.

The Dangerous Classes

American cities have rarely been the results of rational planning, and their growth between 1820 and 1870 was as chaotic as it was rapid. In these decades the population of Philadelphia rose more than tenfold, from 65,000 to 674,000, while that of New York increased from 152,000 to 1,478,000. Less than 7 percent of the American population lived in cities of 250,000 or more by 1870, but those who had moved to cities in the preceding half century had witnessed a growth spurt like nothing before or since.[1]

Growth was helter-skelter, with all classes and nationalities juxtaposed. As Sam B. Warner noted:

> They were cities of store keepers and small sweatshop factories, of businesses run by one boss or a few partners, of the scattering of shops and work rooms among residences, of mixed neighborhoods of rich and poor, native and immigrant, and strong smells and slovenly habits, coexisting with stiff and polished propriety.[2]

A survey of New York's fifth ward after the bloody draft riots of 1863 revealed a population of 25,587 in 3,000 buildings, among which were 48 factories turning out everything from chocolates to carriages, 542 "stores," 234 dram shops (bars), 23 lager beer saloons, 17 gambling saloons, 7 concert saloons, 76 brothels, and 22 policy shops. This happened to be a relatively fashionable district![3]

The physical proximity of opposites shaped perceptions of the mid-Victorian city. Some version of "Lights and Shadows of the Metropolis" was a favorite title for books about urban conditions between 1840 and 1880. A book published in 1868 bore the title *The Secrets of the Great City: A Work Descriptive of the Virtues and Vices, the Mysteries, Miseries and Crimes of New York City*, and contained a description of the clientele of Harry Hill's dance hall, a collection of bankers, lawyers, clerks, sailors, soldiers, thugs, pugilists, prostitutes, and boys.[4] It was the flourishing of vice amid the trappings of respectability that descriptions of the city forcefully projected. The author of *The Women of New York, or Social Life in the Great City*, an exposé based on a mixture of fact and fancy and suffused by equal portions of prudery and prurience, wrote of his book:

> In it the women of the Metropolis are boldly and truthfully unveiled, and every phase of society is thoroughly ventilated. Where sin and immorality have tainted women in high life, and where fashionable wives and beautiful daughters have yielded to the enticer's art, it tears the fictitious robes from their forms and reveals their habits of life, their follies and frailties.[5]

In a similar way, Henry Ward Beecher inserted in his popular *Lectures to Young Men* a "portrait gallery" of urban types—the wit, the humorist, the libertine, the cynic, the dandy—designed to demonstrate that elegant clothes and fine manners were more likely than the peddler's rags to conceal a vicious heart.[6] In great cities "fashion does abuse nature," E. H. Chapin wrote in 1854. "Men we see, so gorgeous and so disguised, that they look like walking chambers of imagery, or cylindrical chess-boards, and we know not whether we behold a party of gentlemen or the intrusion of a menagerie."[7]

Exposés of city life suffered from a fascination with the grotesque, like naturalist novels later in the century, but vice was real enough in the cities. The police commissioner of New York estimated in 1866 that the city had 621 houses of prostitution, 2,670 public prostitutes, and 99 "houses of assignation," estimates he presented to counter the more extreme claims of respectable citizens, including a Methodist bishop who had startled his parishioners with the assertion that there were more prostitutes than Methodists in the city.[8] (Investigation showed that the Methodists were still hanging onto a slight lead.) Gambling flourished too in its "splendid hells." An estimate put the number of major gambling houses in New York City at 150 in 1868, and the *New York Tribune* asserted in the same year that the city had become the gambling headquarters of the nation.[9]

Violence was less easily quantified, but much more threatening to life and limb. New York City had eight major and ten minor riots between 1834 and 1871, the most famous and deadly being the Draft Riots of 1863, when mobs, mostly Irish, virtually seized control of the city for three days, terrorizing the police and yielding only before the massed artillery and bayonets of regular soldiers. So many people were caught up in the draft riots that organized gangs of toughs played a relatively minor role, minor at least in comparison to the riots between the Dead Rabbits and the Bowery Boys at election time in 1856 and again in the celebration of July 4, 1857. Before that there had been anti-abolitionist riots in the mid-1830s, and casual street violence was rife at all times.[10]

Urban vice and crime were no respecters of age. Boys joined men in the gambling houses, pimped for prostitutes, wandered the streets in pursuit of thrills, and joined up with the gangs.[11] According to J. T. Headley, a Victorian chronicler of urban violence, the Dead Rabbits, the largest and best organized of the New York gangs, "were mostly young men, some of them being mere boys." [12] During the anti-abolitionist riots of the mid-1830s a mob of boys threatened a minister.[13] When the Reverend L. M. Pease went to the notorious Five Points district in 1850 to open a mission, he found that all the gangs had affiliates composed not only of teenagers but also of children between 8 and 12—the Little Dead Rabbits, the Little Plug Uglies, the Forty Little Thieves.[14] In 1872, Charles Loring Brace, a representative Victorian reformer, claimed that the "dangerous classes of New York" were its children, usually between 8 and 16 or 17.[15] Over the course of 450 pages, Brace sought to document the suggestion of his Introduction that

> the class of a large city most dangerous to its property, morals and its political life are the ignorant, destitute, untrained, and abandoned youth: the outcast street-children grown up to be voters, to be the implements of demagogues, the "feeders" of the criminals, and the sources of domestic outbreaks and violations of law.[16]

Or, as an earlier observer had written:

> Lads from fourteen to twenty-one are the busiest instigators, the most active abettors, and the most daring perpetrators of offenses against the peace and good order of society. In tumults, street fights, and riotous assemblies in resistance to authority and contempt for law, they generally take the lead.[17]

Brace said that the dangerous classes were recruited not from immigrants but from their children, and he followed contemporaries in locating the cradle of gang violence in New York in the Five Points area, which was populated mainly by Irish immigrants and their children, with a scattering of Italians, native-born whites, and free blacks.[18] Not all of the gangs, however, were composed of immigrant children. Reformers liked to think that crime and vagrancy resulted merely from the inability of immigrant families to adjust to conditions in the United States, but the records of the New York House of Refuge indicate that children of native-born parents also swelled the ranks of "juvenile delinquents," as street vagrants were labeled from the second quarter of the 19th century onward.[19] Crowded conditions in homes and the lure of an emerging gang culture both drove and tempted young people of various nationalities into the city's streets.[20]

Youth in the Early Republic, 1790–1840

Much of our knowledge of poor urban youth in the middle of the 19th century comes from the observations of genteel reformers like Brace. Brace was a dedicated philanthropist and a perceptive observer of his times, but a host of factors colored his perceptions and those of other reformers. For Brace the metropolis was a symbol of all the disintegrating and dangerous forces in American life. He wrote *The Dangerous Classes of New York* in the wake of the Paris Commune, and he made it clear that unless the dangerous classes were controlled, revolutionary mobs would do in America what they had done in France. Further, any reader of Brace will recognize that most of his documentation pointed to a potential for mischief among the young rather than to actual misdeeds. Like most Victorian reformers and, indeed, like many reformers of the Progressive Era, Brace was convinced that vice was addictive and that environment determined character. These convictions led Brace to conclude that street "arabs" who started their careers roaming the avenues and pilfering from vacant buildings would graduate to major felonies. Finally, the physical proximity of different life-styles in large cities made it difficult for reformers to draw clear distinctions and tempted them to lump a variety of life-styles under the rubric "perishing and dangerous classes." [21]

What Brace viewed as a Manichaean struggle between respectability and virtue on one side and a subculture of crime and depravity on the other might have been simply a conflict between a Protestant middle-class life-style which emphasized sobriety and self-restraint and an emerging urban lower-class life-style which valued spontaneity, gang loyalty, and physical prowess. Brace himself recognized that some admirable qualities prevailed among lower-class gang members— loyalty, generosity, resourcefulness. The pet plan of Brace's New York Children's Aid Society, the placing out of city youth on rural farms, ultimately foundered because street boys sorely missed the adventures of city life and found farm life to be dull and suffocating. Moreover, although lower-class life was often violent, the lower classes in antebellum cities had no monopoly on crime or vice. For example, a recent student has called attention to the role of "gentlemen of property and standing" in anti-abolitionist riots. [22]

Finally, in the history of urban volunteer fire companies one can observe a form of lower-class youth culture that was not depraved, pauperized, or criminal. Prior to the professionalization of the volunteer fire companies around the time of the Civil War, their membership was composed of a mixture of boys and young men between 10 and 30. In New York City almost every company had an appendage of "volunteer aides," usually teenagers under 18, too young for regular membership. Sometimes more numerous than the regulars, these volunteer aides bunked in the station houses, courted the favor of regulars with gifts, and dragged tenders to fires. The volunteer aides usually had their own organization and rules, which paralleled those of regular firemen; they had their own captains and foremen, and their own system of fines and penalties. Describing American volunteer companies, an English traveler noted that "the firemen are mostly youths engaged during the day in various handicrafts and mechanical trades, with a sprinkling of clerks and shopmen," young men "at the most reckless and excitable age of life." [23]

Firemen often started their careers when boys. In New York, Charles Forrester began to run with the engines at 10, Carlisle Norwood at 8, Zophar Mills at 13, John Cornwall at 16, and Malachi Fallon "as soon as he could find his legs." [24] Complaints about "these boys frequenting the engine houses" were rife, but less so than outcries against the "riotous and disorderly" conduct of firemen in general. [25] Like antebellum volunteer military companies, fire companies were social fraternities as well as civic agencies. Contemporaries, in fact, thought that they were too social. Whether they actually set more fires than they put out, a view which had some strenuous defenders in the 1840s, fire companies habitually scrimmaged with each other. The more youthful firemen were the worst offenders:

> The engineers had no control over them, and their insubordination, utter lawlessness, and the confusion they created, proved a continual source of annoyance and serious hindrance both to the engineers and the regular firemen, a great majority of whom would gladly dispense with their precarious assistance if by so doing they could be freed from all suspicion of participating in riots caused by these boys. . . . [26]

Almost any occasion would justify a brawl between rival fire companies; such brawls were often little more than gang fights between youth groups from rival neighborhoods. Collisions and brawls between companies most often occurred on the way to fires, with arguments breaking out over which company had the right to put out the fire and collect a bonus from the insurance companies. In Cincinnati, where the companies increasingly had become social centers for young rowdies who delighted in shaking down the citizenry at subscription time, a planing mill burned down in 1851 while ten separate companies brawled up and down the waterfront, an event which directly contributed to the creation of a professional fire department two years later. [27]

By the mid-1850s in New York a combination of police, insurance companies, and property owners were calling for creation of a metropolitan, paid fire department, a demand finally acceded to in 1865. Wherever professionalization replaced the old volunteer companies, the boys were the first to go. In Cincinnati, for example, prior to the creation of a paid force of professional firemen in 1853, some of the companies had been composed entirely of teenagers, but the new metropolitan force's members were almost exclusively between the ages of 25 and 35.[28] In their heyday, however, the volunteer companies had provided an outlet for youthful high spirits, opportunities for display and parades, and a quasi-legitimate form of involvement for youth in civic affairs.

Volunteer fire companies, although containing a narrower range of social classes, were remarkably similar to volunteer military companies. Although the latter were more likely than the fire companies to include lawyers and merchants as well as mechanics and laborers, both fire companies and military companies drew on a broad range of ages for members.[29] Unlike fire companies, which were rare outside of cities, military companies flourished in villages and towns as well as urban centers. But in cities volunteer military companies were as rowdy as the fire companies. There always had been some tomfoolery at rural musters, with no end of drinking and with orders to "fall back" literally obeyed by tipsy privates, but in cities the pattern often contained more violence than burlesque. An abundance of military companies meant that occasions for fighting were also abundant. Moreover, the brawls of the urban military companies, like those of the fire companies, were often thinly disguised gang fights between rival classes, nationalities, and neighborhoods.[30] Indeed, some of the military companies and many of the fire companies had ties to the organized gangs, as well as to each other. Gang members often wore uniforms of sorts and either copied or parodied the names of military companies, calling themselves the "Roach Guards," the "Atlantic Guards" and so forth.[31]

Neither type of volunteer company had formal teaching roles to play, but they did provide their members with a direct view of the sort of men and events that plowboys often complained of missing. The city itself was a teacher, and if the lessons it taught could not be reduced to a textbook, they could still be learned.[32] Growing cities which lacked a superstructure of professional associations provided amateurs in any field with a wide scope for activity. This is just another way of saying that they provided youth with opportunities for participation and observation, for young people were amateurs. They were too young to be elected to official bodies, but that hardly mattered when most official bodies were loosely organized and relatively weak.

The case of theatricals provides an illustration. Although professional companies of actors and actresses flourished in 18th-century America, demands for entertainment in the fast-growing cities provided ample scope for amateur companies, often made up of young people between 13 and 25. To raise money for their libraries, young men's societies at times put on amateur theatricals, using their youngest members to impersonate females.[33] Apprentices also put on public dramas and melodramas. The "Mortonians," formed in Philadelphia in 1812, were mainly "store lads." [34] Thomas Buchanan Read and Edwin Forrest both started in theatricals while apprentices.[35]

Teenagers in cities also viewed the workings of politics from close quarters. They could not vote, but they could run errands for ward bosses and, in the tougher parts of town, act as strong-arm squads on election day. When the Bowery Boys and Dead Rabbits clashed during the election of 1856 in New York, the lines were drawn not merely between rival gangs but between rival parties as well, with the Bowery Boys backing the Native American or Know Nothing Party and the Rabbits supporting the Democrats, led by Fernando Wood. The street gang was a straight if not level avenue to urban politics in the 1840s and 1850s.[36]

Fitting neither Brace's image of a perishing subculture of crime and depravity nor the model of decorous sobriety extolled by Sunday school novels, the life-style of antebellum urban youth displayed an admiration for physical prowess, a high valuation of peer loyalty, and an intense antipathy toward young people of different social classes and ethnic groups. All these traits survived to become characteristic of street-corner society in the 20th century, but in the second quarter of the 19th century they were reflected in the behavior of other groups as well. Antebellum college students, for example, were scarcely strangers to violence, peer loyalty, or class pride. Within cities, moreover, the life-styles of the military and fire companies marked not only the children of immigrants and street waifs but also the children of native Americans and young men drawn from a variety of trades and occupations. For this reason, it is not entirely accurate to describe the behavior of urban youth as a lower-class style. Rather, it became stigmatized as a lower-class style only in the context of an emerging middle-class ideology in mid-19th-century cities. Brace was an articulate spokesman for this ideology, but the latter's main support derived from the influx of Protestant youth from the country to the countinghouses and mercantile establishments of the eastern seaboard.

From Plow to Countinghouse

The growth of commercial exports after the War of 1812 stimulated the establishment of banks, warehouses, and insurance companies, and inevitably created a demand for bankers, warehouse men, and insurance agents. In turn, the growth of cities created a need for more high-ways to get food in and for more grocers and agents to distribute the food once it got there.[37] Boston was virtually rebuilt between 1780 and 1860.[38] Lured by the new opulence of maritime ports, a steady stream of young men and women from the country descended on the cities.[39] New York, overcoming challenges posed by the spectacular growth of other urban centers, emerged as America's foremost city at mid-century.

The explosion of commercial opportunities for young men in cities had a harsh effect on country life. In northeastern states the reputation of agriculture plummeted after 1800. If business leaders readily praised the steeling effects of a rural boyhood, they knew enough to add that the benefits of farm life were reaped only in maturity and only at a distance. For youth on the farm, there was no such retrospect, only dim prospect. "It is not strange," wrote one observer, "that mercantile and mechanical employments are thronged by young men, running all risks for success, when the alternative is a life in which they find no meaning and no inspiring and ennobling influence." [40] Convinced that "agriculture is not the road to wealth, nor honor, nor to happiness," young people left home by the thousands.[41] Discussing their aspirations in life in the late 1860s, two young Virginians saw the choice clearly:

> All the promise of life seemed to us to be at the other end of the rainbow—somewhere else—anywhere else but on the farm. We read history, ancient and modern, and observed that the men who had influenced the world had chosen military, commercial, professional, financial, or industrial occupations rather than farming. And so all our youthful plans had as their chief object the getting away from the farm.[42]

Observers were struck not just by the uprooting of youth from farm life but by the ambition of young men. The concept of calling, which had enjoyed a long history in Calvinist thought, changed its meaning in the first half of the 19th century, acquiring connotations of occupational mobility. No man should be idle, but neither did he have to spend his life at a single job.[43] "Young men think," Emerson wrote, "that the manly character requires that they should go to California, or to India, or into the army." [44] On the eve of the Civil War, Lincoln spoke of the "race of life"; at its close a minister compared life to "a race-course in which a countless number of persons are contending for the prize." [45] Edward Hazen warned of the risks of the age: "many individuals mistake their appropriate callings, and engage in employment for which they have neither mental nor physical adaptation; some learn a trade who should have studied a profession; others study a profession who should have learned a trade." [46] Daniel Drake summed up the preference of the age:

There are others, however, whose paths are eccentric, and they pass out of the orbits of their ancestors, are subjected to new influences both attractive and repulsive. [They may] finally lose all visible connection with the states of society in which they were respectively born and reared. In the lives of such, there must of necessity be decisions, actions and events of greater *relative* importance.[47]

Young men who left home went in all directions, but only those who were bound for cities jolted the pens of moralists from their inkstands. A succession of conduct-of-life treatises addressed to urban youth sold like patent medicines in the three decades before the Civil War. William Alcott's *The Young Man's Guide*, published originally in 1833, ran through 21 editions by 1858.[48] The first edition of Daniel Eddy's *The Young Man's Friend* sold 10,000 copies. In 1857, Albert Barnes reflected on "the unusual number of books that are addressed particularly to young men," and the way in which "our public speakers every where advert to their character, temptations, dangers and prospects with deep solicitude."[49]

In conduct-of-life books youth itself was defined as embracing an indefinite period of years after the final home leaving—"doubling the cape of life," as Samuel C. Griswold called it. A youth was one who had left home for the busy scenes of city life, an event that usually occurred, according to the authors, between ages 15 and 25. Joel Hawes described the audience of his *Lectures Addressed to the Young Men of Hartford and New-Haven* as a "class of young men between 15 and 25 years of age."[50] Youth counselors, if we may so designate the authors of advice books, found the nautical metaphor irresistible. Youth was no longer a way station on the Puritan's highway of life. Instead, it was like "a vessel which has left its moorings in the harbor, and stretched its canvas for a returnless voyage, and floated out on the heaving bosom of the great ocean."[51]

More concerned with techniques of character building than with the practices of commercial life, the conduct-of-life books which appeared between 1830 and 1860 had an unspecific quality that renders them of little value as sources of concrete information about their audience. Similarly, autobiographical recollections of business leaders provide a few insights about the process of migration, but an abundance of false leads. In obedience to the canons of the success cult, businessmen in the 19th century customarily emphasized the discrepancy between their original and ultimate stations in life—a bald form of self-advertisement—and hence were likely to exaggerate their early hardships.

Neither advice books nor autobiographies said much about girls, although girls were as likely to leave home for the city as were young men. Indeed, girls probably left agricultural communities at earlier ages than boys, for girls were less valuable on farms. According to the 1830 census, girls aged 15 to 19 generally formed a smaller proportion of the population of New England villages under 1,500 people than did males of comparable ages, but a larger proportion in cities. The following table compares the ratios for villages in Middlesex County, Massachusetts, with those for the factory towns of Lowell and Waltham and the city of Charlestown.

Age and Sex Ratios, Middlesex County, 1830

	POP.	% FEMALES 15–19	% MALES 15–19
Villages:			
Acton	1,128	3.8	6.3
Ashby	1,240	3.0	5.4
Bedford	685	5.1	5.9
Billerica	1,370	4.2	5.0
Boxborough	474	3.1	5.6
Burlington	446	3.5	2.9
Carlisle	566	3.3	4.7
Shirley	991	3.7	7.1
South Reading	1,311	5.0	6.4
Urban areas:			
Charlestown	8,787	5.5	4.4
Lowell	6,474	12.7	3.2
Waltham	1,857	10.9	5.3

Similarly, in the largest towns of New Hampshire—Portsmouth, Exeter, and Dover—the proportion of females aged 15 to 19 was 7.2, 7.9, and 9 percent, respectively, much higher than the average for the state as a whole, suggesting that teenage girls were drawn not just to factory towns like Waltham and Lowell but to any large population center.[52] "The most intelligent and most enterprising of the farmer's daughters," a contemporary noted, "become school-teachers, or tenders of shops, or factory girls. They contemn the calling of their father, and will nine times in ten, marry a mechanic in preference to a farmer."[53]

The census provides some clues about migration, but more abundant data is contained in the records of some of the fraternal associations for migrants in mid-19th-century New England. The records of one such association, the Sons of New Hampshire, are especially valuable because the published proceedings of the two "festivals" held by the Sons in 1849 and 1853 contain, besides the usual toasts and speeches, registries which list not only the name of each member but also his town of origin in New Hampshire, place of residence in Massachusetts as of the festival date, occupation, and date of his removal to Massachusetts. By tracing the Sons in the manuscript of the 1850 federal census, it has been possible to draw a profile of about a quarter of the association's 2,200 members.[54]

The Sons distributed themselves across the spectrum of occupations, from crafts and industry to commerce, transportation, municipal employment, and the professions. But the Sons were not an exact replica of New England's population. All of them were, obviously, men, and to judge from their names, virtually all must have been Protestants. The membership list, moreover, is top-heavy with commercial, middle-class occupations; clerks, agents, brokers, grocers, traders, and merchants made up about half of the entire group. With the exception of a few laborers, sailors, farmers, "gentlemen," and one wag who listed his occupation as "nothing in particular," the remainder were professional men, skilled and semiskilled artisans, and an assortment of innkeepers, drivers, and stablers.

On balance, then, the Sons were not a microcosm of their society, but a cross section of its middle class, specifically its urban middle class, for most of them lived in Boston or adjoining cities such as Cambridge, Charlestown, Roxbury, and Dorchester. The banquet hall of the 1849 festival was decorated with over twenty sketches representing both the rise and progress of the Sons and the middle-class ethics proclaimed by all the after-dinner speakers. All of the sketches had something to say, but sketch number twenty-one said it all:

> Sketch comprehending all manner of natural obstacles, with a "native" on a pinnacle of rock, as if he had surmounted them all. The rock projects into the river, upon which are steamers and sail-boats. Motto above, "Be wise and rise." Beneath, "He can do anything." [55]

But whatever occupations they pursued and whatever status they had achieved, all of the Sons had left New Hampshire for Massachusetts, and in that sense their experience was representative. New Hampshire, like neighboring Vermont, was known as "a noble state to emigrate from." [56] Unproductive land, an inhospitable climate, and the lure of economic opportunities in Massachusetts depleted the population of many New Hampshire towns between 1800 and 1850. "In some villages," a speaker remarked to the assembled Sons of New Hampshire at the 1853 festival, "not a single young man who has attained his majority within the last ten years, remains at home." [57] Or, as the town historian of Temple, New Hampshire, related in 1860, "there has been a constant emigration of young men dissatisfied with farm life, and imbued fifty years ago, with the enterprising spirit of today." [58] Manhood was New Hampshire's staple product.

By 1853 many of the Sons were old men. Nathan Appleton, one of the wealthiest Sons, was 84, having emigrated in 1794. His brother Samuel was nearly 80 when the first festival was held in 1849. But the majority of Sons had been young men when they first came to Massachusetts, between ages 15 and 25. Within the latter category, the peak was in the middle, between 18 and 22, reinforcing the earlier suggestion that the final leaving of home or "start in life" usually came in the late teens or early 20s. At any period a fair number of Sons migrated at or under age 12, probably as dependents within their families, and a larger number came when 30 or over, as men who had already established themselves in New Hampshire. (Late migration was especially characteristic of professional men—doctors, lawyers, and clergymen.) But most came in youth, and in fact, a very large number came exactly at age 21, suggesting that they may have postponed migration until of age to enter legal contracts or until free of quasi-contractual obligations to parents.

Age at Migration of 574 Sons of New Hampshire

AGE	<12	13	14	15	16	17	18	19	20	21
Number	43	8	16	22	37	29	49	38	42	51
AGE	22	23	24	25	26	27	28	29	30>	
Number	30	27	24	12	12	15	10	10	99	

The typical Son left New Hampshire for Boston or an adjoining city in his late teens or early 20s. He did not bring his parents with him, nor was he likely to be married before migration. He was likely to marry not in his early 20s but between 25 and 30.[59] For such a young man, migration was likely to weaken ties to parents. Visits home were possible, but not easy. In order to visit his parents at Harvard, Massachusetts, only 35 miles west of Boston, young Amos Lawrence had to leave Boston at noon on Saturday, travel after dark to arrive home at midnight, and begin his return at midnight on Sunday to arrive at his place of business by dawn on Monday.[60] Most of the Sons would have had an even more strenuous journey if they decided to visit home. The "start in life" differed from its counterpart today less in its timing than in its irrevocability, for the prospects of ever again seeing one's parents on a regular basis were slender.

While leaving home diluted ties to parents, it might well have strengthened ties to brothers or cousins. Assuming that two individuals who had the same last name and who came from the same town in New Hampshire (except Portsmouth, the largest city) were related, then a fraction under 20 percent of the Sons either arrived in Massachusetts with relatives or, much more likely, had relatives already there when they arrived. The figure of 20 percent, moreover, is probably only the tip of an iceberg. It is derived from analysis of the registry of the 1853 festival, which lists town of origin. It is possible that individuals with the same last name but from different towns were also related. It is likely that some of the Sons had relatives who, for one reason or another, did not come to the festival and sign the register. Some migrants, further, might have lived with or near married sisters when they came to Massachusetts, but there is no way to establish the relationship with certitude. Sons might also have been related to other Sons with different last names. For obvious reasons, the relationship of step-brother was very common in the 19th century, but only a fortuitous discovery in a family register indicates that two of the Sons, James Bowers and L. K. Pierce, were stepbrothers.

The fact that an individual had a relative already in Boston or some nearby town admittedly says nothing about the emotional content of the relationship. Brothers or cousins might have lived at a distance, ignored each other, or disliked each other. The data from the festival registry provides some clues on this issue, specifically with reference to occupational similarities among Sons. In 1853 a majority of related Sons, (57.2 percent) were following essentially different occupations, but a significant minority followed identical or similar occupations (20.2 and 22.6 percent, respectively).[61] The proportion of similar or identical occupations among related Sons might have been higher than these figures suggest. Sons who followed identical occupations when they first migrated might have split up by 1853. In any event, a significant, but certainly not overwhelming, proportion of related Sons pursued identical or similar occupations.

Kin relationships had residential as well as occupational significance. Although only a small proportion of Sons were actually living with related Sons in 1850, over the course of time patterns of co-residence had probably been very important in cushioning the shock of migration for younger brothers or cousins. Relatives who migrated in the 1820s or 1830s might have lived together while each established himself, but one would hardly expect them still to be living together in 1850. To get a fair idea of the real frequency of co-residence, it is better to study just those Sons who migrated shortly before 1850—let us say since 1843—and since our concern is with youth, to study the residential patterns of those who were between ages 15 and 25 on removal to Massachusetts. Of those Sons who fall into these combined categories— that is, who migrated between 1843 and 1850 and who were between 15 and 25 at removal—all but 48 were married heads of households by

1850. Of the 48, 11 were living in 1850 with individuals who were probably brothers or cousins, since they shared the same last name and town of origin. The actual figure might well have been larger since, as noted, there are various ways in which individuals with different family names could have been related. Some individuals who did not live with relatives had them nearby. George Dimond, one of the 48, was a turner from Concord, New Hampshire, who came to Boston in 1845 at age 20. The festival register indicates that Oral Dimond, a turner from the same town, had arrived 15 years previously. Whatever their relationship, the Dimonds lived in the same ward, but not the same house. Three others also had probable relatives in the area but were not living with them in 1850.

What about the remaining 33 Sons who were not living with relatives and who had no known relatives in the area? Did they come to Boston without any contacts, or were there other people waiting to receive them? The case of D. R. Everett provides one clue. The festival register lists him as living in Boston in 1853, engaged in the butter and cheese business. But in the 1850 census Everett was discovered living in Billerica with Rufus Clement, a retired merchant, who happens also to have been a Son and to have come from Everett's home town, New London in Merrimack County. Since New London had a population of only 945 in 1850, it seems likely that Everett's family knew of Clement and dispatched their son to live with him. Similarly, Robert L. Crosby, a lawyer who came from New London in 1849, lived with Benjamin Seamens, a grocer who had migrated from the same town in 1837. The case of two clerks, David and Edward Fox, illustrates still another possibility. They came from different towns, Center Harbor and Meredith, but the same county, Belknap, and might have been cousins. At the time of migration they were fairly young, 13 and 16 respectively. Since they arrived in Charlestown, Massachusetts, in the same year, neither was likely to have been much help to the other in getting established. But the 1850 census reveals that they resided with (and probably worked for) Zadoc Bowman, a merchant who had come to Charlestown from Center Harbor in 1825 at the age of 15. Interestingly, Zadoc lived next door to Dexter Bowman. Like the two Fox Sons, both Zadoc and Dexter Bowman signed the festival registry. The Bowmans were probably related, although they came from different counties. Dexter Bowman was 24 when he came to Boston in 1818, seven years before Zadoc. It seems likely that the elder Bowman had performed the same kind of services for Zadoc as the latter performed later for the Foxes.

The remainder of the 48 Sons who migrated between 1843 and 1850 (and who were between 15 and 25 at migration) lived in households which contained neither known relatives nor former heads of household from their hometown. But even in these cases some patterns can be deduced. Young strangers in the city do not appear to have sought out just any boardinghouse. George Blandin, a driver, lived with his employer, a stablekeeper. More commonly, Sons resided in boarding-houses run by innkeepers from New Hampshire, or top-heavy with young men from northern New England who followed occupations similar to that of the Son who resided there. Slade's Hotel, for example, was not a hotel for transients but an apartment hotel with married and single boarders, about half of whom were from New Hampshire. Lucius Slade, the innkeeper, had migrated from Cheshire County in 1844 and later attended the Sons' festival. H. L. Dunklee, one of the 48 Sons, was not from Slade's town but probably searched out Slade's establishment as a suitable place for a youth from New Hampshire. The other boardinghouses which contained Sons in 1850 were usually either run by individuals from New Hampshire or contained mainly young men from northern New England. In either case, the boarders themselves were likely to follow similar lines; houses filled with merchants, clerks, traders, and agents, rather than with a promiscuous mixture of occupations, were the rule.

Finally, there were contacts provided by regional rather than kin connections and by contiguous rather than identical places of residence. Young men from New Hampshire tended to congregate in certain wards and neighborhoods. Justus Beals, for example, was an exception to some of the aforementioned patterns, for on arriving from Nelson in Cheshire County in 1849, he boarded in a house that contained eight other boarders, only one of whom was from New Hampshire. No other Beals signed the festival register, and hence it is possible that Justus had no relatives in Boston. But in 1850, Beals was living next door to two other Sons, Samuel Greele and Ira Ballou, who had migrated in 1825 and 1814, respectively. At the festivals, Sons both ratified existing contacts and made new ones. Perhaps this is what a speaker had in mind when he told the audience at the 1853 festival that "a gentleman observed to me the other day, that he objected to these kind of festivities; it was too clanish [sic], altogether too clanish." [62]

Despite the existence of various cushions to soften the impact of migration, life in the city could never duplicate the conditions of country life. Most of the Sons came from villages and small towns which had little if any industry before 1840. Some of the Sons had prior commercial experience clerking in country stores, but this was not quite the same as clerking in a large countinghouse. A boardinghouse, moreover, was not home; indeed, many of the boardinghouses bore no resemblance to any home. Apartment hotels like Marlboro House or Bromfield House or Adams House in Boston's central fifth ward were likely to contain 50 to 100 boarders, mainly young men, along with an astonishing number of servants (44 in Adams House alone). Young men had left home for centuries, but the assumption in the past had been that they would then move into households which resembled the ones they had left, households which contained five to ten people with a head and dependents. But large urban boardinghouses were not substitutes for the parental home. Even in the smaller boardinghouses young men were not dependent merely because they resided with a relative or co-regionalist.

Because of the inevitable shock of transition from country to city, kinship ties and regional chauvinism might well have been more important to migrants than they ever had been at home. In the city they could no longer be taken for granted but had to be cultivated. Further, the occupational composition of the Sons of New Hampshire suggests that kinship and regional ties reinforced economic contacts. The Sons of New Hampshire was in part a business as well as a regional organization. A number of Sons, in addition, joined the Young Men's Christian Association after its establishment in Boston in 1851. The YMCA, a home away from home and a church away from church, appealed primarily to middle-class youth who had recently migrated to the city from the country.[63]

The obvious differences between the behavior of rowdy fire company lads and that of earnest YMCA clerks who regularly attended midday prayer meetings underscore the extent to which youth of different social classes had different life-styles as well as different institutions in cities. In the three decades after 1830, conduct-of-life tracts not only warned urban youth about the traps that awaited the unwary but also contributed to a definition of the life-style appropriate to urban middle-class youth.

"Decision of Character"

Antebellum youth counselors were ambivalent in their response to social change, in the sort of advice they gave, and in their perspective on their audience. At times counselors were carried away by the energy and idealism of youth. "I love to look upon a young man," Daniel Wise confessed.[64] Youth was generous and confiding, Jared Waterbury claimed. To the youthful vision, all nature spreads out her cabinet of beauties and woos him to investigate at every step. Thoughts rush in upon him from every object, and often produce, while the mind is undisciplined, a gush of sensations, and a thrill of delight, which speaks in his eye, but can find no expression on his tongue. In fact, youth . . . is the poetry of existence.[65]

The world, however, demanded more of man than poetry; indeed, Waterbury and other counselors strongly suggested that it had no need at all for poets, or at least for young ones. No one symbolized the poetic, undisciplined nature of youth better than Byron; his poetry and life had a strong attraction for those American young people whose emotional yearnings found inadequate outlet in piety. Longfellow noted in 1832 that every city, town, and village had its little Byron, its self-tormenting scoffer and "gloomy misanthropist in song." Without exception, advice books proclaimed Byron to be the most dangerous model for youth. Who will deny, Wise asked rhetorically, "that Lord Byron's life was a splendid failure." [66] "Among the founders of corrupt dynasties in English literature," Rufus Clark noted in 1853, "we might mention the name of Byron. This author combined, as you well know, the most brilliant intellectual qualities with the deepest moral depravity." [67] So much for romanticism. Youth was attractive, but only to weak minds. Youth was an interesting period of life, a time of high spirits, but also volatile and thoughtless. Youth counselors preferred to play the role of kindly assassins of youthful fancy rather than ardent praisers of youthful energy. "Your spirits flow in rich currents of feeling, and your lively imaginations paint the most inviting pictures of the future," Wise wrote, that "it seems a pity to dim so fair a vision." [68] But Wise was up to the task. He advised his young readers to "control your appetites, subdue your passions, firmly and rigidly practice right principles, form habits of purity, propriety, sobriety, and diligence." [69]

The habit of censuring youth had deep roots in Puritan thought, and even after 1800 it flourished in rural as well as urban areas. "During a ministry of a quarter of a century," a clergyman in rural New Jersey complained in 1828,

> I have been much tried, and have witnessed the trials of many pious parents, on account of the levity and folly of youth generally, from 14 to 22. That period of seven or eight years, which seals the destiny of so many for time and eternity, causes more anxiety to the pious of my acquaintance than any other period. [70]

But both the passage of time and the growth of cities added some new twists. By the 1830s it was not merely the idleness, disobedience, and vanity of youth that was so bothersome, but the tendency of young people to push too quickly into active life. "Nothing can be more foolish or ridiculous," an essayist claimed in 1832, "than the eagerness with which gaunt and gosling-like youths strive to break through the barriers, by which their elders would restrain them, and rush at once into the public arena, where only giant arms and iron nerves can hope to be of any avail." [71] Yet, the same writer had to concede, nothing was more common. "In this goodly age, there are so many ways of making a display by means of superficial or erroneous information, that he must be endued with uncommon strength of purpose, who is able to disregard them." [72] Youth counselors were now more likely to urge prudence rather than humility on their readers, to point to recklessness rather than self-esteem as the soft spot in the young man's defenses. "Place yourself in an attitude of defence," Jared Waterbury cautioned. "Insidious foes lurk around your path. A dangerous enemy lies in ambush." [73]

As authors of cautionary verse, youth counselors relished playing the role of village wise men addressing wayward youth. Everything had once been secure, they claimed, but now all was commotion. John Mather Austin's list of "a thousand means of recreation" gives some notion of their idea of a good time: "the enjoyments of the paternal roof . . . the friendly call—the perusal of interesting and instructive books . . . the summer morning walk to behold the beauties of the glorious day . . . or the evening ramble." [74] They esteemed slow but steady progress; they liked the earnest plodder rather than the flashing meteor.

Their tone suggests that they were not deeply involved themselves in the turmoil of their age, that they were wise and aloof observers at a chamber of curiosities. Nothing is further from the truth. Youth counselors were, indeed, products of their times, often products of its worst features. Solomon Southwick's advice book rivaled any in its praise of simplicity, but Southwick's life had been anything but calm and orderly. After a start as a printer's apprentice in New York City in 1791, Southwick embarked on a career of petty officeholding in New York state politics, as well as on speculative real estate ventures. Caught by the money squeeze in 1817, he went bankrupt and landed in debtor's prison. He spoke with the assurance of experience when he told the Albany Young Men's Association in 1838 to "encourage no more the wild speculator." Southwick might well have valued stability, but his esteem of simple pleasures and humble goals was less a description than a criticism of his own experience. [75]

In different ways, most of the authors of advice books recapitulated Southwick's experience. Their early careers usually provided case studies of the very kind of "versatility" and "indecision of character" which they liked to condemn. Even the clergymen who wrote advice books were often men who had held a succession of pastorates. George Peck, author of an advice book published in 1853, provides an extreme illustration of the common tendency. Between the time of his licensing as a Methodist Episcopal preacher in 1816 and his retirement in 1872, Peck held nearly 20 different pastorates or executive positions in the church. Most clerical youth counselors held three or four different pastorates.[76]

Mobility often characterized more than merely the professional careers of youth counselors. Edwin H. Chapin, a Universalist minister and youth adviser, was the son of a peripatetic physician who drifted from town to town in New York and New England in search of patients. Lacking any fixed home, young Chapin came to Boston in his early teens, finding employment as an errand boy on State Street and recreation in a club which gave theatrical entertainments. "An impulsive and versatile boy needing most of all repression and drill, the aid of fixed conditions and regular habits," his biographer wrote, "he was kept in the constant whirl of events, hurried from scene to scene, drawn into the distracting meshes of diversity and novelty, until his gifts for order and patient application, never equal to his gift of spontaneity, had suffered serious damage." [77] When he came to address young men, Chapin himself placed only negligible value on spontaneity, and reduced conduct to a rigid sequence of duties to self and society.[78]

Youth counselors had a conservative, almost reactionary cast of mind, and yet the sort of advice they conveyed was not really reactionary. No counselor told his audience to leave the cities and retreat to the security of the village; none told young men to abandon trade for manual labor, where the temptations to dishonesty might have been less intense; few followed St. Paul in urging early marriage as a remedy for the lusts of the flesh. Beyond this, youth counselors thought that they saw a way to bridge the gap between tradition and change, between the behavior appropriate to youth and that demanded by the world of affairs.

The key to their resolution lay in the concept of the "decision of character," the title of an influential essay published originally in 1805 by John Foster, an English Baptist minister turned essayist. Foster's essay, which ran through repeated reprintings and re-editions in 19th-century America, marked a critical step in the process by which 19th-century moralists reshaped an old concept under new conditions. Character, once equated with natural physical marks and inborn traits, now came to signify a configuration of moral qualities gradually molded in each person. Foster listed as a fundamental mark of decisive character the possession of "a strenuous *will*" to accompany decisions of thought.[79] The ablest men moved through life with an "internal, invincible determination" and made events "conduce as much to their chief designs as if they had, by some directing interposition, been brought about on purpose." [80] Foster, whose language and ideas bear a striking resemblance to the views of William James nearly a century later, dwelt on the importance of building a vital reserve to strengthen resolution. Nothing was more destructive than "protracted, anxious fluctuation, through resolutions adopted, rejected, resumed, suspended"; that was the careless squandering of the "costly flame" of energy.[81] The goal was to preserve energy so that at the right moment all the reserve forces were primed for discharge:

> How costly a thing is youth's energy; if only it could be preserved entirely englobed, as it were, within the bosom of the young adventurer, till he can come and offer it forth a sacred emanation in yonder temple of truth and virtue. But, alas! all along as he goes toward it, he advances through an avenue formed by a long line of tempters and demons on each side, all prompt to touch him with their conductors, and draw this divine electric element . . . away.[82]

Victorian physiologists later picked up Foster's view of the human body as a closed energy system and applied it specifically to demonstrate that sexual license, particularly masturbation, drained energy and ultimately led to insanity.[83] Foster might have been thinking of the same thing, but he never said so. He did, however, recognize the potentially amoral implications of decisiveness. He had a disconcerting way of drawing his illustrations of decisive personalities from the annals of conquerors and, less frequently, self-made men. At one point he acknowledged the "mortifying truth" that only a perverse conscience could sanction the actions of most men preeminent for decision of character. Disingenuously, he ascribed "to a defect of memory that a greater proportion of the examples introduced for illustration in this essay, do not exhibit goodness in union with the moral and intellectual power so conspicuous in the quality described." [84]

The potential nihilism of the concept of decision of character did not deter American youth counselors from promoting the latter at every turn.[85] Although many authors of advice books were clergymen, and although most tracts contained a chapter (usually near the end) on religion as the foundation of morality, youth counselors were less interested in saving souls than in preaching the absolute value of character. They often argued, in fact, that the effort involved in becoming religious was valuable because it built character. Religion, in other words, was ancillary to character formation, and not the other way around. "Resolution," Joel Hawes proclaimed, "is omnipotent"; every youth needed "a deep, fixed sense of moral obligation." [86] Daniel Wise said that "energy is force of character—inward power." [87] Rufus Clark defined character as "executive force in the soul" and "fire within." One may possess talent, imagination, and good taste, a man may be conscientious and benevolent, "but the propelling power of his being must be energy." [88]

Many factors accounted for the receptivity of youth counselors to the concept of decision of character. Evangelical Protestantism had smoothed the way for John Foster's ideas. Like Foster, many American evangelicals found the passage from promoting religious conversion to celebrating decision of character to be swift and easy. Joel Hawes, for example, came to the genre of the advice book directly from the religious revival. Raised in a poor New England family and apprenticed in his teens to a cloth dresser, Hawes took a religious turn at 18. Resolving on the ministry, he entered Brown University at 20 after a brief period of study to compensate for his lack of formal education. In the 1820s, while pastor of the First Church in Hartford, Hawes summoned Lyman Beecher, the foremost Connecticut evangelical of the day, to fan the fires of religious awakening in his church. From 1826 onward, Hawes presided over periodic revivals which brought large numbers of young men into his church. It was shortly after the first of these revivals that Hawes delivered his original lecture series to young men, adjusting the spiritual message to temporal necessities but keeping the same bias toward decisive commitment which had brought many into his church and which had contributed to his own reorientation of plans in youth.[89] Similarly, Jared Waterbury, long before he turned to counseling the youth of the cities on the conduct of secular life, had composed a book of letters aimed at holding young converts true to their conversion decisions by stimulating "such youth to activity in the cause of Christ."[90] Evangelicals could bring themselves to criticize business practices and an inordinate attachment to wealth; they castigated dishonesty and "Mammonism" time and again. But they were unwilling to criticize the elements of business success, the personal force and enterprising spirit that the world rewarded, for radical individualism had long been a hallmark of evangelicalism itself.

The emphasis of youth counselors on decision of character was congruent not only with the evangelical temper but also with the main objective of advice books: to bridge the gap between traditional values and new conditions. For this purpose, character was not a set of doctrines or even a code of behavior, but an internal gyroscope, a self-activating, self-regulating, all-purpose inner control. By holding up decision of character as an ideal, youth counselors were, in effect, sanctioning a measure of ambition and undermining some of the traditional Puritan hostility to youthful vanity and assertiveness. But even as they did so, they sensed the need to protect their flanks by pounding home the importance of self-restraint. Intolerance of self-indulgence in youth compensated for tolerance of self-assertion as part of the intricate process of value trading that introduced Victorian morality to America.

Conclusion

Youth counselors addressed advice books to young men in general, but they strongly implied that their audience was composed mainly of middle-class young men who pursued mercantile occupations in the city. The protagonists of the brief moral tales which youth counselors often inserted were almost always drawn from the ranks of young merchants and clerks. Despite the censurious tone of most advice books, their authors were speaking to young men of their own social class.

Although youth counselors were unable to define success precisely, beyond implying that it involved the domination of life by the individual, they had no doubts that young men who honed their characters by the practice of self-restraint would become successful. In this respect, conduct-of-life books provided urban middle-class youth with both a goal and a method of attainment.

The advice books also reflected genuine alarm over the moral perils and moral transgressions of their intended audience. The depth of their anxiety made it impossible for youth counselors to embrace the ideal, so widely held during the last two decades of the 19th century, that loyalty to peers was to be encouraged as the first step in building loyalty to society. The mid-century youth counselor viewed every man as an island; his ideal was a hoarding of the self within the fortress of character. But the counselor himself was no more than an island among islands, shouting across to the others to be heard. His position was no less marginal and insecure than that of the urban middle class itself during the 1850s.

Paradoxically, the marginal quality of his position only made the youth counselor more emphatic about the therapeutic value of his panacea, character building. Walter Houghton has shown how the doubt, frustration, and insecurity of one side of the Victorian mind actually nourished the rigidity, dogmatism, and moral absolutism of the other.[91] Similarly, to say that the youth counselor was confident does not mean that he was a simple man living in a simple age.

PART TWO

Toward the
Age of Adolescence,
1840–1900

Albertis Browere, *Mrs. McCormick's General Store* (1844). Troublesome boys were a favorite topic for antebellum artists. Courtesy of New York State Historical Association, Cooperstown, N.Y.

SKETCHED NOVEMBER 1853 AT
THE UNIVERSITY of VIRGINIA

THE STUDENT

It gives me great pleasure to say that, although the vivacity of these blooded colts at the University frequently leads them into all sorts of devilities and excesses, they have almost invariably the manners of gentlemen. P.C. 1853

The Student. P.C. was "Porte Crayon," a pseudonym for David Hunter Strother.

HEAR!

Donnie Cantwell

★ PREACHING SINCE AGE 15 ★ VOTED MOST POPULAR BY 1970 SENIOR CLASS ROANE COUNTY HIGH SCHOOL ★ LISTED IN OUTSTANDING TEEN-AGER BOOK OF AMERICA 1970

★ CONDUCTED AREA - WIDE YOUTH CRUSADES IN FOOTBALL STADIUMS, GYMNASIUMS, AUDITORIUMS, ETC.

EVANGELIST

BETHEL BAPTIST CHURCH
OCT. 25 - 29, 7:30 P.M.

Route 29 North , 4 Miles North of Armhurst

Donnie Cantwell. The young man with the Dickensian name belongs to a long line of American boy evangelists.

BROADWAY, OPPOSITE THE ST. NICHOLAS, AT FOUR OF THE AFTERNOON.

These sketches capture the proximity of age groups and the mixture of refinement, decadence, and brutality in mid-nineteenth century New York City. Reproduced from *Harper's Weekly*, August 29, 1857 (above), and November 19, 1859 (below).

CHATHAM STREET, NEW YORK, ON SUNDAY.

FILIAL REVERENCE.

YOUNG AMERICA, *fresh from School, to expectant Parent (loq.)*. "Aha! Governor! What! starting out your Bristles? Good idea. Let 'em Sprout." *(Parent collapses.)*

The precocity of American boys in the mid-nineteenth century attracted the attention of artists as well as that of travelers and moralists. Reproduced from *Harper's Weekly*, July 18, 1857 (above), and February 20, 1858 (below).

MASTER SPARROW. "Look there, Tom! Young Fred is asleep!"
MASTER SPRAT. "Yes! Poor Little Beggar! What a shame it is to keep such a mere Child as that up so late!"

CHAPTER 5

From Nurture
to Adolescence

FLIGHT from farm to city, the spread of commercial opportunities, and exposure to intense moralism all rendered the period between 1790 and 1840 a distinctive era for young people. The conditions of coming of age in 1840 differed radically from those of 1740 or 1640. Yet, viewed from a different perspective, the entire period between 1640 and 1840 had an underlying unity, for prior to 1840 the immediate environment of young people was likely to be casual and unstructured rather than planned or regulated. In families, frequent departures from home put a limit on direct applications of parental discipline. In schools, brutality and burlesque mixed with slackness and informality. Draconian regulation of youthful conduct in colleges was softened by the fear of officials that students would quit the institution and by the officials' dualistic assumptions about youthful conduct. In any event, the justification for strict discipline in colleges was inapplicable to most youth in most situations. As Francis Wayland argued, the crowded, congregate nature of a large institution brought out all the worst features of youth and demanded tight regulation.[1]

The assumptions and practices which guided the social treatment of youth before 1840 occasionally passed under the rubric "accidental education." Speaking before the American Institute of Instruction in

1831, James Walker warned against the belief that youth be allowed to attain strength and maturity before being put to the trials of life. Such a belief, Walker argued, would counteract "one of the wisest arrangements of nature, according to which every individual is exposed to temptations gradually, and to one temptation after another, and is not thrust on a multitude of new temptations at once." [2] Adults cannot shut youth off from the world, Walker concluded, nor should they allow youth a prolonged period in which to study their roles in private before acting them out in public. [3]

Between 1840 and 1880 a different viewpoint and set of practices crystallized both in America and in Britain. The reformation of the English public schools launched by Thomas Arnold of Rugby was one illustration of the new approach, for Arnold sought to supplant long-standing chaos and brutality with an air of moral supervision and earnest solicitude. No longer were the public schools to be dumping grounds for the dissolute sons of gentlemen, places where they were treated like serfs and often acted like serfs on the rampage. Rather, they were to become nurseries of Christian character. [4] In America, concepts of moral education and practices in Sunday schools, private schools, and public schools were similarly modified under the new dispensation. But everywhere the leading feature was the same: internalization of moral restraints and the formation of character were more likely to succeed in planned, engineered environments than in casual ones.

Behind the various institutional and intellectual changes between 1840 and 1880 lay various demographic and economic forces. Leaders of the urban and commercial sectors of American society insisted that businesslike efficiency replace casual, ineffective, and sporadic applications of discipline in the rearing of the young. At the same time, changes in the social position of women in American society rendered feminine influence a more potent and self-conscious force than ever before in the nurture of children.

Whatever the sources of the new practices, however, their impact was mainly on the years between 7 and 12 or 13. Nothing in theory excluded their application to young people between 13 and 20, but in practice the latter showed little interest in joining institutions which sought to provide completely regulated environments for small children. Indeed, one paradoxical effect of environmentalist doctrines was that they seem to have rendered a variety of educational and religious institutions unattractive to youth. Yet the rising importance attached to the total regulation of the child's environment ultimately contributed to a recognition of the problematic character of the years around puberty. In contrast to antebellum youth counselors, whose focus had been primarily on the 18–25 age group, mid-century advocates of a closer supervision of children often indulged in a romantic view of the child which led them to portray the years around puberty as fraught with peril. What began with attempts to launch a revolution in the treatment of children culminated in a sensitivity to the distinctive dangers of early adolescence.

Moral Education

The idea that moral restraints were most effective when most fully internalized was an old one. It united rationalists such as John Locke in the 17th century with pietists like Philip Doddridge in the 18th, for both Locke and Doddridge viewed corporal punishment and terror as less efficacious than early attention to habit formation and a reliance on withdrawal of affection.[5] But in the writings of a group of philosophers of "natural education" in late 18th-century Britain—Richard L. Edgeworth, his daughter Maria, Hannah More, Sarah Trimmer, and Mary Sherwood—the principle of internalization merged with an emphasis on controlling the total environment of the child. Richard L. Edgeworth was an Irish landowner who became an important disciple of Rousseau and who sought, with indifferent results, to raise his son on the principles of *Émile*. Horace Mann proclaimed that Maria Edgeworth was "universally acknowledged" to be the foremost writer on education since Locke, a testimonial that would suggest an indirect influence by Rousseau on Mann were it not for the fact that in the hands of the Edgeworths the naturalism of Rousseau became so infused with moralism and utilitarianism as to be unrecognizable. For the Edgeworths, naturalism did not mean following the inclinations of the child or deemphasizing bookish education in favor of free development. Rather, it demanded that, instead of ignoring their children or reading lectures at them, parents should induce children to read "moral tales," little novels in which "distinct and useful" information was conveyed to the child through his reading of the actions of fictional children thrust into contrived situations. The moral tales presented "imaginary model situations" and contrasted the consequences of dealing with them wisely or foolishly.[6] British educators of the naturalist persuasion were also conscious that a real environment, the family, could be so regulated as to produce desirable moral effects in children. Appropriately, the Edgeworths began their *Practical Education* with a chapter on the role of toys in the educational environment of the child.[7]

In America the moral tale was embodied in Sunday school novels (which between 1830 and 1860 rolled off the presses of the religious publishing houses like water over Niagara), but the most complete and influential exposition of the determining role of family environment in moral education was Horace Bushnell's *Christian Nurture*.[8] Bushnell passed along a few hints to parents on methods of child rearing, yet strictly speaking, his book was not a child-rearing manual at all. Rather, it was a religious and philosophical treatise that aimed to demonstrate the Christian roots of "nurture," a word which Bushnell used interchangeably with "cultivation" and which had connotations of the growth of plants in nurseries. Bushnell described the family not as a collection of individuals bound together by kinship, property, and duty, but as an active entity in itself, a beneficent force greater than the sum of its parts.[9] Appropriately, he described the influence of parents as deriving from and acting through the procreative process. Procreation not only brought the child into existence but also passed on the moral and physical traits of the parents. Bushnell's interest in eugenics, a subject on which he was ahead of his time, was reflected in his desire to find some intellectual basis for depicting the family as more than a collection of related individuals residing under the same roof.[10] He would have agreed with Catharine M. Sedgwick's observation that "the people who surround us in our childhood, whose atmosphere enfolds us, as it were, have more to do with the formation of our characters than all our didactive and preceptive education."[11] For Bushnell the "organic unity of the family" was not just the result of reason and precept but especially of mood and tone.[12] Although hostile to Calvinism and to revivalism, Bushnell did not hold a romantic view of the child "trailing clouds of glory." Instead, he fluctuated between a Lockean view of the child as clay to be molded and a modified Calvinist view of the child as "somewhat depravated."[13]

Bushnell was a central figure among a group of writers in the 1840s who sought to reconcile the manifest inequality of women in American society with egalitarian democracy by defining a separate sphere of domesticity for women. In this respect, Bushnell was moving down the same avenue as Catharine Beecher, whose popular *Treatise on Domestic Economy*, published originally in 1841, was reprinted almost every year between 1841 and 1856.[14] Both Beecher and Bushnell departed from earlier child-rearing treatises, which had assumed male dominance in the household. Instead, they sought to elevate women to the status of unchallenged custodians of the moral development of children.[15] As a contemporary argued, "it is the province of the mother to cultivate the affections, to form and guard the moral habits of the child."[16]

Mothers, of course, had long had practical responsibility for the care of small children, but in the 1840s and 1850s demographic and economic forces made the cult of domesticity more than a rhetorical flourish. In 1800 the birthrate in the United States was higher than the highest birthrate recorded for any country in Europe. Yet by 1880 it had slumped below those of several European nations. Changes in the total fertility rate, another useful index, underscored the same tendency. A white woman bearing children in 1800, according to such rates, would reach menopause after having experienced an average of 7.04 births. In 1850 she would reach it after 5.42 births, and in 1900 after only 3.56 births. The drop in fertility occurred in rural as well as urban areas; indeed, the decline in rural fertility was the main cause of the decline in national fertility. But the fertility of urban women, starting from a lower base in 1800, remained lower throughout the 19th century. Only in 1930 did rural fertility finally fall to the level of urban fertility in 1840.[17]

The decline in fertility affected the position of married women in a number of ways; since fertility was lower in cities, the effects of the decline were most evident in urban areas. We are all familiar with the long-term effects of these changes. Families today contain fewer children than in the past, and the family's childbearing period is much narrower. But this pattern of two or three children closely spaced did not emerge until the end of the 19th century. In the middle decades of the 19th century, families were stretching out the intervals between children by birth control (abstinence and withdrawal) without practicing conscious family planning. The practice of family limitation, as opposed to family planning, meant that most of the life-cycle of a family was still occupied by childbearing and child rearing, but that longer time gaps would now occur between births, gaps when mothers would be free to devote attention to the conscious nurture of children without the physical and emotional drain attendant upon an endless cycle of pregnancy, birth, recuperation, lactation, and new pregnancy.[18]

The physical movement of population complemented the effects of demographic changes. Most of the migrants to cities in the 1830–1860 period were either young married couples or unmarried youth who would soon enter marriage. Mid-century cities contained a higher proportion of people aged 20–29 than rural areas and a lower proportion of small children and old people.[19] Young married couples who had left behind parents and grandparents on moving to cities formed a ready market for child nurture books of the sort written by Catharine Beecher.

The upgrading of the maternal role was scarcely possible among many poor people; it was most likely to occur in middle-class families where mothers had the undisputed custody of children after fathers left for work in the commercial district. The concept of Christian nurture was essentially a conservative ideal which grew out of fears of atomism and individualism in Jacksonian America. Advocates of maternal influence and of the ideal of the home as a moral agency, with tender love vibrating in every timber, explicitly described their viewpoint as a therapy "in this age of extreme individualism." [20] Even those like Bushnell whose original conceptions were shaped by personal experience came to view Christian nurture as part of a larger ideal of social cohesion and as an alternative to rampant individualism. [21]

"Individualism" is and was, admittedly, a catchall term, one applied to almost any fearful tendency in antebellum society. Bushnell might well have had his eye on something more concrete—the waves of Irish immigration which brought a non-Protestant and often disorderly foreign population to America in the 1840s and 1850s—for he included in the 1860 edition of *Christian Nurture* a chapter on the capacity of the Anglo-Saxon stock to outpopulate its rivals. [22] Others feared acquisitiveness and the commercial spirit. But whatever the specific anxiety, the ideal of Christian nurture was a symbol of the desire of middle-class Americans to seal their lives off from the howling storm outside and to create in family and church the kind of environment that would guarantee the right moral development of children and youth. [23]

The concept of Christian nurture placed a premium on the role of family environment in regulating every step of the child's development so that growth would be smooth and organic. In the middle decades of the 19th century, this concept had a host of literary applications and practical implications, sometimes traceable to the direct influence of Bushnell or comparable authorities and sometimes emerging independently, from the logic of institutional development. As an example of the latter, between 1825 and 1860 virtually all New England colleges responded to the challenge of student disorder by gradually shifting the burden of discipline from harried professors to parents who were now kept abreast of their sons' progress by report cards. As an example of the former, the language of Bushnell and Catharine Beecher suffused biographies and autobiographies of the 1840s and 1850s. These genres began to pay far more attention than previously to the conditioning role of family environment and to the humble and ordinary events of childhood as shaping forces of development. The child was, as ever, father to the man, but now in the sense that childhood formed a mold which determined later development, rather than in the traditional sense that the occurrences of childhood were indications of later direction and prospects. [24]

The mere fact that biographers paid more attention to childhood says nothing, of course, about actual changes in child-rearing practices within the family. Of all institutions the family is perhaps the most difficult to penetrate. But an analysis of changes which occurred in Sunday schools between 1800 and 1860 provides a valuable if oblique line of approach to changes in family values and practices.

Emerging in England in the wake of the 18th-century Wesleyan revivals and imported to America at the turn of the 19th century, the early Sunday schools had a number of distinctive characteristics. First, the laity led the way, with the clergy initially playing a minor role. Not a single minister could be found to address the first meeting of the Philadelphia Sunday and Adult School Union in 1817.[25] Second, Sunday schools were conducted mainly for the poor. As late as 1817, Boston pietists named their Sunday school society the Boston Society for the Moral and Religious Instruction of the Poor.[26]

The first of several changes which were to affect Sunday schools came in the 1820s when, under the impulse of evangelical revivals, Sunday school promoters began to emphasize the possibility of converting children en masse. The managers of the American Sunday School Union exemplified the mood of millennialist expectation when they rejoiced in 1824 that "millions of children and youth have been rescued from the paths of vice and snatched like brands from the burning. . . . [They are] brought beneath pious instruction, and their tottering steps have been directed toward the lamb of God." [27] No longer a philanthropic expedient for conveying the rudiments of morality and literacy to street waifs, Sunday schools were now portrayed as divinely appointed instruments for the regeneration of the nation.

As expectations rose, the clergy took an increasing interest in Sunday school affairs, limiting the role of lay pietists and philanthropists. Individual churches began to introduce Sunday schools as appendages of their regular services. The process began in Connecticut in 1815 and was generally completed by 1819, when the governing body of Congregationalist churches in the state could announce that "Sabbath schools are generally introduced into our congregations." [28] As the role of the clergy expanded, the intended audience of Sunday schools was redefined. The original interest in uplifting street boys gave way to a new focus on the children of regular church members. The unresponsiveness of the poor to the patronizing tone of Sunday school promoters partly accounted for the shift, but a no less important factor was the eager approval bestowed by the local ministers on schools which seemed to guarantee a steady stream of new church members with each rising generation.[29]

As Sunday schools became arms of the churches and agents of middle-class piety, their advocates gradually redefined the meaning of religious conversion. The founders of the Sunday school movement had been uninterested in the topic of conversion, expecting little more than an improvement in behavior from the street waifs under their watch.

As noted, the idea of converting Sunday school scholars became prominent only in the 1820s as a byproduct of millennialism and revivalism.
"Immediate repentance" and "immediate conversion" became slogans
of the movement in the 1820s and continued in high esteem into the
1830s and 1840s. Ambrose Edson put the issue bluntly in 1830: "if it be
a more favorable time to become a Christian in youth than when three-
score and ten years have passed away in sin, who will say that the age
of five years is not better than that of fifteen." [30]

Once planted, the idea of converting children thrived in the fertile
soil of 19th-century sentimental Protestantism, but the vines spread in
so many directions as to obscure the root. Some Protestants sought actively to convert children without really softening their concept of conversion. Edward Payson Hammond, to take the most famous representative of this view, took pleasure in publishing letters from boys who
rejoiced, in the manner of one 13-year-old, that "I have been born
again. I am three days old when I write this letter." [31] Although he conceded that most people associated early piety with early death, Hammond rejected the connection. G. Stanley Hall, who was familiar with
Hammond's evangelistic labors, thought that Hammond's literal belief
in the mass conversion of children was exceptional.[32] Indeed it was, for
even those who sympathized with Hammond preferred to argue that at
most one should pray for rather than induce the conversion of children.

In contrast to Hammond, liberal Christians preferred to drop the
word "conversion" from their theological lexicons or to describe conversion as a noiseless and nearly invisible experience, "the sweet experience of some tender moment, when the prayer is being offered at the
mother's knee; and neither child nor mother may mark the instant of
the change." [33]

Between these extremes, a third viewpoint can be located in mid-
19th-century Protestantism, one which wove features of the other views
into a distinctive synthesis. Briefly summarized, the intermediate view
insisted on the need for a "tangible and manifest" conversion experience as a capstone of childhood nurture, while rejecting as a great
"practical error" the idea that children could not be converted until they
had lived some years in sin or indifference.[34] No longer was a young
man to wait until 18 or 20 before initiating the cycle of conviction and
conversion after some remarkable incident had snapped him out of his
youthful lethargy. The old idea that youth was a time for sowing wild
oats, that an excess of prohibitions in youth merely produced an erratic
adult, had no place in the thought of mid-century moralists. An idea
"more false, more destructive to an exalted character and noble achieve-
ments, cannot be entertained," Rufus W. Clark wrote. As the president
of the Boston YMCA put it in 1857, "even within my own remem-

brance, it was supposed that young men . . . must go through fermentation before they could *afford* to be good." But now they "understand that there is no such necessity, but that they are to carry from the cradle to the grave an unblemished name, with unblemished morals." [35]

Those who sought to combine nurture with piety preferred that religious conversion take place in early to middle adolescence, as a confirmation of antecedent moral influences and guarantor of safe passage through youth, rather than in young manhood, as a traumatic resolution of religious and secular doubts.[36] Conversion was no longer to be a rite of passage from youth to adulthood but a kind of confirmation ceremony at the end of childhood. Various collections of biographies, the observations of contemporaries, and the quantitative evidence gathered by Hall and his associates in the 1890s indicate, moreover, that religious conversion increasingly coincided with the years around puberty in practice as well as theory.[37] What Hall and others were later to call "adolescent conversion" was not a timeless component of Protestantism but a phenomenon which took irregular shape in America during the revivals of the early 1800s and which was later institutionalized in a more regular and attenuated form in middle-class church and family practice toward the middle of the century.

Applied to religious conversion, the ideal of Christian nurture sanctioned a downgrading of the Protestant tradition which had allowed a period of introspection to precede conversion, a period designed to lead the would-be Christian to deeper convictions of unworthiness and sharper sensations of lustrous change. Bushnell himself drew the connection when he counseled Yale students that "one of the great talents in religious discovery is the finding how to hang up questions, and let them hang, without being at all anxious about them." [38] Time adds nothing to the thoroughness of conversion, nor suffering to the end of it, Henry Ward Beecher argued in 1859. The idea that spiritual change, to be genuine, had to be a long process, "dragging itself through weary weeks and months, during which the mind is to pass through much anguish and tribulation, until finally the light shall arise and shine, is simply foolish." [39]

As expectations about the timing of religious experience changed, so did its content. Conversion accounts increasingly took up only a few pages or a few sentences, and often described conversion as little more than a feat of self-mastery. For William Lyon Phelps in Rhode Island, conversion in a Baptist church in the 1870s at age 10 did not even involve that:

> During the year and a half we lived in Providence I was "converted." There were revival meetings at our church, and one evening, when the Reverend Doctor Bixby had been preaching, I stood up when they called

for the unconverted. It was not an explosive experience, but I did feel very happy.[40]

Sunday schools were not the only agencies of religious conversion, but they were important and, in the eyes of their promoters, certainly preferable to camp meetings. Moreover, changes in the organization of Sunday schools after 1830 complemented changing concepts of religious experience. If conversion was to be the result of organic development rather than a sudden paroxysm, the age grading of Sunday schools became desirable in order to facilitate the synchronization of religious experience and levels of development. The earliest Sunday schools had included adults as well as children (sometimes they had more adults than children), but a reaction was under way by 1840, and by 1860 age homogeneity had supplanted age heterogeneity in the Sunday schools of town and city churches.[41] Similarly, details of the Sunday school itself—the books used, the teachers employed, the room arrangements, the time of class—all became prominent in discussions of Sunday schools between 1840 and 1860 as ways to ensure that religious and moral growth would proceed smoothly rather than spasmodically.[42]

In summary, Sunday schools between 1815 and 1860 gradually ceased to be offshoots of Christian philanthropy aimed at the ragged poor and became instead arms of regular churches, designed to induct the children of church members gradually into the full life of the churches. Changes in goals led to shifts in techniques. As less attention was paid to proselytizing among the unchurched, more was given to the physical arrangements of the schools, to the size of rooms, preparation of teachers, quality of books, and age grading of classes. At the same time, the concept of conversion also changed. Originally a topic that had excited little interest, the religious conversion of pupils gradually became a major goal of Sunday schools, first under the influence of the millennialist mood of evangelicalism in the 1820s and later under the impact of the ideal of Christian nurture. In the form it took during the 1830s and 1840s, conversion was to be as continuous as possible with benign influences in childhood, an act of ratification rather than of revolution. The child raised as a Christian and, as Bushnell put it, never knowing himself to be other than a Christian, was to grow up to become the "whole man," the balanced and benevolent young gentleman beset neither by gnawing religious doubts nor by crass commercial greed.[43] He was to exhibit "harmony of character." As Daniel Wise, a youth counselor and also a former president of the American Sunday School Union, put it: "see to it that there are neither excesses nor defects in your character, but a harmonious blending, a delightful symmetry, formed of fitting proportions of every high quality."[44] Describing mid-

19th-century middle-class religious life, William Dean Howells viewed the effects of new ideals more cynically, but probably more accurately:

> Religion there had largely ceased to be a fact of spiritual experience, and the visible church flourished on condition of providing for the social needs of the community. It was practically held that the salvation of one's soul must not be made too depressing, or the young people would have nothing to do with it. . . . The Sunday school was made particularly attractive, both to the children and the young men and girls who taught them.[45]

These changes occurred primarily in towns and cities. Age heterogeneity in Sunday schools prevailed much longer in rural areas, where pupils were often over 15 or even 18 and where managers were forced to complain about the difficulty of attracting children under 15. It is also likely that these changes occurred primarily within the middle class. Admittedly, historians overuse and under-specify the term "middle class." To the extent that the term "middle class" presupposes the existence of a self-conscious proletariat (or peasantry) on one side and a self-consious and flamboyant elite on the other, it is inapplicable to mid-century American cities. But the cities did contain the laboring poor, many of them immigrants, in abundance.[46] The composition of an organization like the Sons of New Hampshire suggests that fraternal bonds tied together not only co-regionalists but men of similar occupations in cities. The extraordinary emphasis on self-denial in advice books was evidence of an effort to indoctrinate a social group with values that would set its members off from the freewheeling style of other social groups in the city. And although it was a religious treatise, *Christian Nurture* was imbued by values which were, if not "middle class," certainly businesslike. Bushnell's argument with "ostrich nurture," with the idea that children could be left to their own devices until rescued by a conversion experience, was that it was an inefficient and wasteful method, and hence had to be supplanted by a new method which made the controlled environment of the Christian family the agency of moral growth. In a similar way, the degree of attention to details of management in Sunday school manuals after 1840 bespoke the same high valuation of businesslike efficiency. Finally, the downgrading of introspection was a valuable asset in the commerical life of towns and cities. The ideals of linear moral growth and organic nurture left no room for a period of sowing wild oats or for prolonged self-analysis. Among the commercial classes of rapidly growing cities, a good name, unblemished morals, and steady behavior could have direct and practical value. Where strangers met and transacted business, outward demeanor was important to gain confidence, but whether a man had finally made certain of his possession of "saving grace" mattered little.

Asylums for the Preservation of Childhood

In both chronology and substance, some striking parallels exist between the transformation of family ideology and Sunday school practice after 1840 and changes in secular education during the same period. The common school revival, led by Horace Mann, Henry Barnard, Calvin Stowe, and others gave public education a mighty push in the direction of environmental control. Here again, the model was European, specifically the Prussian school system, remarkable for its orderly character, and Hofwyl, the Swiss estate of Phillip von Fellenberg on which the educational reformers J. J. Wehrli and J. H. Pestalozzi had developed a major complex of institutions. The various schools at Hofwyl, physically isolated from society and run as boarding schools, inspired Americans as diverse as Mann, George Bancroft, and John Griscom. Bancroft's Round Hill school at Northampton, Massachusetts, became a model for elite American boarding schools such as the Flushing Institute, St. Paul's, and Groton. Unlike academies, where students boarded in town and often worked part-time while in attendance, boarding schools were designed as total environments for the child. The fact that one of the schools at Hofwyl was for delinquent children, moreover, stimulated Griscom, a New York Quaker reformer, to use Hofwyl as a model for the New York House of Refuge, founded in 1826 to provide street urchins with a salutary moral environment.[47] Of course, the mere existence of models at Hofwyl or in Prussia does not account for their grip on the minds of 19th-century American educators. Rather, the values of reformers, which mixed a soft sentimentalism about childhood with a hard bureaucratic preference for order and efficiency, shaped their receptivity to some models rather than others.

The near obsession of the common school revival movement with school architecture and the physical setting of schools revealed both the soft and hard sides of reform values. At times, reformers drew a connection between school appointments and pupil efficiency; better ventilation made better pupils. At other times, a more romantic line of thought asserted that beauty in the schoolroom was itself a preservative of juvenile morals. In 1847 an Ohio school report called for "commodious playgrounds, and attractive objects, inspiring correct taste, elevated feelings, and profitable associations, and conveniences, which would preserve youthful sensibility and morals from injury and pollution."[48] In Michigan, Ira Mayhew called for schoolhouses so carefully constructed and situated that everything offensive would be kept from the sight of children, and he specifically suggested that teenage boys, uplifted by the elegance and beauty of their school surroundings, would be deterred from the "secret vice" of masturbation.[49]

The location of the schoolhouse was important too—not too near the center of town or the highway, for then children would have to listen to the coarse language of teamsters or the taunts of street rowdies.[50] The same applied to high schools. "You are aware that the location of the High School room," the Westfield, Massachusetts, school committee noted in 1850,

> is not peculiarly favorable to moral nor intellectual improvement: The Town Hall above, which is occupied some days each term for town meetings and other purposes, is a great annoyance. The police court room and lock-up underneath may be very useful in some connections, but should be kept at a respectable distance from our public schools.[51]

All of this stood in contrast to colonial practice, when schools had been kept in private dwellings, if not in barns. But relative to other goals of reform, school architecture was only a peripheral concern, an offshoot of a more fundamental desire to make school as coextensive with the life of the child as conditions would allow. Even the insistence of reformers on substituting various types of state and local support for the older system of head taxes on scholars was probably less central to their thinking than their desire to bundle every child warmly in the garment of education, to make school a veritable "asylum for the preservation and culture of childhood."[52]

The goal of making the life of the schools coextensive with childhood had a number of specific implications. The school year was lengthened from weeks to months to the better part of the year. Nonattendance was increasingly defined as deviant, and punished from the 1850s onward by compulsory education laws. The latter, in turn, underscored the special problem posed by the truant, for his absence was intolerable, dangerous to himself and a waste of public money, but his presence could prove troublesome too. Massachusetts found one answer, for in 1862 a state law provided for the incarceration of chronic truants in reform schools, thus preserving the principle of institutionalization.[53] In addition, reformers vigorously insisted on the dissemination of regular, graded school texts. Not only the books but also the teachers needed filtration.[54] To screen teachers, reformers advocated normal schools to ensure the best preparation possible for missionaries to the classroom. Normal schools, further, would guarantee a steady supply of female teachers and hence would foster another goal of the reformers: the introduction of female teachers to winter as well as summer school sessions. If the primary school was "heaven's great nursery," women were its ideal directors.[55] Horace Mann would have agreed with Catharine Beecher when she proclaimed that one of the ugliest abuses that women had to witness was the turning over of tender children "to coarse, hard, unfeeling men, too lazy or too stupid to follow the appropriate duties of their sex." [56]

Economy as well as philosophy conditioned the preference of reformers for female teachers: The latter's willingness to work for less than males helped to persuade local school boards of the advantages of females, but the emerging domination of teaching by women was more than the product of the ageless parsimony of school boards. Strictly speaking, it was not the result of parsimony at all. Reformers were eager to save money wherever they could because their broader ambitions for education were expensive to implement. It cost money to transform a locally controlled nonsystem of education into a centralized and bureaucratically administered pyramid of educational institutions.

The presence of both philosophical and economic considerations in promoting the domination of schools by female teachers underscores the curious mixture of tender sentiment and hard efficiency in school reform. If the consensus on the value of female teachers provides one illustration of this mixture, the process of classification of the schools by attainment and age yields another. Complaints about the difficulty of managing classes that contained a promiscuous assemblage of infants, boys, girls, large boys, big girls, young men, and young women did not begin in the 1840s. But classification of the schools by age and attainment is best viewed, nevertheless, as a byproduct of the common school reform movement. Unlike the college students of an earlier day, for whom teaching had been an avocation, school reformers were not content with random laments or vain musings on what might be, but were men of affairs capable of extraordinary activity in translating ideals into approximations of reality.

The soft side of age grading focused mainly on the presence of tiny tots in the schools and assembled various pieces of medical wisdom to justify the removal of 4- or 5-year-old children from academic pressures. Originally hopeful experiments in the 1820s and early 1830s with "infant schools" had left a bitter taste and the conviction that children under 6 or 7 were unready for the mental and physical demands of formal education. The key document was Amariah Brigham's *Remarks on the Influence of Mental Cultivation Upon Health*, a plea for greater attention to the health of the mind and body than to the cultivation of mental faculties.[57] Brigham warned that "precocious maturity of the mind is nearly always disease"—disease first of the brain, then of the nervous system, and ultimately of the mind in the form of total insanity.[58] Those who pushed small children ahead too rapidly would reap a bitter harvest in later years.

Brigham's viewpoint enjoyed the high esteem of reformers. Ira

Mayhew cited Brigham not only against hothouse education but also against the sort of infant prodigies whose biographies, invariably brief, were circulated by ministers to cheer the faithful.[59] Children who were taught hymns before they could speak and were reasoned with before they could think, Mayhew warned, would meet the same early death or insanity that awaited 4- or 5-year-old "scholars" who were expected to exhibit feats of memorization in schools.

A calculating Yankee mentality represented the hard side of age grading. As long as schools were ungraded, it was difficult to justify the widespread use of female teachers, mainly because of doubts that tender ladies of 16 could manage plowboys of 18 in a classroom. Gradation, on the other hand, would permit the year-round employment of women, with older boys placed in high schools under male tutelage. As the North Andover, Massachusetts, school board argued in 1859,

> had we a High School, we could entrust the care of all the other schools to female teachers, through the year. The advantages of the plan would be great; the smaller scholars, by far the majority that attend school the entire year, would suffer no interruption in their studies by the constant change of teachers. They would have before them as a stimulus a higher grade of school for which to prepare themselves, whilst the older scholars, instead of leaving town or seeking a private school, could pursue the higher branches, such as Algebra, Geometry, Botany, Astronomy, etc.[60]

Aside from stating the logic behind gradation and the introduction of female teachers, the foregoing quotation also underscores some other goals of school reform. Reformers admired symmetry in organization, the ideal of a graceful pyramid of schools, with each level fitting neatly into those above and below. The high school was to give shape and direction to the efforts of the lower schools, and the lower schools were needed to simplify and clarify the functions of the high school.[61]

In addition, although Horace Mann and others at times described education as a cheap form of police, they did not view public education as merely a device to bring social control over the children of the lower classes. Their goals were actually more ambitious. They wanted all children to attend public schools, and they were hostile to private education as such. Their strident insistence on uplifting the moral tone of public schools aimed partly at making such schools attractive to the middle class.

In place of external regulation of conduct by village elders, ministers, or town officials, mid-19th-century moralists substituted the cultivation of character in the regulated environment of family and school. The sources of the new ideology were manifold: rationalist and pietist, British and American, the Edgeworths and Hannah More, Round Hill and Hofwyl, conservative and even radical.[62] Whatever the source, however, the social perception was the same. The growth of cities, increase in population mobility, and rise of egalitarianism, combined with evidence of social disorder, all contributed to the conviction that moral development of the young should no longer be shaped by casual contacts with adults in unstructured situations but had to be regulated at every turn. In the words of Henry Barnard, "a broad, liberal, and cheap system of educational influences, such as schools, books, libraries, lectures, cabinets, etc., must be spread before and around every child, youth, and grown up person in our cities." [63]

School Reform and the Teenager

Changes in education between 1840 and 1880 primarily affected those between 6 or 7 and 13. But what about young people between 14 and 21, the large boys, young men, and young women whose presence had given such a distinctive cast to the old district schools? Part of the answer lies in the practical consequences of age grading. Earlier we saw the broad spectrum of ages in George Moore's Acton school in 1828. The tables below, indicating the age spread in 1860 in the central intermedi-

Ages of Students at Concord Intermediate School, 1860

Boys

AGE	8	9	10	11	12	13	14	15	16	17	18
Number	0	0	3	3	7	7	14	1	4	1	1

Girls

AGE	8	9	10	11	12	13	14	15	16	17	18
Number	1	0	4	4	6	8	3	3	0	1	0

Ages of Students at Concord High School, 1860

BOYS					
AGE	14	15	16	17	18	19
Number	1	4	3	8	1	0

GIRLS					
AGE	14	15	16	17	18	19
Number	2	8	8	3	1	4

ate school and public high school in nearby Concord, Massachusetts, can serve as a basis for comparison.[64]

With variations, this tendency toward the concentration of high school students in the teen years was reduplicated across the country. The major determinant was whether an intermediate school existed below the high school. If so, the high school age range usually ran from 14 to 19; if not, it would more likely be 11 to 17.[65] The presence or absence of intermediate schools, in turn, reflected the level of population concentration. Even in Concord in 1860, outlying schools in sparsely settled areas continued to display the same wide range of ages that characterized George Moore's Acton school in 1828.[66] As a rule of thumb, the school reports of Ohio in the 1850s read like those of Massachusetts in the 1840s; those of Michigan in the 1860s like those of Ohio in the 1850s; and those of Iowa in the 1880s and 1890s like those of Michigan in the 1860s.

Age grading in public schools inevitably affected practices in both private schools and colleges. In place of the mixture of boys, youth, and men in the original academies, academies in the decades between 1850 and 1870 generally tended toward concentration in the teen years.[67] In colleges the entire period from 1850 to 1900 saw a gradual concentration of students in the 18–22 range. Neither the median nor average age at graduation from college actually changed much in the period from 1830 to 1900, but the age spread contracted.[68] In academies and colleges, moreover, the initial changes occurred at the lower rather than upper rungs of the age ladder; the 10-year-olds disappeared from academies before the 22-year-olds did; the "mere boys" of 13 or 14 disappeared from the colleges before the 25-year-olds. As in the public schools, the first casualties of age grading were the "precocious" children further up the ladder than their age and level of attainment entitled them to be.[69]

Although the younger children and youth were eliminated first at each level, concepts of development played no more than a minor role in the process. A bureaucratic preference for order and efficiency and the logic of institutional change were the motivating forces. The concentration of teenagers in high schools and academies occurred because of the systematization of lower schooling.

The debate over the high school did, however, produce its share of references to "adolescence," a hitherto unfamiliar term which began to acquire more specific meanings toward the middle of the 19th century. The common theme was that high schools made it possible to keep children at home longer, especially during the dangerous years of adolescence. One commentator wrote in 1858, "Early departure from the homestead is a moral crisis that many of our youth do not show themselves able to meet. It comes at a tender age, when judgment is weakest and passion and impulse strongest."[70] The words could have come from an advice-to-youth tract, but in this case the writer was using the perils of adolescence to justify sending children to high schools rather than away to boarding schools. Another version of the argument appeared in the pleas of local school committees that public school had custodial functions and that even an ill-equipped public school was superior to the street school.[71]

Since school committees manufactured so many arguments to justify high schools, it is difficult to judge how much significance they attached to any one of them. It seems likely, however, that the argument from adolescence was less a motive for constructing high schools than a promotional appeal to induce parents to send their children to them. One implication of Bushnell's philosophy was that home residence was a precondition for right nurture, and the measurable popularity of Bushnell's writings suggests that the equation of residence and dependency met with a strong response from some segments of American society. A glance at the promotional literature of academies in the same period points to an identical conclusion, for academy spokesmen put part of the blame for the manifest decline of their institutions on the unwillingness of parents to send their children away from home during adolescence. In 1866, Charles Hammond, principal of Monson Academy, conceded that this was the main argument against academies. Hammond then proceeded to argue that the point would have real force only if all homes were ideal, which they certainly were not, and hence that departure from home in adolescence was still necessary.[72] But Hammond was defending a declining viewpoint as well as a declining institution. By the 1870s, apologies for academies had a pathetic ring. In an address delivered in 1877, Calvin Hulbert confined himself to the modest suggestion that academies might still be valuable for rural boys who, ashamed of their rough dress and green ways, could thus avoid exposure to "the sneers of mock-culture, fashion's glitter and tinsell, that so often overpower homely but generous merit" in graded town schools.[73]

Commercial towns and cities were the places most likely to establish public high schools during the middle of the 19th century.[74] Such schools served the needs and met the wishes of a segment of the middle class not only because they assuaged the fears of middle-class parents that their children would be corrupted if allowed the sort of freedom traditionally accorded to academy students, but also because they suited the peculiar conditions of dependency in middle-class families. A commercial agent, for example, did not have the same options that were available to farmers, who had traditionally sent their sons out as farm servants or seasonal laborers in their early teens, or to wealthy merchants, who owned their ships and who could send their sons out as supercargo. The period of dependency in urban, middle-class families was no longer than it traditionally had been on farms, but its content was different, for in urban middle-class families dependency was likely to involve continuous residence under the parental roof, interrupted only by daily trips to a nearby public high school. Small wonder that a Frenchman in the 1870s praised the American high school as a source of continual replenishment of the middle class.[75]

Actual conditions, however, placed severe constraints on the ability of the middle class to use high schools as agents of prolonged dependence. Public high schools unquestionably embodied the goals of segments of the middle class. Their students were drawn mainly from the ranks of children of small shopkeepers, traders, clerks, and professional men; on graduation, they became teachers, clerks, merchants, and college students.[76] But even in populous commercial communities, the places most likely to establish high schools, the proportion of teenagers in attendance was small. Most high schools had entrance examinations, a fact which suggests that those who promoted them as ways to keep youth at home during adolescence did not want their argument taken too literally. In the battle between high standards and universal education, high school officials remained on the side of the former virtually to the end of the 19th century. Moreover, a majority of high school students and an even greater majority of graduates were girls. Boys who attended high school at all were likely to be withdrawn after a year or two and sent to work. Graduation from high school could serve a girl as a passport to teaching, but graduation was still of little importance to a boy unless he planned to enter college. Middle-class families could forgo the labor of their children for a longer period than lower-class families, but not indefinitely.[77]

On balance, the innovations which perfected the educational environment of those between 7 and 13 had a paradoxical effect on those 14 to 21. Wittingly or unwittingly, reformers made education beyond the rudiments expensive in the process of making it systematic. By stretching out the school year they increased the principal cost of education, loss of wages while attending school. And by replacing the casual, seasonal sessions of the old academies with graded sequences of annual courses, they accomplished the same effect with a vengeance. Consistent with their preference for order and efficiency, reformers explicitly argued that it was better for juveniles to attend school for a long term within a single year than for short terms spread out over a number of years.[78]

Finally, by substituting female for male teachers, school reformers committed themselves to a system of discipline based on "moral suasion" instead of corporal punishment and humiliation. At the same time, they had to concede that moral suasion, a rational appeal to a higher moral sense, often did not work with older boys who grew rebellious, scorned lady teachers, and dropped out.[79] A few reformers recommended that women try Quaker repression in class, separating the offender from his peers and giving him the silent treatment; others called for a return to male teachers.[80] But most just threw up their hands in exasperation. "The larger and lustier and more masculine he [the boy] is," an Illinois official stated in 1872, "the more does he surpass their [females'] understanding." [81] Most school officials accepted the logic of their position and acquiesced in the removal of older pupils from school. After all, they had always been troublemakers, and, in any event, earnest reformers had little sympathy with their practical joking. Apostles of efficiency, reformers were bitter if uncomprehending critics of village traditions like the barring out of a master. The schools were better off without these "fast boys, young rowdies, and lazy country boys that go to school just to shirk work at home," a Pennsylvania teacher argued in 1866.[82] Better to put them out to trades, improve our manufactures, and solve our discipline problems, he concluded.

In the 1860s, industrialization and the Civil War alike contributed to the pattern of removal. Teenagers found ample demand for their services in the factories of eastern states such as Massachusetts, Connecticut, Rhode Island, and Pennsylvania, while those who went off to save the Union in the 1860s found their jobs taken by fresh crops of 15- and 16-year-olds.[83] A fraction went on to the high schools, but as a school committee noted in 1862, they were the good boys from nice homes, not the backward and unmanageable boys whose absence from the schools few would miss.[84] The shift did not begin with the Civil War; as early as 1847 the Marshfield, Massachusetts, school committee described the "change that has been gradually taking place in our schools during the last thirty years, by the pupils being withdrawn from them so much younger than formerly." [85] But like other changes, this one was accelerated by the Civil War, and in the early Gilded Age it became a dominant refrain of school boards. Indeed, it was one of the key arguments for the emerging tendency toward rapid and automatic promotions in the larger school systems. If boys were to finish school early, as they must, then it became intolerable that they dally in the lower grades till they were 12 or 13. It was better to move them rapidly through their paces, so that when they left school at 14 they would at least have been exposed to something beyond the rudiments. The superintendent of schools in Boston devoted part of his 1882 report to complaints about 16- and 17-year-olds still in grammar school and urged rapid promotion; a survey of American urban education published in 1885 indicated that most urban school systems were following his advice by pushing boys quickly through the grades up to age 14 and then letting them go.[86]

Earlier we noted some chronological and intellectual parallels between secular public schools and Sunday schools in the middle of the 19th century. One additional comparison is worth noting, for in both cases social change, gradation, and female influence rendered institutions unattractive to teenage boys who were prone to drop out. An unbroken line of complaints by Sunday school officials stretched from the 1830s to the 1870s concerning the difficulty of "keeping the boys." "Boys of twelve or fourteen years have supposed it a necessary indication of manliness to abandon them, and have left the school just at the age when they most needed its instruction and restraints," a Sunday school agent complained in 1832.[87] Forty years later, E. C. Hewett asked "how shall we keep the boys?" [88] In 1876, Asa Bullard, a veteran of Sunday school administration, conceded that "large boys" aged 14 to 17 created special problems:

> There is a class of pupils who are just between the periods of childhood and manhood—large boys—that should receive special attention of the guardians of Sabbath schools. High-spirited, inclined to throw off restraint, often reckless, generally overestimating themselves, and perfectly confident of their ability and wisdom, and somewhat ashamed to be numbered among children, these large boys are not only often inclined to leave school, but are among prominent candidates for ruin and temptation.[89]

Ironically, one institution was having increasing success in "keeping the boys"—the reform school. The earliest American reform schools were the privately inspired and funded houses of refuge established in eastern cities in the 1820s and 1830s. In the 1840s and 1850s, however, a new set of institutions emerged; these were more likely than the refuges to contain "reform school" somewhere in their titles. Unlike the original houses of refuge, reform schools were usually located in the country, were primarily state supported, and aimed more self-consciously at the reformation of juvenile offenders than at providing domicile for street "arabs." The Massachusetts State Reform School for Boys, located at Westborough and created by legislative act in 1847, was the first state-supported institution for juvenile delinquents in the United States, although it also received more than $60,000 in private bequests from Theodore Lyman, a shipping magnate and former mayor of Boston. A similar mixture of public and private support marked the establishment in 1854 of a state reform school for girls at Lancaster, Massachusetts.[90]

The Lancaster school was the first American institution to use the "family system," modeled on a French colony for juvenile offenders at Mettray and a comparable German one (the *Rauhe Haus*) at Horn, near

Hamburg. The founder of the *Rauhe Haus*, a young theology student named Johann H. Wichern, had concluded that a homelike atmosphere would fill a gap in the lives of street waifs who had never known the blessings of a stable home. At Lancaster the girls were grouped into cottages under house mothers, with younger and older children in the same house, as in the family.[91] Ohio's state reform school for boys, established in 1857, was modeled on the Lancaster system.

The Lancaster school differed from most other reform schools in one important respect. The early houses of refuge had taken children at any age up to 20, and Lancaster followed this pattern in the sense that it sought to incorporate age heterogeneity in its cottages. In contrast, most reform schools, and ultimately Lancaster, sought to fix the upper age limit at 14 or 16, for "with puberty comes a strengthening of the bad propensities, and, moreover, a new passion is added, of great power and violence."[92] But the attempt to limit inmates to those under 14 failed. The rise in juvenile crime in cities after 1830 increasingly turned reform schools into dumping grounds for teenage felons and troublemakers. More and more, reform schools became high schools for the lower classes, with a concentration of inmates between 14 and 17. By 1873 the trustees at Lancaster were complaining bitterly about the presence of "older and more corrupt girls."[93] Well they might, for in that year the average age of inmates was a little over 16, with 85 of 110 falling between ages 15 and 18.[94] At Westborough in 1855, 132 of 339 inmates were from 14 to 16 years old at commitment.[95] At Cape Elizabeth, Maine, the age at commitment in 1856 ranged from 7 through 18, but 157 of the 274 inmates were between 13 and 16 at commitment.[96]

Those who sought to reform juvenile delinquents in mid-19th-century America spoke the lofty language of nurture and environmentalism. Reform schools, they claimed, were not prisons but homelike institutions, veritable founts of generous sentiment. In fact, they were prisons, often brutal and disorderly ones. A short story tells a great deal. When an inmate of Westborough set fire to the place in the late 1850s, the boys were quickly transported to a jail recently completed in Fitchburg; in a pinch, the jail was the only comparable social institution.[97] If reform schools differed at all from adult prisons, it was because children could be shipped off to the former not just for crimes but for general vagrancy and stubbornness. The old common law idea that the state had a sort of eminent domain over children (*parens patriae*) meant not only that it could protect children from abuse, but also that it could commit to institutions children who had exhibited criminal or disorderly potential rather than specifically criminal behavior.[98]

From Childhood to Adolescence

We have seen how efforts to mold an ideal environment for children between 7 and 13 rendered the years around puberty more conspicuous. More often than not, the effect of protecting children from contamination by adults was the drawing of a line roughly at the age of puberty through some traditionally broad age groups. This observation underscores the extent to which the social definition of an intermediate stage of development has often depended on a prior perception of new conditions affecting one of the bordering stages of life. As ambitious but green young men flocked from agriculture to urban commercial occupations between 1820 and 1860, for example, youth counselors argued that the new conditions of adulthood required a new conception of the tasks of youth, which they called character building. Similarly, the growing sensitivity of middle-class moralists to the importance of insulating the lives of children led to a sharper perception of the "crisis" which sexual maturation posed to the putative innocence of childhood. As the years around puberty acquired increasing social and institutional significance, an old concept, that of adolescence, acquired new connotations.

Adolescence had traditionally signified one of the rungs on the ladder of life, specifically the life of a young aristocrat, and had acquired over the centuries various associations with the courage of young knights and the perils posed by court life or the grand tour to the virtue of young gentlemen. [99] In addition to its aristocratic connotations, adolescence had long fascinated philosophers who sought to catalogue the "ages" of man, to classify the life cycle by whole or magic numbers. [100] In the 17th century, Pierre de La Primaudaye had debated for line after line the relative merits of 7 and 6 as digits to divide the life cycle. [101]

Whatever might be said about the value of such speculations, American doctors were engaging in them as late as 1825. One especially earnest practitioner of the art stretched his classification from childhood (0–7) to "the age of insensibility, hope, and the last sigh" (99–105). [102] Folk wisdom as well as philosophical musing sanctioned division by 7. American physicians and educators often complained about the "vulgar opinion" of simple people that the body changed all of its parts every seven years. [103]

In its premodern form, adolescence was associated with aristocracy, knighthood, and numerology; in its modern form it has been associated with biology and the middle class. The timing of the change is debatable, but Rousseau's *Émile* marked one turning point, for Rousseau outstripped his predecessors in postulating drastic change at pu-

133

berty. "We are born, so to speak, twice over," Rousseau wrote, "born into existence and born into life; born a human being and born a man." [104] In a single paragraph Rousseau compared the tumultuous change wrought by puberty to a tidal wave and the adolescent to a lion in heat. In America from the 1830s onward a host of physicians, philosophers, and health popularizers followed both Rousseau and European medical texts of the late 18th and early 19th centuries in describing changes at puberty according to the canons of romantic sensibility. [105] "All his feelings shoot into rampant growth and vigor," Orson Fowler wrote of the boy at puberty. "Before half asleep, how much animation and the highest phase of human vigor he evinces! Desires before tame, now become almost resistless. A new set of motives and emotions burst upon him." His "heaving bosom" aches with surplus strength, as he desires to do and become something worthy of himself. [106] The effects on girls were no less dramatic, but totally different, producing a "maiden coyness, a modest bashfulness, a sweet smile, a sentimental reverie, a queenly grace of motion, because queenly inspiration gushes through every look, lisp, and act." [107] Perhaps Fowler rather than the maiden was really in the throes of a sentimental reverie, but the extravagance of his language did underscore his saltatory view of adolescence.

Not only did certain changes accompany puberty, but sexual maturation itself contributed to moral and psychological change. Most medical tracts took for granted a theory of the convertibility of energy: a rise in sexual capacity led to a rise in physical, moral, and spiritual energy. Conversely, anything that dissipated the reserve of sexual energy (for example, masturbation) depleted all other kinds of energy. The important "revolution" which overtakes boys and girls at puberty, Pliny Earle wrote, "sometimes seriously affects the mind, and produces absolute insanity." [108] Sexual maturation and rapid growth overburdened the system, so that the nervous fluid could not perform its functions. Earle actually took a more sophisticated view of the dangers of masturbation than most medical writers of his day, for he suggested that it was more often an effect than a cause of insanity. But in one form or another, the masturbatory insanity theme, which had originated in Europe in the 18th century, kept surfacing in antebellum medical tracts and in "confidential chats" with parents and children on the dangers of secret indulgence. [109]

Although the concept of adolescence took off from the principle that biological change determined other changes in youth, it allowed some scope to social determinants. The psychiatrist Isaac Ray cited intensification of educational pressures, parental indulgence, and errors in diet as causes of disease, insanity, and hysteria in adolescence.

From Nurture to Adolescence

Orson Fowler added premature labor in offices and factories. If you want to wear your children out at 30, Fowler advised, send them to work at 8 or 9, "but if you would have them live to be a hundred, give them the reins till they are twenty or upwards, and allow them to be boys and girls, instead of making them young ladies and gentlemen." [110] All the specific instances, however, went back to some sort of energy depletion. For Ray the danger was that too much cerebral energy would be used up in adolescence; for Pliny Earle it was too much nervous fluid; for Fowler it all became part of a universal law that it was much better for children to ripen late than early, "that the length of life of all animals can be calculated from the age at which they come to maturity." [111]

Thus, adolescence was not merely a dangerous time of life that needed careful watching, but a stage marked too often by overpressure and an acceleration of experiences. Andrew Combe and others who described adolescence during the second quarter of the 19th century strongly advocated delayed development during the teen years, while the word "precocity" increasingly acquired pathological connotations. Precocity was not just a word but a disease, and writers trembled at its "symptoms." Popularized originally in America in the 1830s to describe the pernicious effects of infant schools, the term came to embrace the syndrome of over-rapid development in adolescence.[112] "Emulation" in the form of hot competition for school prizes was thought of as a major cause of epidemics of precocity. The pale-faced seminarian, the sallow damsel, and the infant prodigy had all fallen victim to this peculiar scourge of the Victorian child.[113]

The framework within which Americans wrote about both adolescence and precocity reflected one side of Rousseau's thought to the neglect of another. Although there is little evidence of direct influence, Americans followed Rousseau the romantic rather than Rousseau the psychologist. At points in Émile, Rousseau had penetrated to the ambivalence of adolescent experience by suggesting that the moodiness of a youth was the result of antagonism between the social affections flowering at puberty and the residue of self-love from childhood, so that any frustration of basic wishes was now perceived as an attack on the self. Generosity one moment might turn to hatred the next, because the youth was just starting to work out the implications of his social nature.[114] But at other points, Rousseau fell back on a romantic, naturalist orientation that led him to conclusions at odds with his own analysis. Adolescence need not be a difficult period at all, he argued, if only we do nothing to stimulate the development of the child. A slow and steady regimen in childhood, one that avoided stimulating both sexual curiosity and secular knowledge, would guarantee a noiseless transition from childhood to youth. Rightly cultured, adolescence could become a time of generosity and mercy. Spared exposure to the world during childhood, the youth would be just and wise; spared an immediate gratification of his wants, he would learn resignation.[115]

Rousseau's willingness to propose a prolongation of innocence as a final solution to the problems of maturation marked the path that American moralists were to follow between 1840 and 1880. Perhaps because of their antecedent addiction to the English school of "natural education," Americans relished citing "laws" which proved that children should never be indulged in self-will or pleasure. Social fashion, above all, was the antithesis of natural law. Parents who pushed their girls ahead in school or who packed them off to boarding schools only hastened their decay, warned Elizabeth Blackwell in 1852. Striving to please their parents and teachers, adopting artificial airs and ways, the girls "sinned" against nature in exact proportion to their obedience to fashion. But mistakes usually began even earlier, with the fatal cup of coffee for breakfast, rich foods and sumptuous dinners, or pickles and candy in the lunch box.[116] J. Stainback Wilson turned the conflict between nature and fashion into one between country and city. On one side were simple manners and plain living, on the other stimulating food, balls and theaters, children's parties, lascivious books, "and the whole hot-bed system of city life." The former "tend to retard the appearance of the courses [menstruation]," the latter to stimulate sexual organs into premature activity, "which is followed by premature old age." [117]

The jarring mixture of moralism and naturalism which underlay the medical advice of Wilson and Blackwell bore obvious resemblance to the views of Orson Fowler. Fowler described the laws of health as "self-acting" in the sense that every transgression carried its own penalty.[118] Elizabeth Blackwell argued along similar lines that behind all the laws of nature lay one which dictated that physical and mental growth be synchronized. Every epoch of development had its appropriate task. In youth priority had to go to bodily growth and the storing up of energy. Mistakes in the regimen of youth would be punished in maturity, just as those of childhood met their judgment day in youth.[119]

This sort of naturalism might be called romantic if only because it held country life and village manners in high esteem, but more properly it was a religious form of naturalism, a religion of nature in which sin, repentance, punishment, and salvation had physiological rather than theological connotations. So far from being locked into an antagonistic relationship, medical naturalism and religious pietism were similar in that each juxtaposed nature and fashion. A moral tale bearing the bizarre title "Death at the Toilet" illustrated this synthesis of medicine and piety. Purportedly based on the journal of a physician, it related the gruesome story of a certain "Charlotte _____," a vain, vapid, and selfish young lady of 20 who ignored both the pious entreaties of her widowed mother and the sound advice of her doctor in order to attend a succession of fashionable balls, only to drop dead of heart failure one evening while readying herself for still another social round. The good doctor wove post mortem and funeral sermon into a single ghoulish paragraph:

> On examining the countenance more narrowly, I thought I detected the traces of a smirk of conceit and self-complacency, which not even the palsying touch of death could wholly obliterate. The hair of the corpse, all smooth and glossy, was curled with elaborate precision; and the skinny, sallow neck was encircled with a string of glittering pearls. The ghastly visage of death thus leering at the tinselry of fashion—the vain show of artificial joy—was indeed a horrible mockery of the fooleries of life.[120]

Concepts of adolescence as a distinct, critical, and incapacitating stage of life thus went hand in hand with a number of other attitudes—fear of fashion, a preference for nature's way, a strong feeling for the preservation of innocence, and a proclivity to borrow theological concepts and to recast them in physiological terms.

It is one thing to note this syndrome of attitudes and ideas, another to locate it on the spectrum of society. But the language of contemporaries provides some clues to the relationship between this syndrome and both class and sex roles. With respect to class, a preference for a "natural" regimen in child rearing flourished primarily within the mid-Victorian middle class of small shopkeepers, independent artisans, and self-employed professionals. Such families were likely to contain the preconditions for receptivity to the natural regimen: relatively small numbers of children; adequate leisure time for mothers to devote to a conscious program of child rearing; an intense conviction of the need for self-restraint in expenditure, which undergirded the naturalist's proscription of luxurious foods and children's parties; and a pervasive moralism which represented the aftereffects of the Second Awakening.[121]

With respect to sex roles, it is worth noting that those who warned about precocity were thinking mainly of girls rather than boys. Observers usually agreed, for example, that school rivalry produced much worse effects on girls than on boys. Furthermore, for most of the 19th century, teenage girls were a more interesting literary and psychological topic than their brothers. Adolescent girls were stock figures in novels from *Charlotte Temple* in the 1790s to Fenimore Cooper's *Tales for Fifteen* in the 1820s to Oliver Wendell Holmes, Sr.'s, *Elsie Venner* on the eve of the Civil War.[122] In a sense, girls were the first adolescents; only

137

much later in the 19th century were the normative implications of adolescence applied primarily to boys.

Although medical advisers who warned against precocity focused on overpressure in schools, changes within families lay behind much of the rising interest in adolescence. The ideal of the family as a total environment united by ties of warmth and intimacy applied in theory to children of either sex, but alterations in the position of girls in urban middle-class families gave the ideal a special pertinence to young ladies. In rural families female children were valuable as baby-sitters, nurses, and cooks; by the 1820s they were also valuable as wage earners in factory towns like Lowell. In mid-century middle-class families, in contrast, the value of girls was less evident. Declining birthrates and the availability of cheap Irish servants cut into some of the traditional functions of teenage girls, while the influx of immigrants into factory jobs after 1840 removed the seal of respectability from labor in mill towns. Conduct-of-life tracts aimed at young ladies of quality between 1840 and 1860 contained none of the exhortations to decision of character that marked comparable tracts intended for young men. Rather, the former urged the resolute practice of self-culture on girls simply as a way to fill up time.[123]

The increasing if still limited popularity of public high schools provided the urban middle class with the perfect institutional outlet for its teenage female children, since high schools provided tuition-free education in language and science at places near home. For girls the opportunity costs of advanced education were negligible; hence, they persisted longer in school than did their brothers. But the education of girls beyond puberty was more than just a necessity created by their superfluous position in households. The same revolution which upgraded motherhood virtually to the level of a profession also sanctioned the appropriation by women of control over cultural life. During the middle decades of the 19th century, the world of novels and poetry became as much a part of the sphere of women as the tasks of child rearing and school teaching. As a corollary, girls were not merely to be educated but educated thoroughly, to the point where fluttering eyelids would no longer conceal a vacant mind. Foreign travelers in America often commented that American girls were better educated than American men and far more sprightly in conversation, just as they observed that American fathers made sacrifices for their daughters that they would not think of making for their sons.[124] Possession of an educated daughter became a sort of prestige symbol, a crude form of conspicuous consumption.

Their predominance in public high schools explains why girls were the focus of medical advice, but not its content. Hostility to precocity and a proclivity to dwell on the radical changes wrought by puberty developed mainly on the romantic and unorthodox fringe of American medicine rather than at its orthodox core. Most of the individuals who portrayed puberty as incapacitating were unusual if not eccentric. Combe and Fowler were popularizers of phrenology; Isaac Ray and Pliny Earle were psychiatrists or "alienists." The periphery, whether represented by homeopathy, phrenology, mesmerism, or health fads was much more avant-garde then the core, more receptive to a naturalist orientation and to a saltatory theory of adolescence. [125]

The fact that critics of precocity so often praised nature's way—no city living, no hothouse education, no chocolates, no rich food, no luxury of any kind—might justify classifying them as rural bigots set against modernizing trends in their society. The trouble is that they were usually just the opposite, well educated and in the forefront of change. Alienists like Isaac Ray and Pliny Earle were better educated than most physicians of their day. Orson Fowler can be characterized as a popularizer of phrenology or as a popularizer of new ideas about health. Either way, he was an entrepreneur. The heated presses of his publishing house in New York City sent off tracts of every sort in every direction. Elizabeth Blackwell, who sounded such ominous warnings against city life, fashion, and a stimulating diet, was the first American woman to graduate from an orthodox medical school. She belongs on most lists of notable American women of the 19th century, although she probably would not have made any list had she taken her own advice literally.

Inasmuch as medical and educational advisers on precocity and adolescence were not rural reactionaries, how can we account for the conservative character of the advice they offered? Their views might be an accurate reflection of the acceleration of life experiences of average children and young people in the 19th century. In view of the presence of child prodigies like Phoebe Bartlett and precocious leaders like Jefferson and Hamilton no one could assert that precocity was a new phenomenon of the 19th century; but Victorian critics were concerned with ordinary children who were increasingly being exposed to precocious experiences, not with prodigies. The indictment of precocity by these critics, however, depended not only on the reality of precocious experience (the evidence for which need not be recapitulated) but also on the assertion that precocity led to insanity. Was this true? It is possible that increased regulation of the child's total environment might have produced psychologically more dependent and less mature young people, vulnerable if not insane. One could argue, for example, that such young people, denied conventional outlets for their desire for autonomy, took refuge in the fantasy world of 19th-century adventure literature, in the stories filled with sentiment, seduction, violence, pirates, Indians, desperadoes, and young stalwarts who brazenly cut loose from family ties and made their own way. These were the staple topics of the New York *Ledger* and similar weeklies during the 1850s, 1860s, and 1870s. The *Ledger* had an astonishing circulation of 400,000 in 1860, and a contemporary affirmed that "nine-tenths of the readers of all papers of this class are boys and girls between the ages of ten and twenty." [126]

Yet a taste for sensational literature was not itself a sign of debility, certainly not the sort of debility against which medical and educational writers warned. Previous generations of young people might have devoured the same sort of literature, had it been available. Moreover, the circulation totals of the *Ledger* and similar publications were far too great to have been the result of changing socialization patterns which even in 1860 were more an ideal than a reality. Foreign travelers at this time continued to be struck by the maturity and adult orientation of American young people rather than by their vulnerability and immaturity. [127]

All of this prompts a turn to the possibility that when an influential group of mid-Victorian writers linked adolescence, precocity, debility, and insanity, they were speaking symbolically rather than descriptively. While they could point at times to unnerving academic pressures on youth, such pressure was in their eyes no more than a specific example of their general perception that American life was frenetic and itself marked by overpressure. Social critics of the Jacksonian era and after saw an excess of haste and commotion in their society, too many centrifugal forces and not enough cohesion. [128]

From this broad symbolic framework, individual writers could draw various specific applications. Elizabeth Blackwell could warn against the dangers of fashionable education which emphasized superficial accomplishment; Orson Fowler could campaign against parents who encouraged their sons to enter lowly clerkships on grounds that any white-collar position was preferable to manual labor. In each case, adolescence was becoming a sort of symbolic battleground. That is, a disposition was developing to measure the effects of various educational and social attitudes by their invigorating or debilitating impact on youth.

The 19th-century debate over female equality provides an especially revealing illustration of the way in which apprehensions about particular doctrines were expressed in symbolic formulations related to adolescence. Through sentimental novels the American public had absorbed an image of the adolescent girl as sensitive, "tremulous," "susceptible to every gentle emotion of the soul," and "delicately alive to friendship." At the same time, a cohort of moralists sought to connect the sentimental portrait to the complexity of sexual maturation in girls, which not only accounted for females' distinctive psychological characteristics but also sentenced them to a separate sphere.[129] Boys might have problems during adolescence, but only if they abused their sexual faculties by masturbation. For girls, in contrast, it was the normal functioning of the system, the "revolutions" which accompanied puberty, that created difficulties.

Present in medical and educational literature before 1860, all these assumptions became much more explicit in the postbellum period. E. H. Clarke's *Sex in Education; or, A Fair Chance for the Girls,* a polemic against coeducation published in 1873, provides an excellent illustration of some of the Victorian prejudices concerning female adolescence.[130] Between the onset of puberty and the end of female adolescence at 18 or 20, Clarke argued, menstruation demanded that young girls be allowed prolonged periods of rest, more prolonged and regular than any system of coeducation could sustain. In a variation on the hydraulic theory of energy used earlier by writers on masturbatory insanity, Clarke insisted that the loss of energy during adolescence was so severe as to preclude serious study. Coeducational colleges ran the risk of turning out learned young ladies whose "generative" processes were in a sorry state of disrepair, young ladies like a certain "Miss D____," who went to college in good health but who could not cope with the demands of textbooks and of that equally stern taskmaster, nature, that she "build and put in working order a large and complicated mechanism." Miss D____'s decline was both predictable and lurid; first pain, then torture, misery, paralysis, and hysteria.[131]

Clarke's book was interesting, but not nearly so interesting as the replies which rolled off the presses with such alarming speed as to suggest that Clarke had touched a raw nerve rather than merely advanced a new hypothesis.[132] Clarke's disingenuous tone rightly infuriated his antagonists, for under the guise of giving girls a fair chance he sought to deny them equal opportunities for education. A few opponents protested the bluntness of his language, his preference for saying "undeveloped ovaries" rather than "withered flowers." But on balance, the replies were distinguished less by disagreement with his method of attack than by acceptance of many of his leading assumptions, specifically that adolescence was a troubled time of life, especially for girls, because of academic pressures and the demands of physical growth. Their differences from Clarke concerned emphasis rather than basic outlook. Some thought that biological change was less important than the "custom of public exhibitions, and the unnatural excitement which is oftentimes kept up to stimulate the susceptible thought-machine of the child and youth into abnormal activity."[133] Mary E. Beedy defended coeducation for providing a mental occupation for girls and thus correcting their all too strong tendencies toward hysteria.[134] Caroline M. Dall hoped that copies of Clarke's book would not fall into the hands of girls, for it might only incline them to hysteria.[135] Others thought that provision of proper rest periods for girls within a coeducational setting would be sufficient concession to nature. To the extent that Clarke's respondents departed from his views about adolescence, finally, it was to insist that a "correct" (meaning natural) regimen in childhood would solve whatever problems adolescence might pose. If only girls did not have their paper doll parties at 8 or 9 years of age, if only education of the will commenced early, older girls would not go the way of Miss D____.[136]

Clarke was not the first doctor to use case histories of doubtful authenticity to censor female ambition. The lamentable Miss D____ was a cousin of Charlotte ____ mentioned earlier. But there were some differences. Charlotte's funeral sermon was delivered by her doctor, but her ultimate executioner was a woman, Martha Clark, from whose *Victims of Amusement* the story was extracted. E. H. Clarke, on the other hand, was a manly sort of man, the type who liked womanly women who did not have to be told where their sphere was. Further, in the case of Charlotte, her vanity rather than her ambition brought about her undoing. By 1873, however, with coeducation an established fact in many state universities and threatening to spread to the East, the specific ambitions of Miss D____ to rise in the world were seen as part of an emerging pattern. Appropriately, E. H. Clarke put the concept of adolescence to more specific and practical use than his predecessors. Indeed, his insistence on being specific accounted for the storm that blew up around *Sex in Education.*

Clarke gave the concept of adolescence some practical applications, but there were limits. Coeducation, after all, survived and flourished. English visitors like Sara A. Burstall might have found some of the justifications for coeducation a little strange (it would make the boys behave better), but they could not deny the wide acceptance of coeducation in high schools and colleges by the 1890s. Nor could they ignore the lame quality of arguments against it, like that of the president of Vassar who insisted that American youth of either sex needed the sort of tranquil repose offered by single-sex institutions. Clarke may have won a battle, but he lost the war.[137]

More generally, the concept of adolescence was often devoid of practical effect even when it had practical applications. In the 20th century, concepts of adolescence have justified the institutional segregation of youth, but in the middle decades of the 19th century the implications of the idea of adolescence were, if anything, anti-institutional.

Those who complained about the hurry and worry of school life could do little more than call for the construction of gymnasia and for more attention to health. The remarkable amount of attention given in schools to student health struck Sara A. Burstall as a no less distinctive feature of American secondary schools than the practice of coeducation.[138]

Conclusion

At the time E. H. Clarke was writing, social and economic changes were in motion which would make "adolescence" a household word in middle-class families by the early 1900s. But in the middle decades of the 19th century the word was still unfamiliar. As late as 1854, Roget's *Thesaurus* equated adolescence with "being out of one's teens," with manhood, virility, and maturity—with everything, that is, but childhood and senility.[139] A number of advanced physicians and a few educators in the more highly urbanized states used the concept, but with nothing like the scope and scale it later acquired.

These obvious limitations, however, only serve to make the period between 1840 and 1880 a more enticing field of study, for the origins of an idea can be at least as instructive as the later stages of its development. From this perspective, several implications are worth drawing out. The concept of adolescence, from the beginnings of its modern form, was usually intertwined with a romantic view of childhood, with articulate fears of modern life, cities, overpressure, and overcivilization. In the form it assumed in mid-century, the concept of adolescence was the creation of a distinctive mind set, an expression of a mélange of nostalgia and anxiety, and in its crudest mold an embodiment of Victorian prejudices about females and sexuality.

CHAPTER 6

Dead-End Jobs
and Careers

IN the 20th century a combination of technological advance and prolonged education has contributed to a stretching out of the period of dependency. Young people must now serve their time as dependents just as they did in agricultural communities in the 17th and 18th centuries, where, for different reasons, the period of dependency was also lengthy. Between these extremes lies much of the 19th century and a slice of the 20th, roughly the period from 1820 to 1920, when the development first of commercial and later of industrial opportunities made it possible for young people to achieve adult economic status at relatively early ages. Paradoxically, it was during the final decades of this intermediate period, from 1890 to 1920, that the institutions which have effectively delayed the achievement of adult status by youth since 1920 were first developed. The impulses which created these institutions of adolescence grew out of an industrializing society in which young people were still deeply involved in the economy. To understand how the impulses arose, it is necessary to study the changing position of young people of different social classes during industrialization.

Yet industrialization itself was not a sudden process, nor were its effects monolithic. Most crafts passed through several distinct phases of industrial development, with each phase having its own special effect

144

on the economic position of youth. Moreover, industrialization in America was not superimposed on a simple and austere agricultural economy but on a complex and speculative one. Between 1810 and 1850, for example, the proportion of the labor force in farming dropped from around 80 percent to around 55 percent; most of the refugees from agriculture in this period did not enter manufacturing establishments but went into trade, construction, and service.[1] To understand the effects of industrialization on young persons and on the decisions which were to alter their economic and social position, therefore, we must distinguish the impact of increased reliance on machinery from the long-standing changes wrought by the decline of agriculture.

All of this makes it difficult to describe the effects of industrial change. Was the demand for juvenile labor increasing, waning, or increasing in some fields and waning in others? A beginning can be made by looking at one issue on which a consensus existed in the 1880s. Apprenticeship, everyone agreed, was in decline.

Apprenticeship and Boy Labor

"Machinery has advanced, apprenticeship has declined," a carpentry union official claimed in 1886. "I have made inquiries, and fail to hear of a single instance of an indentured apprentice," he added. "The law is a dead letter in our trade. There is scarcely the appearance of an apprenticeship." [2] State labor reports in the 1880s echoed the refrain. Apprenticeship had lost its educative functions because of the introduction of machines. Whatever its length, the period once devoted to apprenticeship was now taken up with little more than machine tending. Apprentices had become, in effect, child laborers. "The number of trades in which that class called helpers are employed is increasing every year," Charles Peck wrote in a New York labor report, "and the extent to which they tend to increase the supply of mechanics has become a serious question to many trade unions." Peck gave as an example the experience of the molders, where "great complaint" was made about the practice of skilled mechanics taking on assistants only to find one day that slack times had prompted employers to lay off journeymen and to keep on the helpers. With poetic justice, the process would culminate a few years later with the helpers, now approaching manhood, forced out by a new crop of green hands. Industrialization thus created a vicious circle, with each new generation imperiling the position of its predecessor.[3]

Confusion over terminology marked many discussions of apprenticeship in the 1880s and 1890s. Worried that cheap boy laborers would displace adults from jobs, unions often sought to regulate the number of apprentices in a particular trade, while management claimed that few apprentices were actually employed. In a sense both sides were right, for industrial conditions did accelerate the demand for boy labor in some industries, but management often omitted the designation "apprentice" in describing these juvenile laborers. A number of studies at the end of the 19th century pointed out that in many trades the number of apprentices was actually below that allowed by the union, but that, paradoxically, the problem created by the preference for juvenile labor was growing apace.[4]

The acceleration of demand for cheap boy laborers was particularly intense during the early stages of industrialization, those marked by the concentration of workers into factories and the subdivision of tasks. During these initial phases, industries had a consuming appetite for teenage laborers. Data compiled by Carroll Wright in Massachusetts in the 1870s indicate that the same pattern often prevailed even after the introduction of high-speed machinery in the more advanced stages of industrialization. In the highly mechanized textile mills of Adams and Lawrence, young men between 16 and 20 made up 45.7 percent and 62.3 percent of the male work force 16 and over. In the boot and shoe industry, 41 percent of all Massachusetts-born females at work were between 16 and 20. Other industries contained lower but still significant proportions of teenagers. Young men aged 16 to 20 comprised 24.1 percent of the workers over 16 in nail factories, 23.1 percent in metallic goods factories, 38 percent in rattan factories, 37.5 percent in rubber factories, and 29.5 percent in agricultural tool factories.[5]

The Massachusetts data on age groupings by trade used the categories "15 and under" and "16 to 20." For our purposes the categories "16 and 17" and "18 and over" would have been more useful, for a young man usually demanded adult wages at 18. What happened to young men who started in factories at 12 or 14 upon reaching 18? One possibility was to stay on at near apprentice wages. "In many cases," a New York labor report noted, "the so-called 'apprentice' or 'helper' . . . is actually a young man who, by age, though not by expertness, should be a qualified journeyman."[6]

It was, of course, possible to move into some other line of work, but such moves yielded few gains in income or status. The switch from factory to craft encountered sharp and usually successful opposition from unions eager to exclude cheap juvenile labor. The Massachusetts data indicate that skilled crafts virtually excluded teenagers in the 1870s. In carpentry, cabinet making, brick making, blacksmithing, and masonry, for example, young people aged 16 to 20 comprised less than 20 percent of the work force 16 and over. In cities, where unions were strongest, the proportion of youth was below the already modest state averages. In Worcester, for example, it stood at 6.1 percent in carpentry, against a state average of 7.2 percent in that trade.[7] So zealous were craft unions in guarding their adult members from juvenile competition that the employment of apprentices rarely became a cause of strikes. In factories, unions were often either nonexistent or too weak to do anything about cheap juvenile labor; in the crafts they were usually strong enough to prevent the issue from arising. The infrequent strikes occasioned by issues related to apprenticeship were nearly always in skilled or semiskilled crafts where journeymen who worked on contract for employers put up staunch resistance whenever the latter sought to force on them a high ratio of apprentices.[8] This left one final alternative, the pursuit of casual labor. Between 1865 and 1900 the ranks of unemployed veterans who flooded into New York, Philadelphia, Chicago, and other great cities after Appomattox were swelled by hordes of young tramp laborers who drifted from place to place and job to job.[9]

The introduction of high-speed machinery did not always accelerate the demand for cheap labor. Sometimes it had the opposite effect, with the availability of cheap adult labor and the complexity of the machinery itself the determining factors. In Newark, for example, the proportion of boys aged 15 to 20 in crafts declined sharply with the introduction of machinery in the 1850s. Industrialization led employers to seek cheap labor, but adult immigrants rather than teenagers were the preferred source, for the boys were too unsteady in their habits and too prone to switch jobs, get into fights, and grant themselves holidays.[10] The case of printing provides an illustration of the role played by complexity of machinery: the rapid spread of linotype machines in the 1890s led to the displacement of unskilled and often young hand compositors, mainly because the output of the machines depended on the skill of the operators. In the manufacture of bottles, apprentice glassblowers managed to survive the first phase of industrialization, which saw the introduction of semiautomatic machinery, but not the second, marked by the use of totally automated machines after 1900.[11]

Thus, some phases of industrialization intensified the demand for young laborers, while other phases did not. Because of the chronological overlap of phases, observers saw conflicting pieces of evidence, but rarely the whole picture. They complained about idle and dissipated youth in one breath and about exploited youth in the next. The only point of agreement was that apprenticeship was in decline.

Most observers in the 1880s thought that apprenticeship was afflicted with a terminal disease. The same observers indulged in a romantic portrayal of "the plodding, sober apprentice of a generation or two ago," an earlier age when youthful apprentices had developed their skills under the attentive supervision of master mechanics.[12] Perhaps every generation thinks that its predecessors lived in a more stable time; certainly every generation of the 19th century thought that the Golden Age of youthful subordination had just ended.[13] In reality, however, complaints about the loose and unsystematic character of apprenticeship went back to the 17th century. The whole of the 19th century—and not merely its last two decades—heard a litany of complaints about aspects of apprenticeship and about journeymen who took on excessive numbers of apprentices without thought to their own employment prospects.[14] As a variation on the theme, the New York *Working Man's Advocate* complained in 1844 that strikes which led to higher wages had a negative effect, for "by alluring other young men from the ploughtail," they merely resulted in flooding the market.[15] Shortages of adult labor during the Civil War caused journeymen to strike against an overreliance on boy labor by employers.[16] Further, even assuming that apprenticeship in the 1830s had a more instructive nature than in the 1880s, the statement would apply only to youths who could enter the better craft apprenticeships, and such entry in the 1830s was often conditioned by family connections. The great majority of American young people in 1830 were stuck in some form of servitude, especially farm servitude, during their early and middle teens; in such servitude, apprenticeship had no more meaning than in a factory of the 1880s.

Although apprenticeship had never provided the sort of universal and smooth transition to adult occupational status that observers in the 1880s depicted, for various reasons the clearest perception of both the dangers and inadequacies of apprenticeship occurred only after the Civil War. The changes, in other words, pertained as much to the eye of the beholder as to the object of vision. Prior to large-scale industrialization, the extensive use of apprentices, often called "berkshires" or "two-thirders," developed principally in occupations like iron molding, where journeymen worked on a piece rate basis; the journeymen hired apprentices directly, without consulting either the furnace proprietors or the employers, who provided patterns and purchased the finished product. Berkshires were potential threats to the status of journeymen, but since the latter did the actual hiring, they had little reason to view berkshires as clear and present dangers. Rather, journeymen routinely raided their rivals for berkshires who knew enough about the craft to be useful but not so much as to be intimidating.[17]

Only the relatively advanced stages of industrialization, marked by the introduction of high-speed machinery, turned a long-standing potential threat into an immediate and real one. In the shoe industry, for example, half-trained apprentices had flooded the trade during periods of rapid expansion after the War of 1812, but they made only inferior products that sold cheaply, and they were the first to be laid off in dull times. The introduction of steam power in the boot and shoe industry during the 1860s, which followed completion of an earlier stage of development marked by the concentration of workers into factories, sent many of the journeymen scurrying to the Order of St. Crispin, a trade union that sought to regulate the use of "green hands" in the industry. As Blanche Hazard noted, in 1867 "the green hand, the untrained shoemaker, might be a mere machine operator and beside turning out good work, could usurp the journeyman's place or else reduce his wages. Manufacturers, with hosts of unskilled laborers to call upon, need not compete with each other and send up wages." [18]

The gradual concentration of workers into factories purchased added efficiency at the price of altering the relationship between apprentices and journeymen, for the latter were now strictly employees, devoid of even the appearance of freedom, while the former, still subordinate in theory, were no longer necessarily under the control of journeymen. [19] Ironically, if intimacy between journeymen and apprentices was breaking down, in one respect their social positions were converging, for increasingly each was a wage earner rather than a jobber. Independent jobbing, particularly in the fabricating trades, was one of the last casualties of the Industrial Revolution in America. Down to the Civil War, for example, cigar makers remained largely independent of employers who purchased and marketed their output, with dissatisfied journeymen merely setting up in business on their own. [20] In metal fabricating, jobbing long survived the concentration of workers into factories. As early as 1798, Nathan Starr, who had received a government contract to make swords, entered into subcontracts with independent journeymen who worked inside his plant at Middletown, Connecticut, to supply him with scabbards and the like. In the early 19th century this "inside contracting system," with its unique combination of later factory and earlier jobbing stages, spread among the more important machine tool builders and metal fabricators in the Northeast. [21] But by the 1880s the logic of specialization and efficiency, the desire of capitalists to exert control over every phase of production, was undermining jobbing at every turn. [22]

Thus, while the constituents of the crisis were present earlier, it was only in the 1880s that all of the various strands came together in the large, impersonal factory where apprentices and journeymen were alike consigned to the ranks of an industrial proletariat, and where teenage helpers posed a constant threat to the wage-earning abilities of young adult journeymen. For an industrial proletariat of this sort, the traditional fetish of self-culture had little relevance, for self-culture had been implicitly tied to at least something like self-employment. Whereas the promoters of mechanics' institutes in the 1830s had assumed that the improved artisan could command both the respect and patronage of the commercial world and that the workbench was a route into the class of independent producers, the growing scale of industry relegated this kind of ambition to the realm of shattered dreams. Increasingly, the higher-ups in American industry rose not from the workbench but through successive layers of management. In 1876, Francis A. Walker ridiculed the idea that each rising generation produced a "disposable fund" of workers who, "eagerly watching the prospect of industry in its several branches," silently and swiftly moved into openings. Freedom to move, Walker argued, was mere illusion. The artisan was, for example, free to move only to other artisan jobs. "The man who is brought up to be an ordinary carpenter, mason, or smith, may go to any of these callings or to a hundred more, according as his taste prompts or the prospect of remuneration attracts him." But in practice he has no power to compete "in those higher departments of skilled labor for which a more elaborate education and larger training are necessary, for example, mechanical engineering." The reality, Walker concluded, was that the entire population did not compete for all occupations. Instead, there was a series of "industrial layers superimposed on one another," with the members of the several strata effectively isolated from each other.[23]

Like most of his contemporaries, Walker exaggerated the degree of mobility possible earlier in the century. But industrialization did make the existence of self-contained layers more conspicuous than ever before, just as industrialization and the growth of cities made unemployment more conspicuous.

A consensus was growing among observers of the economic scene at the end of the 19th century that ambitious youth should not enter occupations in their early teens. Observers complained that youth were being forced into "dead-end" jobs, and that a prolongation of education, even if only for two years, would make all the difference. In 1906 a Massachusetts commission concluded that children who entered the job market after leaving school at 16 did notably better in the long run than their peers who hastily answered any one of hundreds of newspaper advertisements for "a lad around 14."[24]

Was this assertion valid? The commission, unfortunately, made no effort to determine whether it was the two extra years of education in themselves or the family resources that made possible those two extra years which accounted for the difference. Moreover, the commission spoke too glibly about the availability of occupations in which earnings rose with advancing age. The assumption that one's wages should rise with age is widespread today, so much so that a recent addition to the long line of federally subsidized vocational programs was christened "career education" in order to convey the impression of open-ended wage possibilities. At the other extreme, most people in preindustrial American society did not have careers; a man was likely to be making as much at 40 or 50 as he had been at 18 or 20. The same was often true even after the Industrial Revolution. A study which correlated wages with age in a Philadelphia factory between 1890 and 1930 indicated that earnings peaked at around age 25 but declined thereafter.[25] But industrialization did increase the number of nonmanual jobs in the service sector; between 1870 and 1910, jobs of this kind increased more rapidly than goods-producing jobs. The number of people employed in professions, for example, rose from 230,000 to 1,150,000, and those in trade, finance, and real estate from 830,000 to 2,760,000; jobs in manufacturing establishments grew by a lesser proportion, from 2,250,000 to 6,300,000.[26] There was more need than ever before for clerks, bookkeepers, accountants, engineers, lawyers, and business managers. Not all of these jobs offered the prospect of significantly rising earnings with advancing age, but they were usually better paying than factory jobs.[27]

The growing number of open-ended jobs held by adults served only to underscore the grim condition of youth pushed into dead-end jobs. Critics who assumed that the position of youth in the economy was deteriorating at the end of the 19th century misread some of the indicators, for young people had long performed dull service jobs, especially in agricultural communities. But the gap between those jobs and the newer opportunities now broadened, leaving the teenage boy in a dead-end job more conspicuous than at a time when the sort of work he performed differed little from that of his elders.

To view the same point from a different perspective, the closing decades of the 19th century saw the emergence of a sharp difference between the opportunities available to middle-class and working-class youth. The difference was detectable by the 1870s; it would become much more pronounced as America moved toward the status of a mature industrial society. The most attractive new jobs were opening up in the white-collar sector of the economy; the least attractive new positions were in factories. The prerequisite for access to white-collar jobs was possession of formal education to age 14 and preferably to 16 or 18. Parents sufficiently wealthy to forgo the labor of their children during early and middle adolescence guided their offspring through a more prolonged period of schooling and thus qualified them for desirable jobs. Poor parents, on the other hand, had to rely on the labor of their children for support, and could not afford the opportunity costs of even slightly prolonged education.

In late 19th-century America, class differences often involved differences in nationality as well. Americans of native stock were more able to afford the opportunity costs of prolonged education than were immigrants or their children. Labor reports of the period often complained about the flooding of some trades by immigrant children. There was some bitterness that native Americans could no longer gain their livelihood by honest manual labor, but expressions of bitterness were usually tempered by the realization that the latter had more alluring opportunities elsewhere.[28]

To take note of these differences in opportunities at the end of the 19th century is not to romanticize the early part of the century as a time of equal opportunity for all. Social class had *always* conditioned the nature of available opportunities. In 1820 or 1830, superior family resources had aided advantaged youth in manifold ways, by providing, for example, the sort of personal contacts in distant cities which young men like the Sons of New Hampshire could turn to advantage, or by equipping young men with enough capital to make a start toward the status of independent enterpriser. But prior to the late 19th century, class differences had not been reflected primarily in the early and middle teens. Youth of different classes had worked side by side on farms and in small machine shops, even though their ultimate destinations differed. After 1880, in contrast, middle-class parents had to adopt a different strategy, that of placing children in their early teens on the track of formal education.

The Prolongation of Education: A Labyrinthine Way

Only in the latter part of the 19th century did the sheer length of time passed in the setting of formal education become a major determinant of one's economic prospects. Earlier in the century an important distinction had existed between those who attended school at all and those who did not, but among the former, persistence in school bore little relation to family status or life prospects. The son of a merchant was likely to be finished with his formal education at 14 or 15, while the 18-year-old "large boy" was still in district school. Similarly, the son of a well-placed lawyer was likely to have finished college by 20, the age when a poor youth would only be arriving at the decision to attend college. Even at the end of the 19th century the correlation of prolonged schooling and enticing job opportunities was far from perfect, but a truncated education was likely to lead to a poor job. The more attractive crafts did not want anyone under 16. Advertisements for bookkeepers or accountants were usually addressed to those around 16 or 17, if not older. The colleges did not want anyone who had not attended secondary school, and employers were increasingly prone, as we shall see, to look to the colleges as sources of managerial recruits. Thus, while the son of an unskilled laborer who somehow managed to stay in school until 16 might not thereby have improved his job opportunities, the boy who dropped out at 12 or 14 was in serious trouble.[29]

Schools served the needs of business in a variety of ways. As the informal machine shop with a dozen journeymen and apprentices gave way to the modern business corporation, education provided a form of certification for young people. A diploma could act as a kind of letter of introduction. (In contrast, the old academies did not even have graduations.) What did a diploma certify? Certainly literacy, but also manners. Reformers in the 1840s had nothing against good manners, but they had been interested primarily in implanting in youth the seeds of moral self-regulation. For moral principles, school officials in the Gilded Age substituted deportment, immediate and visible behavior in the classroom. Manuals on school discipline in the 1870s and 1880s were extraordinarily detailed, reading almost like manuals of etiquette. To some extent, the near obsession with deportment reflected a desire to socialize and to Americanize immigrants and their children, but nothing in the school manuals of the Gilded Age restricted the concern with outward behavior to the children of immigrants. Rather, school officials were convinced that boorishness would work to the disadvantage of any child, native or foreign.[30]

Yet elementary and high schools were more than socializing agencies. By preparing young men for professional schools, formal public education in the late 19th century also served to quench the thirst of business for specialists and technicians, and, incidentally, to undermine the network of "old boy" affiliations that controlled access to some enticing lines of work. By stimulating demand for increased numbers of mechanical engineers, for example, industrialization placed unbearable pressures on the traditional method of training engineers through apprenticeships in small, closely knit machine shops. To an increasing extent, the high school and professional school rather than the shop became the popular access route to the mechanical engineering profession. Older shop-trained mechanics dismissed these formally educated engineers for their supposed mediocrity and "averagism" while clothing themselves in the purple of elitism and creativity. The shop remained the preferred access route for sons of prominent engineers, while the high schools and professional schools tended to attract young men from middle-class and lower-middle-class backgrounds.[31]

Mechanical engineering was distinctive because of its formidable tradition of shop culture. At the other extreme, in medicine the traditions of apprenticeship were relatively weak, those of formal education relatively strong. It was probably not an accident that medicine was the most accessible profession before the late 19th century, for the presence of scores of medical schools even before 1860 reduced the need for young men to find patrons to sponsor them in apprenticeships.

Between these extremes, various occupations and professions were turning to the model of formal education in the 1880s and 1890s. The number of professional schools established between 1876 and 1900 in law, medicine, pharmacy, dentistry, and veterinary science was more than double the number established from 1851 to 1875. Only in theology did the rate of establishment of new schools fall off after 1876. Taking the six professions together, 498 professional schools existed in 1898, as against 284 in 1875. A survey of American education published in 1900 listed "scientific, technical, and engineering schools" separately from "professional" schools, although engineering was taking on most of the characteristics of a profession by 1900. If we add the technical and engineering colleges onto the professional schools, the growth rate of professional education after 1876 becomes astounding, but still not so remarkable as the proportionate increase in the number of professional students between 1878 and 1899; 988 percent in dentistry, 142 percent in medicine, 249 percent in law, 87 percent in theology. Further, the most notable upsurge took place in the latter part of the period, between 1888 and 1899. The number of medical students rose from 11,000 in 1878 to 13,000 in 1888 to 24,000 in 1899; in law the comparable figures were 3,000 to 3,700 to around 12,000.[32]

The explosion of professional education provides a further clue to the growth of the high schools, for not only did the professions and high schools grow at roughly the same rate over the same time span, but the high school became the principal route to professional schools. The linkage between the two was established by entrance requirements which were becoming much more rigorous and precise than the traditional demand for a "good academical education." Of course, there were still gaps between theory and practice and between the practices of different states. As late as 1900, Pennsylvania and New Jersey required only a common school education as a prerequisite for medical school, while Virginia asked only for "evidence of a preliminary education." But in states like New York and Illinois, graduation from a four-year high school course was becoming the normal prerequisite.[33]

Admissions requirements established one point of contact between the high school and the professional school, but the similarity between the two types of institutions ran deeper. We have seen that by 1850 the contours of the high school fundamentally differentiated it from the old academies. Where the academies had been loosely structured institutions with abundant ties to the workplace, the high school followed the model of the reformed common school in providing a systematic, orderly, regular type of education. To a much greater extent than had been true of the academies, attendance at public high schools meant postponement of entry into work. One sign of the attraction which the concept of efficiency had for late 19th-century educators was that the issue between regular and irregular (or "accidental") education was played out anew in the development of professional education, with regularity once again the winner.

The earliest instance of a collision between two different ideals of professional education lay in a change which took place at the United States Naval Academy in the 1850s. Established in 1845, the Naval Academy had originally been a cram school for midshipmen preparing for examinations that would qualify them as ensigns. Most of the students in the 1840s had already spent years at sea. The academy did not exist to make men out of boys, although most of the students were teenagers. Rather, its purpose was technical and limited, the preparation of young men for an examination. Appropriately, the discipline of the 1840s was loose, with middies often not even bothering to wear uniforms and with an occasional duel between students a tolerated if not recommended practice. Conditions were rough, but no rougher than what middies had already encountered at sea, where traditionally they had boarded in steerage, eaten with common sailors, endured a variety of hazings, and developed a ritualistic code of insubordination.[34]

The transformation of the academy began in the 1850s under Superintendent George P. Upshur. Upshur believed in strict discipline, with an end to middies drifting down to breakfast at 9 o'clock in their dressing gowns. He also belonged to a new breed of naval officers oriented toward steam power and naval engineering, and accordingly desired a more regular curriculum sequence which left little room for the unsystematic practices of an earlier day. During the 1850s the academy lost its character as a cram school and it became instead a totally structured environment, in the fashion of contemporary boarding schools, for midshipmen whose ventures to sea would henceforth be confined mainly to practice cruises and whose education would be gained through a consecutive four-year course sequence.[35]

During the next half century, issues roughly analogous to those which had arisen at Annapolis during Upshur's tenure as superintendent developed in a variety of professional schools. In medical education, for example, the proliferation of medical schools began in the 1820s and 1830s, but for a long time formal medical education complemented rather than replaced on-the-job training. The usual custom was for a young man to attend a session at some medical school (or become an apprentice to a doctor), then practice for a period, and then attend another session to obtain the M.D. degree; in effect, this meant that a half-trained doctor "practiced" on patients before completing his education. If this sort of training jars the modern temper, it was accepted in its day as consistent with the preeminent position of shop training. By the 1890s, however, professional associations were pushing, in some cases successfully, for the principle of consecutive study, with formal education to be completed before entrance into practice. As Abraham Flexner was to show in 1910, the content of even a consecutive course of medical study left much to be desired, but the ideal of total preparation as a prelude to practice was gaining support in professional thought during the 1890s.[36]

Two distinct viewpoints likewise emerged among those who sought to replace the tradition of shop culture in mechanical engineering with formal education. One group of educators promoted the type of engineering school which sought to train scientifically competent engineers by emphasizing calculus and physics at the expense of the sort of adeptness in handling tools that could best be acquired in practice. For the other group, the ideal was an institution like the Worcester Free Institute, with its subordination of abstract education to the actual sale in local markets of products made by students in the school shop. Here again the future lay with the less utilitarian, more formal type of school typified by the engineering colleges springing up at land grant universities.[37]

Even a broad definition of a profession would probably not have included business in 1900, and yet commercial education developed on a track which ran roughly parallel to medicine and engineering. Commercial schools had their origin in the antebellum period, when the flood of young men from the country seeking city clerkships overwhelmed the merchants, who had traditionally trained their own clerks. To that extent, commercial schools served some of the same functions as high schools, except that the former were more likely to attract adults. During their first half century of development, commercial schools focused almost exclusively on teaching specific and fairly rudimentary skills like penmanship, simple bookkeeping, and business arithmetic.[38] By 1897, however, J. E. King of Rochester, New York, could claim that the business school had to cease being a clerk factory and educational repair shop and launch instead into "real business training." [39] Edmund J. James, the foremost spokesman for and historian of business education in the late 19th century, could point by 1900 to a "broadening view of what the business school may do." [40] As James noted, more than an upgraded curriculum was to mark the new business school. The quality of preparation of both teachers and students was becoming important. In the early days of business schools, the teachers were businessmen whose qualifications consisted almost entirely of job experience, but in the 1890s the trend was toward "pedagogical ability" and the hiring of college graduates as teachers. The aspirations of business schools to higher status at the end of the century led to an escalation of admission and attendance requirements. In New York the regents of the state university used "previous preparation" and "persistence of effort on the part of the students" as criteria for formal recognition. [41] James aptly summarized the process:

> This recognition [from the regents] is not only honorable in itself, but is important as indicating for this work the beneficent effects which have come to other kinds of educational effort through guidance and supervision by that distinguished corporation. The advantages that have accrued to elementary, secondary, and higher education, general and technical, public and private, in New York through state inspection . . . may now be obtained by commercial. [42]

James's remarks underscore the extent to which the pressures for change in the educational system were exerted from the top down, as well as from the bottom up. The regents not only registered business schools but also allowed them to give diplomas or certificates, with the distinction between the two species of parchment "the requirement of graduation from a registered high school, which attaches to the diploma but not to the certificate." [43] In a similar way, the high school became the indispensable access route to the more formal, prestigious, and less shop-oriented type of engineering school, but it was not necessary for more casually structured schools like the Worcester Free Institute. [44]

The burgeoning of certification requirements after 1880, which accompanied the proliferation of professional schools, had less to do with the growing complexity of occupations than with the attitudes and ideals of promoters of professional education. The raising of preprofessional and professional standards in the traditional professions had the effect of stimulating emulation by other, less well established groups. James and other spokesmen for business education repeatedly pointed to the presumably greener pastures of law and medicine as a justification for raising standards in business. From the opposite direction, pressures from public education forced business schools to imitate the bureaucratic organization of public schools or face loss of recognition. [45] The adoption of certification requirements thus became a way to close the gap between the rising educational bureaucracy and the older professions on one side, and the aspirations of newer occupational groups seeking professional status on the other.

The number of young men and women who rose to the higher steps of the educational ladder was still small in 1900. The revolution initiated with the doubling of the public high school population in the 1890s was still far from complete as late as 1930, when high school students embraced only about half of the 14- to 16-year-old population. The proportion of the population aged 18 to 21 in institutions of higher learning (graduate and undergraduate) rose sharply in the final decades of the 19th century and doubled between 1900 and 1920, but even in the latter year it was only 8.09 percent.[46] Yet by 1900 the consequences of the systematization of education, particularly education beyond elementary school, were becoming evident in the career lines of young men entering professions.

Fast Starts, Long Avenues

In order to gain insight into the effects of economic and educational changes on career patterns, I have examined three collections of biographies of late 19th-century lawyers. The first collection chronicles the lives of lawyers who practiced in Illinois, usually outside of Chicago, between 1870 and 1916; the second and third, lawyers who practiced in Chicago and New Jersey during approximately the same period.[47] The results (summarized in Tables 1–5) point to a number of interesting conclusions. First, despite the upgrading of professional standards in the late 19th century, lawyers were generally younger at entrance to legal practice than their counterparts in antebellum New Hampshire. An especially dramatic reduction occurred in the number of very late starts (28 or over). Second, lawyers born after 1870 and lawyers born in the larger population centers were younger at entry to practice than those born earlier or born in any period on farms. Obviously these factors were complementary; those born later in the century were less likely to be born on farms. Yet even farmboys were quickening their gait as the century wore on. Third, lawyers who practiced in Chicago were younger at entry to practice than those who practiced elsewhere in Illinois, regardless of the size of town of origin.

Why should the fact that an individual chose to practice in Chicago rather than somewhere else in Illinois have made a difference in his de-

TABLE 1
Age at Entry to Practice of Illinois Lawyers

AGE AT ENTRY	18–24	25–27	28 AND OVER
Total: N = 400	43.3%	33.7%	23.0%
Born pre-1860	39.5	30.1	30.4
Born after 1875	50.1	41.8	8.1
Born on farms, any period	32.0	37.0	31.0
Born on farms after 1870	44.2	34.9	20.9
Born in places of under 2,500 population *	43.2	42.4	14.4
Born in places of more than 5,000 population *	53.2	33.4	13.4
Born in places of more than 30,000 population *	59.7	27.9	12.4

* SOURCE: U.S. Census of 1870

TABLE 2
Comparison of Illinois and Chicago Lawyers Born in Midwestern Towns of 3,000 Population or Less * (N = 256)

AGE AT ENTRY	18–24	25–27	28 AND OVER
Practiced in Illinois outside of Chicago	45.0%	33.5%	21.5%
Practiced in Chicago	58.3	29.2	12.5

* SOURCE: U.S. Census of 1870

TABLE 3
Chicago Lawyers by Region of Origin

AGE AT ENTRY	18–24	25–27	28 AND OVER
Total (N = 275)	52.7%	34.2%	13.1%
New England	40.0	38.8	21.2
Middle Atlantic	51.2	24.8	24.0
Midwest	62.1	23.5	14.4
South (incl. Md. and Ky.)	90.5	9.5	—

TABLE 4
Chicago Lawyers Born Outside the South (N = 268)

AGE AT ENTRY	18–24	25–27	28 AND OVER
Born in towns of under 3,000 population *	47.2%	35.1%	17.7%
Born in towns of more than 10,000 population *	65.0	24.4	10.6

* SOURCE: U.S. Census of 1870

TABLE 5

New Jersey Lawyers

AGE AT ENTRY	18–24	25–27	28 AND OVER
Total (N = 240)	67.9%	21.8%	10.3%
Born pre-1860	56.0	25.1	18.9
Born 1871–1880	68.2	22.8	9.0
Born 1881–	86.1	11.1	2.8
Born in eight largest towns of the state, or in cities of more than 30,000 population outside of state *	79.7	14.9	5.4

* SOURCE: U.S. Census of 1870

velopment? That more opportunities for winning fame and fortune existed in Chicago can be taken for granted, but our focus here is not on the achievement of fame but on the first uncertain flapping of wings, regardless of outcome. Perhaps Chicago attracted more energetic types, those willing and eager to break out of familiar molds. Perhaps the abundance of opportunities for legal practice in a large city reduced the dependence of young men on patrons and sponsors. Whatever the cause, however, the various factors cited were interwoven rather than antagonistic. In the course of the 19th century more and more individuals were born in cities or drawn to cities to practice.

Personal considerations such as the untimely loss of a parent, a timely turn of luck, idiosyncrasy of character, initiative or its absence—all these condition the velocity of one's movement. But personal and environmental qualities cannot always be neatly separated. Different environments affect attitudes as well as options. Modernization of the eduational system and the growing compartmentalization and specialization within professions and occupations after 1870 meant not only that young people were locked onto certain tracks early but also that they had relatively few inducements to switch tracks. The rewards for obedience to the sequence were tangible, more so than ever before, while the difficulties involved in duplicating the juggling acts of individuals like Alfred Poore, the young man who earlier in the century had wandered from occupation to occupation, were formidable.

Paradoxically, the same economic transformation in the late 19th century which opened new avenues to youth lengthened the avenues themselves. Randolph Bourne, the foremost American philosopher of youthful radicalism in the early 1900s, once noted that his contemporaries had "a very real feeling of coming straight up against a wall of diminishing opportunity." [48] In a suggestive study of success literature, Richard Weiss called attention to the presence at the end of the 19th century of a feeling "that the ordinary man had fewer opportunities than at an earlier time." [49] Much of the nostalgia for the "country boy" in late 19th-century thought associated the past with freedom and spontaneity, qualities now presumably in decline. These observations raise an important question: Why did a generation experiencing an explosion of opportunities perceive them to be eroding? Part of the answer lies in the fact that the perception of declining opportunity was rarely unequivocal, since opportunities might be contracting in one field while expanding in another. But part of the answer also lies in the fact that men had to submit to new kinds of discipline in the late 19th century if the benefits of opportunity were to be reaped. More time had to be spent in school, and in a much more systematic type of schooling. Even after the termination of formal education, moreover, a young man might find himself caught in the bureaucratic web of a large business corporation. "Nowadays," Bourne wrote,

> professional training is lengthy and expensive; independent business requires big capital for success; and there is no more West. It is still as true as ever that the exceptional man will always "get there," but now it is likely to be only the exceptional man, whereas formerly all the able "got there." [50]

Bourne overstated his case, but he had a point. There still was a West, and all the able had not always succeeded in the past. But the white-collar bureaucrat, if he had been nurtured on the ideal which associated high status with self-employment, could well have been left with a feeling of inadequacy because of his inability to get to the top of the pile.

To make one's mark in the world is, of course, a relative concept, but the physical perimeters of a small village or small partnership in the 1850s put more of a limit on the number of people one had to impress than did a large city or sprawling industrial complex in 1900. Modernization gave young men greater impetus in making their "start in life," but it also made it difficult for those on the rise to come to general notice much before age 40. As Eugene R. Whitmore wrote, "until the age of forty, much of a man's time is spent as an apprentice—as an assistant to someone." [51]

Whitmore's observation reflected not only the growth of business bureaucracy during the later stages of industrialization but also the changing age structure of the population, especially in large cities. In 1820 or 1840 a young man in Philadelphia or New York who glanced around would see mainly other young men. Compared with rural areas, antebellum cities contained a lower proportion both of children and of adults over 30. In 1840 white people aged 20–29 formed 45.6 percent of the white population aged 20 or over in cities of 100,000 or more; by 1890 the comparable proportion was 36.7 percent; by 1910, 33.6 percent. By 1930, more people in large cities were in the 30–39 age bracket than were between 20 and 29, and almost as many were between 45 and 64. If our young man of New York or Philadelphia looked around in 1930, he would see himself as an island of youth in a sea of age.[52]

A principal consequence for youth of this aging trend was the imposition of horizontal age layers over the younger brackets. The presence of greater numbers of middle-aged people in society meant that an upwardly mobile youth had more bodies to climb over on his way to the top. As career trajectories flattened off, the term "middle age" itself changed its meaning. Early in the 19th century, middle age had signified no more than the "meridian" of life, the halfway point between life and death. But after 1900 it was used increasingly to indicate a stage of life rather than a signpost on the highway of life—specifically, the years between 40 and 55 when a managerial executive would either reap the dividends of his early "apprenticeship" or stagnate. One writer described the middle-aged man as the "keystone of modern suburban development, being in a noticeable majority on the commuters' trains and at taxpayers' meetings." He was the main burden-bearer of civilization, but he was also entering the "real awkward age." [53]

Young people of all social classes felt the impact of the economic and demographic changes of the late 19th century, but the most articulate response to these changes came from spokesmen for the middle class. A configuration of distinctive values and ideals emerged in advice-to-youth books after the Civil War: the glorification of physical strength, the need to build in youth a reserve of vital energy, the value of ascetic self-discipline, and the importance of prolonging the period of preparation for manhood. In modified form these values were to suffuse middle-class youth organizations between 1890 and 1920.

The Tasks of Youth

Conduct-of-life books in the first half of the century had extolled prudential virtues and "balance of character," as well as "decision of character," but after the Civil War a new emphasis began to infiltrate such volumes. In 1865, for example, Daniel Eddy of Philadelphia brought out a new edition of his popular advice book, *The Young Man's Friend*.[54] In the first edition, published in 1855, Eddy had assumed that character, depicted essentially as a principle of balance and equilibrium, was sufficient armor against the allurements of vice. The second edition, in contrast, read more like an early draft of Josiah Strong's nationalist manifesto, *Our Country,* for Eddy not only prophesied that by 1900 "the stars and stripes will wave from the rocky abutments of Newfoundland to the Isthmus of Panama," but urged that America's mission demanded that its youth exhibit energy—specifically, physical energy—rather than mere self-restraint.[55] Most persons, he conceded, viewed physical power as belonging only to the sensual, animal, and brutish. "When you speak of muscular development, they think of Heenan, Morrissey, and Sullivan, knights of the ring." [56] But Eddy rejected the prejudice and emphasized the value of physical culture as the very foundation of character. "What mudsills are to a building, muscular development is to manhood," he wrote.[57] Eddy was so convinced of the challenge facing young men in the late 1860s that, even when he was not specifically calling for physical culture, he lapsed into rhetorical declarations of the value of force and energy. Two analogies, neither of which appeared in the original edition, illustrate perfectly Eddy's new perception of the menacing environment confronting youth. The first compared life to a racecourse in which innumerable competitors were scrambling for the prize. The second, aimed at reminding his readers of the qualities now needed for success, compared man to a steam engine, with muscle power providing the ironwork, brain the engine power, and steam the force "which puts all its wheels in motion, causes all its shafts to turn, and all its parts to beat in harmony." [58]

To say that in subsequent years others elaborated on the theme of physical training suggested by Eddy is to understate the point. More accurately, increasing numbers of youth counselors were obsessed with physique and fitness. The commonsensical recommendations of antebellum advice books that young men pay heed to the demands of the body for rest and relaxation gave way to a cult of body building. William Mathews's chapter on "decision" in his *Getting on in the World* drew heavily on the ideas of John Foster, but Mathews then criticized Foster for failing to emphasize the connection between constitutional firmness and decision of character. Decisiveness was now less a moral quality than a muscle.[59] In a similar way, Kenneth H. Wayne's *Building the Young Man* virtually reduced character building to a handmaiden of physical culture.[60]

As the association between physical culture and character building sharpened, the connection between a country boyhood and one's prospects for success in life became fixed. God made the country, man the city, William Cowper had said, and Americans agreed. Country life was natural, simple, and moral, and the country boy was free of the foppish affectation of his city counterpart. But after the middle of the 19th century the idealization of rural life began to change. Country life retained its innocence but now took on new qualities in the popular imagination. A rural boyhood, many now argued, would not only protect innocence but build strength and endurance for the struggle ahead. In the hands of success mythologists, country life became a kind of tuition-free school for success.[61]

For those so unlucky as to be born in cities, educators provided a series of surrogates for country experience. Regular periods of exercise, a Connecticut school superintendent argued, would instill "promptness, endurance, and agility," the birthright of farm boys but qualities to be inculcated consciously in city boys.[62] Manual training, the principal embodiment of the idealization of rural life in late 19th-century education, was now pruned of its traditional association with the education of delinquents and deviants and advanced as valuable for city youth regardless of class. Various impulses fed into the manual training movement in the 1880s and 1890s: dissatisfaction with the bookish curriculum of the schools, anxieties about the decline of apprenticeship, and a desire that America hold its own in commercial and industrial rivalries with the European powers. But those who advocated manual training on grounds of economic practicality and utility had to fight successive and often losing battles with others for whom the character-building functions of manual training reigned supreme.[63] The latter claimed that manual training would teach the sort of respect for hard work once instilled by farm labor, and would knock those "false ideas of social ambition" out of city boys at a time when "the ambition for easier lives and more genteel employments, and the silly but common notion that labor is menial, that the tools of the trades or of the farm are badges of servility, have greatly lessened apprenticeships." [64]

These comments suggest that both country boyhood and manual training, the genuine article and the surrogate, were envisioned as counterforces to the mad scramble for wealth in the late 19th century, and indeed, a reactionary spirit often did suffuse discussions of both. Yet on balance, success mythologists were able to sanction both country boyhood and the drive for success by depicting the former as providing the reserve power needed for achievement of the latter. A country boyhood became in their view the basis for dynamic manhood.

The more writers dwelled on a vision of dynamic manhood as the key element of success, the more vividly they portrayed the insidious agents of corruption: too much sleep, too much food, and above all, too much sex. Any sex was too much for John Harvey Kellogg, superintendent of the Battle Creek Sanitarium and a recognized authority in the Gilded Age on diet and regimen. Kellogg's popular *Man, the Master-*

piece built on a tradition of 19th-century Protestant thought which had associated masturbation with loss of vitality, but the sort of regimen he prescribed to conquer secret vice was more sadistic than ascetic.[65] In what might be termed a Puritan's theory of dreams, Kellogg devoted page upon page to describing a regimen that would avert not only conscious masturbation but even the erotic midnight reverie. First of all, one had to keep the will finely tuned during the waking hours by practicing self-denial, so that the will would react at night like an alarm clock, snapping the youth out of his dream in time to prevent nocturnal emissions. Beyond this, Kellogg advocated the following: drinking hot water, six to eight glasses a day, to help the system evacuate itself before sleep and thus to eliminate "irritating" congestions; urinating several times each night (same purpose); avoidance of alcohol, tobacco, tea, and coffee as dangerous stimulants to lecherous thoughts; cold enemas and hot sitz baths every day; wearing a wet girdle to bed each night; and kneading and percussion of the abdomen each day to keep the bowels light and lively.[66]

Kellogg was not the first American to equate medical and divine "laws," nor the first to suggest that the natural and perfect penalty for self-abuse was impotence ("by an immutable law of nature, we are ultimately deprived of any faculty which is grossly abused"[67]). A few antebellum youth counselors such as John Todd had voiced comparable fears of sexual indulgence. Yet by the 1880s, ideas like Kellogg's were pushing toward center stage. *Man, the Masterpiece* was itself a success tract disguised as a treatise on health and physiology; a chapter on the workings of the stomach succeeded one on "how to make life a success." At times, moralism gave way to momentary lapses into religious terminology. Straining for the right metaphor to underscore the value of the daily cold water douche, Rev. C. Cuthbert Hall compared it to baptism![68] The mixture of Protestant moralism, religion, health, and success was incongruous, but behind it lay a distinctive paradox of late 19th-century thought. The same writers who exhorted youth to rise in the world were usually critical of business enterprise, associating the latter with luxury and corruption and advocating extreme self-denial in youth. Kellogg was no exception. He associated city life, frailty, and intellectuality with sexual indulgence, and rural life with sexual restraint. Kellogg generalized even beyond village life; all things natural and wild—Indians, savages, even apes—were chaste. It was as if the road to the boardroom ran through the jungle.[69]

Although Kellogg represented some important currents in late 19th-century thought, in one respect he looked backward rather than forward, for it was the negative function of will power as an agent of self-denial which most attracted him. After 1890, success writers dwelled increasingly on the positive and transcending functions of will power, arguing that the meager endowment of original nature had to be supplemented by psychic energizing. Frank C. Haddock's popular *Power of Will* and *Business Power* drew heavily on the methods of New Thought, an increasingly fashionable system of mind cure, to elevate the significance of will and "magnetic" power in the drive for business success.[70] Self-improvement was no longer the piecemeal process of acquisition prescribed by earlier youth counselors, but a "dynamic assertion of will and tapping of mysterious yet scientifically controllable inner energies."[71] Orison S. Marden, another leading success writer around 1900, used New Thought to counsel unflappable optimism in the face of adversity. Common to each writer was a realization that the world was no longer malleable, that in an age of gigantic enterprise and astonishing economic changes, a young man needed more than the mere endowment of original nature.[72]

Recognition of the limits of nature did not enable success mythologists to write more realistically or coherently about the actual prospects of the young man facing life than had youth counselors in the second quarter of the 19th century. Marden's *The Young Man Entering Business* advised its readers in one chapter to plug away at one occupation for years, but in the next chapter it warned about the dangers of sticking to one line. At one point in *Choosing a Career*, Marden told young men to acquire special training before picking a career; some fifty pages later he exhorted them to choose a career on the basis of its capacity to stir the latent enthusiasms of the soul.[73] Books like these were inspirational rather than programmatic; they provided pep talks rather than marching orders. Unintentionally, they illustrated the unhinging effects which the rise of modern business corporations had on those nurtured on the ideals of an older world of small partnerships.

Others, however, were beginning in the 1880s and 1890s to explore the implications of economic changes for the start in life. Books on how to choose careers, which rolled off the presses with increasing frequency after 1890, bore some resemblance to the success tracts and were pervaded by many of the latter's values, but they broke new ground by the technique of assembling experts from different occupations to describe conditions in their specialties. Cautiously at first, and later systematically, such books downgraded the importance of both introspection and the parental hunch as the sole bases for choosing occupations, substituting a sober respect for the wisdom of professionals. Whitelaw Reid used the classic metaphor of a ship at sea, but he gave it a new orientation:

> Too often, however, it is the case that the predilections of immaturity are inimical to the best interests of the individual, who may elect to adopt a career for which he is naturally unfitted, and in which, if he escapes failure,

he can never hope to achieve any great degree of success. Not to every parent, though, is given the clarity of vision which will enable him to perceive the unwisdom of a boy's choice, or, if perceiving it, the ability to lead him gently to the path which it is best he should take. For want of just such penetration the ocean of life is full of many human wrecks, hulks battered on the rocks of misguided effort. And it might easily have been that a few words, spoken in the right way and at the proper moment, would have directed the buoyant bark of youth into the smooth waters of progress and achievement.[74]

Besides seeking to introduce a less emotional tone into discussions of career choices, Reid was also implying that decisions made before the order to advance were more important than a reckless willingness to go on marching straight into the line of fire.

Thus, two viewpoints coexisted around 1900. Young men were told as never before that to push ahead they needed almost demonic energy, yet they were also told that success depended on careful choice in the first place. The two viewpoints were in some ways complementary. By elevating the importance of vital reserve and self-consciously acquired traits of personality, success mythologists such as Marden subtly shifted emphasis from time spent on the stage of life to time spent in preparation. Similarly, Whitelaw Reid located the key to success in the original career choice rather than in later maneuverings in the business world. For Marden or Reid, youth was ideally a time of preparation rather than involvement. Antebellum youth counselors had limited their comments on early preparation to occasional declarations of the value of proper habit formation in childhood. Even though their audience was composed of young men in their teens and 20s, they had had little to say about the later stages of dependency. Writers such as Marden, in contrast, spent nearly as much time describing the physical and moral regimen appropriate for success as detailing conduct required in the world of affairs. "Tough timbers must come from well-grown, sturdy trees," Marden wrote in a book whose subtitle, *to Inspire Youth to Character Building, Self-Culture and Noble Achievement*, defined its goals.[75] In this "strenuous age," he claimed elsewhere, men must either push or be pushed. "The projectile power of your ambition depends wholly on the vigor of the determination behind it. What you accomplish will depend on the amount of life energy, of enthusiasm and will power you put into your efforts to achieve."[76]

Success writers in the late 19th century were often hostile to the prolongation of formal education on grounds that it had a softening effect on youth, but they were receptive to the idea that the quality of youthfulness be prolonged. At its simplest level, this idea took the form of a recommendation that more time be spent in preparation, regardless of the exact constituents of preparation.[77] But success mythologists also argued for the prolongation of youth as part of the prolongation of enthusiasm for life. Insisting on the value of pluck in the face of barriers, they praised the qualities of youthfulness—courage, daring, and high spirits. The young man's task was no longer to prune himself of youthful effervescence but to prevent the incursion of boredom and cynicism in adulthood. The artless and ingenuous warmth of youth, they argued, was preferable to the calculating spirit of maturity.[78] A youth counselor of the 1850s would have argued that enthusiasm was a characteristic of youth, but he would then have added that it was just such zest for life that ruined young men by the thousands.

It is ironic that the period between 1890 and 1910, which saw success cultists vying with each other in proclaiming the need for manlier men to confront the struggle of life, should also have witnessed the flowering of the opposite ideal, that youthfulness as a quality be indulged, that youth be prolonged. One of the few contemporaries who glimpsed this incongruity in success literature was Randolph S. Bourne. Bourne's *Youth and Life* explicitly contrasted the "rational," success-oriented approach to living—the idea that life was a series of obstacles to be surmounted by orderly plans of attack—with the "experimental," youth-oriented idea that life was "a laboratory where its possibilities for the enhancement of happiness and the realization of ideals are to be tested and observed." [79] In Bourne's view the desire to prolong the "detached enthusiasm" of youth as an end in itself would follow upon recognition that life was a continuous process of discovery rather than a planned march toward fixed values.[80]

Bourne called for radical youth to lead the way to the experimental ideal, but his call met with little response.[81] Like British youth, American youth between 1890 and 1920 followed the path of conformity rather than rebellion.[82] America had its share of discontented youth, but unlike Germany, America had no *Wandervogel*, no organized movement of rebellious and alienated young people.[83] The business world bewildered many, but most pressed ahead, perhaps armed with one of Orison S. Marden's inspirational tracts, but avoiding, one might hope, the clammy embrace of one of John H. Kellogg's wet girdles.

The Tasks of Parents

Just as economic changes altered the conditions of success for upwardly mobile young men, they created new imperatives for families. If not a sufficient cause of success, a prolongation of education into the teen years was becoming a necessary precondition. Yet to prolong education for even a few years beyond puberty meant that families would have to relinquish support from their children. The more systematic education became, the less possible it became to attend school randomly or seasonally, in the fashion of antebellum academy students. Parents would have to forgo the earnings of children, moreover, at a time when those earnings often provided their margin of security. Today, parents look at middle age as a time when their teenage children will place an extraordinary drain on family resources. In 19th-century families the opposite was true; teenage children were economic assets and were expected to compensate by their earnings for the fact that they had been economic liabilities when young. A survey of working-class family budgets in Massachusetts in the 1870s indicated just how vital this sort of compensation was. Children between 10 and 19 provided, on average, a quarter of family income, and more than a third of the income in families headed by unskilled workers. Further, to parents the most valuable working years of a child were not those under 12, for available opportunities at such early ages were meager, nor those over 18, for at that age working-class children customarily left home and boarded out for a few years before marriage. Rather, the critical time was between 12 and 17, the very years to which secondary education laid claim.[84]

In some ways, working children in the late 19th century differed little from their predecessors in the early 19th century, for children had always been expected to work. But parental perceptions of the importance of the wages of working children were likely to be much sharper in 1880 than in 1820. The decline of apprenticeship made it both difficult and unnecessary for young people to leave home at 12 or 14 to live in the house of a master. Available evidence indicates that after midcentury it became more common for urban lower-class young people to live at home during their teen years and thus to exert a drain on family resources, which had to be compensated for by earnings.[85] In addition, urban working children in the 1880s did not compensate their parents by performing seasonal services around a farm but by bringing in measurable weekly wages. Finally, unlike the farmer, who at least had a farm to fall back on, urban parents who rented three or four rooms in a tenement could point to few tangible pieces of property or signs of economic security besides wages. To forgo the wages of children had become increasingly necessary (if children were to get ahead), but also increasingly painful.

The opportunity costs of education—the loss of wages while the children attended school—put prolonged education beyond the reach of children in most families during the closing decades of the 19th century. It is difficult to say at just which income level the cutoff came, for parents with two or three teenage children might well have been able to educate one of them, despite modest resources. But any kind of prolonged education was usually beyond the reach of all but the upper levels of the working class and the middle class. At a time when increasing numbers of middle-class parents were sacrificing the labor of their children in favor of prolonged education, most working-class parents and children remained caught up in the sort of productive-contractual relationship that had once characterized family life in all social classes.

The interplay of these forces created a number of unique pressures in late 19th-century households. Lower-class households, once free in the sense that children left home at early ages, experienced new tensions as the period of home residence extended further into the teen years. It was no accident that by the 1890s observers of slum life were struck less by the vagabonds, homeless children, and street urchins who had captivated Brace than by the existence of a stable street-corner society composed not of wanderers but of neighborhood toughs who preferred the life of the street to the "pestiferous tenements" of their parents.[86]

In middle-class homes economic change had different implications. Parents who chose to sacrifice the earnings of their children to advanced education demanded that this sacrifice be repaid not in wages but in obedience to the demands of school and society. The extraordinary emphasis on achievement, purity, and self-restraint in success tracts suffused both middle-class family values and the institutions created for middle-class young people in the 1880s and 1890s. The following chapter will describe some of these institutions, but at this juncture it will suffice to note that the impetus behind the creation of institutions for adolescents came from men and women whose values approximated those of the success writers. The values of success writers and those of the architects of new institutions for youth, such as the Boy Scouts and church youth societies, were complementary in many ways. Each group located the social evils of the day in big cities; each preferred the virtues of the country boy; each celebrated Puritan thrift and self-denial; each castigated political and economic corruption; and each, finally, saw value in prolonging the period of preparation.

The linkage between the success cult and youth work was often personal as well as intellectual. John H. Kellogg wrote books in the 1880s which mixed physiology and the ideals of success; by 1915 he was coauthoring school texts on physiology with Michael V. O'Shea, perhaps the leading entrepreneur of adolescence after 1900. The connection which Kellogg established between asceticism and chastity would have met with a positive response from General Robert Baden-Powell, the founder of the Boy Scouts, who believed that the stimulation of perspiration was a guarantor of chastity and that, presumably in cold weather, a twice daily washing of "the racial organ" in cold water was equally therapeutic. Frances E. Willard, whose Women's Christian Temperance Union played an important role in organizing the activities of boys and girls in small towns of the Middle West, established Kellogg as the Union's director of physical education. Francis E. Clark, the founder of the Young People's Society for Christian Endeavor, one of the major late 19th-century Protestant youth organizations, did double duty as a success writer. So did Luther H. Gulick, the man who in the 1890s provided the theoretical justification for the growing YMCA interest in work with boys. A multivolume series of books published in 1910 and designed to advise parents on the best ways to raise children and young people bore the title *The Foundation Stones of Success*. G. Stanley Hall took a place second to none in his hostility to any soft or debilitating regimen for youth in his trumpeting of body building as the foundation of character, reserve force, and indomitable will. In a talk before a YMCA audience, Hall retranslated his biblical text to read "worship the Lord in the beauty of healthfulness." [87]

Conclusion

The Industrial Revolution in America had the effect of giving economic significance to two turning points in the lives of youth. The first was between ages 12 and 14, the period which had become the usual school leaving age in urban areas even before major industrialization. The second turning point was at about 18 for working-class youth, who at that age sought adult wages, only to find in many cases that employers intended to keep them on merely as helpers at apprentice wages. For middle-class youth the same turning points were important, but for different reasons, for in order to take advantage of the new economic opportunities they had to stay in school during their teens.

Economic change thus made the teen years conspicuous in a way they had not been in the 1820s and 1830s, when "youth" signified the ages of home leaving between 15 and 25, rather than school attendance from 14 to 18. But industrialization did more than render the teens conspicuous; it made them vital, and it demanded that families eager for their children to rise in the world take steps that would segregate their young people from the world of casual labor and the dead-end job. Even before 1870, demographic changes caused by steadily declining birthrates had created a kind of family in which self-conscious nurture rather than remote "government" of children was a possibility, but industrialization now made nurture vital for teenage boys as well as for young ladies and small children.

The steps taken by middle-class families between 1880 and 1900 to guarantee their children's access to attractive jobs involved more than merely sending them to high school. The middle-class values of self-restraint and self-denial evident both in conduct-of-life books and medical tracts at mid-century were now asserted in extreme form, and conscious efforts were made to enforce obedience and dependency. In the 1820s and 1830s, independence in youth, a willingness to strike out on one's own, had been a precondition for success for young men like the Sons of New Hampshire. By 1900 such desires for independence and autonomy were viewed as prescriptions for failure.

CHAPTER 7

Against Adulthood:
College, High School, and
Christian Youth "Activities"

IT WAS IRONIC that the trumpeting of manliness and will power in late 19th-century success tracts should have become one of the impulses behind the establishment of institutions for adolescents, since the adolescent was a stranger to manliness, at least insofar as manliness meant intellectual and spiritual maturity. Middle-class values at the end of the century downgraded maturity and intellectuality in youth while upgrading physical prowess and perpetual becoming. The word "manliness" itself changed meaning, coming to signify less the opposite of childishness than the opposite of femininity.

Changing expectations about the behavior of youth could be glimpsed in success literature which substituted the glorification of strenuosity and will power for a sober assessment of the elements of maturity, but they were most fully revealed in the institutions for young people created within colleges, public high schools, and Protestant churches between 1880 and 1910. Although significant differences in goals and structure separated colleges, high schools, and church youth societies, the vectors of change were parallel. The development of a sponsored extracurriculum in colleges had a strong impact on secondary schools, while after 1900 attitudes and practices that emerged in church youth societies in the 1890s influenced not only secular youth organizations but also high schools. In all of these institutions, moreover, rhetorical glorifications of strenuosity and will power coexisted with the thrusting of youth into positions of extreme dependence.

College "Life"

The expansion first of secondary schools and later of graduate education in the late 19th century had eroded some of the traditional functions of the college and had prompted a few individuals to call from the 1860s onward for the abolition of collegiate education.[1] So far from disappearing, however, the college gradually solidified its position as part of the multifaceted university. Abraham Flexner underscored the irony in 1908 by calling attention to "on the one side, a formidable array of scholars, laboratories, publications; on the other, a large, miscellaneous student body marked by an immense sociability on a common-place basis and widespread absorption in trivial and boyish interests."[2] The continued vitality of the college was strange mainly because, more than any other educational institution of the time, it seemed to insulate itself from the roaring business world outside its portals. True, the college had long been a cloistered institution paying little heed to the utilitarian demands of the business world. The remarkable aspect of the college's development after 1890 was that it continued to insulate itself at a time when business was more eager than ever before to recruit college graduates.

Insularity took a variety of forms in late 19th-century American colleges. The ideal of communal living, which had disintegrated in the face of the needs and desires of antebellum students, revived under the impetus of new prosperity. The construction of new residential facilities once again made colleges centers for the living as well as the learning experiences of youth. Part of the insularity lay in the curriculum, which, despite sundry efforts at reform, continued to be top-heavy with classical and general culture courses. But insularity now extended to the extracurriculum as well. Nothing better illustrates the insularity of the latter than the preeminence in the 1890s of campus "activities." Sports, dramatics clubs, debating societies, fraternities, and even religion were essentially college activities among college students in the 1890s; that is, these activities began and ended within college gates. The extracurriculum became a form of surrogate involvement, a substitute for attendance at comparable activities in the world outside the college. The major exception to this statement actually reinforces it, for to the extent that college activities of the 1890s reached beyond the college, it was to other colleges. This was the age not only of organized sports and organized debating clubs but also of intercollegiate sports and debating. Even religion went intercollegiate in the late 19th century with the creation of the intercollegiate YMCA.[3]

As student life became more insular, it became less acrimonious. Riots became less common and much less violent than those of the 1830s and 1840s, perhaps because discipline was relaxed. Fewer students now had to march grudgingly to eight o'clock chapel, and fewer engaged in open sedition against college authority. Occasional battles against the vestiges of "parentalism plus" disturbed a few institutions, especially some of the more remotely situated and conservative liberal arts colleges, but even these confrontations were relatively free of the violence and mayhem which had once been the inevitable outcome of student rebellion.[4]

More apathetic than hostile toward college authorities, students in the 1890s were also less prone than their predecessors to oscillate between intellectual extremes. Clashes between deism and pietism in the 1790s or between atheism and theism in the 1870s gave way to the bland and conforming student bodies of the 1890s. The change was often most noticeable at elite institutions. Describing Yale at the end of the century, Henry Seidel Canby had no difficulty encompassing student life in the space of a chapter, yet he took pains to distinguish between several different types of professors within a single English department.[5]

In comparison to antebellum students, those of the 1890s were more bland and even tempered, less prone to fits of melancholy and violence. In part, the difference arose from the dissimilarity in the economic prospects faced by early and late 19th-century students. The student who told Henry Adams that his Harvard degree was worth money in Chicago spoke for the later generation of students, a generation that had fewer reasons to doubt the purpose of college education than did the generation of the 1830s and 1840s.[6] Students in the 1890s, especially those at prestigious colleges and universities, could confidently view college education as a pleasant interlude on a well-marked path which led to positions in business management on graduation.

A dose of romantic activism complemented the insularity and homogeneity of student life. Canby recalled:

> We were strenuous without thought to ask the reason why. For all but the congenitally lazy, the songful hours over beer steins, the country walks, and the midnights of intimate talk, were interludes (like our lessons) in a tense activity. The cry in our undergraduate world was to do something.[7]

So freshmen hurried through the halls seeking news for the college paper. Athletes struggled to make teams. Boys with a knack for business managed orchestras, sports, and even cooperative pants-pressing companies. The activist mood came over religion too. Yale men sang: "what the hell do we care what the people say, we are, we are, we are the Yale YMCA." [8] In part, too, romantic activism and muscularity were outgrowths of a kind of adolescent bravado, subliminal expressions of contempt for the extreme emphasis on decorum instilled in late Victorian households. [9]

A measure of boyish seriousness accompanied romantic activism. Undergraduate pranks which embodied burlesque declined. Officials and students alike viewed team sports less as outlets for high spirits than as useful forms of preparation for the competitive business of life. The combination of romantic activism and boyish seriousness reinforced the prevalent homogeneity and conformity of college life. At Bowdoin, William De Witt Hyde made each of the students in his class write out a personal religious creed, not to form the basis of a controversy but as the initial step toward arriving at a consensus. [10]

Increasingly, faculty and administrators sanctioned aspects of the extracurriculum, especially team sports and fraternities, as agents of moral development. The president of Princeton justified team sports as "gentlemanly contests for supremacy," marks of true manliness, and concluded that the Christian who equated depression of spirits with piety was becoming extinct. [11] President Tucker of Dartmouth confessed that he had never been able to see a healthier agent of moral development than organized athletics. LeBaron Russell Briggs of Harvard described a football team as a perfect democracy. Eugene Richards argued that athletics made the college into a little republic, "a means of preparation for the responsibilities of life in the larger republic outside the campus." [12]

The same arguments sanctioned fraternities. Julius Seelye of Amherst praised the fraternity for sublimating the rivalry of individuals into good fellowship. Andrew White of Cornell thought that membership in fraternities bred a sense of responsibility and hence made men out of boys. "The badge which each member wears fixes his responsibility; to be less than a gentleman is to disgrace it and to injure the fraternity." [13]

These statements indicate that some administrators were growing more tolerant of students, or at least of the boyish traits of students. But they should not obscure the fact that official control was now extended over the extracurriculum as never before. Tutors no longer peeked over transoms and through keyholes; presidents no longer made miscreants kneel and pray for divine forgiveness and guidance. But while the forms of control were no longer obtrusive, the scope of control expanded. Administrators sanctioned fraternities, but only after they had succeeded in pruning them of some of their more brutal and secret practices.[14] In athletics, too, student control gave way in the 1890s to tripartite regulation by faculty, alumni, and athletes.[15] Debating societies were now advised and often run by faculty members who readied their speakers for intercollegiate clashes, a practice which led some to charge that for practical purposes the professors at rival colleges were engaged in the debate.[16] Paradoxically, while the student mood was romantically activist, the traditional independence of the extracurriculum withered.

No one better typified the new mood of college officials than Hyde of Bowdoin, the "boy president" who rode around town on a bicycle with a tennis racquet under his arm and who affected an air of easy informality with his students.[17] His brief book of 1898, *The Evolution of a College Student*, traced the development of a fictitious student, Clarence Mansfield, through letters to his parents and friends.[18] Clarence changes from a homesick freshman to a rebellious, sports-loving, arrogant sophomore to a skeptical junior who flirts with atheism and socialism. This might have been strong medicine for parents, and indeed would have been had not Hyde diluted the dose by turning Clarence into a paragon who acknowledges that a stiff economics course has knocked the giddy socialism out of him and who affirms that he is suitably (if rather vaguely) religious. Clarence even talks his fiancée out of entering settlement house work, disclaiming "ascetic, egotistical self-sacrifice." [19]

Hyde's point was not only that college education was an inoculation against socialism and skepticism but also that the rebelliousness of students was a normal part of growing up. Thus, the erratic thinking and behavior of students needed understanding rather than censure:

> The college student is a being of infinitely complex and swiftly shifting phases which external description is powerless to catch and reproduce. The only way to portray his deeper nature is to place him in intimate and confidential relations and let him "give himself away." This kinetoscopic picture is presented in the hope that it may assure over-anxious parents that not every aberration of their sons is either final or fatal.[20]

By applying the concept of evolution to the psychological and moral development of a student, Hyde was able to defuse many of the traditionally menacing aspects of student behavior as well as justify the official tolerance and cooptation of the student extracurriculum in the 1890s. The decline of pietistic religion probably made it easier for him to take a more generous view of student aberrations, for college presidents no longer viewed themselves as shepherds of undergraduate souls, obligated to practice a more rigid system of discipline than could be found in most homes. As a corollary, the decline of college revivals in the 1880s cut both students and faculty off from the one practice that had traditionally brought them face to face, and spurred the search for new forms and concepts of control.[21]

The new tolerance of the student extracurriculum and the acceptance of a normative view of development (in place of the old idea that vice was addictive) reflected the spectacular growth of college enrollment between 1850 and 1900. In 1850 there were 38.1 undergraduates for every 100,000 people; in 1900 the figure was 123.3 per 100,000. In absolute terms the same period saw a jump from 8,837 undergraduates to 77,085. Although the upward curve began earlier, the 1890s witnessed a quantum leap: undergraduate enrollment increased 38.4 percent from 1890/1891 to 1894/1895. Growth was partly the result of the more advanced stages of settlement in the western states, where the base in 1850 had been near zero. Proportionately, the most rapid rise took place on the Pacific coast and in midwestern states such as Ohio, Indiana, Illinois, and Michigan. Moreover, the turn toward coeducation, which began in state universities after 1860, brought a new constituency to the university. But even individual colleges in the East, many of which resisted coeducation, felt the pressure of rising enrollment. Between 1850 and 1890, Harvard's enrollment rose from 358 to 1,552, Princeton's from 251 to 850, Columbia's from 135 to 573, and Pennsylvania's from 95 to 490.[22]

Traditional methods of control, based on tutorial attentiveness and close supervision, were suited to small student bodies where no class contained more than fifty members and where the president knew all of the students by name. The expansion of college enrollment made it nearly impossible to apply the old methods of control, even if the faculty had the desire to do so. Inherited ideas had sanctioned the primacy of the class as a moral and administrative unit; even the more conservative college presidents in the early 1800s had tolerated hazing as a way to brand newcomers with a sense of group identity in a particular class. But the growth of student enrollment after mid-century undermined the class both as a moral and administrative unit. Secret societies, fraternities, and intercollegiate sports all cut across class lines. The effects of increasing size were evident even before 1870 in a decline of tutorial supervision, but it was only after 1880 that administrators sought to come to terms with new forms of student organization and to direct them to acceptable ends.[23]

Rising enrollment helps to explain the willingness of college presidents to accept the principle of socialization by the peer group, but the facts of growth and of the survival of the college are themselves puzzling. As noted, some educators had thought that colleges would simply disappear with the expansion of secondary and graduate education. A debate which broke out at the 1904 meeting of the prestigious Association of American Universities illustrates some of the arguments used to justify the college's continued existence. The debate took off from a semantic issue. What should be the exact application of terms such as "college," "graduate education," and "professional education" within universities? President Hadley of Yale thought that the term "college" should apply to technical schools as well as to schools which taught liberal arts and sciences, and that "graduate education" should apply only to postbaccalaureate research under a professor of liberal arts or sciences. Munroe Smith of Columbia challenged Hadley, observing that the distinction between graduate and professional training was breaking down. "The graduate department is practically becoming a school of professional training; and in the so-called professional faculties we can see the beginnings of the development of the research idea." [24] Smith went on to insist that technological schools were bound to be raised to the level of the older professional schools and of the graduate schools, rather than continuing to run on a track parallel to the college. The drift, he concluded, was to put the new professions (like engineering) on the same level with the old professions, to infuse both professional and graduate education with the spirit of research, and thus to come "logically to a distinction which puts on one side the academic college, and on the other side the university, in which are grouped all these schools of professional training that are more or less imbued with the research spirit." [25]

At this point in the debate, Charles W. Eliot of Harvard sought to resolve the issue by introducing still another semantic distinction, between a sampling or "schoolboy" stage and a university stage marked by specialization along career lines. "And there is nothing between—nothing." [26] Andrew West of Princeton made the obvious rejoinder: "I wonder where President Eliot would get his argument for the college as an American undergraduate institution, if the sampling is concluded at the end of the secondary school state, before the student gets to his undergraduate course." [27] In such a case, what justification would there be for insisting that the student take a college degree before entering professional school? Eliot argued in reply that college education was, in effect, an early stage of specialization, a time when the student could acquire background knowledge as a prelude to professional school. The law student had to know history, economics, government, and language before he could study common law, and the best place to learn these was in college. Coming almost full circle, Eliot concluded with a plea that all universities require the B.A. degree as a prelude to professional school. West was put down, but he would not stay down. What about the students who had no intention to prepare for professions? Why should they go to college? Eliot conceded that in the last graduating class at Harvard a majority of students went straight into business, but he argued that business itself was becoming an "intellectual calling" like the learned professions, and hence that the college degree was appropriate for it too.[28]

Eliot's argument, which would have been ludicrous in 1860 or 1870, had substance by 1904. For much of the 19th century, business had preferred young men with practical, on-the-job knowledge rather than cosmopolitan university men. Indeed, business had often preferred boys to young men. An informed observer of the practices of New York merchant houses in mid-century noted that business sought young clerks of 14 or 15, straight from district schools, rather than older college graduates.[29] But business attitudes were changing in the 1890s. Corporations were increasingly prone to recruit college men for managerial positions. The few spokesmen for the business community who blasted the college gave inadvertent evidence for the opposite view. R. T. Crane, a strenuous critic of college training for businessmen, sampled business opinion in 1901 in order to demonstrate the inutility of college education, but a majority of his respondents either endorsed college education or expressed no opinion, while sixty of sixty-five graduates polled by Crane affirmed that any financial sacrifices they had made to attend college had more than been offset by their later success.[30] Crane himself was over 60 at the time, and clearly spoke for a dwindling minority. The only argument made elsewhere against graduates was that an overdose of self-love made them reluctant to serve apprenticeships on the lower rungs of the managerial ladder, an argument which presupposed that a demand for their services existed.[31]

The writings and testimonials of business leaders and success writers in the early 1900s suggest that, on balance, business saw innumerable credits and few debits in college education. Success writers such as Orison S. Marden reported that his books had induced young men to stay in or return to college despite initial disappointment.[32] Few saw much value in Crane's assertion that the energetic youth who started in business at 16 would build up an insurmountable lead over his rivals who wasted their youth in college. Most agreed, rather, with the president of a large paper company who said that "the college student ought to excel the young man whose education has been confined to the high school," or with the Wall Street banker who believed that, other things being equal, the collegian would outstrip the nongraduate.[33]

Business was not indifferent to technical education, and some institutions owed rising enrollments to their ability to provide scientific and engineering courses to eager students. Down to 1890, for example, no pattern marked the vocational choices of graduates of Pennsylvania State College, but between 1890 and 1900 from 50 to 60 percent of its graduates entered engineering. After 1895, Westinghouse, which along with General Electric controlled much of the market for electrical engineers, hired its experts and executives directly from engineering schools.[34]

In contrast, proponents of college education placed only marginal emphasis on its ability to impart either practical training or familiarity with business principles. Rather, businessmen responded positively to the romantic activism of the collegiate extracurriculum and to the general, culture-oriented curriculum, believing with Charles A. Dana that "there is nothing more advantageous to an able youth than to be thrown into contact with other youths in the conflict for study and in the struggle for superiority in the school and in the college."[35] The world of corporate management needed a man who thrived on competition and who could make difficult decisions in a cool and detached way, a man with "knowledge, traditions, and ideals that do not spring from the monotonous routine of his early humble positions."[36] Further, business believed that the college man was poised as well as energetic, possessed of personal and social qualities as well as competitive drive. As Walter Dill Scott argued, a college graduate could handle men as well as things.[37]

Uppermost in the minds of both business leaders and educators after 1890 were the intangible benefits of college education. Organized sports and clubs could instill a spirit of competition, while college education bred ideals and higher ambition. Simon Nelson Patten of the University of Pennsylvania called attention to the ideals of "efficiency, economy, generosity, and service" instilled in college, and concluded that college was a better antidote to greed than the old morality of self-denial.[38] Patten's litany of Progressive virtues was echoed by others and blended nicely with the mood of many business leaders who sought for the corporation the lofty image of a service institution rather than that of a mere convocation of dollar chasers. Henry Dwight Sedgwick claimed in 1908 that the aim of college education was to teach boys to become "good, heroic, wise, pure, honorable gentlemen," and then conceded in the next breath that these words had "rather a rhetorical and fantastic sound."[39] Perhaps they did, but Henry Seidel Canby described the typical alumnus of his generation as a man who argued for the general culture courses despite his dim memory of their contents and keen recollection of his difficulties with them. Such courses "gilded the profit-making system and made it fit for a gentleman."[40] Like the strenuous extracurriculum, the curriculum itself was most valuable when least specialized. It fitted a man for life not by reason of any particular skill it taught him, but because of the invisible qualities it instilled. Apologists for college education in the early 1900s rivaled success cultists in proclaiming the importance of building a vital reserve of surplus power as well as social poise in preparation for active life. As a corollary, it was not any single course but the atmosphere of college "life" that really mattered.[41]

The terms and phrases popular among college advocates in 1900 were not at all like those of 1870. In that year, Noah Porter of Yale had defended college education as a device to prolong youth, but he equated youth with innocence and described entrance into the college portal as a kind of passage into Eden in an age of individualism and aggressive commercialism. Forty years later, Clayton S. Cooper's soporific *Why Go to College?* praised college education for instilling "realism," by which he meant candor rather than technical aptitude, the distaste of Tom Brown or Dink Stover for sham and hypocrisy.[42] Underneath the lightheartedness and seeming listlessness of the undergraduate, Cooper asserted, "one may discern the real American undergraduate, energetic, earnest, expectant, and strenuously eager for those great campaigns of his day and generation in which the priceless guerdon is the 'joy of working.' "[43] For Cooper, college was a time to cultivate the qualities of energy and manliness that would prevail in the battle of life. Or, as Charles Thwing wrote:

> The various concerns of the student—athletic, social, dramatic, musical—represent fields in which he may prepare himself for winning his Gettysburgs; and it may be noted in evidence that some of the greatest constructive works of modern times, requiring bravest daring and the most intrepid confidence in oneself and in mankind—such as the building of railroads, telegraph and telephone lines, great bridges—have been among the triumphs of college men.[44]

Thwing's words underscore an ambivalence which runs through much of the literature on college life in the late 19th century. Although Thwing used the language of military conquest to describe the tasks of business leaders, others (and Thwing himself elsewhere) recognized the importance that social qualities were coming to have. Business leaders and success writers still spoke of strenuous achievement, but in the latter stages of industrialization the need was less for supermen who rose by demonic energy and unflinching will than for men who could coordinate and harmonize the various parts of a modern business enterprise. The rise of team sports to preeminence among college activities in the 1890s was at least partly the result of their ability to combine in perfect measure the qualities of strenuosity and cooperation.

From College to High School

The willingness of business leaders to accept the arguments of college officials was significant for two reasons. First, it helped guarantee that jobs would be awaiting graduates whose preparation had consisted mainly in baptism by total immersion in college life. Second, the obvious cash value of a college education encouraged emulation of college practices in public high schools. The extracurriculum of the late 19th-century college, with its features of activism and insularity, became a model for the extracurriculum of the early 20th-century public high school. The high school had its music and dramatics clubs, its speech and debating societies, its sports and fraternities, and its student government associations. At the high school in Cambridge, Massachusetts, for example, the methods for controlling athletics were modeled directly on the techniques of nearby Harvard.[45] High school debating societies rather slavishly emulated the practices of late 19th-century colleges, subordinating spontaneous discussion to trench warfare, with faculty coaches acting the role of generals and often foot soldiers. One commentator protested that high school debating was so regimented that it had virtually become a sport, a game played according to exact rules. The only difference, she added, was that in the hundred yard dash the athlete and coach parted ways at the starting line, while in debating the coaches often wrote the speeches and virtually ran the race.[46]

By the 1920s, management of the high school extracurriculum had become a flourishing subdivision of the science of education. "Experts" on the extracurriculum formed virtually a profession within a profession.[47] But during the early years of the 20th century, when the extension of the social role of the school was just starting, misunderstandings were frequent. Ella Flagg Young related that her original expositions of the value of social activities in school met with bewildered looks from veteran teachers who thought that she was defending the right of students to play cards.[48] She could do little more than reply about the value of "co-operative power." Webster Cook of the high school in Saginaw, Michigan, began a speech on "Deportment in the High School" with a conventional call for teachers to make the establishment of order—tautologically defined as the quality of orderliness—the foundation of school government, but then launched into a twilight zone by suggesting that there was actually a much more fundamental meaning of school order, one that resembled the French military concept of esprit de corps, "a mass spirit in which each individual surrenders himself and which, except so far as they have surrendered, is always different from

183

the spirit composing the mass." [49] The trouble with the traditional idea of school order, Cook argued, was that it neglected the spirit of the school; outwardly conforming behavior might conceal a vicious heart. The job of the teacher was to get at the soul of the school; for this end, activities—or, more accurately, the channeling of activities toward common goals—constituted a valuable means. So too was a softening of the forms of discipline. Given a choice between sticking on a point of order and promoting school spirit, it was always better to choose the latter, for order would take care of itself if only the heart had been touched: "it is better to forego a point for the time being than seriously to alienate our school." [50]

On the surface, and only there, school authority was weakening in the first decade of the 20th century, as the Spencerianism which had been a feature of school manuals two or three decades earlier gave way to calls for a sympathetic understanding of the student's viewpoint. Florence Milner actually compared the teacher to a host or hostess, the students to invited guests in the classroom—a far cry from in loco parentis.[51] But if the exercise of authority was becoming less obtrusive, its scope was now much greater, for authority was being extended as never before over the spare-time pursuits of students.

The rate of change varied from school to school, but as a rule of thumb, the more receptive the administrators of a school were to theories which emphasized the social functions of education, the more likely they were to experiment with the regulation of student social life. The University of Chicago High School provides an apt illustration, since the university was a leading center of educational progressivism during the first decade of the 20th century. In 1907 the dean of the high school, William B. Owen, proposed a "programme of enlargement of the functions of the school to include the general social training of the child," words that could as well have been extracted from the writings of John Dewey.[52] Three years later, Franklin W. Johnson described the results of Owen's experiment at the high school. Not only had faculty members been assigned to advise every student club, but even the meeting times of activities were now regulated. Music clubs met on Monday, science and literary clubs on Tuesday, and so on. The tentacles of control extended to dances too, for to discourage students from patronizing sleazy dance halls in the neighborhood, the school conducted its own socials, with teachers and parents present in abundance to ensure "frequent and general mixing" of partners.[53]

The mood of college life rather than the sum of its parts was a magnet for secondary schools in the early 1900s. Throughout the 1880s and 1890s the reading public had been inundated by a wave of articles and books laying bare the *sanctum sanctorum* of secret societies, fraternity life, and team sports on the campus. Articles on Skull and Bones or Hasty Pudding were not meant for alumni, who knew as much as they needed or wanted to know about the collegiate subculture, nor were they describing new developments, for most of the organizations had flourished for decades. Rather, they were aimed at parents who were nongraduates but who were beginning to entertain thoughts of a college education for their children.[54] Small wonder that high school officials often complained that public secondary schools were victimized by the irresistible image which the colleges projected.[55]

For most young people who reached secondary school during the early 1900s, high school marked the end of formal education, a fact which makes it unlikely that high schools were merely imitating colleges. Most schoolteachers and principals had taken the normal school route rather than the college route into teaching; in origin they were closer to the lower than upper middle class.[56] Their rhetoric, too, had a sober and earnest ring, unlike the speeches of college presidents who celebrated the gentlemanly qualities of resourcefulness, courage, and heroism. Yet one of the remarkable features of the American college in the 20th century has been its ability to woo a middle-class clientele into institutions whose physical trappings are often aristocratic—the manicured lawns, Gothic buildings, academic pomp, and sporting ethos. Similarly, one of the notable features of the early 20th-century high school was the way in which the realities of terminal education at age 16 or 18 coexisted with aspirations for college education. One study of a midwestern high school indicated that, while most of the students were sons of laborers, farmers, or petty merchants, most aspired to be doctors or lawyers, career goals which demanded college education.[57] Other studies showed that, despite the introduction of the elective system (pioneered by President Eliot at Harvard) into high schools between 1900 and 1910, most students still opted for traditional courses. The proportion of high school students taking Latin, for example, actually rose at a time when many were arguing that high schools could flourish only if they became more utilitarian, and at a time when academic psychology was downgrading the "mental discipline" arguments long used in defense of Latin.[58]

Although public high schools around 1900 copied the practices of colleges in sundry ways, efforts to turn high schools into social and cultural as well as academic centers for youth cannot be entirely explained by the principle of emulation, since the high schools diverged from the collegiate model in several significant ways. At a time when college officials were eager first to clean up and then to sanction fraternities, high school authorities were making repeated and often successful efforts to destroy them. The abolition of secret fraternities and sororities was, for

185

example, one feature of the attempt to coordinate the social activities of youth at the University of Chicago High School. In 1906 the Supreme Court of Washington upheld a school board's decision to bar members of a high school fraternity from participation in all sponsored school activities, even though the fraternity met at the homes of members after school hours.[59] Fraternities, a school official wrote bluntly in 1917, "encourage wrong attitudes and a spirit of disregard for the established order."[60] In comparison with college presidents of the 1890s, who did not object to occasional skylarking by the undergraduates, high school officials in the early 1900s were virtually obsessed with instilling conformity and obedience in students.

A second distinguishing feature of the high school extracurriculum was the central place that student self-government occupied in it. Attemps to introduce student government into colleges after 1880 had usually foundered on the indifference of students themselves who, like their antebellum counterparts, desired less rather than more contact with agents of authority.[61] The rise of student government in high schools fit the mood of Progressives who were convinced that students had to learn the principles of government if bossism and corruption were to be driven from American cities. As Joel H. Spring has noted:

> Education responded to what was perceived to be the disintegration of human relationships in the growing urban environment by attempting to use the schools as a new focal point for community life. The image of the city was similar to the one applied to other corporate bodies. Specialization and the interdependence of the city required both a cooperative individualism and a coordination of individual tasks.[62]

Behind the growing importance of the Progressive ideal that society be run on bureaucratic principles lay the same transformation in the nature of economic organization which had contributed to the growth spurt of high schools after 1890. In the 1860s and 1870s both cities and businesses had been run with little attention to bureaucratic principles. A figure like William Marcy Tweed rose to power in New York not by defending or even defining the public interest but by appeasing all of the private, fragmented interest groups of the city. Tweed's New York, Seymour J. Mandelbaum has written, contained "a series of elites that commanded the respect of many limited 'publics.' The fragmentation of power and respect curtailed the work of administrative agencies which attempted to regulate a complex environment in the general interest."[63] Business leaders often sought reform, but their ambitions were frustrated by the fact that their own business experience did not equip them to run a complex city government. "Business firms expanding their scope in the later decades of the century encountered many of the same problems which had earlier plagued the city. The benefits gained from the division of labor were dissipated by a breakdown of the administrative mechanism." [64] As businesses grew in scale after 1870, the initial response of entrepreneurs was to redouble their efforts to keep abreast of all the details of the operation, but by 1900 many business leaders had come to recognize the impossibility of the task and had turned to the model of bureaucratic organization, with separate managers for each subdivision all working toward common goals.

Bureaucratic methods of organization, which developed toward the end of the 19th century in business, influenced both colleges and high schools. Administrative specialties developed in the former during the 1880s and 1890s. With enrollments growing, it became impossible to divide students into small bodies under a single administrator; instead, the responsibilities of administration were divided among several officers, each performing a single duty toward all the students. [65] The emergence of "experts" on the extracurriculum was one phase of the same development in secondary schools, but a more important effect was the growing belief among educators that participation in a supervised extracurriculum would teach both a mastery of wholesome individual skills and a cooperative spirit. [66]

Public high school officials spoke of like-spiritedness, but they often imposed like-mindedness. The years between 1900 and 1920 witnessed the virtual destruction of student autonomy wherever the high school was transformed into a total environment for teenagers. Student self-government conveyed the semblance of power without its substance, for principals kept an absolute veto over anything worth vetoing. [67] For those middle-class young people privileged to attend high school, the status of studentship was becoming nearly coterminous with that of youth. Of course, it was still possible for a young person to acquire a political education without playing out the charade of student self-government. The avenues from street gangs to politics were still paved in 1900, just as they had been in the days of Boss Tweed, who rose from a street gang to leadership of a volunteer fire company to alderman, congressman, and mayor. [68] In Boston during the 1890s, settlement house workers described the way in which boys still graduated from South End street gangs to young men's political and social clubs at age 18. [69] But for a segment of middle-class youth in 1900, this was no longer an approved route of access to politics.

It is difficult to believe that the organization of the social life of youth around high schools occurred merely because educators desired it. For generations, educators had desired all sorts of things, only to be frustrated by student hostility. Attempts to impose arbitrary discipline on college students between 1800 and 1850 had been met by repeated student strikes and rebellions which had brought professors and presidents to their knees. Academies, too, had often been the scenes of student strikes before 1880. In the 1860s, Samuel Train Dutton, then a student at a coeducational academy in New Hampshire, deliberately violated a rule which forbade male students from joining in the games of female students and played croquet with the young ladies. As a result, Dutton was suspended and forbidden to graduate with his class. In retaliation, the class threatened to strike, and Dutton was quickly reinstated. Dutton then went on to Yale, graduated, and became a highly successful school administrator, first in South Norwalk, Connecticut, and later in Brookline, Massachusetts. In each place Dutton built a reputation for success in organizing the social activities of young people around the school; in neither did he experience any serious opposition from students.[70]

A brief comparison between two manuals on school discipline—one written by Hiram Orcutt in 1871, the other by Frances M. Morehouse in 1914—underscores the change which came over student behavior between 1870 and 1920. A veteran of decades of academy teaching, Orcutt entertained old-fashioned ideas about discipline, including a preference for appeals to the Bible as a way to reach the conscience of the student. But Orcutt conceded that reading from scripture would be of little avail against the main problem which most teachers faced, the student rebellion. Rather, rebellions had to be put down quickly "by stunning, crushing blows."[71] Like many schoolmasters of his day and earlier, Orcutt saw himself as a kind of pugilist whose success depended on an ability to paralyze his numerically superior opponent with a single devastating blow.

In contrast, Frances M. Morehouse, who was supervisor of high school teaching at the Illinois State Normal University, addressed herself to a different problem: the disorganized and subterranean dissent manifested by the widespread inhaling of chloroform by high school students and the practice of shooting heroin and cocaine.[72] Actually, addiction to narcotics was widespread in 19th-century America, and not merely among youth. Patent medicines often contained opium, leading individuals to addiction at early ages. But Morehouse was not describing the inevitable addiction which came with overuse of medicinal elixirs, nor the solitary experimentation with laughing gas, but a fad among high school students, "a fad before the teachers are aware that it has been introduced."[73]

It is impossible to gain a solid conception of the extent of experimentation with or addiction to narcotics among high school students in the early 20th century, and hence impossible to generalize that the assertive and aggressive impulses behind student rebellions in earlier generations had given way to the despair behind dope addiction. But rebellions were becoming comparatively infrequent in the late 19th century. Whether in college or high school, students were becoming less violent, more tractable. Why? Perhaps because authority itself was so much more firmly entrenched by 1900. High schools and colleges now served vital functions in training men for desirable positions in the economy. A college education, once valuable only for entry into the learned professions of law, medicine, and the ministry, was now a passport to the higher levels of business management as well as to the newer professions and professional schools, while high schools were major turnpikes to colleges. Students who engaged in mass rebellions against school authority were now faced with the loss of more than a piece of parchment. Indeed, the fact that college and secondary school officials were increasingly able to substitute sweet reasonableness for the mailed fist was a sign of their growing power, for it was no longer necessary to intimidate students with vainglorious shows of force when so many more subtle agents of control were at hand. Perhaps, too, young people who had been exposed to the even and consistent regimen of middle-class Victorian homes, a regimen which substituted appeals to reason and conscience for corporal punishment and humiliation, were less likely than their predecessors in the 1820s and 1830s to oscillate between extremes of deference and violent rage. Whatever the cause may have been, the acquiescence of young people in the transformation of the school was an apt instance of youth making its own history.

The contours of student social life in the early 20th-century high schools were shaped not only by the ambitions of principals and the acquiescent mood of students but also by the desires of parents. Dutton and others involved in the expansion of the social role of the school often commented on the value to them of parental cooperation. By 1900, parents' associations sponsored by the conservative National Congress of Mothers were beginning to play a formal role in supervising both high school students and their activities. The heavy emphasis on conformity and obedience in early 20th-century secondary education reflected the desires of parents who were eager to ensure that their teenage children did not deviate from the course that would steer them successfully between the Scylla and Charybdis of boy labor and the dead-end job. [74]

The Youth Savers

Another set of values behind the creation of institutions for youth in the 1880s and 1890s was muscular Christianity. Imported from Britain, muscular Christianity flowered in the "young people's movement" in

Protestant churches during the last two decades of the 19th century. In retrospect, muscular Christianity seems worth little more than a passing glance, at least in comparison to secondary education, which has experienced such astonishing growth since 1900. Yet, at the time, its influence and that of the institutions it spawned affected far more young people than did public high schools, a fact which becomes less surprising if we recall that pietists in America had long professed a deep interest in the moral welfare of youth. In many ways, muscular Christianity was the final act of a melodrama which had been playing to packed houses for much of the 19th century and which, in its several scenes, had exhibited sundry attempts by evangelical Protestants to "save" youth from cities, gambling dens, grog shops, and bawdy houses. By any measure, the final act was the worst.

Promoters of Christian youth organizations during the 1880s and 1890s persistently misunderstood the precedents for and significance of their achievement. John H. Vincent wrote in 1892 that "there never has been a time in the history of the Church when so much attention has been given to the organization and discipline of young people as now." According to Vincent, "we are just beginning to distinguish between children and young people and to order our efforts in the line of this recognition." Another spokesman claimed that before the young people's movement the church had been a stranger to its youth. A Methodist called the Epworth League the most remarkable development in the history of the church. Whatever the goals of the movement, hyperbole was its style.[75]

The young people's movement grew impressively. The Epworth League, organized in 1890, had over a million members by 1895. Christian Endeavor, originally Congregationalist but ultimately dominated by other denominations, embraced nearly 850 local societies and 30,000 members in 1885 and grew to 660,000 by 1890. The Student Volunteer Movement, begun in 1886, formally organized in 1888 under the aegis of the evangelist Dwight L. Moody, and committed to the "evangelization of the world in this generation," had sent over a thousand missionaries into the field by 1898.[76]

These figures appear to support Vincent's assertion that youth was suddenly being discovered by the churches, but a closer examination permits no such conclusion. Such rapid growth was possible only because of the prior existence of young people's societies in churches, societies now federated into national organizations. National organization was new, but not the principle of separate organizations for youth. As early as 1675, for example, the church in Norwich, Connecticut, had stipulated that all males and females 13 and over "shall frequent the meetings appointed in private for their instruction, while they continue under family government, or until they are received into full communion in the church." [77] A treatise on religious education published in 1814 advocated a rigid separation in all parishes of children 14 and under from "youths" over 14.[78] For much of the 19th century, Sunday schools had contained special classes for teenagers. Whatever the distinctiveness of the young people's movement, it did not lie in a sudden discovery of youth.

Although precedents for church youth societies existed, the period between 1880 and 1900 was important, for in these years Protestant churches attempted, as never before, to take over the spare-time activities of youth. This was less the result of a sudden discovery of youth than of factors intrinsic to Protestantism at the end of the century. In prior decades, local and semi-permanent church societies for young people rarely existed outside the eastern states, mainly because the settlement of the frontier put severe limits on the spread of institutional Christianity. Even in the 1850s, Protestants in rural villages in Michigan could complain that "we have no Sabbath, no minister, no gospel, no schools of any kind"; between 1840 and 1870, Methodist work in Illinois and Wisconsin was principally missionary work.[79] Further, nearly half the 360 Methodist missions reporting in 1850–1851 were in the older conferences of the East; many were in communities whose original population had been depleted by wholesale migrations.[80]

By the 1880s and 1890s, however, many communities in the Midwest were reaching a level of ecclesiastical sophistication attained much earlier in the East. A settled and secure ministry replaced the earlier reliance on periodic revivals, informal class meetings, and peripatetic circuit riders. The growth of Sunday schools was one measure of the change which saw large areas of Protestant America shift from the tactics of the revival to the structured activity of the institutional church. After spectacular growth in the 1820s and early 1830s, the Sunday school movement received a severe jolt from the Panic of 1837 and subsequent depression. Rallying briefly during the 1850s, the movement declined again during the Civil War. By the 1870s, however, the curve was rising again, and this time there were few reverses. In 1830 there were 570,000 Sunday school scholars in the United States and Canada; in 1880, 6,949,454; in 1893, 11,669,956. All of this occurred at a time when Protestantism was declining in relative importance in large cities; that it occurred at all was the result of changes outside the great cities, particularly in the Midwest and, to some extent, the Far West.[81]

Intellectual changes complemented institutional changes. New theological currents, named "evangelical liberalism" by one scholar, sanctioned the primacy of moral rather than religious goals and broke with the old evangelical idea that the experience of "saving change" would guarantee moral rectitude. The ideal "progressive" church of the late Gilded Age was one that busied itself with federating members, including young people, into associations for self-improvement or recreation.[82] A study of an Indiana village, published in 1912, described the effects on a single community of the changing role of the church. The principal recreations of the period between 1840 and 1860 had been boxing and wrestling matches among the youth. As late as 1863, local churches sponsored only 14 percent of the social events reported in local papers. By 1910, in contrast, churches sponsored 70 percent of all social events in the village.[83]

These changes occurred primarily outside of large cities, but fear of the metropolis provided the emotional thrust behind the organization of young people's societies. Evangelicals feared great cities. The metropolis was too heterogeneous to allow the sort of moral oversight possible in villages and towns. In the eyes of evangelical Protestants, a combination of immigrants and the liquor interest dominated cities. In the Gilded Age, metropolitan wet populations repeatedly beat back efforts of town and village abstainers to impose prohibition. Prohibition became the symbolic issue over which differences in the cultural and moral values of the native and immigrant populations were fought out. The young people's movement, dry as a stone, was in large measure a response of the native Protestant population to the challenge of the city, but a response which aimed less at elevating the moral tone of the metropolis than at building a moat around villages and towns, the places in which evangelical strength was rising rather than declining.[84]

The primary burden of organizing church social activities fell on the pastor, but at every turn he could draw on church women for support. Not only were churches taking over youth acvitities, but women were often becoming the agents of control. The moral influence of women had long been accorded primacy in the raising of children, but after 1870 female influence in the institutional church scored a number of important gains. In 1886 the Methodist Women's Home Missionary Society appeared. Women increased their influence in the foreign missions as well. By the 1880s roughly half the foreign missionaries sent out by the Methodist Church were women. No female moral society of the antebellum period ever attained the degree of influence of the Women's Christian Temperance Union, which began its work in 1874 and which was joined in the 1880s by the Anti-Saloon League.

Frances Willard, the remarkable leader of the WCTU during the 1880s and 1890s, once said that the difference between the early and late 19th-century temperance movements was the difference between a straight line and a circle. She suggested by the analogy that temperance had given up its reliance on mass pledges and direct exhortation and had instead allied itself with other causes, thus seeking to remove the opportunities as well as the desire for indulgence in liquor. In her eyes, the task of "purifying" the environment had several elements besides temperance. She launched the WCTU into a host of reforms including suppression of the sale of cigarettes to boys, raising the age of consent, and organizing mothers' clubs. In 1885 the WCTU established a department of social purity, headed by John Harvey Kellogg and his wife, and thus linked itself to a campaign which, beginning in the 1870s with isolated attempts to prevent state legislatures from licensing and regulating prostitution, swelled into a national crusade aimed at purification of the entire society through the advocacy of premarital chastity. For purity reformers, sexual abuse was the source of all evil. Accordingly, the goals of sex education in the family and vigilant supervision of the child's environment became even more important than the suppression of prostitution. The WCTU, by far the most effective organization in expanding the scope of purity reform, attacked not merely private tippling but the atmosphere of public indecency.[85]

The WCTU met with its warmest reception in the Midwest, but an institution of eastern origin, Chautauqua, provided the liaison between the WCTU and other reformers. Chautauqua, the name of a lake in southwestern New York, became the title of an adult education movement that developed out of a normal school for Sunday school teachers established in 1874.[86] John H. Vincent, one of the founders of Chautauqua, went on to become the chief spokesman for the Epworth League as well as for Sunday school reform. Temperance was ever a prominent topic at Chautauqua summer sessions. Frances Willard was the first woman to appear on Chautauqua's platform other than as a speaker on Sunday school topics; the third summer session in 1876 was less a school than a temperance convention.[87] By the early 1900s temperance Chautauquas were invading Iowa and Nebraska, always with the local patronage of the WCTU and the Anti-Saloon League.[88] But Chautauqua was more than merely a center for temperance agitation. By 1886, Chautauqua featured a host of model young people's societies—cadet corps, reading clubs, even a "Look-up Legion" to build character in boys. The curriculum of boys-work at Chautauqua included many ideas later popularized by the Boy Scouts.[89] Not the least of these was physical training as a solution to youthful vice; one of its historians suggested that if Chautauqua had had a coat of arms, the appropriate symbol would have been a dumbbell.[90] Chautauqua had significance as a force behind the organization of youth work, but for our purposes it is most valuable as a microcosm of the groups coalescing behind youth work in the late 19th century: Protestant laywomen, Sunday school promoters, and temperance advocates.

The difference between the early and late 19th century lay not merely in the extension of ecclesiastical control over the spare-time activities of youth but in the increasing erosion of the principle of voluntary association by youth. The young men's societies of the 17th through early 19th centuries had been organized by young men themselves; the young people's movement of the 1880s and 1890s, in contrast, consisted entirely of adult-sponsored youth organizations. Francis E. Clark, the founder of Christian Endeavor, unwittingly underscored the change when he mentioned that an antiquarian friend had given him a copy of a sermon delivered by Cotton Mather in 1724 in which Mather had praised religious societies of youth.[91] Clark proceeded to use Mather's point to advertise Christian Endeavor. In fact, Mather's sermon had consisted of two separate addresses. The second, cited by Clark, was a proposal for a model constitution for religious societies of young men, but the first was a sermon on the occasion of the founding of a voluntary association of youth that Mather delivered originally not in 1724, when he was nearing the end of his life, but in 1679, when he was only 16.[92]

Christian youth organizations of the late 19th century downgraded not only voluntarism but intellectuality and spirituality as well. One sign of the direction was the preference of leaders of the young people's movement for "training" rather than "edification." To train youth for church work became a principal slogan of individuals like Francis E. Clark, but neither Clark nor the other leaders were able to define what role in the church young people were to be trained for. Clark offered a list of vapid possibilities: "training in public prayer and confession of the very simplest yet sincerest sort; training in work for others on the lookout and social committees; training in preparation for the prayer-meeting committee; training in temperance and missionary zeal and different sorts of Sunday school work." [93] Even when spokesmen for the young people's movement outlined specific goals, they were so general as to be meaningless (e.g., the immediate conversion of the world) or so trivial as to be ludicrous (e.g., running errands for the pastor). One stalwart of the movement gave unwitting evidence of the quandary when he proclaimed that Christian Endeavor would endure through the ages because of the exact and precise quality of its ideology, an ideology built on "pledged endeavors, united endeavors, and systematic endeavors." [94]

Clark insisted that the difference between training and mere edification was the difference between activity and passivity. In fact, edification had long been associated with the focus of young people's societies on self-culture, an active though not necessarily strenuous objective. Cotton Mather's text for his address to young men had been "edify one another" (1 Thessalonians 5:11). In contrast, nothing in Clark's outline of the function of Christian Endeavor displayed even the faintest interest in self-culture. Clark did not want young people to spend their time reading or worrying about their spiritual condition. Nor did his concept of training include participation by youth in church affairs. He did not want young people to become evangelists or missionaries. He was content to urge that they take an interest in the missions. In effect, he substituted busywork for participation. In 1904, William B. Forbush, a Congregationalist pastor, reported that only in a small fraction of churches did any plans exist for incorporating the activities of young people's societies into church affairs.[95] Christian Endeavor had become a halfway house for youth who, while technically converted, were not assimilated into the active life of the church. According to Forbush, the problem was not ministerial hostility but perplexity in local churches "as to how to find enough activities in the church really worth while which have not already been pre-empted by others older and more competent." [96] He did not add, although he might well have, that by substituting busywork for spiritual concern the young people's movement had left itself defenseless against this very difficulty.

In view of the structure of Christian Endeavor and similar organizations, the significance of the concept of training lay less in youthful activism than in its connotation of an adult-youth, superior-inferior relationship. An illustration of this was the importance attached throughout the young people's movement to the development of surrogates for the involvement in church affairs. The most notable of these surrogates was the pledge, usually a commitment to live cleanly and to obey orders, which virtually all of the youth organizations demanded of initiates. Adult leaders waxed eloquent on the character-building effects of the pledge, on its "hard, rigid, cast-iron" quality.[97] No account of the progress of the movement was complete without a reprinting of pledges in an appendix. Since conversion narratives earlier in the 19th century had often concluded with a declaration by the convert of his pledge to some course of action, the pledges of the young people's movement invite comparison with the conversion cycle of the early 1800s. But the comparison cannot be pushed very far. The Christian Endeavor pledge, to take the most famous example, was not the product of any kind of self-analysis. It was devoid of theological content and nearly devoid of moral content. It was not a pledge to do anything in particular. The act of pledging and the ardor it summoned up were more important than what was being pledged. In other words, the focus had shifted from content to process and from involvement to substitutes for involvement.

Consistent with their emphasis on ardor and training, spokesmen for the young people's movement had an incurable fondness for military metaphors. Indeed, between 1870 and 1910 the use of military models for the education of youth reached a high point of popularity. A disproportionately large number of the private schools established in America during these years relied principally on military drill to inculcate discipline. Both in America and Britain, moreover, the attitude of religious leaders and the religious public toward the army had shifted after mid-century from hostility to broad sympathy. Out of the Crimean campaign came stirring biographies of soldier-saints like Hedley Vicars, while the Civil War in America had witnessed the rise of various types of voluntary religious work among the troops.[98] Julia Ward Howe's "Battle Hymn of the Republic" revived military imagery in hymnody no less than contemporary British hymns like Sabine Baring-Gould's "Onward Christian Soldiers." Dwight L. Moody, who had labored as an evangelist for the army and navy committee of the YMCA, brought his militaristic vocabulary to Britain in 1867 and acted later as impresario for the American debut of Christian activists like Henry Drummond, an earnest Scot whose addresses in the 1880s inspired the early conferences of the Student Volunteer Movement.[99]

Puritans, it is true, had always been fond of comparing the saints to an army, but early 19th-century evangelical literature had made very little use of military metaphors. As an evangelical commented in 1832,

to the greater number of persons to whom we can offer illustrations of Christian topics, no language sounds so idly, no figures appear so insignificant, no forms of commonplace so "flat and unprofitable," as those which represent in a military character, the exertions by which men are to evince themselves the servants of God.[100]

In contrast, the national conventions of organizations such as Christian Endeavor and the Student Volunteer Movement resounded with a drum-and-trumpet Christianity which probably made some youthful members wonder whether they had not accidentally wandered into the halls of a regimental armory. The church had learned, a Baptist spokesman declared in 1892, to appeal to the "soldier-like" instincts of youth.[101] Christian Endeavor members were routinely compared to soldiers and reminded of the exploits of Civil War heroes whose courage and ardor had withstood the test of the winter marches of the 1860s.[102] Theodore Cuyler, a leader in Christian Endeavor, applied the same analogy to the distinction between conversion and sanctification, claiming that "conversion is simply an enlisting in the army of Jesus. The battles and hard bivouacs are yet before you."[103] J. Ross Stevenson told the Student Volunteer Movement's 1898 convention that "we may liken this to a council of war, in which we take account of the field to be won, the opposing forces to be met, the agencies we are to employ, the enlistment that is needed, the equipment we must have, and the spiritual authority which must be recognized." [104] John R. Mott told the same convention that "tomorrow morning we shall fling out the battle line through all the length and breadth of the United States and Canada, and within a few months . . . it will extend to the very ends of the earth." [105] Mott was a little fuzzy about the exact mission of the troops; he suggested a motley array of causes ranging from the liberation of 200 million Chinese women from "enslavement" to the suppression of gambling in Latin America. But wherever his troops were going, they were moving in step. So too were those of James Vance, a Newark minister, who addressed the 1906 convention of the Student Volunteer Movement with the ringing declaration that "we can hear the blare of trumpets, the roll of drums, the tramp of soldiers, and the voice of our great Commander as He sends us to the front with 'Forward, march!' " [106]

The admiration for paramilitary organization implicit in such language represented a sharp break with the evangelical tradition. Evangelicals had never shown high esteem for the antebellum volunteer military companies; rather, they had viewed the latter as little more than social clubs for vicious youth. Further, evangelical Protestants had long condemned the strut and swagger implicit in military education for feeding the vanity of youth, the very thing that had to be repressed. [107]

Any comparison between antebellum military companies or military schools and late 19th-century paramilitary youth organizations in churches breaks down quickly. The volunteer companies had been formed by young men themselves, while organizations like the Boys' Brigade in the 1880s and 1890s were strictly adult-sponsored, created and controlled by men for the benefit of boys. Further, the volunteer military companies had had various functions to perform. Despite all the imbibing that went on in them, the volunteer companies had acted from time to time as police, militia, and ceremonial reception committees. The Boys' Brigade, on the other hand, had no military or even civil functions to perform. As its defenders pointed out, in an unintentionally double-edged argument, the charge of militarism leveled against them was unfair, since the Brigade was not really training boys to be soldiers but to be better boys.

If we compare Christian youth organizations of the late 19th century with the private military schools established before 1850 by Captain Alden Partridge and his disciples, a similar transformation can be seen. Here is Captain Partridge writing words in 1825 that could as well have been composed in 1895:

> Under a military system, subordination and discipline are much more easily preserved than under any other. Whenever a youth can be impressed with the true principles and feelings of a soldier, he becomes as a matter of

course, subordinate, honorable, and manly. He disdains subterfuge and prevarication, and all that low cunning which is but too prevalent. He acts not the part of the assassin, but if he have an enemy, he meets him openly and fairly.[108]

But Partridge next moved to a discussion of the standing army, "that bane of a republic, and engine of oppression in the hands of a despot," and concluded that military education served the key function of training soldiers for the militia. It was this part of Partridge's argument that could not have been echoed by a spokesman for the Boys' Brigade later in the century, for the latter had no goal in mind beyond the character-building function of military education. No longer a technique for training militia, military regimen in the 1880s had acquired an exclusively socializing function.

The leaders of late 19th-century Christian youth organizations often extolled youth for intrinsic idealism, heroism, and chivalry. Amos R. Wells argued that boys responded naturally to the pledge required by Christian Endeavor to live life in earnest, because the pledge appealed to their innate chivalry: "They treat the pledge as a knight of old treated his knightly vow." [109] Many of the branches of the young people's movement employed chivalric and/or military imagery in their titles. The "Captains of Ten" sought to promote "loyalty to Christ." The Princely Knights of Character Castle, founded in 1895 for boys aged 12 to 18, sought to inculcate purity, patriotism, and heroism, and had offices such as "herald" and "keeper of the dungeon." At times, church organizations fused militarism and chivalry. The Church Temperance League was modeled on the paramilitary Boys' Brigade, but its members were divided into Young Crusaders, aged 8 to 16, and the Knights of Temperance, aged 16 to 21.[110]

A correlative of this disposition to extol youth as a quality, to praise young people for putative idealism and heroism, was an inclination to censure boys and girls who simulated adult behavior. Despite a professed interest in character building, the organizers of church youth societies had no tolerance for precocious youth. Young men who became religious in 1820 or 1830 had not been expected to profess a viewpoint any different from that of adult believers. Perhaps youth might not grasp religious principles as fully as adults; perhaps youth would display greater recklessness or ardor. But young people were not supposed to profess a lesser version of the creed of adults. Christian Endeavor and similar branches of the young people's movement, in contrast, were religions in themselves—religions of boyish ingenuity, naïve idealism, and adolescence.[111]

From "Stranger Youth" to Adolescent Boy

The foremost evangelical youth organization of the 19th century, the YMCA, could trace its lineage directly back to 1844, when a group of London clerks founded the first Association, and indirectly to the long tradition of young men's societies like the ones Cotton Mather had founded in the 17th century. But the YMCA changed its focus and ideology so completely in the last two decades of the 19th century that by 1900 it was scarcely distinguishable from the other arms of the young people's movement.

The original goal of the YMCA was to provide spiritual comfort and practical assistance to the young men who flooded the cities in the 1850s. "How is the stranger youth armed to meet the attack of worldly excitement and sensual allurement?" Daniel Lord had asked in 1852. His answer, the provision of watchful care for the young stranger, shaped the scope and thrust of the Associations which sprang up in American cities in the 1850s.[112]

In its early years the YMCA contained a broad range of ages. The minimum age was usually set at 15 or 16, and some men as old as 35 or 40 were admitted. In practice, the great majority of members before 1860 were in the 18–30 age bracket. What later became known as boys-work either did not exist at all or took the form of occasional rescue missions for street rowdies. As late as 1865, a YMCA convention passed a resolution criticizing boys-work, even the sort of city mission work that did not involve the incorporation of boys into the regular organization of the Association.[113]

The boys-work movement had its orgins in the late 1860s but began in earnest only after 1880. During the 1870s, boys-work in most communities was under the control of women, the same sort of genteel ladies who took the lead in the WCTU and similar organizations for the suppression of vice; in 1879 a writer in the *Watchman* argued that boys-work would have to be led by other boys or by women, for in most communities adult males would not waste their time on institutions for juveniles.[114] But within a decade, various associations had established boys-work departments, usually run by male secretaries. The rise of boys-work coincided with the emergence of a group of professional secretaries in the YMCA, men like Robert McBurney, Richard C. Morse, and L. L. Doggett, who rescued the Association from its post–Civil War doldrums by the application of business techniques. The professional orientation of the secretaries guaranteed that boys-work would be organized "efficiently," which meant in practice that it would be kept

199

separate from the other branches of the Association, less because of a romantic idealization of boyhood than because Association organizers were usually happiest when they could break a whole unit into digestible parts.[115]

Boys-work from the 1880s onward bore little resemblance to the Association's early experiments with missions to street rowdies. The boys recruited in the 1880s and 1890s were not pariahs neglected by fashionable churches, but were increasingly middle-class in origin.[116] This shift in focus came easily to the Association, for its regular membership had always been composed of middle-class youth. Formal studies of regular members in the 1890s confirmed what Association leaders had long suspected: YMCA membership was top-heavy with young merchants and clerks, and day laborers were in short supply.[117]

The boys who came under Association supervision after 1880 varied in age from town to town and city to city. In Pulaski, Tennessee, boys-work encompassed ages 9 to 20; in Dayton, Ohio, 13 to 20; in Washington, D.C., 14 to 20. With the introduction of sophisticated organizational techniques, however, boys-work tended to stabilize in the 8–16 age range.[118] Local associations traditionally had made adult membership available to boys at 15 or 16, although in practice the Association had aimed primarily at those in their late teens and up, rather than at those in their middle teens.[119] Prior to the rise of boys-work, however, the presence of a minority of 15- and 16-year-olds in the Association had no normative implications. Middle-class clerks who came at 15 to a city and applied for membership in the Association had shared the experiences of older members, becoming, so to speak, junior partners of the same corporation. But as Association tentacles ranged downward to boys-work in the 1880s, the 16-year-old who joined now no longer straddled the lower steps of an escalator but was, instead, incorporated into an essentially self-contained and adult-sponsored organization for juveniles. In this respect, Association boys-work resembled branches of the young people's movement like the Boys' Brigade, for the Brigade, no less than the boys-work department of the Association, focused on teenagers to the exclusion of young adults in their 20s.

The mixture of rural nostalgia and paramilitary organization which was to pervade boys-work during the late 19th and early 20th centuries can be detected as early as 1881, when the boys' department of the Brooklyn YMCA launched the first of a series of annual excursions to the upper Hudson River. None of the boys is known to have recorded his observations, but the experience must have been jarring. First there was the trip up the still beautiful if no longer sublime Hudson, then, on arrival, a march in step to special barracks where the juvenile army was quartered. Whether jarring or not, the combination of trips to the country and tight organization was to reappear again and again in ensuing decades.[120]

At first, no theoretical justification for the scope or content of boys-work existed. During the 1880s many of the boys' leaders were fundamentalists, and boys' meetings were as filled with the Holy Spirit as with nature walks and marching orders. A radical change began only toward the end of the 1880s, with the inspiration provided in Britain by Henry Drummond and in America by Luther H. Gulick.

Drummond was born in Scotland in 1851, the nephew of a tractarian. Despite an erratic record at the University of Edinburgh, he resolved to study for the ministry of the strongly evangelical Scottish Free Church. In his youth, Drummond fell under the influence of William Ellery Channing and Ralph Waldo Emerson, deriving from them an optimistic belief in individual will power and the possibilities of religious growth which he then combined with the traditional evangelism of the Free Church. During the 1870s, Drummond became a lecturer on natural science at the University of Glasgow, and from that vantage point he attempted a second and riskier reconciliation, that of science and religion. In *The Natural Law in the Spiritual World* Drummond sought to establish the fundamental congruity of scientific and religious phenomena by suggesting that the laws of growth and regeneration, so evident in the natural world, were recapitulated in the spiritual world, specifically in conversion, regeneration, and the growth of character.[121] Drummond claimed that his method had been inductive: he had first noted natural phenomena and then marked their congruity with spiritual experiences familiar to every Protestant. The linkage was provided by "life," a word Drummond used mystically and interchangeably in either department without pausing, as his biographer noted, to inquire whether the two kinds of phenomena had anything more in common than a name.[122]

The Natural Law in the Spiritual World sold 120,000 copies in Britain and far more in America. Drummond's willingness to confront the most pressing intellectual problem of his day accounted for part of the book's success, but Drummond also benefited from the prior familiarity of the American religious public with his work as an ardent follower of Dwight L. Moody and Ira Sankey. Deeply moved by the American evangelists during their successful Edinburgh revivals of 1873, Drummond became their foremost Scottish disciple, stirring young men everywhere with his warmth and, incidentally, raising generous sums of money to finance the expansion of the YMCA. Drummond was so impressed by Moody and Sankey that, on first visiting America in 1879, he passed up an invitation to dine in Boston with Longfellow and Oliver Wendell Holmes, Sr., in order to visit the evangelists in Cleveland.[123]

In the 1880s, Moody took the lead in introducing Drummond to American college audiences and particularly to the Student Volunteer Movement, which Drummond actively promoted during the rest of his life and for which he became a patron saint after his premature death in 1894. In the summer of 1887, Drummond addressed rapt audiences at the Northfield Conference, which was staged under Moody's auspices but which reached a stratum of the educated public that Moody had never been able to penetrate. To the extent that American college students could still be stirred by religion, Drummond was the man who stirred them more than anyone else. Contemporaries agreed that the man was bigger than his books, that his presence radiated a spiritual force rarely encountered since the days of the circuit riders. Drummond's American visit of 1887 turned into a triumphal procession; requests for appearances and lectures poured in upon him from college presidents, pastors' associations, women's clubs, and teachers' organizations.[124] Charles Thwing characterized the nature of Drummond's appeal: "his youth, his ease of approach, his ability, his simplicity, his method of satisfying the reason before attempting to arouse the feelings or to move the will—appeal with special persuasiveness to college men." [125]

No late 19th-century evangelical sought more vigorously than Drummond to harmonize evolutionary science and religion, just as no evangelical sought more earnestly to reconcile traditional Protestant techniques of moral suasion with progressive theology. The new evangelism preached by Drummond combined the old emphasis on personal responsibility with a modern disposition to mute the proclamation of man's unworthiness. But Drummond's accomplishment was, at best, an artful juggling act, more an illustration than a resolution of the crisis confronting evangelicalism in the late 19th century. He could claim in one breath that "all formal religions are efforts to escape spirituality" and that *"the new Evangelism must not be doctrinal,"* and in the next that "with regard to doctrine, . . . let me say at once we must recognize it as one of the three absolutely essential possessions of a Christian Church." [126] His ideas were so amorphous that, on visiting Harvard, he was innocently amazed to find that he and the Unitarian professors agreed on most religious issues.

Most of Drummond's work in America was with college students, but even before he came to America in 1887 he had become involved in Britain with boys-work, specifically with the Boys' Brigade, which he served as honorary vice-president and which he founded in Australia and promoted in America. Like other evangelicals of his day, Drummond sought always to appeal to the animal spirits of the boy, or rather the Boy, for Drummond always capitalized the word. He was convinced that attempts to cultivate directly the qualities of intellectuality and spirituality in boys would go for naught, just as he was convinced that the army drill and uniforms of the Brigade were in tune with "Boy nature." [127]

Drummond constructed a bridge from traditional evangelicalism (which had censured youth as a quality) to late 19th-century evangelical Protestants, who were prone to celebrate youthfulness. Luther Halsey Gulick, fourteen years younger than Drummond, built an equally important bridge from the evangelical youth work of the 1890s to the more secular youth organizations of the Progressive Era.

Born in 1865 in Honolulu to Protestant missionary parents, Gulick attended Oberlin College and took a medical degree at New York University. In 1887 he moved to Springfield, Massachusetts, to conduct summer courses in gymnastics at the School for Christian Workers (later American International University), run by the YMCA. Gulick went far beyond his co-workers at Springfield in his belief that gymnastics and team sports had spiritual as well as hygienic value. Team sports encouraged "heroic subordination of self to the group," a quality which he viewed as essentially religious. Gulick's idea of religion, in turn, had no room for introspection or piety.[128] "The religious life," he wrote, "must be energetic, enthusiastic, and executive." [129] Gulick portrayed Christ in terms indistinguishable from those of Thomas Hughes, author of *Tom Brown's School Days* and *The Manliness of Christ;* Christ was not meek or gentle but forceful and dynamic, the first muscular Christian.[130] In the thought of Hughes and Gulick, boyishness and manliness came together in opposition to feminine qualities. Thomas Arnold of Rugby would have viewed a reference to the "manly boy" as a contradiction, but for Hughes and Gulick the manly boy became the embryo of the muscular Christian.

More than anyone else, Gulick (who designed the YMCA emblem, a triangle symbolizing spirit at the apex and mind and body at the feet) was responsible for directing boys-work toward organized games. Gulick argued that team sports were natural to Anglo-Saxon boys during adolescence. Compared to Drummond, Gulick was uninterested in military metaphors, but he was no less representative of the sort of man attracted into boys-work at the end of the 19th century. Something in the nature of the muscular Christian, either of the athletic or military variety, seemed to carry him into boys-work at the end of the 19th century. The highly structured environment which characterized boys-work was the perfect outlet for men who had fallen into religious skepticism without losing either the moral absolutism or the spiritual enthusiasm that had long marked the evangelical mind. Even Gulick's best friends thought he was "somewhat a czar" because of his insistence on directing activities, but Gulick could have replied that boys, with their simple, nondoctrinal religious sentiments, needed nothing so much as a czar to direct them.

During the 1890s, Gulick's ideas encountered opposition from conservatives within the YMCA, and Gulick ultimately found secular youth work a more congenial atmosphere than the one provided by the lingering piety of the late 19th-century Association. In 1903, Gulick became the director of physical education activities in the New York City public schools. Still later, he became one of the directors of the Boy Scouts of America, an organization formally established in 1910, while his wife was founder of the Camp Fire Girls. Gulick's personal odyssey was representative of the general tendency, for after 1900 boys-work increasingly cast off its evangelical clothing. But even before this shift had occurred, Gulick's ideas received a powerful buttress from the work of the first professional psychologists of religion in America.

The Religious Psychology of Adolescence

It was symptomatic of the keen interest of evangelical Protestants in youth throughout the 19th century that most of the early explorers of adolescent psychology came to the field from the direction of religion rather than education or criminology. G. Stanley Hall, whose interest in religious psychology was partly the result of his own experience and partly the result of the influence of his mentor, William James, claimed as early as 1881 that adolescence was almost exclusively the time of religious conversion.[131] Students of Hall, including Arthur Daniels and James H. Leuba, sought to document Hall's claims in various articles published in the *American Journal of Psychology*.[132] In the preface to his *Psychology of Religion*, Edwin D. Starbuck acknowledged Hall's influence, and in a number of books published between 1900 and 1917, George Coe of Northwestern University explored the relationship between youth and religious sentiments.[133] By the time Hall published *Adolescence* in 1904 he could draw on the work of twenty-five different scholars.[134]

Religious psychologists at the end of the 19th century were imbued by a positivistic preference for studying religious affections in the context of physiological and psychological impulses. "If religion has any reality," Leuba wrote, "it must express itself in psychic and physiological phenomena. The work of a true Science of Religion, as we understand it, is to find out what these subjective manifestations are, and then to treat them as it would any other psychic fact." [135] Coe made a similar point in 1902 when he proclaimed that religion was essentially an experience, "a set of determinable impulses and aspirations, feelings and desires, tendencies to do and to believe and apparent responses to the same on the part of supposed divinity." [136]

This was strong medicine, and at first glance it would seem that religious psychologists were using positivism to destroy the foundations of religious belief. Virtually all the psychologists, however, would have rejected such an interpretation of their goals. By demonstrating the relationship of affective, spiritual, historical, anthropological, and physical forces in the behavior of individuals, religious psychology arrived at a species of pantheism. As Coe put it, the authority of religion depended on its ability to produce a self-certifying life, a form of consciousness "that needs not go beyond itself to find its reasons for existing, because it has within itself something of the Ultimate and Eternal." [137] Similarly, Leuba's positivism concealed a mystical strain: "Neither the theories nor the external practises, rites or ceremonies, but the deeper subjective realities experienced by the individual constitute the material out of which the New Revelation will issue." [138] The content of the New Revelation remained a little uncertain, but it certainly would not include the "noetic" or intellectual side of religion. The most evanescent aspects of religion, he argued, were its intellectual formulations, a category into which he placed "the idea of the soul, of the future life, of God, etc." [139] What was left in Leuba's thought was a universal sense of sin or incompleteness, followed by a release into a state of moral harmony, with religious conversion the specific agency of release.

Coe, Leuba, and Hall himself were each trying to make peace with God in an age of skepticism, but in such a way as not to relegate religion to the role of handmaiden of character development. By proclaiming everything as religious, they were able to thrust religion back into the picture while simultaneously blurring its contours.

Given their interest in religious experience, religious psychologists were inevitably drawn into a discussion of conversion in adolescence, for the latter had long been the usual "season" of awakening. Searching for a way to ground religious experience in evolving human nature, they found in adolescence an ideal field of inquiry not only because of its long-standing association with religious enthusiasm but also because it was so obviously a time of growth and change. If, more than any other stage of life, adolescence illustrated evolutionary growth, and if the adolescent was naturally religious, then it could be argued that evolving human nature was religious.

The first step, taken by all the early religious psychologists except William James, was to prove that adolescence was universally a time of religious awakening. Such proof usually began with the assemblage of data on the age of conversion, derived from questionnaires submitted to evangelical church bodies. In *Adolescence,* Hall presented the tabulated data gathered by his students, but took pains to remind his readers that he had been the first to demonstrate the connection between adolescence and conversion. Strictly speaking, this was true, for previous religious spokesmen had never seen the need to demonstrate statistically what everyone already knew.[140] It is ironic that Hall tried to establish his paternity of so sickly a child, for no degree of statistical compilation could conceal the obvious bias of the method—all of the questionnaires were distributed among evangelicals, and whatever conclusions emerged were applicable to evangelicals alone. In a notably lukewarm introduction to Starbuck's *The Psychology of Religion,* William James observed that the data, "sincere in its general mass," was dictated by the particular phraseology of the evangelical *Volksgeist.* [141]

James's cautionary words were lost on Hall, who insisted that the origins of religious enthusiasm in youth lay in the one universal experience of adolescence, sexual awakening. It was not coincidental that the age of sexual maturity and religious conversion was the same, Hall claimed, for the rise of sexual potency convulsed the whole system and threw the adolescent into storm and stress.[142] Only those who thought of sex as a vile thing, Hall said, could think that religion was in any way degraded by revelation of its intimate relationship to sex. Sex was only the expression of love, and love was the essence of religion. In the end it all came out neatly: the adolescent was simultaneously sexual and amorous, the pure enthusiast in search of truth and beauty. "Youth seeks to be, know, get, feel all that is highest, greatest, best in man's estate." [143]

Behind such lyrical rhetoric lay a belief that the adolescent neither knew himself nor was understood by others. The sexual awakening, Hall argued, jarred youth out of egocentricity, but the transition from self-absorption to social behavior was neither smooth nor inevitable. If nature stretched the soul of the adolescent, it also cautioned obedience and sacrifice, so that the adolescent was always left with a sense of incompleteness and melancholy. Religious concern grew out of this basic dualism of adolescent response, but at the same time it helped to forge identity by directing amorphous drives and instincts toward love and service. Religious conversion was, thus, not only a normal outgrowth of adolescent experience but a "cure" of sorts for storm and stress. To prove his point, Hall referred to the evidence of several hundred personal narratives collected from his students that affirmed the pattern of antecedent despondency and succeeding exhilaration. When we recall that the traditional "steps" of conversion had always located the blackest time of night just before dawn, we can see the wisdom of James's observation that the data assembled by religious psychologists said more about the Protestant *Volksgeist* than about the psychodynamics of human development.

Hall at times described adolescence as a preparation for maturity, but his focus was on the process of becoming, and he often had difficulty conceiving of any fixed outcome of growth. In his thinking, conversion did not mean being "saved," nor was it merely a valuable moral device which guaranteed safe passage through youth to the more important stage of adulthood. Rather, it was the best expression of all that was praiseworthy in the quality of youthfulness; it was the agency by which both the instinctive drives and spiritual feelings of adolescence were brought into harmony. Whether conversion actually came in adolescence or not, it should. "It may suffer displacement up and down the age scale. Its true place is in the adolescent years." [144]

Hall was a patron saint for YMCA "liberals" such as Luther Halsey Gulick and often spoke at Association conferences. Despite obvious doctrinal differences with the Association, Hall was able to praise it for its conception of the unity of physical, moral, and religious development. Hall was also familiar with the young people's movement in Protestant churches, and in *Adolescence* he devoted part of a chapter to it, assuming the stance of sympathetic critic. He praised the enthusiastic spirit of the societies, as well as the tendency of their ritual to promote solidarity among youth. Hall's only criticism of the young people's movement was that it placed excessive spiritual pressure on youth.[145] This was a strange criticism in view of the hostility to introspection and intellectuality which marked the movement. Indeed, it was paradoxical that evangelical interest in encouraging deep religious experience in youth was at a historic low point in the 1890s, the very time when religious psychologists began to take an interest in conversion during adolescence.

Because of his close connection with the YMCA, Hall saw his ideas disseminated rapidly by Association organizers and seized upon by Sunday school officials who had lines of contact to the Association. From the 1870s onward, Sunday school organizers had been emulating the bureaucratic methods of public school administration, but the work of religious psychologists provided them with a sophisticated psychology hitherto lacking. A little book published in 1913 aptly illustrated the coalition of administrative impulse and psychology. Intended as a textbook, *The New Convention Normal Manual for Sunday School Workers* was billed as the work of experts in Sunday school education.[146] For present purposes, two aspects of the *Manual* are significant. First, it contained eighty-odd pages on the nature of the pupil. Earlier editions of the manual had outlined the functions of teachers, but the new edition sought to integrate lessons and stages of development. On page after page, the authors sliced the pupil into chronological segments and then tucked him into physical, mental, social, and spiritual compartments of development. Even the most dimwitted teacher could have followed the accompanying chart. The fact that the *Manual* was published by the conservative Southern Baptist Convention is its second notable feature. Nothing better illustrates the rapid dissemination of religious psychology than the latter's penetration by 1913 to a body durably resistant to any sort of theological modernism.

The motives of those who molded adult-sponsored youth organizations in the 1890s were complex. Gulick was a great lover of sports, a man who enjoyed the game for the sake of the game. On the day of his death in 1918, his wife chose not to cancel a play festival scheduled in advance.

> A bright day dawned, a memorable one in the lives of the campers. It was water carnival day, and Dr. Gulick lay dead in his house on top of the cliffs at the water's edge. The sports were held; death was not allowed to interfere.[147]

At the other extreme, Henry B. Wright, a professor at Yale and prominent YMCA spokesman, organized a baseball team for boys in 1903 and participated avidly, although "he never cared much" for the game:

> He learned to field well, and every day one winter he practised swinging two heavy bats in order to get his muscles trained for it. This he did in the cellar, guiding his swing on the mortar rows between the bricks. In the end he batted above the average. He played the game because of the friendship it afforded with men whom he loved and wanted to reach.[148]

Homoerotic drives might have impelled Wright and others into boys-work. Fears of women and even of sexuality itself pervaded the published literature of the young people's movement. Leaders often complained that boys deteriorated under feminine influence, just as they proclaimed that boys who indulged in masturbation would, literally, disintegrate. Solitary vice was

> the crime of innocence that benumbs the conscience and kills with its unkindly blast the flowers of early piety. The crime that blanches the cheek, that shakes the nerve system into ruin, that clouds the intellect, that breaks down the integrity of the will, that launches emasculated ruin into asylums of hopeless insanity, collapsing in premature death.[149]

It is possible that boys-workers refused to allow their charges the sort of relaxed relationship to women or to sexuality which they themselves had been unable to attain.

PREVIEW OF THE SECOND DIVISION—THE PUPIL.

General	The BEGINNER is considered as follows:	The PRIMARY PUPIL is considered as follows:	The JUNIOR PUPIL is considered as follows:	The INTERMEDIATE PUPIL is considered as follows:	The SENIOR PUPIL is considered as follows:	The ADULT PUPIL is considered as follows:
I. PHYSICALLY.						
Energy	1. Restless	1. Active	1. Energetic	1. Energy Lessened	1. Energy Greatly Increased	1. Endurance
Physical Dependence	2. Dependent	2. Less Dependent	2. Growing Independence	2. Self Sufficient	2. Self Reliant	2. Aggressive
II. MENTALLY.						
Attention	1. Attention Brief	1. Attention Growing in Power	1. Voluntary Attention	1. Voluntary Attention Strengthened	1. Attention to the point of Application	1. Attention to the point of Concentration
Curiosity	2. Curiosity	2. Curiosity Strong	2. Inquisitive	2. Investigative	2. Independent thinking	2. Original Research
Memory	3. Memory but Slightly Developed	3. Memory Rapidly Developing	3. Verbal Memory at Height	3. Memory Based on Association of Ideas	3. Logical Memory	3. Philosophical and Practical Memory
Imagination	4. Imagination "Run Riot"	4. Imagination Imitative	4. Imagination Toned Down	4. Imaginative Literature a Delight	4. Imagination Productive of Ideals	4. Imagination Creative
III. SOCIALLY.						
Play	1. Plays Alone	1. Plays with Companions	1. Plays with the Gang	1. Plays with Team	1. Plays as Exhibition of Skill and Strength	1. Plays for Recreation
Egoism	2. Self Centered	2. Sensitive	2. Social Nature Developing	2. Self Conscious	2. Self Sacrificing	2. Service
IV. SPIRITUALLY.						
Religion	1. Impressionable	1. Conversion a Possibility	1. Great Evangelistic Opportunity	1. Religious Crisis	1. Choice of Service	1. Life of Service

Note—This Chart in enlarged form, wall size, for class use, may be had from the Sunday School Board.

Such an interpretation is obviously speculative and, taken in itself, could scarcely account for the magnitude of the growing adult control over the activities of youth. The young people's movement grew out of the intersection of a host of factors rather than from any single motive force. The combination of rising school enrollments and expanding economic opportunities in the Gilded Age in effect reduced the number of occasions in which boys of 14 or 15 and young men of 20 or 25 would occupy a common status or situation; this helps account for the predominance of teenagers and the absence of older youth in most late 19th-century organizations for young people. Many of the characteristics of the young people's movement—the overwrought rhetoric, the emphasis on perpetual motion, and the inability to define goals for youth—grew out of the intellectual decadence of evangelical Protestantism at the end of the 19th century. George Coe diagnosed the disease:

> the evident decay of the revival, the alienation from the Church of whole classes of the population, the excess of women over men in Church life, the apparent powerlessness of organized religion to suppress or seriously check the great organized vices and injustices of society, the failure of the Sunday school to make people or even its own pupils familiar with the contents of the Bible.[150]

E. G. Lancaster suggested the therapy: "the pedagogy of adolescence may be summed up in one sentence. *Inspire enthusiastic activity*." [151]

For all the talk about activity, however, the motive force behind church youth societies in the 1880s and 1890s was defensive, a desire to shield young people from contamination by the alien culture of big cities and immigrants. A set of values which can be located in medical and educational literature as early as the 1840s and 1850s had finally found embodiment in institutions. A common thread which ran through college "life," the high school extracurriculum, and Christian youth organizations was hostility to precocity, to adult behavior in youth. As it acquired institutional forms, the long-standing fear of precocity changed its shape. The avoidance of precocity no longer entailed merely the removal of intellectual pressures and social stimulants from youth, but the creation of a self-contained world in which prolonged immaturity could sustain itself. Adolescent life has value "in and of itself," a commentator wrote. "Its degree of perfection is not measured by the closeness with which it resembles maturity." [152]

Conclusion

One common thread running through youth organizations in colleges, high schools, and churches in the late 19th century was adult leadership. Another was passivity, although this quality was more evident in high schools and churches than in colleges. A third was insularity, for in youth organizations of every stripe, young people were to practice their adult roles without direct engagement in adult affairs. There were differences between the values of the upper-middle-class and upper-class families which could afford to send their children to prestigious colleges and the lower-middle-class families for whose young people high school provided terminal education, just as there were differences between the freedom within insularity allowed to college students and the obedience within insularity demanded of high school students and members of church youth societies. However, these differences should not obscure the fact that until the first few years of the 20th century most youth organizations in colleges, schools, and churches were intended only for middle-class youth. They were essentially defensive institutions that sought to demarcate the life-style of youths of a certain class from those young people of different social classes. In this respect the religious psychologists had special significance, for while they took their cue from church youth organizations, they were among the first to argue that adolescence should become a universal experience.

PART THREE

The Era
of Adolescence,
1900–Present

The change from pious to muscular student styles was reflected in the decor of student rooms at Hobart College, circa 1890–1910. Photos courtesy of Geneva, N. Y. Historical Society.

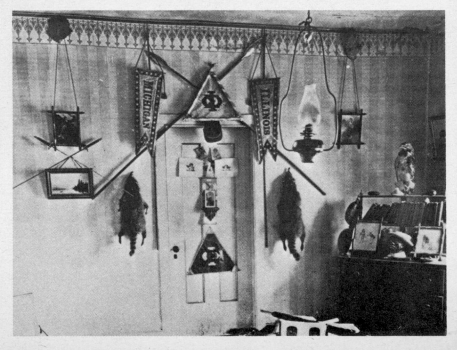

Late nineteenth- and early twentieth-century public high schools modeled many of their activities on those of the colleges. This is the Geneva (N. Y.) High School team of 1910. Courtesy of Geneva, N. Y. Historical Society.

Abbot Thayer, *The Virgin* (1893). James Flexner noted that Abbot Thayer "specialized in glorifying the American girl. With little wings, she was a fairy; with big wings, an angel; nude, she was the spirit of the Water Lily; dressed, Virginity." Courtesy of Freer Gallery, Smithsonian Institution.

"Oh, eyes!" he whispered, softly. "Oh, eyes of blue!"

Suddenly William saw himself in his true and fitting character.

Between 1890 and 1920 artists depicted youth of both sexes as innocent and ingenuous. The young man is William Sylvanus Baxter, protagonist of Booth Tarkington's *Seventeen*. These illustrations, from the first edition, show Willie daydreaming about the insufferable, baby-talking Miss Lola Pratt and, in a melancholy mood, assuming the attitude of Sydney Carton.

Prior to 1864, boys under eighteen could legally enlist as musicians. The exploits of some, like Johnny Clem, "the Drummer Boy of Chickamauga," who entered the army at nine, became famous. Reproduced from *Harper's Weekly*, December 19, 1863.

By World War I, boys were only playing at war. Above, Boy Scouts practicing wall scaling, New York, 1917. Below, Junior Naval Reserve on maneuvers, Central Park, N. Y. C., June, 1918. Photos courtesy of U.S. War Dept. General Staff, National Archives.

Boy Scouts guarding recruiting posters, N. Y. C., 1917. Courtesy of U.S. War Dept. General Staff, National Archives.

Boy Scouts selling Liberty Bonds, Boston, circa 1918. Courtesy of U.S. War Dept. General Staff, National Archives.

Boy Scouts burning German-language newspapers in Brooklyn, June, 1918. Courtesy of U.S. War Dept. General Staff, National Archives.

CHAPTER 8

The Invention
of the Adolescent

THE ERA of the adolescent dawned in Europe and America in the two decades after 1900. In America, Britain, and Germany these decades witnessed the appearance of both the institutions and psychology that were to govern the social treatment of youth for much of the 20th century. Attitudes and concepts which had appeared within the middle class in the 1880s and 1890s now pushed beyond the perimeters of that class in the shape of efforts to universalize and to democratize the concept of adolescence. A biological process of maturation became the basis of the social definition of an entire age group.[1]

The simultaneous development in different nations of the institutions and psychology of adolescence had some common characteristics and sources. In both America and Britain, for example, the collapse of voluntarism in youth organizations was first evident in denominational youth societies during the final two decades of the 19th century and then took secular form after 1900 in organizations like the Boy Scouts. In many countries, recognition of differences in the opportunities available to middle-class and working-class youth and the arrival of advanced stages of industrialization combined to displace young people from the job market.[2] Demographic changes, too, contributed to growing social interest in adolescence. In the United States and Europe, moderate declines in the birthrate between 1800 and 1850 turned into precipitous plunges by 1900.[3] Not only were mothers having fewer children, but births were now spaced more closely together than in the middle of the century. By 1900, urban areas were displaying a pattern of closely spaced children which approximated the modern pattern of childbearing within a narrow span of the family life cycle.[4] As the spacing of children contracted, a type of family was created which had little precedent, the family in which all the children were teenagers. There were, of course, other possible age ranges within the context of close spacing—all the children between 3 and 7, or between 8 and 12. But a second demographic characteristic of the late 19th century, the aging of the population, gave special prominence to the family marked by a predominance of teenage children. Between 1840 and 1900 the proportion of people aged 45 to 64 in the American population nearly doubled.[5] In other words, more men and women survived to see their children become teenagers.

Yet despite the similarity of demographic and economic forces in a number of countries, in no two countries did either the experience or the institutions of adolescence take the same form. To grasp this one has only to compare the primitivism and alienation of the German *Wandervogel* movement, young people in all-out revolt against the stifling constraints of Wilhelmine middle-class family life and the fierce intellectual pressures of the gymnasium, with the conformist nationalism and boyish cheerfulness of the British Boy Scouts or with the coeducational sociability of the American high school.[6] Further, although the middle class played the key role in shaping the institutions of adolescence from nation to nation, the history of the middle class differed from country to country. In America a potent middle class produced during these decades the Progressive reform movement, marked by purpose, optimism, and even a streak of utopianism, qualities that bore little resemblance to the anxieties of the German middle class, trapped between a threatening proletariat on one side and a hostile aristocracy on the other. And even in America the massive reclassification of young people as adolescents and the creation of institutions to segregate them from casual contacts with adults were not the results of a clear and consistent social movement but of a coalition of different types of people with different and often conflicting motives.

Despite these differences, between 1900 and 1920 both the concepts and institutions which have dominated youth work for the last half century took shape, almost final shape. G. Stanley Hall's *Adolescence*, published in 1904, was the seminal book, but direct radiations from Hall's work formed just one element in the process.[7] All sorts of individuals—earnest humanitarian reformers, boys-workers, nervous parents, school bureaucrats, and academicians—stumbled onto the study of adolescence after 1900, sometimes drawing inspiration from Hall, sometimes not. But no sooner had they all converged than they parted company, going off in separate directions and to new interests. They left young people holding the bag, so to speak, for the institutions created in the early 20th century survived to become an enduring form of custody for youth long after the ideas and impulses which created them were laid to rest.

The Awkward Age

At the center of the change was the adolescent—vulnerable, awkward, incapacitated by the process of maturation, but simultaneously the object of almost rhapsodic praise, the very bud and promise of the race. Adolescence, according to Hall, was a new birth, a wiping clean of the slate of childhood. Echoing Rousseau, Hall viewed adolescent experience as torn by dualisms which disrupted the harmony of childhood; hyperactivity and inertia, social sensibility and self-absorption, lofty intuitions and childish folly. The antithetical qualities of adolescence demanded, in turn, a removal of pressures for adultlike behavior. Hall insisted that the misbehavior and eccentricities of young people be viewed as normal outgrowths of biological maturation rather than as inexcusable departures from a fixed standard of behavior. In this respect, Hall desired a prolongation of adolescence, so that the human possibilities of the period might be realized. Although deeply indebted to Darwin, Hall preferred a normative view of adolescence to a normative view of natural selection. That is, many qualities of adolescence, such as religious enthusiasm, idealism, altruism, moodiness, and inertia, had little immediate value in the struggle for survival, but they had to be allowed free play, a full draining out or catharsis, before safe passage to maturity was assured. Hall argued that adolescent faults—even serious ones like running away from home or breaking and entering—were the outgrowths of instinctive urges, and that a regimen of repression would only cause recrudescences later on in a more menacing form.[8]

Although Hall's ideas had numerous antecedents, *Adolescence* was a highly personal document, reflecting the life and concerns of its author more than any single intellectual tradition. Like many intellectuals of his generation, Hall had outgrown his early dalliance with theology and a later flirtation with philosophy before developing a positive passion for psychology. For Hall, psychology was a new theology, a discipline in which ultimate issues of life and mind could be studied as part of a vocation without interference from institutional churches and authoritarian traditionalism. Nowhere else could one deal with ultimate questions so scientifically. As Hall's biographer has noted, the central intellectual problem of his career lay in his inability to yoke questions about the nature of mind and man with the methods of laboratory psychology; but Hall's failure resulted more from the incongruity of the elements than from any lack of eagerness on his part.[9]

During the 1890s, Hall underwent a series of personal crises: the loss of his wife and a child in a fire, the near collapse of Clark University (which he headed), and his continued failure to find in laboratory psychology the kind of synthesis of material and spiritual phenomena he had sought. Although *Adolescence* contained lumps of half-digested data about growth measurements and the age of menarche, Hall actually wrote the book during a period of romantic release, when he had finally given up his search for the Holy Grail in a laboratory. Appropriately, he rested his theory of adolescence on the principle of recapitulation, which had enjoyed a long history in the biological doctrines spawned by the romantic movement. In Hall's version, recapitulation postulated that the child passed through or retraced in its development the course already taken by the "race." Taking his cue from the fact that some of the materials used by children in play, sand and wood, were once the tools of primitive man, Hall speculated that adolescence corresponded to a period in prehistory marked by large-scale migrations. For the race and for the individual, it was a time of upheaval, giving rise to myths and sagas, poetic descriptions of the traumatic uprooting. In a similar way, the dictates of racial experiences attracted the adolescent to tales of heroic leaders and battles. Some contemporaries thought that Hall was speaking figuratively, but he understood the law of recapitulation literally. The adolescent was not merely like savage man. An almost Jungian collective consciousness determined aspects of adolescent behavior which were responses to inexorable commands out of the past.[10]

Although the concept of recapitulation had roots before Darwin, it could be harmonized readily with the prevailing evolutionary orientation of American psychology in the late 19th century. Its nonempirical character rendered it suspect to some, but its astonishing scope blended nicely with the mood which lay behind the cosmic philosophies of individuals like Herbert Spencer, Lester Frank Ward, and John Fiske. The doctrine justified the prolongation of adolescence, the removal of pressures for accelerated development, although it was also a source of some repressive conclusions. Hall used recapitulation both descriptively and normatively, without any awareness of contradiction. At times he insisted that all individuals passed through fixed stages of development; at other times he conceded that many did not but should be forced to anyway. *Adolescence* was replete with familiar warnings about the dangers of precocious development in cities, but in a number of places Hall admitted that modern youth really desired the fast pace of urban life. Adolescence was the age "when the average boy, and still more the average girl, is most averse to farm and even to country life. The social instincts are strong, and so too is the love of excitement and living in groups." [11] This must have been a painful admission, for Hall had always preached the futility of quarreling with an instinct. His response was to propose ways to make the city more like the country—nature trips, playgrounds, sports—all designed to distract youthful attention from opulent and meretricious urban culture. [12]

Hall's contradictory attitudes toward education illustrated the interplay of liberalism and repression in his thought. In *Adolescence* he called for more inspirational teaching in high school. Let history be the story of heroes, and physics the study of cosmic forces rather than abstract formulas. Appropriately, he assailed industrial education, just then coming into fashion, for its ruthless subordination of youth "to the tool, machine process, finished product, or end in view." [13] But at one point he conceded that industrial education had a firming effect on the young. "Instead of seeking soft, ready-made places near home, such education impels to the frontier, to strike out on new careers, to start at the bottom and rise by merit, beginning so low that every change must be a rise." [14] Despite the violence it did to youthful spontaneity, industrial education fitted "flabby, underdeveloped, anemic, easy-living city youth" for the struggle for life. [15] Later, in his two-volume *Educational Problems*, published in 1911, Hall repeatedly associated industrial education with conservation, and urged the former as a therapy for the waste of natural resources and as a corrective to youth's softness and dissipation.

The more Hall convinced himself that the old virtues of ruggedness and courage were reborn in industrial education, the more he blended his defense of the latter with an apology for military training. The waste involved in war was inexcusable, Hall argued, but none should ignore the role of war in promoting "robust physical and moral training." [16] Military training not only taught the efficient conduct of war but also inculcated habits of efficiency. Yet war was more than an anvil of habit formation:

> To be chosen by the state, taken away from the home environment, and made to serve the fatherland with a possibility of offering up life upon one's country's altar gives seriousness, poise, and right orientation, implants not only love of flag but esprit de corps and regimentation. [17]

These were Hall's words in 1911; the approach of World War I only made him more extreme on the subject. In fact, as early as 1881, Hall had written about his joy at seeing a line of German schoolchildren marching in step.[18] Ambivalence about freedom and regimentation ran all through his writings, early as well as late. In part, it reflected his ambivalence about his own boyhood. At times Hall sang the praises of rural boyhood in the fashion of William Dean Howells, but at other times he conceded that his own boyhood had been unhappy, marked by his inability to love or even to like his father, by stark fears that he would have to pass his life in the drudgery of farm service, and by shame and self-accusation over the fact of his own sexual maturation. In Hall's boyhood home in Ashfield, Massachusetts, the genitals were always referred to as "the dirty place" and he recalled wrapping his penis in bandages at night to prevent emissions. But the most wounding event, according to Hall, occurred during the Civil War, when his father bribed a doctor to declare Hall medically unfit for service and then, to make doubly certain, purchased a substitute. Hall pointed to his mortification as a turning point which gave him a "tremendous stimulus to atone by service" for his failure to enlist. But little in his later writings suggests that his atonement took the form of service, at least in any philanthropic sense. On the contrary, he accepted many of the postulates of social Darwinism and wrote scathingly about the weak and unfit. His failure to go to war certainly made Hall seek a moral equivalent, but one which took the form of trumpeting the virtues of fitness and discipline throughout his life.[19]

Hall's own life experiences accounted for some of the contradictions in his view of adolescence, but so did the cultural milieu of late 19th-century America. A profound ambivalence about the changes through which America was passing marked the 1890s, the decade in which Hall worked out his psychology of adolescence. If growing worship of the ideal of social efficiency indicated an acceptance of the values of machine culture, in other moods Americans seemed to want to be rid of it all, to return to primitive nature. The era produced Frederick W. Taylor and scientific management, but it also produced Edgar Rice Burroughs and Tarzan. Its foremost political leader, Theodore Roosevelt, built battleships, the symbol of the potency of the machine, but also wrote about the wild West.[20]

Hall stood conceptually as well as chronologically poised between two centuries. Despite the trappings of recapitulation theory, Hall's insistence on the value of a moratorium in adolescence resembles more recent formulations of the needs of youth. But in other respects Hall's ideas about adolescence were just a culmination of concepts that had flourished in less systematic form for much of the 19th century. This is true not only of specific themes (such as adolescent conversion and the dangers of precocious development in cities) but also of the saltatory theory of adolescence itself. Most 20th-century psychologists have broken with Hall on the latter point and have preferred to stress the continuity of development from childhood to adolescence. Accordingly, they have assumed that Hall's view of radical change at puberty was just another of his idiosyncrasies. Yet there was nothing idiosyncratic about Hall's saltatory view of adolescence. One unifying characteristic of 19th-century ideas about youth and adolescence was the assertion that some sort of radical change was likely to occur at puberty; vestiges of this disposition survived into the 20th century not only in Hall's synthesis but also in the attitudes of ordinary people. As late as 1929, Leta Hollingworth observed:

> It is still common to see parents cherishing the belief that some magic change will take place in their unfortunate children at puberty. The parent of a feeble minded, nervous, or sickly child is frequently heard to say, "he (or she) will likely be all right when he (or she) 'changes.' " This myth of a re-birth of personality at puberty is by no means confined to the uneducated as mere folklore. Physicians themselves, even in our own day, often advise parents of feeble minded or otherwise unfortunate children that the latter "will be all right after puberty." [21]

Both the contradictions in his views and the fact that he dressed old ideas in the latest fashions enabled Hall to influence radically different types of people. *Adolescence* was the starting point even for those who rejected the substance of Hall's message. Specifically, Hall's influence extended to four distinct areas: the movement to organize the spare-time activities of middle-class boys and girls in adult-sponsored youth organizations; parents' manuals which sought to guide the management of teenagers in middle-class and upper-middle-class homes; educators who had to manage the teenagers who were flooding public high schools; and the vocational guidance movement, which sought to bridge the gap between classroom and workplace.

Building the Boy

Hall's psychology of adolescence met with an especially zealous response from boys-workers, for whom Hall provided both a justification of their efforts and, it would seem, an articulation of their innermost thoughts. It was among boys-workers that some of the most repressive aspects of Hallian psychology found an attentive audience.

The Era of Adolescence, 1900–Present

Boys-work in the early 20th century covered a broad range of activities. Some of these had originated in the attempts of Victorian reformers to salvage street urchins from slum life in the middle decades of the 19th century. Others had started in the 1870s with efforts to gather impoverished city youth into boys' clubs which employed a mixture of prayer meetings, penny savings banks, manual training, and cadet corps to attract members. Still others had developed only after 1880 in the attempts of the YMCA to organize the leisure time of schoolboys. Further, because boys-workers rarely distinguished between actual or merely potential criminal behavior, the line was not sharply drawn between boys-work and the reform of juvenile justice embodied in the movement after 1900 to establish juvenile courts. Reformers continued to apply the term "child-saving" to a host of diverse enterprises, including juvenile courts, reform schools, settlement house clubs, boys' clubs, and playgrounds.[22]

Despite a plethora of activities and precedents, boys-work in the first two decades of the 20th century contained some unifying impulses and objectives. One common theme was the relinquishment of any vestiges of pietism. Protestant clergymen continued to play a disproportionately large role in boys-work after 1900, but religious conversion and prayer meetings virtually vanished as topics in the literature of boys-work. Second, after 1900 boys-workers persistently sought to develop techniques applicable to young people of all classes. Victorian reformers like Charles Loring Brace had not been concerned about the children of their own class. When they thought of child saving, they thought of the poor. Similarly, leaders of Christian youth organizations like Christian Endeavor recognized sharp differences between their own attempts to protect children of respectable church members and the goals of urban boys' clubs, which contained perhaps 800 to 2,500 street rowdies gathered in an uneasy truce. In contrast, boys-workers after 1900 cast their net broadly, in the hope that boys of all classes would respond to military drill, team sports, and civic education.[23]

A corollary of these tendencies was that boys-workers became increasingly interested in the psychology of adolescence, a psychology that detached the needs and interests of youth from class and ethnic forces and tied those needs and interests to a universal experience of maturation. Imbued with a belief in social reconstruction through civic education, boys-workers were especially attracted to Hall's conviction that peer loyalty and civic duty were in harmony. As Alvan F. Sanborn wrote, "properly handled, the 'gang' conscience of the boy may become the civic conscience of the man." [24] The most glaring defect of Hall's psychology, its subordination of class and ethnic factors to biological ones in the process of socialization, paradoxically accounted for part of

222

its appeal to boys-workers, for it reassured the latter that once they had grasped the psychodynamics of adolescence and had learned to direct the gang instinct to social ends, they would achieve the sort of success that had long eluded middle-class Protestants who sought to "reach the boys." There was certainly an element of low comedy in the way in which boys-workers catalogued types of gangs and types of games. William B. Forbush's *The Boy Problem,* which carried both an introduction by and the intellectual imprint of G. Stanley Hall, contained a chart of the "instincts utilized" by various types of boys' organizations.[25] The Boys' Brigade, for example, appealed to "chs., CLN, EML, IMT, loy, PHY, PUG, soc." That is, it utilized chastity, loyalty, and sociability to a slight extent, and cleanliness, emulation, imitation, physical activity, and pugnacity to a major degree. By the way, the Brigade, according to Forbush, appealed to only 10 percent of the boy's interests and instincts, a poor showing alongside the Captains of Ten, which appealed to 40 percent of his capacities. In a similar way, J. Adams Puffer, whose indebtedness to Hall was no less obvious than that of Forbush, was probably the first man in history to become an authority on blindman's buff and hide-and-seek.[26] But behind such curious applications of scientific technique lay the authentic enthusiasm of boys-workers in the early 1900s for a psychological system that subordinated class and religious differences to a principle of biological maturation.[27]

Although their interest had been stirred initially by boys' clubs sponsored by city churches and settlement houses, boys-workers like Forbush and Puffer increasingly rallied around a new organization, the Boy Scouts, founded in Britain in 1908 by General Robert Baden-Powell and established in the United States in 1910. As early as 1902 the American naturalist Ernest Thompson Seton had founded the Woodcraft Indians to give city boys a taste of country life, but Baden-Powell's inspiration derived less from American models than from his own experience in the Boer War and his subsequent conviction that British boys needed the sort of toughening that outdoor life could provide.[28]

In his early writings Seton had valued nature study for its own sake. He thus bore some resemblance to William R. George, who turned a fresh air camp for city boys into a self-governing junior republic in upstate New York, for George too thought that the natural setting was valuable in itself. But neither Seton nor George was destined to shape the course of boys-work in the early 1900s. The boys-workers who responded to Hall's psychology were deeply suspicious of George's experiment; in their view the gang might be a democracy but not a parliamentary republic.[29] The American scouting movement followed Baden-Powell rather than Seton. In both America and Britain rigid organization, authoritarian control, and a disposition to view outdoor life as little more than a tool for toughening muscle fiber marked scouting between 1910 and 1920, so much so that radical intellectuals in the United States voiced fears that scouting was no more than a capitalist plot to train a new generation of armed strikebreakers.[30]

Those who shaped the scouting movement in America repeatedly pointed to Hall's writings for support; small wonder, for *Adolescence* contained interminable passages on the need for loyalty, courage, and steeling discipline. Hall often criticized the softness of home life, a theme which became a near obsession among boys-workers and scouting leaders. David Snedden, a leader in the vocational education movement, noted that scouting appealed mainly to boys from middle-class urban and suburban homes "whose home environment is often so formal and respectable that only surreptitiously and, perhaps, illicitly, can the cruder and more masculine expression of the various 'virtues' find outlet." [31] Edgar M. Robinson described "the disadvantage of the boy who has been coddled all his life and kept so carefully wrapped up in the 'pink cotton wool' of an over indulgent home, till he is more effeminate than his sister, and his flabby muscles are no less flabby than his character." [32] Hall, moreover, had written very little about girls, a bias fully reflected both in the literature on boys-work after 1900 and in the masculine orientation and sexual segregation of scouting. Girls can never experience, wrote J. Adams Puffer, " 'the hour of glorious conflict, when the blood leaps, and the muscles rally for mastery,' the decent manly pride in taking one's punishment and 'fighting' it out as long as one can stand and see." [33] It was a boy's world, not a girl's and not a man's, a fact which prompted H. W. Gibson, a YMCA tractarian and boys-worker, to reduce all of adolescent psychology to something called "boyology." [34] Finally, Hall's doctrine of recapitulation seemed to justify the sponsorship by adults of essentially nonadult activities for youth. Henry S. Curtis, a disciple of Hall's who was active both in scouting and in the playground movement, claimed that scouting's provision of a quasi-tribal life for boys was "an almost complete proof of what is known in education and anthropology as the recapitulation theory." [35]

The nature of the scouting movement provides one illustration of the mentality of boys-workers in the early 20th century; the course of the playground movement provides another. The founder of the playground movement, Joseph Lee, was born into the Brahmin aristocracy, the son of a passionately conservative partner of Lee, Higginson, and Company, and a graduate of Harvard's class of 1883. In the 1890s, Lee became involved with the work of the Massachusetts Emergency Hygiene Association, which had been experimenting with school gardens and playgrounds as remedies for the effects of urban crowding on the play life of boys and girls. Lee resolved to make the organization of play facilities his lifework, but his contribution lay less in organization than in popularizing a philosophy of play which both inspired field workers and connected the playground movement with the body of Progressive reforms aimed at juveniles. As Lee's brother-in-law, Richard C. Cabot, wrote in 1914, play had become a religion. Or as Lee's co-worker Henry S. Curtis put it, a playground was not a place but an idea.[36]

Borrowing heavily from Hall and from Luther H. Gulick, Lee believed that the play instinct was a residue of an earlier and more natural stage of development, the "barbaric and predatory society to which the boy naturally belongs." [37] Games and athletics, Henry S. Curtis wrote, "are the activities of our ancestors conventionalized and adapted to present conditions. They are reminiscent of the physical age, of the struggle for survival, of the hunt, of the chase, and of war." [38] Another spokesman for the playground movement described the playground as "the interpreter of race tradition." [39]

For Joseph Lee, play was neither a preparation for life nor a release from work, but life itself; all work should be so suffused by play instincts that any distinctions between work and play would become purely verbal. The trouble was that modern conditions frustrated play instincts, not because boys had no place to play but because a bureaucratic and specialized society run by experts provided few outlets for instinctive drives. The tragedy of civilization, Lee wrote, was "that the end of all our labor and our ingenuity has been, for the great majority of men and women, the defeat of that inner life which it is our dearest object to promote. Man is a stranger in the modern world." [40]

In such moods Lee resembled Jane Addams who, in *The Spirit of Youth and the City Streets,* had written of an irrepressible conflict between man and industrial society, a conflict whose most severe effects fell upon youth.[41] Jane Addams abandoned the old custom of describing the city merely as a perilous environment in which young people lost their virtue; instead, she focused on the absence of an organic connection between work and play in the city. A dull and dehumanizing industrial regimen drove young people to seek both excitement and pathetic forms of self-expression in recreation. Foreshadowing ideas later developed by Lewis Mumford and Van Wyck Brooks, Addams contrasted the need for recreation with the meager opportunities for legitimate entertainment in the city. For most city youth, she said, the theater was "the only possible road to the realm of mystery and romance," the only place where young people could satisfy a craving for a higher conception of life than that provided by the world around them.[42] But the pleasures of the theater would never suffice. Theaters contained the seeds of seduction and promoted the separation of age groups in play, a unique feature of the modern city, she thought, and one which contrasted with "the old dances on the village green in which all the older people of the village participated." [43]

The Spirit of Youth enjoyed the high esteem of those who sought remedies for the divorce of work and play in modern life. Richard C. Cabot claimed that Jane Addams had taught her generation the holiness of play; William James described passages of the book as immortal.[44] But the only practical conclusion which *The Spirit of Youth* yielded was the need to bring the spare-time activities of youth under adult supervision. Addams herself wrote the introduction to Louise deKoven Bowen's *Safeguards for City Youth at Work and at Play*, a book which reduced Addams's hymn to play to a gradgrindian utilitarianism and which, specifically, advertised the activities of the Juvenile Protective Association of Chicago in licensing and supervising amusement houses as alternatives to penny arcades and vaudeville shows.[45] Similarly, Joseph Lee, for all his praise of spontaneous play, made effort upon effort to ensure that the games played in playgrounds would be carefully regulated. Henry S. Curtis claimed that he was converted to the principle of organized play when he realized, while watching some boys at play, that no one was trying to win and, even worse, no one seemed to care what the score was. Edward J. Ward reduced it all to an aphorism: "a playground is not a playground without supervision." [46]

The movement to regulate the spare-time pursuits of children and young people during the Progressive Era provides an illustration of the divergent types of people drawn into reform after 1900. Jane Addams was the very director-general of humanitarian Progressivism. Louise deKoven Bowen was representative of the upper-class urban ladies who sought to impose Victorian moral standards on lower-class youth.[47] Joseph Lee was not only an aristocrat but also an uncompromising racist, convinced that weaker races were staining the purity of the Anglo-Saxon strain by their thoughtless embarkation for America. While Lee occasionally rose to a perception of the dehumanizing effects of industrialization, he was at heart an antimodernist, a highborn gentleman convinced of the decadence and degeneracy of his society and age. What the world needed, he said, was more steel and less flab in its young people. Like Hall, Lee praised the moral value of war; he was still praising it in 1921.[48]

Of all the spokesmen for organized play and regulated recreation, Lee was not only the most conservative but also the one with the greatest influence. In part, his influence was simply the result of his persistence in the pursuit of a single idea, in contrast to individuals such as Jane Addams, who moved on to other interests after the publication of

The Spirit of Youth. Moreover, Lee's influence was not confined to the vandalized steel cages which urban playgrounds became; it also affected the organization of extracurricular activities in schools. His persistence contributed to his influence, but so did the fact that he and other playground promoters came along with an elaborate ideology at the very moment when educators were becoming intensely interested in the organization of spare-time activities in schools. By elevating the significance of play, Lee strongly reinforced the disposition of educators to utilize sports, dramatics groups, debating societies, and music clubs as agencies for the cultivation of social cooperation among students.[49]

Lee's bloodcurdling rhetoric was a far cry from that of school bureaucrats who genuflected at the altar of education for life adjustment, as distant as General Baden-Powell from Mr. Chips or Miss Grundy. Lee, it is true, had caught the beginning of the strenuous collegiate subculture at Harvard in the 1880s, and the image of college life had an undeniable impact on secondary education. But spokesmen for the latter were likely to echo the language not of Lee but of Jay B. Nash, who reassured the National Education Association in 1921 that "the whole problem of child engineering becomes, then, a problem of conservation of leisure time for physical efficiency and the training of citizenship." [50]

Through scouting and through the organization of the school extracurriculum the ideas of boys-workers in the early 1900s reached a primarily middle-class audience. Later studies documented the predominance of middle-class participation in scouting and school activities, but even before 1920 boys-workers saw the signs of their failure to reach lower-class youth. Hall noted that the latter were indifferent to team sports that were supposed to build social cooperation, and preferred instead just to punt a football up and down the street.[51] Hall glimpsed an aspect of street life that continually eluded boys-workers, for what the latter saw as evidence of lower-class depravity was actually an autonomous lower-class tradition which could be traced as far back as the second quarter of the 19th century and which valued physical prowess, spontaneity, and defiance of authority rather than self-restraint and an orientation toward abstract goals. The innumerable studies of lower-class youth in the Progressive Era rarely turned up evidence of a pattern of felonious behavior. Instead, middle-class reformers had to content themselves with documenting the petty misdemeanors that were inevitable in crowded urban areas.[52] For example, Progressive reformers often complained that street boys pilfered from vacant buildings, a harmless act unless one viewed it from the perspective of the addictive theory of vice so dear to the hearts of Victorian and Progressive reformers alike.

Failing to comprehend the self-sufficient quality of lower-class life, boys-workers were doomed to repeated frustrations. In many ways this outcome was ironic, for boys-workers who responded to Hall's psychology had seen it as a justification for their efforts to reach boys of all social classes. Even more ironic was the fact that boys-workers were often sharp critics of the emphasis placed on politeness and decorum in middle-class homes. They actually admired the rowdy and resourceful street boy, although they continued to use the language of conquest, "winning the boy," to describe their successes.[53] The frustration so evident in the strained rhetoric of the young people's movement in the 1880s and 1890s spilled over into early 20th-century boys-work, so much so that one suspects that successful encounters with lower-class boys gave boys-workers new confidence in their own virility.[54]

From Child Study to Adolescence

Although many of the leaders of American psychology in the early 20th century—men such as William James, James M. Baldwin, John Dewey, and E. L. Thorndike—were largely indifferent to his work, Hall's thinking had a profound impact. The enthusiastic response of boys-workers accounted in part for Hall's influence, but boys-workers occupied a self-contained and often eccentric universe. However, Hall also had an audience composed of parents and teachers, one to which he had been appealing ever since the 1880s, when he had launched the child study movement in America.

At its highest level, child study was an attempt to answer scientifically such old questions as the relative role of nature and nurture in child development, as well as newer ones concerning the origin of ideas and emotions. In the latter respect, child study's debt to Darwin was significant, for from a Darwinian perspective the child became an artifact to study for insight into the evolution of ideas and emotions. Darwinism also bequeathed to child study a heavy emphasis on instinct and a downgrading of consciousness, biases evident in Hall's doctrine of recapitulation. For a brief period of time in the 1890s, child study promised to become a major academic discipline. Hall, who developed both the recapitulation theory and his initial formulation of the stages of childhood while active in the movement, took the lead in organizing child study on a state and regional basis. His efforts were aided by his students at Clark University and by figures such as Dewey, George H.

Mead, Earl Barnes, and others. Collectively, students of the child contributed a more tolerant view of childhood faults, now portrayed as the outcome of a collision between natural instincts and arbitrary adult standards.[55]

If child study produced a few rays of light, it also yielded blanket upon blanket of heat. Few of the important figures in American psychology were able to translate their initial interest into genuine enthusiasm. James, for example, thought that child study was too abstract and analytical to be of much value to teachers, and he distrusted the questionnaire method through which parents and teachers were to supply psychologists with details about child development. Dewey was critical of the movement's tendency to pile up data on the assumption that a revelation about nurture and education lay just around the corner. Baldwin criticized Hall's preoccupation with instinctive drives in development at the expense of conscious imitation of adult models. But child study flourished despite the indifference or hostility of some of the field marshals. It flourished because the rank and file, the parents and teachers who filled out questionnaires and flocked to speeches by Hall or his students, treated it with an almost religious reverence.[56]

Child study appealed primarily to conservative middle-class mothers shocked by the strident feminism gaining ground in the late 19th century but simultaneously eager to become involved, however vaguely, in work for social betterment. Hall was the featured speaker at the first session of the National Congress of Mothers in 1897, an organization with close ties to child study and sharply hostile to women who pursued careers outside of the home. Hall would scarcely have disagreed with Mrs. Theodore Birney, the Congress's founder, when she claimed that only women who lacked the training to evolve the "beautiful possibilities of the home" found motherhood monotonous.[57] (Although the bearer of a new enlightenment, Hall dressed whatever he said in pious references to home and motherhood.) The National Congress of Mothers was also a shrill advocate of purity reform. Mrs. Birney, its founder, was a leading purity reformer; she had received the inspiration to save the race through the child and the child through purity while attending a mothers' meeting in Chautauqua, New York.[58] Indeed, child study was the perfect answer to criticisms so often made in the 1890s of leisured ladies who selfishly restricted the size of their families and ignored their social responsibilities, for it provided the same kind of upgrading of motherhood as a role that religious enthusiasm had provided in the early 19th century.[59]

By 1904, when *Adolescence* appeared, child study was in decline, dismissed by many professional psychologists as a fad and increasingly ignored by Hall himself.[60] Between 1900 and 1920, leadership of the remnants of the movement passed into the hands of "experts" who were less likely to be academic psychologists than professional guidance counselors, men who launched profitable careers advising parents on the problems of childhood and adolescence. The private papers of Michael V. O'Shea, one of the most prolific authors among the family counselors and the first entrepreneur of adolescence, consist almost entirely of correspondence with publishers concerning projected series of advice books. From his base at the University of Wisconsin, O'Shea edited the popular *Childhood and Youth Series* brought out by Bobbs Merrill of Indianapolis and described as "the first systematic attempt to give to parents, teachers, social workers, and all others interested in the care and training of the young, the best modern knowledge about children in a manner easily understood and thoroughly interesting." [61]

The experts who contributed to O'Shea's series were a mixed lot. Their number included E. A. Kirkpatrick, a student of Hall's and a professor at a state normal school in Massachusetts, who advised parents on how to instill in their children a sense of financial responsibility; Irving King, professor of education at the University of Iowa, who contributed *The High School Age;* C. Ward Crampton, director of physical education in the New York City schools, whose *Anatomical and Physiological Age* sought to substitute a system of age measurement based on levels of physical maturation for mere chronological age; and William Healy of the Juvenile Psychopathic Institute, whose contribution to the series, *Honesty,* paved the way for his subsequent studies of juvenile delinquency.[62]

Beyond the stated purpose of popularizing modern psychological insights about the child, no single thrust marked the various contributions to the series. But a similarity in methodology—specifically, a tendency to assume that the process of growing up presented a succession of problems for parents to solve before the child could fully develop its personality—pervaded the series. In place of the direct confrontation between counselor and youth in the conduct-of-life tracts of the 1850s, the *Childhood and Youth Series* substituted the chat between parent and expert. As a corollary, the youth became virtually a passive spectator at his or her own socialization, so much so that it became necessary to give young people the impression that, despite appearances, they actually could play a role. As Irving King wrote:

> The second practical point is to produce in the youth a thoughtful attitude toward these changes [at puberty], that his own help may be enlisted in rounding him out into efficient manhood. If unpleasant or harmful dispositions emerge, he must find in his adult associates sympathy and help rather than condemnation. Although he may not be wholly responsible for the attitudes and moods that develop now, he must be led to see that he is largely responsible for their continuance. He must feel that now more than ever before *he can take a direct hand in his own development.* [63]

Dorothy Canfield Fisher's contribution to the series, *Self-Reliance*, aptly illustrated the change, for her subject was as traditional as her approach was novel.[64] For Fisher, self-reliance was no longer a virtue to be impressed by exhortation or example but a social skill to be acquired in situations contrived by parents. She urged, for example, that 14-year-olds be given a role in planning family trips, subject to their parents' advice and veto. Let young people "determine the routes and estimate beforehand the amount of money that will be needed, and, as soon as possible, let them handle some of the actual details of the transaction."[65] Like Irving King, who described adults as "associates" of youth, Fisher favored relaxed, intimate, and informal relationships between parents and children; yet, like King, she presented ample evidence of the disparity between parent and child under modern conditions.

Fisher's lack of interest in self-culture was not the result of any perception that young people lacked opportunities for independent activity. Pointing to the "instinctive repugnance felt by many parents to what they consider a premature initiation of children in adult activities," she added that as long as adult occupations consisted mainly of paring potatoes and baking bread, feeding cattle and pitching hay, few dreamed that there was anything unnatural or precocious about children who did their share. But now that corresponding adult activities included buying railroad tickets, using a timetable, ordering meals in hotels, sending packages by parcel post, and sending telegrams, "we feel that we do not want our boys and girls to be made 'little old men and women' by too great assurance in handling these modern processes."[66] It was, in other words, the nature rather than the absence of activities that created the problem.

One source of these ideas was the medical texts of the 1840s and 1850s, which had repeatedly portrayed adolescence as a time of incapacity. Where self-culture books had merely observed that at puberty youth acquired more energy, and hence greater capacity for good or evil, the concept of adolescence, ever since the antebellum period, had associated puberty with psychological turbulence and moral incapacity. A second source was the Bushnellian ideal of the family as a moral environment greater than the sum of its parts. Fisher was so strongly committed to the principle of family cooperation that she voiced some mild criticism of the Boy Scouts for taking young people out of the home. But the line from either antebellum medical tracts or Bushnell to Dorothy Canfield Fisher was filled with twists and turns. Bushnell was a distant rather than an immediate ancestor of Fisher. Bushnell had concerned himself mainly with small children rather than with teenagers, while antebellum medical texts, obsessed as they were with diet and regimen and with a morality of self-denial, bore little resemblance to Fisher's idea that parents carve learning situations for teenagers out of the body of routine familial tasks. There were important differences, too, between the child study movement of the 1890s and Fisher's *Self-Reliance*; for child study, despite its scientific penumbra, actually carried over ideas about child rearing which had been commonplace in America ever since the second quarter of the 19th century. Child study seminars of the 1890s echoed the long line of American parents' manuals that had aimed at the production of self-controlled little stoics by the agency of early habit formation.[67] Fisher, in contrast, addressed herself less to early habit formation and to techniques to implant an autonomous conscience than to the acquisition of social poise and personality skills.

Fisher's viewpoint had some precedents in the period before 1910. In the 1890s, for example, James R. Miller, a prolific author of advice books, had substituted advice in the art of living at home for exhortation to character building.[68] But this was a minority opinion in an age when most advice books continued to give priority to the development of self-control. Fisher was digging, in other words, in fallow if not virgin land, for personality rather than character was her keynote. A movement like child study provided her with an audience of attentive and self-conscious mothers, but it did not determine the direction of her thought.

What did, then? As long as historians assumed that prior to the latter part of the 19th century families were extended, multigenerational, and very large, and that the period of dependency was short, it was relatively easy to account for different philosophies of human development by pointing to changes in family structure. The differences between Ralph Waldo Emerson and Dorothy Canfield Fisher on the subject of self-reliance could be viewed simply as reflections of the differences between loose extended families and intimate nuclear ones. Children in cities lost their economic value. Parents consciously restricted the size of their families. Small families nurtured a more self-conscious approach to the socialization of children, just as the loss of economic functions made a new approach to child rearing necessary. Further, as children stayed at home longer, adolescent rearing became as important as child rearing. Fisher presented a version of this argument when she observed that the traditional instructors in self-reliance—splitting wood, stoking stoves, weeding gardens, and making money—had disappeared under modern conditions which thrust children into passive and receptive stances rather than active and purposive ones.

This explanation has the advantage of coherence, but its defects have become increasingly evident. The nuclear rather than the extended family predominated in the distant past, while cities in the 19th century, so far from destroying extended families, actually gave rise to them in many instances.[69] Moreover, dependency had often been lengthy in agricultural communities. Whatever differences existed between the position of young people in families in 1800 and 1900 cannot be reduced, in other words, simply to a prolongation of dependency. Nor does the fact that by 1900 dependent children were more likely to be attending school than working entirely account for manifest changes in the meaning and method of self-reliance. In the antebellum period, for example, conduct-of-life books aimed at young ladies in their teens had portrayed their audience as living at home in a nonproductive, dependent relationship,the exact condition of many middle-class boys in 1900, and yet had propounded for these girls a version of the self-culture advice so often directed at independent young men.[70] Finally, Fisher's insistence that modern life forced passivity on children has to be set against her admission that the real difficulty lay in the nature of adult activities rather than in the availability of tasks for youth.

Structural changes within the family certainly had some effect on changing values in child nurture. The unproductive dependent boy who lived continuously at home was a rarity in 1800, a commonplace by 1900. Demographic changes already described, changes which greatly increased the likelihood of families containing only teenage children, contributed to the emergence of a separate class of manuals advising parents on ways to socialize teenagers. But the most valuable key to explaining the differences between the Emersonian and Fisher versions of self-reliance lies in economic history—specifically, in changes in family strategy dictated by the sharp rise in the number of salaried, white-collar employees. We have seen how the industrial revolution in America increased the number of salaried professionals, managers, salesmen, and clerks. In the late 19th century the differentiation of economic opportunities available to middle-class and working-class youth had compelled middle-class families to place their children on the track of formal education beyond puberty. But a full consciousness of the implications of economic change for youth of different classes developed only gradually. It was not until 1912 that a German, Emil Lederer, coined the term "new middle class" (*Der Neue Mittelstand*) to distinguish white-collar professional and clerical employees from Marx's petty bourgeoisie of small traders, shopkeepers, self-employed professionals, and independent artisans.[71] Child nurture tracts directed at the old middle class, the petty bourgeoisie, had sought to inculate perseverance and stoicism rather than tactfulness and social skill. The old middle class wanted its children to be readied for the slings and arrows of the marketplace, for the sudden reversals of fortune that businessmen in the 19th century could scarcely avoid. The new middle class, in contrast, looked to a future in which its children would be bureaucrats rather than entrepreneurs. It was no longer sufficient to keep children free of temptation; they had to be prepared for roles in complex organizations in which they, like their parents, would be associates rather than leaders.

The idea that passage from childhood to adolescence was a problem to be managed artfully by parents under the influence of professional counselors was still on the periphery of American thought about family relationships when Fisher published *Self-Reliance* in 1916. Even within the boundaries of the middle class it had to compete against rival methods which continued to place an exorbitant premium on habit formation in early childhood and against the mood of muscularity and strenuosity that animated boys-work. But in the decade after 1910, Fisher's ideal found a new and durable source of support in the allegiance of educators who were simultaneously confronting new conditions in the classroom.

Adolescence and Education

By 1890 the teaching profession, if teaching could be called a profession, had reached a point in its development which guaranteed a warm reception to a figure like Hall, a transmitter of academic wisdom who sympathized with the practical problems of the classroom teacher. The rapid growth of the teaching force after the Civil War had not been accompanied by any corresponding adjustment in attitudes toward teachers, especially female teachers, who now formed the great majority of classroom instructors but who were still forced to listen to speakers at meetings of the National Education Association address predominantly female audiences as "gentlemen." [72] Child study appealed to teachers for the same reasons as Herbartianism and other storms which swept across the educational landscape after 1890. "I have some most interesting letters from teachers in New York State," Charles H. Thurber said in 1896, "expressing their gratitude that they can cooperate in even so small a way in some large work. It is a great thing for any one to be associated with large enterprises." [73] If teachers needed "contact with the best men of the best minds in other callings," child study provided it. [74] By upgrading the importance of both childhood and psychology, Hall in effect upgraded teaching. As one of Hall's students wrote, child study was "primarily for the teacher, secondarily for children, incidentally for science." [75]

Although anything that Hall said or wrote met with instant praise from the corps of teachers who flocked to his addresses, the response to his views on adolescent psychology in high schools was at best ambivalent. High school principals and teachers were familar with Hall's ideas, either directly through his writings or indirectly through listening to his students, who often spoke at educational conventions.[76] Those in a position to shape the curriculum had ample opportunity to absorb Hallian psychology but held it at arm's length. At the root of their skepticism lay Hall's failure to define the change from childhood to adolescence in a manner satisfactory to men presiding over a revolution in secondary education.

Between 1890 and 1920 the public high school was the critical institution in American education. It was growing proportionately more rapidly than any other institution, but its goals were the least well defined. In 1893 the Committee of Ten, chaired by President Eliot of Harvard and generally reflecting the viewpoint of the universities, had proposed a continuation with some modifications of the traditional classical and academic orientation of the secondary curriculum. Twenty-five years later, with Eliot in retirement, enrollment booming, and the tide turned, the *Cardinal Principles of Secondary Education* virtually ignored intellectual development as an educational goal, subsuming it under "command of fundamental processes" and relegating it to a minor position in a new educational firmament whose brightest stars were health, vocation, citizenship, and worthy use of leisure.[77]

Behind the prolonged discussion of the goals of secondary education between 1890 and 1920 lay the expansion of enrollment, partly the result of increasingly sophisticated technology, which displaced many young people from the job market, and partly the result of compulsory education laws which, by limiting the hours of employment for 14- to 16-year-olds, discouraged employers from hiring them.[78] "The whole tendency of the times, therefore, is to drive children under sixteen out of work and into school," the Fall River school board noted in 1914.[79] But the mass reclassification of young people in school as adolescents was more than a simple by-product of rising school enrollments. Rather, the reclassification grew out of the goals of a group of social educators who first appeared on the scene in the early 1900s but who reached their peak influence between 1910 and 1925.

Social education was a rubric broad enough to cover vocational education, education for social efficiency, and education for life adjustment. Although distinctions could be drawn among the varieties of social education, differences did not run very deep. Charles Prosser, who popularized life adjustment education, was also secretary of the National Society for the Promotion of Industrial Education, while David Snedden, a vigorous defender of vocational education, had been a student of E. A. Ross, whose *Social Control* became a handbook for social educators of all stripes.[80] All the varieties of social education, moreover, agreed that schools had to prepare young people for membership in social and economic groups rather than for individual success. In this respect the goals of social educators resembled those of many Progressive reformers, who also preferred a society of cooperating groups to the individualism of the success cult. Yet while Progressive ideology and social education shared several points of congruence, the motive force behind the latter came from factors either within or bordering on secondary schools themselves. The expanding social role of the high school in the 1890s and early 1900s provided social educators with a model on which to build in later decades (see pp. 183–189). The vision of the high school as a kind of socializing agency also appealed to secondary educators because it justified cutting the leading strings that had long bound high schools to college entrance requirements. While the high school extracurriculum often took its cue from college life, secondary educators were an increasingly self-conscious group eager to get out from under domination by colleges.[81] Finally, the emphasis in parents' manuals such as Fisher's *Self-Reliance* on the acquisition of social poise and personality skills conditioned middle-class parents to accept the socializing role of the high school.[82] At each point the interplay of social forces reinforced intellectual preferences.

Dancing along the line which separated Victorian and Progressive attitudes toward adolescence, Hall had less to say to social educators than to the muscular Christians who took up boys-work. His plea for more inspirational teaching of traditional subjects fell on the deaf ears of educators in full flight from the ideal of intellectual education. His occasional declarations of the steeling value of both child labor and flogging, neat expressions of the more repressive side of his thought, only widened the gap between him and social educators. Hall's defense of military training met with a mixed response. A few experiments were launched, but educators played down the element of preparation for real war. When Lieutenant Edgar Z. Steever formed a volunteer corps in a Cheyenne, Wyoming, high school in 1911, he justified it along the lines of the play and gang instincts and had each squad assigned a sponsor from among the girls of the school.[83] Even during the war most educators failed to generate much enthusiasm for military drill. As a committee of the National Education Association expressed it in 1917, it was an "educational and moral offense to snatch him [the boy] from the natural life of boyhood and place him in what ought to be a man's job, and thus expose him to the risk, if not certainty, of mental and physical injury." [84]

Hall's ideas on two issues, sex education and health, had a measurable influence on education, but social educators left their distinctive stamp on each. The American Society for Sanitary and Moral Prophylaxis and the American Social Hygiene Association, organizations whose very titles underscore the excruciating obliqueness that marked discussions of sexuality before 1920, reinterpreted Hall's call for the sublimation of sex drives into an assurance that the dissemination of "scientific" information about sex would inoculate young people against the erotic drives themselves. Similarly, social educators like Clarence Kingsley, the principal author of the *Cardinal Principles*, equated health with brushing the teeth rather than with the sort of whole-souled and whole-bodied vitality envisioned by Hall. As late as 1924, Calvin O. Davis described adolescence in Hallian terms ("a time when the human organism is torn by conflicting forces; when racial instincts of untold power contend for mastery; when sex urgings rage and call for satisfaction"), but then concluded that the primary need of secondary education was better sanitation in school buildings.[85]

Although Hall's specific ideas met with indifference or hostility, a half-baked version of his general beliefs paradoxically rode the coattails of social education. Educators convinced that "the modern community is not real enough, not sufficiently organized to provide the old-time social integrations as a matter of course," were receptive to a view of young people as adolescents—that is, confused, weak, and incapable of coming to maturity merely through observation of adult models in casual situations.[86] Committed in theory to the resolution of all social conflicts by the voluntary cooperation of groups, and believing that the practical task of the high school was to coordinate its curriculum with that of the elementary school, social educators sought to remove every possible occasion of stress on the child in school. As a corollary, they responded negatively to Hall's view of radical change at puberty and positively to E. L. Thorndike, Irving King, and the other writers who emphasized the continuity of development between childhood and adolescence.[87] Clarence Kingsley concluded that modern psychology had demonstrated "that the development of the individual is in most respects a continuous process and that, therefore, any sudden or abrupt transition between the elementary and secondary school or between any two successive stages of education is undesirable.[88] By the time Chapman and Counts published their major work on education in 1924, the battle was over. Indeed, it had never really been fought. The goal of secondary education, the author's proclaimed, was the education of all youth (now invariably referred to as adolescents), a goal which demanded that socialization should be the primary goal of education and that "the high school should continue on a higher level the work of the elementary school." [89]

By equating high school education with the education of adolescents, Chapman and Counts noiselessly ratified a subtle but important shift in the scope of the concept of adolescence as a principle of social organization. Although G. Stanley Hall had been disposed to extend adolescence into the early 20s, boys-workers and child labor reformers, reflecting the age group that concerned them, usually limited the application of the concept of adolescence to the years between 12 and 16. Educators, on the other hand, had no reason to establish 16 as the outer limit as long as high schools contained many aged 17 to 19. Without any real debate, adolescence was merely extended to apply to secondary school students of any age. In effect, the high school became the age escalator of adolescence, as a stage of life was defined in terms of a stage of schooling (see p. 254).

As educators extended the practical application of the concept of adolescence, they also reshaped the goals of psychology. Although the architects of adolescence often announced their intention to understand and to sympathize with the problems of adolescents, a major effect of the psychological interest in adolescence after 1890 was the creation of new ways to regulate youthful behavior. Between 1890 and 1920 adolescent psychology became as much a method for controlling the behavior of young people as a tool of description and explanation. A manual on school discipline by a district superintendent in New York City aptly illustrated the direction that adolescent psychology was taking. "The principal will develop some automatically working analysis which he will apply to each case as it comes before him," the author wrote.

A logical scheme to follow is:
(A) What type is the pupil?
    1. Normal
        If so (a) are school conditions normal?
                (b) are personal conditions normal?
    2. Abnormal
        If so (a) is he supernormal?
                (b) is he subnormal?
(B) In which ontogenetic stage is the pupil?
    1. The ascent of childhood
    2. The plateau of childhood
    3. Prepubescence
    4. Adolescence
(C) From which instinct group is the specific offense derived?
    1. Self-preservative
    2. Reproductive [i.e., sexual]
    3. Gregarious
    4. Adaptive

The same specific offense will naturally be handled very differently when committed by an adolescent abnormal boy, for instance, and by a normal girl on the plateau of childhood.[90]

Finally, in addition to extending the scope and changing the goals of adolescent psychology, social educators altered its nature. Whereas Hall had recognized stress in youth as a necessary and even desirable sign of an emerging identity, social educators like Irving King, Clarence Kingsley, and others substituted the noiseless acquisition of civic responsibility and social poise. In effect, they sought the elision rather than the prolongation of youth.

Adolescence and Vocational Guidance

Vocational tracts in the late 19th century broke new ground by disseminating concrete job information, but their authors usually held traditional assumptions about the way in which the final choice was to be made. The boy was to study the material, of course, but then to look within himself and assess his own aptitudes and interests before making his decision. Vocational counselors in the 1890s had suggested that young people should look before leaping and avoid complete reliance on parents, who might only pass along folksy misinformation; but they had believed that both final choice and antecedent introspection were the obligations of youth. In contrast, social educators tried not only to soften the passage from elementary to high school but also to ease the transition from school to the job market, a goal which led them to criticize old methods of job selection and to devise a new answer, vocational guidance.

The vocational guidance movement was the creation of Frank Parsons, socialist, author, lawyer, teacher, candidate for mayor of Boston, and civic reformer. Stumbling into vocational counseling more or less by accident, Parsons opened the Vocational Bureau in Boston in 1907. Actually, Parsons was in many ways a transitional figure. He retained the old distinction between mere work and vocation, with the latter connoting a higher purpose which specific jobs contributed to but did not entirely encompass. His technique was to assist introspection. The youth was told to write out a self-analysis; the counselor would then explain various jobs to him and help him find out more about himself through homemade tests measuring reaction time, reading speed, and other skills. Out of all of this, the youth would then experience a Pauline grasping of his mission in life.[91]

The methods of Frank Parsons were obviously a mixture of old and new, but on one issue he was uncompromising. He was convinced that the difficulty in making intelligent vocational choices lay not only in misinformation but also in the extravagant hopes and expectations which success tracts raised. Boys nurtured on books like John G. Edgar's *The Boyhood of Great Men* were unfitted for a world in which there would necessarily be more Indians than chiefs.[92] Accordingly, Parsons believed that interests and aptitudes had to be correlated with opportunities. Thus, the vocational guidance movement underscored the ambivalent attitudes of Progressive reformers toward late 19th-century success mythology. On the one hand, the architects of adolescence lifted bodily passages about the value of purity, self-discipline, and heroic preparation for life from success tracts; on the other hand, through movements like vocational guidance they sought to protect young people from the kind of insistence on "executive force" and immediate choice that traditionally had pervaded those same success tracts.

Parsons died in 1908. In the next decade and a half, the movement which he created was to undergo a major facelifting which left any resemblance to the original impulse unrecognizable. Meyer Bloomfield, a former student at Harvard of Paul Hanus, transformed vocational guidance from a local offshoot of private benevolence into a national movement connected both to big business and the educational bureaucracy.

In the case of business, the impulse came from the cult of efficiency, as represented by Frederick W. Taylor, the founder of scientific management in America. As business grew in scale, responsibility for hiring passed from the owners to the department foremen, on whose shoulders rested responsibility for cutting down the high turnover rates which plagued many industries. Efficiency experts argued that cutting turnover would raise profits and build a more loyal labor force, and that the use of scientific techniques would increase the chance of locating the right men for the jobs available. By 1910 a number of industries were basing employment policies on various psychological tests, the most popular of which was a system of phrenological analysis developed by Katherine Blackford, who promised efficiency increases of 100 to 1,000 percent for users of her system.[93]

Dissatisfaction with the abstract manual training courses which had been introduced after 1870 in many schools increasingly disposed educators to rival business in support for vocational testing. One survey indicated that Minneapolis schools had become prevocational schools for the training of the social classes which least needed it. According to the study, only one-tenth of recent graduates actually went directly into occupations for which their courses in manual training were at all preparatory, while half went directly into college. When interviewed, most students expressed the belief that manual training was a preparation for the engineering school of the Univerity of Minnesota.[94] Along different lines, a Massachusetts commission reported in 1906 that manual training was failing to stop boys from dropping out of school, and that the only answer was specific vocational training, which would reach the classes which most needed it—the boys about to enter the job market at 12 or 14, rather than the middle-class clientele of manual training courses.

The difficulty was that most skilled trades did not accept boys before age 16 or 18, while lower-class children still left school at 12 or 14. This important gap of two to four years created all sorts of problems for educators. Some advocated junior high schools, which became increasingly popular between 1910 and 1920, as agencies that would encourage lower-class youth to stay longer in school. Others sought to push trade training down into elementary schools, so that boys at 14 would be ready to take a skilled or semiskilled job, assuming that one could be found. But neither of these approaches was altogether satisfactory. Trade unions were suspicious of junior high schools, believing that they would create an invidious distinction between the middle-class youths who could attend senior high schools and the working-class youths who would be forced into the junior version. Trade training in elementary schools was expensive if taken seriously and worthless if not.[95]

At this point vocational guidance entered the picture, for the movement provided a nice balance between social demands and individual needs. If one could get a boy of 8 or 9 thinking about his future, the so-called "life-career" motive, then the shock of transition to the job market would be eased. John M. Brewer argued that vocational guidance would prolong the vocational immaturity of the child.[96] Ernest R. Henderson lyrically dwelt upon the possibilities of vocational guidance as a solution not only for problems of adjustment to the marketplace but also for the "symptoms" of adolescence, "the high rate of elimination from school at that time, . . . the unrest, the questioning of adult values, the beginnings of 'storm and stress' that characterize the commencement of the age of independence, of adolescence."[97]

As the vocational guidance movement merged into the broader movement for social education, the former's promoters relied increasingly on the expert advice of psychologists who provided both intelligence tests and crude preference tests on the confident assumption that while boys could not be expected to engage in self-analysis, professionals could measure interests and aptitudes and line up pegs and holes merely by administering batteries of examinations. The coincidental rise of interest in psychological testing contributed to this, as did the assumption that the first step in the "treatment" of adolescence was to reduce the number of decisions that nervous and excitable young people had to make. The result was that by 1915 vocational guidance had completely turned away from the assumptions of Frank Parsons about the value of introspection and individual responsibility.

Ironically, just as vocational guidance was becoming a national movement, the foundations of confidence in psychological testing began to collapse. In 1912, E. L. Thorndike could argue that the interests of a boy or girl were symptomatic of present and future abilities.[98] But three years later, Frank M. Leavitt pronounced the results of psychological testing to be meager.[99] In the same year, another writer ridiculed researchers who entered schools with the assumption that tests would show the exact job for which a 14-year-old was fitted, when in fact tests could reveal only the range of jobs he might fill.[100] By 1920 skepticism about the possibility of measuring interests independently of on-the-job activity had sliced Thorndike's position to pieces. Psychological testers, many recognized, were trying to take a picture of the soul. Too often "intrinsic interest" was confused with passing fancy. Testers had ignored the distinction betweeen interest and aptitude and had at best located the unfits rather than the misfits.[101]

Like many movements, vocational guidance outlived its original ideology. Guidance survived as a minor part of school counseling, but in the 1920s the major focus shifted from education to industry. The distinction between vocational guidance and vocational selection, too often blurred in the early years of the movement, now became explicit. Max Freyd noted in 1923 that vocational guidance focused on the individual and his interests, vocational selection on picking the most suitable person for a job. Freyd thought that vocational selection had the brighter future, as well he might, for his employer was not a school board but the advertising firm of J. Walter Thompson.[102]

Not all of the idealism went out of vocational guidance in the 1920s, but its stalwarts increasingly redefined their goals to the point at which they became meaningless. Brewer and others talked increasingly about guidance for all ages rather than merely for youth. As Benjamin Stolberg noted in 1922, "the more lyric reformers would extend vocational guidance through life. Indeed, life to them is a schedule between vocational and avocational supervision."[103] In this respect the course of vocational guidance was identical to that of Joseph Lee's playground movement. As evidence mounted to challenge Lee's original belief that supervised play would remedy a host of social problems from unemployment to delinquency, he shifted his interests in the 1920s from youth to adults and from playgrounds to ways to occupy leisure time. As the high hopes of the youth savers of the 1900–1920 period were gradually eroded, the institutions which they created survived in an

242

ideological vacuum and became agencies for custody rather than character building.

Conclusion: The Hollow Youth

The key contribution of the 1900–1920 period was not the discovery of adolescence, for in one form or another a recognition of changes at puberty, even drastic changes, had been present long before 1900. Rather, it was the invention of the adolescent, the youth whose social definition—and indeed, whose whole being—was determined by a biological process of maturation. Although one can identify different and sometimes conflicting impulses behind the invention, all sorts of links existed among the various inventors. Joseph Lee connected boys-work to social education, just as G. Stanley Hall formed a bridge between academic psychology on one side and parents and pedagogues on the other. The fact that a large number of individuals who started from different directions were able to converge on the adolescent made it easy for them to think of adolescent behavior as a universal phenomenon, lurking in the heart of every boy and waiting only for the opportunity to reveal itself.

To speak of the "invention of the adolescent" rather than of the discovery of adolescence underscores a related point: adolescence was essentially a conception of behavior imposed on youth, rather than an empirical assessment of the way in which young people actually behaved. The architects of adolescence used biology and psychology (specifically, the "storm and stress" thought to be inherent in youth), to justify the promotion among young people of norms of behavior that were freighted with middle-class values. One of these norms was conformity, whether in the inculcation of "school spirit" in secondary schools or in the implanting of "loyalty" and "hero worship" in the team sports of boys' clubs. Another was hostility to intellectuality, evident both in the *Cardinal Principles of Secondary Education* and in the muscular Christianity which imbued movements like scouting. A third norm was passivity, although the rhetoric of boys-workers might appear at first to belie this. But if boys-workers praised aggressiveness (the "pugilistic" instinct), they insisted at the same time that it be directed only against other boys in the context of highly regulated team sports.

While a number of underlying values serve to connect the sundry explorers of adolescence between 1900 and 1920, one basic split was evident, between those who continued to look on youth as a time for grappling with growth, development, and life purpose, and those who looked primarily to parents and society for solutions to the problematic nature of youth. For the latter, the ideal was a kind of hollow youth, devoid of inner crisis—an ideal that naturally reinforced the perception of youth as a problematic time of life.

In general, this distinction can be reduced to one between Hall and some boys-workers on one side and social educators and parent counselors on the other. It can also be reduced to a distinction between vestigial remnants of the 19th century and the direction to be taken by our own. When social psychologists like Edgar Z. Friedenberg, Joseph Adelson, and Elizabeth Douvan complained during the 1960s that a succession of noiseless simulations of adulthood had replaced the sort of intense crisis about career plans and moral values once thought to be appropriate to youth, they were merely expressing the negative effects of what had been a positive social ideal for early 20th-century educators. [104]

CHAPTER 9

The Age of Adolescence

A GUIDING assumption behind the efforts of educators and youth workers between 1900 and 1920 was that adolescence should become a universal experience. Yet even in 1920 most young people in America were unfamiliar with the institutions of adolescence. Variations in regional and class life-styles affected the rate of penetration of the new institutions and attitudes toward youth as much as they affected the dissemination of the automobile and telephone. Towns and small cities proved to be much more responsive to the institutions of adolescence than were rural and metropolitan areas, while a mixture of apathy and antipathy continued to mark the attitudes of lower-class youth. Yet by 1950 the revolution in the treatment of young people was largely complete. In the three decades after 1920 virtually every state extended the legal protection provided by the juvenile court to those between 16 and 18 or 20. In effect, adolescence became a legal as well as a social category. In 1920 leaders in scouting still measured membership by the thousands; in 1950 they measured it by the millions. Confronted by a declining demand for their labor, especially during the Depression, boys as well as girls prolonged their education; the proportion of the 17-year-old population graduating from high school rose from 6.4 percent in 1900 to 50.8 percent in 1940 and 62.3 percent in 1956. Between 1920 and 1950 the reformers and clergymen who comprised the original architects of adolescence passed from the scene, but new groups, led by local boosters, made the regulation of young people's activities a matter of civic pride.

While the dissemination of the institutions of adolescence occupies a central position in any account of age relations since 1920, its importance should not obscure other developments. By a kind of Hegelian dialectic, adolescence seemed to generate its opposites. Even as it became almost impossible to avoid exposure to the institutions of adolescence, many young people voted with their feet and resolutely pursued life-styles that deviated from the ideal of conformist and ingenuous adolescence. In addition, between 1920 and 1950 changes were occurring in socialization patterns and family relationships within the middle class, changes which were to have a profound influence both on the institutions of adolescence and on the conditions of coming of age during the 1960s and 1970s.

Adolescence in Town and Country

Those who explored the psychodynamics of adolescence and created its institutions between 1900 and 1920 assumed that the growth of cities and of adult-sponsored institutions for youth were closely connected. The architects of adolescence themselves stood at the end of a line which stretched and twisted far back into the 19th century and which had always associated city life with traps for unwary youth. We have already had occasion to observe how age grading of schools developed much more rapidly in urban areas than in sparsely settled areas, where one-room schools took all comers well into the 20th century. Moreover, the work ethic as applied to youth flourished longer in the country than in the city. Even after the mechanization of agriculture, farmers were able to keep their boys busy feeding chickens, gathering eggs, and repairing fences. A belief that spare time should involve the production of something useful imbued organizations such as 4-H in farming communities. August Hollingshead noted in the 1930s that 4-H Club meetings in Elmtown were oriented toward individual projects rather than toward simulation of life on a long-dead frontier.[1]

In addition to the work ethic, some features of the old patterns of age heterogeneity have survived in isolated rural areas in our own time. A study of Kentucky mountaineers has described the way in which boys and unmarried young men between 16 and 35 customarily gather at the village store to exchange stories and gossip.[2] Older patterns of youthful migration have also survived in rural areas. Summarizing in 1939 the results of various studies carried out in the early 1930s, Robin

Williams observed that in rural areas young people were still prone to leave home at any time from early adolescence until their mid-20s, with the peak coming at age 18. As in the 1820s and 1830s, girls left home at younger ages than boys; children of tenant farmers left at earlier ages than those of landowning farmers, but when the latter left home, they tended to move greater distances, to the city rather than to the next village.[3]

In some rural areas, the survival of older terms for the stages of development reflects these unchanged development patterns. In *Plainville, U.S.A.*, Carl Withers summarized the terms applied to different age groups in a small (pop. 275) midwestern farming community at the end of the 1930s.[4] At times, all offspring of whatever age were called children or youngsters. The latter term insulted no one under 20, but "children" had vaguely pejorative connotations as applied to teenagers. More acceptable substitutes included "lads," "young people," and "children big enough to start sparkin' " (courting).[5] Plainville expected its young men at the "sparkin' " age to "sow wild oats," a tolerance broad enough to cover some premarital sexual experience, but nice girls were not to engage in sexual experimentation, and it was thought better for boys who picked up girls or patronized prostitutes to do their sowing in adjoining towns.[6] While tolerance of sowing wild oats has declined over the course of time, rural people and some evangelical churches in the South and Southwest have continued to hold to the belief that a young man must first go through a period of fermentation before marrying or joining a church.[7]

Withers selected "Plainville" for study partly because of its small size and partly because of its virtual isolation from modern American life. In view of its isolation, it is not surprising that Plainville was unfamiliar with "adolescence"; the word did not exist in the Plainviller's vocabulary. Not only were Plainvillers unfamiliar with adolescence, but they also lacked a word to describe the period between the attainment of sexual maturity and the attainment of full adult status. "Young people" was at times applied to teenagers, but its proper reference in Plainville was to young married couples without children or to courting couples. In other words, Plainville had no term for youth as Americans understood that concept during the first half of the 19th century. The reasons for this omission are open to speculation, but elsewhere in *Plainville, U.S.A.* Withers provided some clues. The age of marriage for males in Plainville was usually between 20 and 22, earlier than the national median for males in 1940 (24.3) and much lower than the national median for males in 1890 (26.1). At the same time, the scope of formal education, even in Plainville, encompassed the period up to 16 or 18. This combination of a falling marriage age and a rising school age had so compressed the age group once designated by "youth" as to strip the latter term of any conceptual significance.[8]

The fact that even in a town as isolated as Plainville new social patterns coexist with the old greatly complicates any attempt to analyze the dynamics of social change. For example, it is not at all clear that the institutions of adolescence appeared first in large cities, next in smaller cities, then in towns, and finally in villages and rural areas. Some of the characteristics of the 20th century's response to young people—the emphasis on their passivity, the regulation by adults of their spare-time pursuits, and the prolongation of education—emerged first in towns and small cities in the East and Midwest toward the end of the 19th century. The key agents in promoting adult-sponsored youth organizations in the 1880s and 1890s were, as noted, Protestant clergymen and organized Protestant women's groups like the WCTU, groups which sought to turn towns into fortresses of morality in contrast to the sinful metropolises. Spurred by the threat of the metropolis, town and small city churches reached a level of institutional sophistication during the final decades of the 19th century which permitted them to set the tone of local morality rather than merely to declaim against local immorality (see pp. 191–192).

After 1900 a new force, the organizational genius of the YMCA, supplemented the efforts of church groups in sponsoring youth organizations in villages and towns. Although the Association was composed mainly of laymen, it rarely challenged ministerial or feminine control of youth organizations; indeed, many ministers passed directly into work for the Association. But the YMCA did bring to youth work a flare for management and a zeal for promotion of community organizations that could operate free of the hindrances usually associated with the office of village pastor. At the same time that it was taking an interest in urban boys-work, the Association committed its energies to support the country life movement, the effort to revitalize village life along Progressive lines. Liberty Hyde Baily of Cornell University's Agricultural College was the most eloquent spokesman for the country life movement, and Theodore Roosevelt was its most influential advocate. But Protestant churches took an equally active interest in the movement, and the actual field work was often carried out by YMCA agents, men cut from the same pattern as urban boys-workers.[9] The pages of *Rural Manhood*, an Association journal with a mandate to popularize the YMCA's country life activities, contain abundant accounts of the way in which Association field agents induced local ministers and village officials to launch "progressive" institutions like the Boy Scouts, Girl Scouts, and Camp Fire Girls, all in an attempt at "the socialization of rural minds."[10]

Even in G. Stanley Hall's hometown of Ashfield, Massachusetts, which still had fewer than a thousand people in 1918, Association agents were active in organizing youth into arts and crafts clubs. Nor was it merely a matter of arts and crafts. Historical pageants aimed at reminding youth of the nation's heritage were promoted as zealously for country as for city youth. By 1920, Joseph Lee's Playground and Recreation Association of America stood ready to provide the YMCA with a "complete list of plays, pageants and operettas for young people, as well as suggestions for songs, dances, carols, costumes, and community programs." [11] It also stood ready to provide the kind of professional direction of activities for children and youth that the Association so valued. "There was considerable aloofness at first," an Association account of a historical festival at Lycoming, Pennsylvania, noted in 1914, "but this was soon broken up by the well organized corps of play leaders under the direction of the Secretary for Rural Recreation of the National Playground Association and the State County Work Secretary of the Young Men's Christian Association." [12]

Conservative morality identical to that maintained by city youth workers accompanied the institutions of adolescence to the countryside. The following statement is from an article on rural delinquency, but with the change of a few words it would be indistinguishable from contemporary discussions of urban delinquency:

> He [the country boy] hears the vile talk of the farm hands. He hears his father's discussion at the dinner table about animals. He is alone much of the time, often passing along dark roads. Vulgar language, when his girl playmates run a crossfire of it to get to an outhouse during recess, opens the way quite easily for vulgar acts as they walk along the silent and lonesome highway five days a week on their way home or to school. [13]

Before 1920, complaints about boys between ages 12 and 17 idling around confectionaries and train depots were the village equivalents to laments about city boys frequenting movie parlors and vaudeville shows. After 1920, village and town youth leaders bemoaned the moral perils posed by movies and automobiles as anxiously as did their urban counterparts. [14]

YMCA organizers found support for their efforts to "socialize" villages and small towns from the social-gospel-oriented Federal Council of Churches, especially from its Commission on Church and Country Life, which conducted various surveys of rural conditions during the Progressive Era and thereafter ardently promoted the turning of churches into community service organizations. Despite the combined efforts of the YMCA and the Federal Council, the spread of community service agencies into open country and village areas was often slow—slow, that is, except for adult-sponsored youth organizations. In a survey of rural social institutions in 140 villages, J. H. Kolb and Edmund deS. Brunner reported that the greatest rise in community organizations between 1924 and 1930 occurred in the category of "youth-serving" societies; such organizations increased during the six-year span from an average of 1.2 to 2.6 per village.[15] Interestingly, this growth spurt came at a time when many adult organizations, particularly fraternal lodges, were in decline. Although Kolb and Brunner noted the changes without comment, Brunner must have been elated, for he had begun his career as a country pastor under the influence of the social gospel and had worked as a secretary for the country church commissions of both the Moravian Church and the Federal Council before moving into the burgeoning field of rural sociology.

The mechanization of agriculture, especially after 1920, might have indirectly facilitated the work of rural sociologists and YMCA field agents by eliminating many of the functions traditionally performed by farm youth, and thereby creating a need to find surrogate roles for them. But this type of explanation is ultimately as unsatisfactory when applied to rural areas as when applied to urban areas. The mechanization of agriculture did more to accelerate the flow of farm youth to cities than to erase demand for the labor of those who remained. Social workers themselves claimed that they were seeking to revitalize rural institutions and to restore the warm and cohesive quality of rural life. Yet the institutions which they created lacked historical roots in the countryside. In promoting play pageants for country people—and (of all things) nature trips for country boys—social workers were actually projecting onto the countryside the fantasies of rural life long entertained by the urban middle class.[16]

The ideology behind urban boys-work, moreover, made the transition to the countryside relatively intact. It is true that the conditions of country life demanded some modifications of the practices of youth organizations and obviously shaped the program of 4-H, which by 1940 was the foremost youth organization in open country areas. Unlike most other youth organizations, 4-H and the similar Future Farmers of America received active federal sponsorship from the Department of Agriculture, and the 4-H program was much more project-oriented than that of the Boy Scouts. But the original impetus for 4-H resembled that of other youth organizations. In *The 4-H Trail*, William H. Kendrick cited John E. Alexander as one of the two founders of 4-H. A follower of G. Stanley Hall, Alexander also happened to be the author of *The Boy Scout Manual* and the leader of the Young People's Division of the International Sunday Schools. Kendrick's presentation of the 4-H program drew heavily on ideas about adolescent psychology popular among urban boys-workers in the first two decades of the 20th century.[17] The accompanying table, taken from *The 4-H Trail,* underscores both the need of boys-workers for a system of psychology and their willingness to accept a barbarously simplified schema.[18]

BOY AND GIRL LIFE KEY

LIFE STAGES	AGE	INSTINCTS	LEARNING	INTERESTS	IMPELLING FORCE
INFANT	1-6	RACIAL SELF-PRESERVATION	INSTINCTIVE	BODY ACTIVITY	OTHER CHILDREN PARENTS
BOYHOOD GIRLHOOD	6-12	IMITATION-PLAY CURIOSITY-TEASING	PUT THROUGH TRIAL ERROR	PLAY-PETS CHUM	SCHOOL PARENTS ASSOCIATES
YOUTH	12-17	GANG SPIRIT SELF CONSCIOUS	TRIAL ERROR COMPARISON	PLAY CHUMS CONSTRUCTION	GANG LOYALTY
YOUNG MAN WOMAN	17-21	WANDERLUST SEX	TRIAL ERROR IDEAS	RECREATION WORK	INDIVIDUALISM
ADULT	21 +	PARENTAL	IDEAS	JOYFUL LIFE WORK	HABITS REASON

THE RULE OF A BOYS LIFE IS LOYALTY TO THE GANG

By 1941, one Boy Scout troop in five was located in villages or open country; in the same year, 4-H enrolled 1,380,000 young people aged 10 to 20, of whom about a fifth were 16 or over. The spread of youth organizations outside of large cities was swift, but not always quiet. Opposition to secular youth organizations ran strong in some areas. Fundamentalist Protestants consistently opposed organizations such as 4-H, the Boy Scouts, and the Camp Fire Girls, even when the latter appeared under church auspices. Fundamentalists viewed such organizations as secular agencies that merely distracted attention from the primary issues of sin and salvation. The fact of fundamentalist opposition helps to explain why the progress of adult-sponsored youth agencies has long been retarded not in rural areas as such, but in areas of rural fundamentalism, especially in the South. The same was true in late 19th-century organizations such as Christian Endeavor, for, while by no means exclusively urban, they developed much more quickly in the North than in the South.[19]

The Zenith of Adolescence

In metropolitan areas, size and diversity have placed limits on the ability of adults to regulate the activities of youth; a combination of fundamentalism and population dispersal have placed some limits on the scope of adult-sponsored activities in villages and open country areas.[20] But towns and small cities of 5,000 to 50,000 people usually have a substantial cohort of young people and cohesive civic leadership from boosters, councilmen, school officials, and clergymen. As early as 1902, William B. Forbush recognized the potential of the town and small city:

> If it be true, as I think it is, that the places in America in which it is most desirable to live are the large towns and small cities, one great reason why this is so is because it is possible in such places so to coordinate the religious, intellectual, social and physical life of the community, not for boys only but for all, that there shall be no barriers between them, but that all shall be for the harmony of well-rounded human development.[21]

Forbush proved to be a minor prophet. A survey conducted by the Boy Scouts of America in 1942 revealed that scouting met with its greatest success in small cities of 10,000 to 100,000 people.[22] During the 1920s, boosters began to displace clergymen as scoutmasters.[23] In *Middletown* the Lynds described a similar relationship between booster spirit and the organization of activities for young people. Comparison of the 1894 and 1924 high school yearbooks revealed the spectacular growth of athletics during the period. "The high school, with its athletics, clubs, sororities and fraternities, dances and parties, and other 'extracurricular activities,' is a fairly complete cosmos in itself, and about this city within a city the social life of the intermediate generation centers."[24] According to the Lynds, Middletown used the high school to celebrate itself. Far from challenging the orientation toward sports and school spirit, local boosters actively promoted it. Contacts between adults and youth, while frequent, were now more likely to occur in the pep rally than in lifelike situations of the workplace.

Adult sponsorship of youth activities has reached its apex in the Middletowns of America rather than in its big cities or small villages. A metropolis could scarcely rival the network of youth organizations described by Hollingshead in "Elmtown," a town of 6,000 people, if only because the controlling agents of youth organizations—churches, local boosters, and fraternal lodges—have never held the same position of eminence in larger cities. Hollingshead provided both the fullest description of the results of the institutionalization of adolescence in the 20th century and a demonstration of the strong relationship between social class and membership in youth organizations. According to Hollingshead, Elmtown's institutions competed for the allegiance of youth with no more than a loose ideology of making "good citizens" out of boys and girls to tie their efforts together. The Boy Scouts, for example, although nominally sponsored by the churches and the American Legion, were really controlled by a clique of civic leaders, all Protestants and nearly all from Hollingshead's Class II, made up of business and professional men who attached high value to the manipulation of local politics and to membership in civic organizations.[25] The Scouts and Camp Fire Girls were usually from the top three classes on Hollingshead's ladder, a fact which illustrates the middle-class orientation of youth organizations and which complements Hollingshead's conclusion, supported by other studies, that participation in church-sponsored activities by youth rises with social class.[26]

Elmtown's churches played a role in sponsoring youth activities, but Elmtown's youth were neither notably religious nor notably skeptical of religion. Nearly every church in town had some sort of society for young people, complete with membership cards in a national body, oaths, dues, pins, and constitutions.[27] But for most youth "the church is a community facility like the school, the drug store, the city government, and the bowling alley."[28] Partly as a result of this, few of Elmtown's youth experienced much soul-searching on the subject of religion. The only exception to this generalization was the Lutheran Church, whose minister thundered against the seductions of the world and portrayed the pains of hell with a vividness that had an unhinging effect on some Lutheran youth. But the more common Elmtown response was that of the Methodist ministers, who were concerned only that young people join special church organizations designed for them. On balance, Elmtown's youth found little in the structure of community organizations to jar them from the passivity and acquiescence which seemed to be their main characteristics. Hollingshead's judgment was devastating but accurate:

> By segregating young people into special institutions such as the school, Sunday school, and later into youth organizations such as Boy Scouts and Girl Scouts for a few hours each week, adults apparently hope that the adolescent will be spared the shock of learning the contradictions of the culture. At the same time, they believe that these institutions are building a mysterious something variously called "citizenship," "leadership," or "character," which will keep the boy or girl from being "tempted" by the "pleasures" of adult life. Thus the youth-training institutions provided by the culture are essentially negative in their objectives, for they segregate adolescents from the real world that adults know and function in. By trying to keep the maturing child ignorant of this world of conflict and contradictions, adults think they are keeping him "pure."[29]

The Era of Adolescence, 1900–Present

At one point in *Elmtown's Youth*, Hollingshead described adolescence as a sort of no-man's-land, devoid of clearly defined status and roles. Elmtown's young people could work at 14 but not vote until 21. According to the motor vehicle bureau, maturity came at 15, the age at which young people were allowed to operate an automobile. The law held that above age 14 a person had the same legal responsibility as an adult, but then added that between 14 and 17 he could be tried as a juvenile delinquent rather than as an adult criminal.[30] In the long view, however, legal anomalies like these existed before the 1930s. It is not just in the 20th century that adolescence has become a legal no-man's-land. Over time, the change has actually been in the direction of a more precise definition of the teenager's role and status, a definition which takes its cue from the high school. Membership in the high school, Elmtown's foremost adult-sponsored youth organization, shaped local perceptions of youth's place even though only a third of Elmtown's youth reached high school and only half of these graduated.[31] In a real sense, a youth who dropped out of high school ceased being an adolescent. Instead, he became a young adult, severing his ties to whatever youth organizations he had joined while in school and slipping noiselessly into the occupational underworld of Elmtown.[32]

Adolescence, Delinquency, and Youth Culture

The identification of adolescence with high school studentship was a powerful force in shaping the experience of growing up during the second quarter of the 20th century. Yet throughout the same period the ideal of conformist and ingenuous adolescence was only one among a number of life-styles which competed for the allegiance of young people. Adolescence acquired the status of an official code, but its acceptance did not preclude the emergence of subcultures, or cultures within a culture. One of the most enduring of the subcultures was that of the street corner gang and juvenile delinquency, both features of American urban life since the second quarter of the 19th century.

As a social reality and legal category, juvenile delinquency antedated the age of adolescence, but the rise of interest in adolescent psychology led to new views of delinquency. Throughout the last quarter of the 19th century and first two quarters of the 20th, positivism was the dominant school of criminology both in Europe and in America. In a sense, positivism ruled without reigning; the specific incarnation of positivism currently enthroned changed from time to time, but the guiding assumptions were the same. In the late 19th century the Italian criminologist Cesare Lombroso sought to identify criminals and delinquents on the basis of such physical characteristics as head shape. With the erosion of belief in this kind of anatomical determinism after 1900, new forms of determinism arose. Between 1910 and 1920, for example, the "mentally defective delinquent" took his place in the pantheon of "criminal types." Other investigators looked for the cause of delinquent behavior in the environment, whether the absence of playgrounds or, in the more sophisticated formulations of the "Chicago school" of sociologists in the 1920s, in the "social disintegration" of the urban no-man's-land around factories and businesses. In the 1920s a number of psychologists challenged this ecological determinism by arguing that delinquency was necessarily the product of particular personality patterns. Common to all of these views, however, were the twin features of positivism: a disposition to shift attention from delinquency, a legal infraction, to the motivation of the delinquent, a physical, social, or psychological type; and a belief that delinquents were as different from conventional youth as a colony of lepers from a brigade of marines.[33]

It should be clear that the mentality which created the delinquent as a type resembled that which created the adolescent as a type. In each case, certain physical or mental traits were labeled appropriate or necessary correlatives of delinquency or adolescence, and then used to explain the behavior patterns of young people. A variation on the theme was the affirmation that delinquency originated in a perversion of the normal psychological patterns of adolescence. In 1904, G. Stanley Hall had argued, for example, that delinquency resulted from the conflict in adolescence between the "savage" propensities of youth and civilized conventions.[34] Twenty years later, Ben B. Lindsey, a Denver juvenile court judge, traced the sex delinquencies of high school girls to the imbalance between physical and mental development in adolescence.[35] Although he rested his case on nothing so misty as the law of recapitulation, Lindsey's language betrayed the typological determinism so characteristic of the times:

> Long experience enables me usually to pick these victims of early [physical] maturation at sight. There is an indefinable something in the eye, a something about the mouth that tells the tale, particularly when there has been an actual sex experience. Usually when I see such indications in children, I talk with them, get their confidence, and find that I am seldom wrong. I wish it were possible for me at this point to explain with precision how I detect these cases. But I can't.[36]

At first glance, some of the sociologists who downplayed the psychological constituents of delinquency in favor of an assessment of its origins in the urban environment might appear to have avoided this sort of typology. Yet a central flaw in the literature on delinquency produced by the Chicago school in the 1920s and 1930s was the assumption that the seeds of adult criminality were sown in youth gangs. In his celebrated study of 1,313 Chicago gangs, for example, Frederic Thrasher portrayed Chicago gangsters of the 1920s as the progeny of youth gangs.[37] On this point any reader of Thrasher or of comparable studies of urban delinquency is entitled to a measure of skepticism. Al Capone and Dion O'Bannion might once have belonged to youth gangs, but most gang youth did not graduate to the world of the Syndicate. Studies of recidivism in the 1920s revealed that most young people hauled before juvenile courts and pronounced "delinquents" did not subsequently embark on careers of crime, yet most students of delinquency were guided by the suspicion voiced by William Healy and Augusta Bronner that "a vast deal of crime has its roots in tendencies established during the years of youth or even childhood."[38]

However flawed the logic, the idea that the psychological or social constituents of adolescence caused delinquency and crime had a number of important practical applications between 1900 and 1940. It established that boys and girls, regardless of social class, were potential delinquents and hence needed close supervision during adolescence. Appropriately, the first generation of juvenile court legislation conferred on these courts power to deal with an extraordinarily broad range of infractions, not just indictable offenses but mere departures from decorous behavior, such as the use of obscene language.[39] To complete the circle, Clifford Shaw and Henry D. McKay defined as a "delinquent" any young person brought before a juvenile court for any offense, whether or not the charge was actually sustained.[40] Further, the link between adolescence and delinquency served to justify the upward extension of the age jurisdiction of juvenile courts between 1899, the date of the founding of the first juvenile court in Illinois, and 1930. By that date most states had extended the maximum age under which a young person could be brought before a juvenile court from the 16th to the 18th birthday.[41]

The positivist mentality spawned convenient justifications for the extension of state control over juveniles, but it ultimately did more to obscure than to illuminate the subculture of delinquency in the 20th century. It was never really clear, for example, whether the Chicago school of sociologists was trying to explain the origins of street corner society as such or its delinquent activities.[42] Over the course of time, delinquency, narrowly defined as a legal infraction committed by a minor, has known neither class nor regional barriers, while urban youth gangs have been primarily a feature of urban lower-class society.[43] Positivism did not just blur the distinction between delinquency and youth gangs; by emphasizing the role of poverty rather than ethnicity in generating gangs, it also portrayed youth gangs as predatory rather than protective. Thrasher noted that a single ethnic group usually dominated the various Chicago gangs which he described, but then downgraded the importance of ethnicity.[44] In contrast, a recent study by Gerald D. Suttles of a slum neighborhood in Southside Chicago has indicated that membership in a gang provides young people of a particular ethnic group with the sort of personal knowledge of their peers on which confidence can be built.[45] A similar impulse probably motivated the youth gangs described by Thrasher and Brace before him, for these gangs usually concentrated on defending their own territory rather than on striking into alien neighborhoods.

Despite his blind spots, Thrasher recognized that gangs provided their members with a self-contained status hierarchy, an insulated world in which members won from their peers recognition of qualities ignored by school and society. Thrasher skillfully used the tools of social science to lay bare the structure of gangs, but the details of their organization were less important than the fact that gangs were organized. Victorian reformers had occasionally glimpsed similar qualities of organization, but as long as they were transfixed by the image of the nomadic street boy, they were unable to recognize consistently the subcultural dimensions of gang life, the fact that the gang was a rival form of society with its own ethics and even etiquette. It was just this self-sufficient quality of gang life which continually frustrated the efforts of reformers in the century after 1850 to break up gangs or to turn them toward more wholesome activities, efforts which form a continuum of failure from Brace's New York Children's Aid Society to settlement houses and later attempts by scouting leaders to reach lower-class youth.[46]

Most of these efforts rested on the assumption that the gang was an embryonic form of delinquency and criminality, an assumption which acquired the status of a scientific postulate in the years between 1920 and 1950. As late as the 1960s, major studies continued to confuse youth gangs and delinquency. One by-product of this confusion was that relatively little attention was paid to the similarities between the behavior of gang youth and that of conventional middle-class young people. Chicago youth gangs of the 1920s, for example, often contained the same gradation of junior, senior, and young adult branches as the adult-sponsored youth organizations into which middle-class young persons were herded after 1890. Gang members frequently had their own argot and songs. The same could be said of *The Boy Scout Manual* which, among other accomplishments, has introduced successive generations of middle-class youth to a set of terms and skills appropriate to scouting but not much else. Thrasher noted that youth gangs in Chicago valued the cunning of the con artist; the scout was supposed to display the cunning of an Indian. Similarly, Thrasher observed that gang members placed a high value on physical prowess, peer loyalty, and even chivalry, all attributes of the ideal scout.[47]

Admittedly, this is stretching the point. To stretch it any farther would be to obscure the obvious difference between the gang and the sponsored youth organization. In the former, members esteemed qualities like physical prowess and cunning as marks of adult status, badges of precocious manhood; the latter justified inculcation of the same traits to distract young persons from the temptations of modern life and to keep them frozen in adolescence. Yet the comparison can be pushed in another direction, for in the 1920s one can detect increasing similarities in content as well as form between the culture of the gang and a developing subculture among middle-class youth.

Since the end of World War II, investigation into the youth subculture has become virtually an autonomous branch of sociology. Disagreeing both on its scope and its relationship to adult culture, sociologists have usually agreed that the middle-class youth subculture enforces on participants conformity to norms, customs, modes of dress, and language fads that are different from those of adults. Although most students have viewed the youth subculture as a relatively recent development, the 19th century did spawn a variety of youth subcultures, from the intense male comradeship of college fraternities to the ebullient style of the fire company lads. The distinguishing feature of the middle-class youth subculture of the 1920s was its emphasis on physical intimacy between boys and girls. During the 1920s the greater freedom of young people toward sexuality sparked a profusion of books and articles on "our rebellious youth." Articles on "flaming youth" swept aside the solicitude for exploited minors that marked the period between 1900 and 1920. To speak of youth in the 1920s was to speak of their behavior, not their treatment. Like gang youth, middle-class young people were investigated as if they inhabited another planet, while moviemakers projected an obviously marketable image of Jazz Age youth. The titles tell the story: *The Perfect Flapper* (1924); *The House of Youth* (1924); *The Plastic Age* (1925); *The Mad Whirl* (1925); *Mad Hour* (1928); *Our Modern Maidens* (1929); *Our Dancing Daughters* (1929).[48]

In the 1920s the supposed maladjustments of adolescence became a favored explanation for the deviance of flaming youth as well as of delinquent youth. Just as lower-class youth could joke about the boy sentenced by the juvenile court to have his adenoids removed, a psychologist could ask his middle-class audience "what ails our youth?" [49]

Tradition had associated adolescent debility with hothouse academic pressures and the temptations of urban sophistication, but in the 1920s the terminology of modern psychology supplanted the rhetoric of Victorian moralism in the equation. There was less talk about adolescent girls driven to insanity by competitive conditions in schools, and much more about the vulnerability of young people in a society marked by changing moral standards. "Institutions everywhere are in flux," Miriam Van Waters wrote. "In morals the old is not dead and the new is not strong enough to stand, and youth dances into the streets, eager and untaught, and impatient with the hubbub of voices trying to remake the social order." [50] Yet these changes in vocabulary often concealed a fundamental continuity of values. The disposition to contrast the stability of the past with the frenetic quality of modern life was as strong in the 1920s as in 1850 or 1900. W. I. Thomas contrasted the "small and spatially isolated communities of the past, where the influences were strong and steady," with a modern individualism which forced a plethora of choices on young people.[51] Miriam Van Waters updated the 19th century's juxtaposition of the sturdy yeoman and the city slicker by distinguishing wholesome labor in factories from service industries where "there is a perpetual demand to please, soothe, flatter and interest tired adults." [52] Margaret Mead contrasted the problematic character of adolescence in America with the blissful Samoan version. In Samoa the worst of times became the best of times; "the whole tradition of Samoa is against forcing any aspect of life." As a result, "adolescence becomes not the most difficult, most stressful period of life, but perhaps the pleasantest time the Samoan girl will ever know." [53]

One drawback of this type of analysis was that it failed to fit evidence turned up by students of middle-class youth in the 1920s, evidence that pointed to continuity rather than discontinuity in most middle-class young people's path to adulthood. Both the Lynds and Hollingshead, for example, were struck by the absence of storm and stress among young people in the communities which they studied.[54] A second flaw of such theorists was that, like the students of delinquency, they displayed an incurable propensity to offer universally applicable theories to explain a kaleidoscope of customs and attitudes. As a result, in each case it was often unclear just what was being explained at a given time. For this reason it is important to attempt to draw a balanced portrait of the changing sexual and social practices among middle-class youth in the 1920s.

"They do scandalous things and hold improper opinions," a contemporary wrote of youth.[55] Ben B. Lindsey's *The Revolt of Modern Youth* assured readers that for every discovered case of sex delinquency, another thousand remained hidden in the invisible empire of the sub-

terranean sex life of youth.[56] In their study of Middletown the Lynds
contrasted the early-evening deadline of buggy rides and chaperoned
group parties of the 1890s with the exclusive boy-girl pairing of high
school dances in the 1920s.[57] Certainly the movie house and automobile
gave young people new types of social liberty. College men decorated
Tin Lizzies with signs like "capacity, ten gals." A resident of "Mine-
ville," a community studied by Albert Blumenthal in the 1920s, commented that "the main thing is that everybody has automobiles these
days and the fellows would rather take some 'Jane' out in the country
alongside the road and have a petting party. They say that summer is
the time to do your stuff and you've got to have an automobile to get
much."[58]

Movies and automobiles were not the only sources of the new social liberties. More young people than ever before, particularly young
women, were attending high school and college. The number of female
students receiving bachelors' degrees had risen steadily since 1890, but
even by 1920 it was still only 16,642. Ten years later the number had
tripled to 48,869, while the comparable figure for men more than doubled in the same decade.[59] Since the middle of the 18th century, college
students and their appointed overseers had been tussling over the propriety of regulations governing propriety; the struggle continued
through the 1920s, but under new conditions. The president of the University of North Dakota banned cheek-to-cheek dancing in 1920, but he
could scarcely have stuffed himself into the back seat of a Tin Lizzie to
measure how close was close. Nor was he likely to get much help from
his faculty. The foundation of the American Association of University
Professors in 1915 symbolized the growing group consciousness of professors and their increasingly academic rather than institutional identification. In female colleges, chaperonage gradually weakened in the
1920s; in many colleges, compulsory chapel requirements were softened. Fraternities and especially sororities, legitimized on most campuses before 1900, added more chapters in the 1920s than in either the
preceding or succeeding decade, and provided initiates not only with
substantial insulation from supervision but also with opportunities to
entertain members of the opposite sex. From their inception in the second quarter of the 19th century, fraternities had been middle-class
equivalents of the youth gangs, no less likely to make trouble and no
less suffused by a spirit of peer loyalty. But in the 1920s the homoerotic
impulses so much a part of the Victorian college scene collapsed with
the onset of mass coeducation in higher learning. College yearbooks,
with pictures of varsity lettermen arm in arm, gave way to the
drawings of bathing girls and near nudes in college humor magazines,
and to this ditty celebrating the charms of a new collegiate Miss Muffet,
who sat on a tuffet:

Drinking her whiskey and gin,
Along came a spider and sat down beside her,
Said she, "It's the D.T.s again." [60]

Changes in the 1920s extended to the substance as well as form of sexual mores. A questionnaire submitted to 792 married couples by Lewis Terman in 1938 turned up some striking differences in the sexual behavior of different generations of women. The proportion of women who had experienced sexual intercourse before marriage rose from 13.5 percent of those born before 1890 to 26 percent and 49.8 percent, respectively, of those born in the two decades after 1890. Fully 86.4 percent of the women in Terman's study born after 1910 had premarital sexual experience. Terman's data revealed a less striking but still significant rise in premarital sex experience among men in the same periods. [61] Similarly, data worked up from Albert Kinsey's researches into American sexual behavior in the 1940s indicated that women born after 1900 were twice as likely as those born before 1900 to experience coitus before marriage. [62]

Like the blind men and the elephant, investigators of changing sexual mores in America described discrete units rather than the whole picture. Both the Terman and Kinsey samples were top-heavy with college graduates, and might have contained other biases as well. [63] For several reasons, it is important to recognize this middle-class bias. Newer customs like necking and petting, which permitted physical intimacy without coitus, developed mainly among middle-class youth, and had little discernible impact on lower-class youth until after World War II; during the 1920s and 1930s, lower-class boys fluctuated between relative indifference to girls and sexual intercourse, without the intermediate stage symbolized by petting. In addition, to the extent that middle-class youths were likely to experience premarital coitus, they were simply accepting sexual mores long common among those of lower social status. Historians who have studied the incidence of premarital pregnancy among all social classes between 1860 and 1940 have discovered that the rate was fairly constant, and that only a modest differential separated it from the rate of premarital intercourse for college-educated women born after 1900. [64] Further, even within the upper strata of the middle class, changing sexual mores certainly antedated the 1920s. Terms like "necking" and "petting" entered the vocabulary before the Jazz Age. Ladies' magazines had been running articles on the flapper since 1910. Similarly, intellectual changes which both sanctioned and stimulated a more candid approach to sex were launched before 1920 in the writings of young rebels like Randolph Bourne, Max Eastman, Margaret Sanger, and Floyd Dell. [65]

Not only were there precedents for the sexual mores of young people in the 1920s, but the changes, whenever they began, affected the middle and upper middle classes as such, adults as well as young people. Middle-class women born after 1900 were more likely than their predecessors not only to experience coitus before marriage but also to experience divorce after marriage and frequent orgasms within marriage.[66] Gertrude Atherton's popular novel *Black Oxen* (1923), whose plot hinged on a gross exaggeration of the possibilities of rejuvenation by glandular surgery, appealed to an audience of middle-aged women who desired to become more rather than less like their daughters.[67]

Not radicalism but a particular kind of self-consciousness seemed to mark the mood of middle-class young people during the 1920s. Mark Schorer has noted that "no figure of the past fifty years is more familiar than that of the moon-calf, the sensitive and misunderstood adolescent who is driven into his brooding, introspective life by the bleak, inapposite realities of the world around him." Schorer's description, of course, fits only the more reflective members of the generation of American young people born around the turn of the 20th century, young men like Philip Selaby, the protagonist of Stephen Vincent Benét's semi-autobiographical novel, *The Beginning of Wisdom* (1921). Self-consciousness also took other forms, from cheek-to-cheek dancing, public smoking, and public drinking to the self-pitying spokesmen for "youth's point of view" who strutted across the pages of magazines with growing frequency. Whatever its form, however, self-consciousness reflected the peculiar experience of a generation more insulated, investigated, and regulated than any of its predecessors.[68]

The self-consciousness of youth in the 1920s can best be characterized as an aspect of subcultural rather than countercultural behavior. The distinguishing feature of counterculturalism is its programmatic quality, the presence of an ideology that defends deviant behavior in the name of some progressive ideal. Randolph Bourne's *Youth and Life*, published in 1911, was one of the first documents of the countercultural tradition, for Bourne juxtaposed the spontaneity and daring of youth with the arid conventionality of adulthood and sided emphatically with the former. Even before Bourne, Julius Langbehn in Germany and G. Stanley Hall in America had contrasted the raw vigor latent in youth with the soft degeneracy of modern civilization. Yet although countercultural philosophies were available in the 1920s, nothing like a spontaneous youth movement emerged in America. Opinion polls of middle-class youth, both in the 1920s and after, consistently failed to turn up any real evidence of intergenerational discord; such polls revealed that young people were somewhat more tolerant than their parents of petting and necking, but otherwise held conventional attitudes about the evils of promiscuity and "sex irregularity." As late as 1963, Bennett Berger could conclude that "there is absolutely no good body of data on adolescents . . . which indicates the existence of a really deviant system of norms which govern adolescent life." Indeed, a few sociologists have proclaimed that the idea of an adolescent culture is merely a myth.[69]

Yet such a claim is ultimately as nearsighted as the insistence of countercultural philosophers that young people were about to storm the Bastille of conventionality. The behavior of flaming youth stood poised between conventionality and unconventionality, marked by what David Matza has called drift. "Drift," Matza has written, "stands midway between freedom and control. Its basis is an area of the social structure in which control has been loosened." [70] Matza has applied the concept of drift to juvenile delinquency, but his idea helps to explain some of the paradoxes in the behavior of flaming youth in the 1920s, paradoxes embodied in the Middletown girl who stayed out every night of the week, occupied her spare time reading "true love" romances, and yet was an "indefatigible" Sunday school teacher and church worker. She broke no laws, but she fitted Matza's description of delinquency:

> Delinquency is after all a legal status and not a person perpetually breaking laws. A delinquent is a youngster who in relative terms more warrants that legal appellation than one who is less delinquent or not at all so. He is a delinquent by and large because the shoe fits, but even so we must never imagine that he wears it very much of the time. Delinquency is a status and delinquents are incumbents who intermittently act out a role. When we focus on the incumbents rather than the status, we find that most are perfectly capable of conventional activity.[71]

This point leads to a final analogy between the gang and the middle-class youth subculture. Not only did the behavior of each stand poised between conventionality and unconventionality, but in each case the type of unconventional behavior indulged in seems to have represented a premature assertion of adulthood against adult-sponsored definitions of the role appropriate to the pure and innocent adolescent. Admittedly, the connection between fraternity skylarking and adult behavior was often tenuous, but a growing acceptance of impulsive hedonism and sexual daring cut across age groups in the 1920s. To a far greater extent than adult-sponsored youth organizations, both the gang and the middle-class youth subculture gave young people access to the symbols, if not always the substance, of adult status.

If, as we have suggested, generational conflict was neither unique to the 1920s nor unusually intense in that decade, why was so much importance attached to it? One clue lies in the fact that those who began books and articles by asserting that youth and age were clashing as irresistible force and immovable object usually ended by acknowledging that young people were confused by the ambiguous standards of adults and needed more sympathetic understanding from their parents. A reviewer of Samuel Hopkins Adams's novel *Flaming Youth*, an updated version of *Charlotte Temple* with a suburban adolescent girl carried to the brink of seduction every other week, praised it for showing that modern young people were at heart serious, "that they are fighting through a knowledge of themselves and of life, and that through freedom comes the opportunity to accept a standard of living—not because it is inherited but because it has been tested and found personally satisfactory." [72] As some contemporaries recognized, there was an odd mixture of alarm, tolerance, and plain curiosity, not to mention a substantial dose of voyeurism, underpinning the investigative curiosity about youth. Anne Temple could only explain the combination of alarm and tolerance in magazine literature by ascribing it to "nothing more or less than a preoccupation with the nature of [youth's] sex life." [73] Adults who were unsure of their own standards could neither impose them on youth nor sanction whatever youth did. In a society where the old was not yet dead nor the new strong enough to stand, to postulate a conflict of generations and then to disarm the conflict by calling for sympathy with the problems of youth gave adults a basis for savoring the new without giving up the old.

The Strange Career of Adolescence, 1930–1970

The Depression of the 1930s submerged the flapper, but both the lower-class youth gangs and the middle-class subculture survived hard times. In the 1930s attendance at high school became a kind of cure for inflated unemployment rates among teenagers. [74] Meanwhile, adult-sponsored youth organizations continued to add recruits. By 1942, 96.5 percent of all potential scouting districts had been organized; the Boy Scouts of America claimed nearly a million more members in 1942 than in 1932. [75] Nor did the iconography of adolescence show much change. A manual for teenagers published in 1948 displayed a photo of six grinning and well-scrubbed high school students; the caption, seemingly cribbed from an elementary primer, read:

> Making the team, qualifying for a part in the school play, getting parents to treat them more like growing-up persons—these are some of the immediate concerns of these boys and girls. You will see more of, and get better acquainted with two members of this group. Meet Larry, who is kneeling in front, and Betty, the girl in the back who is looking on with obvious approval. The lucky dog, Kiltie, belongs to Betty. [76]

Yet these elements of continuity should not obscure a dramatic change which occurred in the experience of adolescence between 1930 and 1970, for in these decades the age group primarily affected by the institutions and subculture of youth dropped and contracted. Signs of the change were evident in the 1930s, when the Tin Lizzies of college campuses in the 1920s gave way to the jalopies of high school students; but after World War II affluence multiplied the number of two-car families and made it easier for 16-year-olds to win driving privileges originally reserved for 18-year-olds. Since 1945, acquisition of a driver's license has become the rite of passage for middle-class American young people. A continued drop of about four months per decade since 1850 in the age of menarche, combined with a sharp drop in the age of marriage between 1940 and 1960, contributed to patterns of earlier dating and the earlier wearing of brassieres and cosmetics in the 1950s and 1960s. By 1970 these activities often began for girls at 12 or 13 rather than at 15 or 16, and were sustained in part by the precocious social climate of junior high schools, institutions which became common only after 1945.[77]

Musical and clothing fashions also gave evidence of the declining age of the adolescent group. The bobby-soxers, usually between 15 and 18, who mobbed performances by Frank Sinatra in the 1940s gave way in the 1960s to the gaggle of teenyboppers, aged 12 to 15, who goggled at the Beatles. By 1960 the record trade distinguished only two age groups; subteens (ages 9 to 13) and "adults" (14 and over.) In contrast, fashion designers still distinguished a teen market (ages 13 to 15) from subteens (ages 10 to around 13) and juniors (16 and up). But the direction of change was clear. During the 1930s, high school boys gradually abandoned the wearing of knickers, which in 1900 had been the distinctive garb of boys 10 to 18, and relinquished them to the 10-to-14-year-olds; in the 1950s the casual wear of teenagers supplanted knickers even for the latter age group. Clothes designers in the 1950s and 1960s could rely on the data gathered in the burgeoning field of teenage market research, initiated by Eugene Gilbert. Like Dwight Lyman Moody, Gilbert began life as an enterprising shoe salesman. But Gilbert's calling was not to lead prayer meetings of young men; rather, it was to harmonize the efforts of merchandisers and the whims of teenage consumers. Paradoxically, between 1945 and 1960, the years when Gilbert was building his market-research empire, teenagers between 16 and 19 grew less conscious of clothing fashions. Fashion advertisements in *Seventeen* increasingly had to compete with advertisements for household furnishings, a reflection of the fact that by the late 1950s, 18 had become the single most common age at which American girls married![78]

The transformation of the adolescent group affected not only the youth subculture but youth institutions and street gangs as well. The removal of millions of young men aged 18 to 30 to military service in World War II seems to have marked the end of the pattern of graduation from street corner gangs to young men's social and athletic clubs and the underside of politics, although the beginnings of this transformation certainly antedated the war. By the 1950s, moreover, a new type of gang appeared in both Western Europe and the United States—the Teddy Boys in Britain, the *Halbstarke* in Germany, the *blousons noirs* in France, and the motorcycle gangs in America, all of which were more predatory and less protective than street corner gangs. In America the motorcycle symbolized the outcast status of the Hell's Angels. So did their initiation rite, the dumping of buckets of excreta on the heads of candidates.[79]

Of all the changes in the adolescent age group since 1945, those which affected adult-sponsored youth organizations are the easiest to measure, simply because such institutions have used membership rolls to measure success. The annual reports of the Boy Scouts of America indicate that since 1945 scouting has been in a prolonged quandary because of its growing inability to recruit even middle-class teenagers. In contrast to the Girl Scouts, which never had been able to attract many teenagers, the early scouting movement had considerable success with boys aged 12 to 17. A survey in 1924 revealed that 42.2 percent of all Boy Scouts were aged 14 or over, while 50.8 percent were 12 or 13. A comparable survey in 1967 indicated that only 19.6 percent of all scouts were 14 or over. In the same year, more than one-third of all scouts were exactly 11 years old, an age rank which had been allowed admission to the Boy Scouts only since 1949, and then only as a response to the declining number of teenage scouts. The expansion of the Explorer program for boys 14 and over took up some of the slack, but the proportion of Explorers to all boys aged 14 to 16 registered virtually no gain in the 1950s and 1960s, while in 1954 the membership of the Cub Scouts (aged 8 to 10) for the first time surpassed that of the Boy Scouts.[80]

It is often said that we live in an age of prolonged adolescence, but it is obviously not adolescence that is being prolonged, at least not the sort of conformist and ingenuous adolescence that emerged as a moral ideal and social experience between 1890 and 1920. Beginning in the 1930s and increasingly since 1940, both sponsored institutions for young people and the youth subculture have affected a progressively younger age group. But if adolescence is waning, what is taking its place? There are only two possible answers: a more pronounced adult orientation on the part of young people, or a different kind of youth orientation. Oddly, a plausible case can be made for each.

The idea that young people have become more adult-oriented during the last few decades does not only rest on the fact that the juvenile activities of traditional youth organizations no longer seem to appeal to youth. As early as the 1930s, for example, observers detected a new mood of seriousness among college students. Depressions, of course, have a way of making people serious, but in reporting on the results of an exhaustive survey of the attitudes of college students in 1936, the ed-' itors of *Fortune* called attention not only to the anxiety of college youth about future employment prospects but also to a new degree of intellectual curiosity and political sensitivity and to a muting of the self-conscious swagger about sex and liquor so common in the 1920s.[81] Political radicalism remained a negligible force on college campuses throughout the 1930s, but there was less of the studied indifference to professors that had long characterized student life, and more of a taste for fine music, literature, and even learning.[82] In addition, there was far more continuity between student life in the 1930s and that of the 1940s and 1950s than is often realized. Perhaps political radicalism has been used too often as the sole criterion of seriousness. Communist cells, prominent in a minority of universities during the 1930s, disappeared in the 1950s, but the influx of veterans after 1945 and the growth of urban universities serving lower-middle-class clienteles did much to perpetuate the sober mood of the 1930s. The veterans were uninterested in the collegiate rituals of adolescence which had developed between 1880 and 1930, and the streetcar students could not afford them.[83]

In many ways, student radicals of the 1960s bore no resemblance to any of their predecessors. Far more radical than students of the 1940s and 1950s, protesters in the 1960s were more activist in temper than the radical students of the 1930s, who often acquiesced to adult direction of their efforts. Yet if one takes the long view and compares the attitudes of college students in the 1930–1970 period with those of students in the preceding four decades, the outbreak of radicalism in the 1960s can be seen as a bulge on a continuum of growing seriousness which stretched back to the 1930s and has endured into the 1970s. Student protesters of the 1960s did succeed in adding a new dimension to seriousness, for they were not merely earnest and inquisitive but emphatic that their desires for autonomy be recognized. Not only did protestors display scant interest in the rituals of college life which had intrigued earlier generations of students, but they ardently demanded a greater share of the governing power in the institutions which most affected their lives.[84]

The political consciousness and intellectual sophistication of student radicals in the 1960s derived in large measure from the distinctive socialization patterns of the upper-middle-class families from which most of them came. In general, the growing maturity of middle-class young people since 1930 has coincided with the rising importance in

The Era of Adolescence, 1900–Present

America of the new or bureaucratic middle class, and of the distinctive child socialization patterns of this class. Where the child study movement of the 1890s had sought to inculcate obedience, self-control, and stoicism, child-rearing manuals in the 1920s and 1930s paid more attention to the social arts and free personality development. Increasingly, the ideal was a kind of family life which would allow for flexibility as well as nurture.[85]

One attitude which appeared to connect the new and old middle classes was child-centeredness, as illustrated by the organization of activities for juveniles, participation in the PTA, and support for better schools. But there were two important differences. First, the new middle class preferred the organization of activities for the child as well as for youth. In *Crestwood Heights*, a study of a Canadian new-middle-class community in the 1950s, Seeley, Sim, and Loosely described the "high degree of institutional activity" experienced by children aged 5 to 12.[86] Almost from the cradle, the Crestwood child was directed through a series of age-graded associations designed for physical, mental, and emotional needs at each stage of development. A second difference between child-centeredness in the new and old middle classes lay in the purposes of organized activity. The Crestwood child was being put through his paces not to keep his character pure but to develop his social and intellectual skills. In contrast to the game playing of youth organizations spawned by the old middle class, the new-middle-class life-style sanctioned the acquisition of skills that would be useful later on, dancing and tennis rather than knot tying and Indian lore. Herbert J. Gans has aptly characterized this style as child-centered but adult-oriented.[87]

A probable effect of these changes in socialization techniques was the emergence of a kind of young person bored by the institutional rituals of adolescence and free of serious parental pressure to join the old type of adult-sponsored youth organization. Miller and Swanson demonstrated in 1958 that differences between techniques of child socialization in the old and new middle classes were authentic. The declining appeal of scouting to teenagers since 1945 has already been noted. In 1960, James S. Coleman observed that students at the high school in "Executive Heights," a new-middle-class suburb, displayed both a revulsion from the institutions of adolescence and a disenchantment with the passive dependency imposed on them by schools. It is fair to add that even within the old middle class, the extreme emphasis on purity and discipline so pervasive in the ideology of youth organizations around 1900 has been weakening since the 1920s.[88]

One could leave it at that, with the growing seriousness of middle-class youth since 1930 reinforced by the changing direction of child socialization techniques in the same period, were it not for abundant evidence that young people have also become more psychologically detached from society. The direction of child socialization has been toward egalitarianism in family relationships, but not consistently toward encouragement of an adult orientation. Alongside families which have been child-centered but adult-oriented, there has flourished a type of family which is both child-centered and child-oriented, which has sanctioned contact between parents and children mainly around the interests of the child. Further, although the age group primarily affected by the institutions of adolescence has been dropping, a high degree of institutional segregation has continued to shape the experiences of young people. Some of the effects of this institutional segregation can be seen in the changing purposes of the adolescent subculture and the emergence in the 1960s of a distinctive postadolescent youth culture.[89]

The post-1920 adolescent subculture differed from youth subcultures of the 19th century in two ways. First, youth subcultures in the 19th century were often class cultures, not only because they drew on young people of similar backgrounds but also because they often expressed themselves primarily in antagonism toward young people of other classes or nationalities. In contrast, the adolescent subculture often expressed itself in a self-conscious grasping after the symbols of adult status and in admiration for young people who challenged adults, expressions represented as fully by reckless driving in the 1950s as by public kissing in the 1920s. Second, to a far greater extent than in 19th-century youth cultures, the post-1920 adolescent subculture expressed itself in the construction of a system for evaluating peers which bore little resemblance to the criteria used by middle-class adults for evaluating either each other or young people. In this sense, the adolescent subculture has not been hostile to adult values so much as indifferent to them. The fact that 19th-century youth subcultures contained a much broader range of ages than the adolescent subculture helps to explain these differences, but an equally important distinction can be drawn between the adolescent subculture in the 1920s and that of more recent decades. The relaxation of moral standards and the dissemination of a laissez-faire attitude toward young people have conspired to reduce in importance the necessity to challenge conventions brazenly, while leaving the adolescent society, viewed simply as a self-contained and insulated value system, more or less intact. In this sense, recent decades have witnessed the growth of the more passive and acquiescent facets of the adolescent subculture and the relative decline of its more active and aggressive features.[90]

Just as the continued expansion of secondary education provided the institutional buttress to sustain the adolescent subculture, so the expansion of graduate education in the 1960s nurtured a postadolescent youth culture which Kenneth Keniston dubbed "postmodern," a style that mixed the attainment of psychological adulthood with an unreadiness to become involved in conventional occupational and family life. Although Keniston believed that such postponement of entrance into life's work was a new phenomenon, a possibility created by the affluence of postindustrial society, postmodern youth resembled those antebellum young men who similarly experienced a prolonged delay between the achievement of psychological maturity and the "start in life." Yet the differences between the two types of youth were substantial. Postmodern young people were the privileged children of the upper middle class, not impoverished young men in flight from the plow or workbench to the ministry or bar. The latter had displayed a strong measure of vocational ambition, although they often lacked the means to achieve their goals; the former customarily viewed the world of conventional occupations and professions with a mixture of apathy and disdain.[91]

Although postmodern young people were a new force in American society in the 1960s, some of their customs and attitudes resembled those of the adolescent subculture of the 1940s and 1950s. A few of the similarities are obvious but also superficial. For example, dress and language fads, long a feature of the adolescent subculture, suffused campus life in the 1960s. Other convergences were more subtle and more significant. The extreme hostility of student counterculturalists in the 1960s to high academic achievement, conventional status seeking, and meritocracy resembled the tendency of the adolescent subculture in the 1940s and 1950s to restrict goals to a level attainable by all. Another significant convergence lay in the high value attached by counterculturalists to physical and emotional intimacy with a few members of the opposite sex.[92]

What Willard Waller once called the "rating and dating complex" existed on a few American college campuses before 1920 but first flourished in the 1920s, especially at state universities where sorority row was likely to be as long as fraternity row. Rating and dating challenged not only traditional courtship and chaperonage but social visiting as well, for it substituted a search for thrills without obligation for supervised dances and restrained conversation over tea. During the 1940s, rating and dating moved on a broad scale down to the high schools, where it soon met a challenge from "going steady," a monopolistic practice which blunted the free-market competition inherent in dating. "Going steady" superficially resembled the college custom of fraternity and sorority "pinning"; the difference was that pinning was really an embryonic form of engagement, while "going steady" simply removed competition from the quest for intimacy. A high valuation of intimacy, warmth, and total frankness also characterized the preferred peer group of student counterculturalists in the 1960s. The latter can be compared either to rating and dating or to going steady, with some obvious differences in each case. But if the quest for intimacy and psychic attachment to peers is made the basis for comparison, the similarities between going steady and love in the counterculture are notable.[93]

In the late 1960s counterculturalist spokesmen like Theodore Roszak and Charles Reich sought to weave the various threads of postmodern youth culture into a coherent philosophy which sanctioned a separate sphere for youth in the same way that Victorian moralism sanctioned a separate sphere for women. Although the themes of counterculturalism were disparate and often elusive, any listing of its constituents would have to include: rejection of the putative values of technocracy, such as the pursuit of expertness, status, and success; philosophical subjectivism (consciousness as determiner and source as well as judge of experience); a preference for a mystical and almost magical view of reality; the cult (as opposed to mere practice) of sexual freedom; and a high valuation of either privatism or communalism, with the latter taking the form of "authentic" face-to-face relationships rather than impersonal and "exploitive" relationships.[94]

In thus raising postmodern youth culture to the level of a philosophy, counterculturalists unwittingly placed themselves in a tradition which went back to the 1920s, to Randolph Bourne and G. Stanley Hall, to Victorian youth counselors and medical moralists, and ultimately to Cotton Mather's jeremiads on the "rising generation." The characteristic which has unified this tradition has been its disposition to assume that the behavior and values associated with a small fraction of young people carry the seeds (good or bad) of future change and thus reveal the fundamental tendencies of the times. As a corollary, consciously or unconsciously, subscribers to this tradition have used their judgment of youth as the basis of advocating that change take one form rather than another. Because society has always been changing and because young people during the last two centuries have been well positioned to take advantage of these changes, there has always been a grain of truth in such assertions. The flaw in this way of thinking has been less its proclivity to indulge in sweeping generalizations on the basis of nonrandom samples than its persistent misapprehension of the attitudes of even those young people whom it identifies as historically significant. For history suggests that convergence and symbiosis as well as divergence and antagonism have marked the relationship between generations, and between the subcultures unique to particular groups within each generation.

Philosophers of the counterculture fell prey to a pair of over-simplifications: that adult and youth values are fixed and exclusive categories; and that young people must be listing one way or the other. In reality, American society has long contained various adult and youth subcultures which have interacted in ways still only dimly understood. For example, the urban Bohemias which developed in a number of American cities in the century after 1850 were populated mainly by adults; only in the last few decades has Bohemianism become the style of an important segment of our young people.[95] In other instances, patterns of behavior which were once general have survived mainly among young people. A custom such as migrating (or tramping) has had a kaleidoscopic history: first, an economic necessity for most people in preindustrial society; later, a practice of both upwardly and downwardly mobile youth in the 19th century; next, increasingly abandoned by middle-class youth during the more advanced stages of industrialization and stigmatized as an unfortunate by-product of the stressful character of adolescence; later, abandoned also by most working-class youth as unions brought job permanence and security; today, practiced out of necessity by the very poor of all ages and out of preference by alienated youth of the privileged classes. The religious revival appeared initially among all age groups; later, among young people of all social classes; still later, among lower-class adults and youth. Placing out children with relatives and friends, once practiced by all social classes, survives today mainly among poor urban blacks.[96] The historical relationship between generations and between social classes within generations is more like a snake dance than a yawning chasm.

These observations suggest that if young people have become more like adults, adults have become more like young people. The changes in the direction of flexibility in child socialization were, after all, initiated by adults, just as the lineage of many of the values esteemed by promoters of the counterculture goes back beyond the youth culture of the 1960s to the writings of middle-aged philosophers like Dwight Macdonald and Paul Goodman. It would be ironic if, at a time when many of the old institutions of adolescence are in manifest decline, spokesmen for the counterculture succeeded in creating a more sophisticated if no less pernicious version of adolescence, one that sanctions the isolation of youth from adult roles not because such roles "tempt" or "corrupt" the young but because they fail to provide scope for freedom and spontaneity.

NOTES

Chapter 1

1. Dean May and Maris A. Vinovskis, "A Ray of Millennial Light: Early Education and Social Reform in the Infant School Movement in Massachusetts, 1826–1840,"in Tamara K. Hareven, ed., *Family and Kin in American Urban Communities, 1800–1940* (New York, forthcoming); "Plymouth Church Records, 1620–1859," in *Publications of the Colonial Society of Massachusetts* 22 (1920):378; quoted in Henry Barnard, *Pestalozzi and His Educational System* (Syracuse, 1881), p. 397; "The Proper Time for Sending Children to School," *Common School Journal* 13 (August 15, 1851):248; on Alvan Hyde, see Heman Humphrey, *Revival Sketches and Manual, in Two Parts* (New York, 1859), p. 132; William Gilmore Simms, ed., *The Life of Nathanael Greene, Major-General in the Army of the Revolution* (New York, 1861), pp. 21, 28–29; Cotton Mather, *Youth in Its Brightest Glory* (Boston, 1709), pp. 3–6.

2. Cotton Mather, *The Best Ornaments of Youth* (Boston, 1707), pp. 22–23, 25; Mather, *Repeated Warnings: Another Essay to Warn Young People Against Rebellions That Must Be Repented Of* (Boston, 1712), p. 4; *Journal of the Life and Religious Labors of John Comly, Late of Byberry, Pennsylvania* (Philadelphia, 1853), pp. 8, 11; *Every Youth's Gazette* 1 (January 22, 1842).

3. David Barnes, *Sermons* (Boston, 1815), pp. 44–70.

4. "The Visit," *Western New York Baptist Magazine* 2 (February 1817):154; "Revival of Religion in Rupert," *Connecticut Evangelical Magazine* 5 (September 1804):113.

5. J. William Frost, *The Quaker Family in Colonial America: A Portrait of the Society of Friends* (New York, 1973), chap. 7.

6. Wiley B. Sanders, ed., *Juvenile Offenders for a Thousand Years: Selected Readings From Anglo-Saxon Times to 1900* (Chapel Hill, 1970), pp. 60–62.

7. "Minutes of the Committee and of the First Commission for Detecting Conspiracies in the State of New York, 1776–1778," *Collections of the New-York Historical Society* 58 (1924):169; on Increase Mather, see "Biographical Sketch and Diary of Rev. Joseph Green, of Salem Village," *Historical Collections of the Essex Institute* 8 (June 1866):166n.

8. Francis Walett, ed., "The Diary of Ebenezer Parkman," *Proceedings of the American Antiquarian Society* 74, pt. 1 (April 15, 1964):46.

9. *The Life and Adventures of John Levy* (Lawrence, Mass., 1871); William Otter, *History of My Own Times, or the Life and Adventures of William Otter* (Emmitsburg, Md., 1835).

10. The greatest change in family size since 1790 has been the decline by nearly 100 percent in families of seven or more members; see U.S. Bureau of the Census, *A Century of Population Growth: From the First Census to the Twelfth* (Baltimore, 1970), p. 12. While family size has changed over time, historians have modified the older view of very large,

extended families giving way to small, nuclear ones; see Philip J. Greven, Jr., *Four Genera-tions: Population, Land, and Family in Colonial Andover, Massachusetts* (Ithaca, 1970), pp. 15–16, 121, 220, and John Demos, *A Little Commonwealth: Family Life in Plymouth Colony* (New York, 1970), pp. 64, 68, 192, 194. Greven found a range of family types from nu-clearity to extension in Andover. He observed that kinship was a major factor in deter-mining social relations and in regulating social conduct, but added that the basic house-hold was most often nuclear, with kin living nearby in the community (p. 16). See also Peter Laslett, "Size and Structure of the Household in England Over Three Centuries," *Population Studies* 23 (July 1969):199–223.

11. For an illustration of the kinds of arrangements made for orphans, see *Autobiog-raphy of Benjamin Hallowell*, 2nd ed. (Philadelphia, 1884), p. 15; for the radical changes in female cohort mortality between 1830 and 1920, see P. R. Uhlenburg, "A Study of Cohort Life Cycles: Cohorts of Native-Born Massachusetts Women, 1830–1920," *Population Stud-ies* 23 (November 1969):407–420.

12. Peter R. Knights, *The Plain People of Boston, 1830–1860: A Study in City Growth* (New York, 1971), chaps. 2, 4, 7.

13. Anson Tufts, "Rev. Edwin H. Chapin, D.D., LL.D.," *New England Historical and Genealogical Register* (hereinafter *NEHGR*) 38 (April 1884):122.

14. Asahel C. Kendrick, *The Life and Letters of Mrs. Emily C. Judson* (New York, 1861), pp. 1–20; George T. Day, *The Life of Martin Cheney* (Providence, 1853), pp. 6–31.

15. "Memoirs of Isaac T. Packard," *The Guardian* 3 (February 1821):45.

16. "Some Records of Deaths in Bedford, Mass.," *NEHGR* 62 (January 1908):69–73; "Deaths at Edgartown, Mass.," *NEHGR* 53 (January 1889):102; Bernard Farber, *Guardians of Virtue: Salem Families in 1800* (New York, 1970), p. 177.

17. Elias Smith, *The Life, Conversion, Preachings, Travels and Sufferings of Elias Smith* (Portsmouth, N.H., 1816), p. 22; Samuel A. Foot, *Autobiography*, 2 vols. (New York, 1873), vol. 1, p. 10; "Send Your Children to the Summer School," *School Journal and Vermont Ag-riculturalist* 3 (May 1849):4–5.

18. *The Mother's Magazine* 1 (January 1833):3.

19. Adelaide L. Fries, ed., *Records of the Moravians of North Carolina*, 8 vols. (Raleigh, 1922–1954), vol. 1, pp. 420–421.

20. Constance N. Robertson, *Oneida Community: An Autobiography, 1851–1876* (Syra-cuse, 1970), pp. 311, 315–316.

21. Philippe Ariès, *Centuries of Childhood: A Social History of Family Life*, trans. Rob-ert Baldick (New York, 1962), p. 368 and passim; David Hunt, *Parents and Children in His-tory; The Psychology of Family Life in Early Modern France* (New York, 1970); Evarts B. Greene and Virginia D. Harrington, *American Population Before the Federal Census of 1790* (New York, 1932), pp. 98–99.

22. Edmund Morgan, *The Puritan Family: Religious and Domestic Relations in Seven-teenth-Century New England*, rev. ed. (New York, 1966), p. 77; see also Roger Smith, "Early Victorian Household Structure: A Case Study of Nottinghamshire," *International Review of Social History* 15 (1970):68–84; John R. Gillis, *Youth and History: Tradition and Change in European Age Relations, 1770–Present* (New York, 1974), pp. 16–18.

23. William C. Gannett, *Ezra Stiles Gannett, Unitarian Minister in Boston, 1824–1871: A Memoir* (Boston, 1875), p. 17; Otis P. Lord, "Memoir of Asahel Huntington," *Historical Collections of the Essex Institute* 11 (July–October 1871):833.

24. "Rev. Henry Griswold Jessup, A.M.," *NEHGR* 59 (1904, suppl.):xcvi.

25. Walett, ed., "The Diary of Ebenezer Parkman, 1745–1746," *Proceedings of the American Antiquarian Society* 72, pt. 2 (October 16, 1962):189.

26. Gillis, *Youth and History*, pp. 16–17; James R. Newhall, *The Legacy of an Oc-togenarian* (Lynn, Mass., 1897), p. 114; Elias H. Johnson, ed., *Ezekial Gilman Robinson: An Autobiography, With a Supplement by H. C. Wayland and Critical Estimates* (New York, 1896) pp. 10–13; John E. Todd, ed., *John Todd: The Story of His Life, Told Mainly by Himself* (New York, 1876), pp. 53–54; William Stickney, ed., *Autobiography of Amos Kendall* (Bos-ton, 1872), p. 11.

27. Octavius B. Frothingham, *Theodore Parker: A Biography* (Boston, 1874), p. 25.

28. Ibid., pp. 26–27; see also Smith, *Life, Conversion, Preaching*, p. 119, and Jason Whitman, *A Memoir of the Rev. Bernard Whitman* (Boston, 1837), p. 34.

29. Edgar J. Sherman, *Some Recollections of a Long Life* (Boston, 1908), p. 13; Solon J. Buck, *William Watts Folwell: The Autobiography of a Pioneer of Culture* (Minneapolis, 1933), pp. 40–43; *Memoirs of the Life and Religious Experience of Ray Potter, . . . Written by Himself* (Providence, 1829), chaps. 1–2.

30. *General Catalogue of the Officers and Students of the Phillips Exeter Academy, 1783–1903* (Exeter, 1903); *Catalogue of the Trustees, Instructors, and Students of New Ipswich Academy, 1831* (Keene, N.H., 1831); Joseph Dow, *History of the Town of Hampton, New Hampshire,* 2 vols. (Salem, Mass., 1893), vol. 1, p. 493. The Exeter catalogue lists ages. For the other academies, I have deduced ages from family registers in town histories.

31. *Catalogue of the Trustees, Instructors and Students of Pinkerton Academy, Derry, N.H., 1850–1851* (Boston, 1851); *Catalogue of the Trustees, Instructors and Students of Leicester Academy, Massachusetts, 1862–1863* (Worcester, 1863).

32. Bernard Bailyn, "Education as a Discipline: Some Historical Notes," in John Walton and James L. Keuthe, eds., *The Discipline of Education* (Madison, 1963), p. 135; Theodore R. Sizer, ed., *The Age of the Academies* (New York, 1964).

33. *Catalogue of the Trustees, Instructors and Students of Leicester Academy, Massachusetts, 1838* (Worcester, 1838), passim; George Moore, "Diaries," 4 vols. (Harvard College Library), vol. 1, October 31, 1829–January 24, 1830.

34. *A Catalogue of the Officers and Students of Haverhill Academy, 1837* (Concord, N.H., 1837). Using various sources, I have traced the occupations of fathers of thirty students at Haverhill. Nine were merchants or involved in "general trade"; five were lawyers; two were innkeepers and two were cabinetmakers; one was a banker and one was a furniture dealer; three were listed merely as "Capt." and one was a "Capt." and a farmer; two were in tanning; four were farmers. All of the farmers held town office.

35. Moore, "Diaries," vol. 1, March 28, 1828.

36. Warren Burton, *The District School As It Was* (Boston, 1833).

37. On merchants see Kenneth W. Porter, *The Jacksons and the Lees: Two Generations of Massachusetts Merchants, 1765–1844,* 2 vols. (Cambridge, 1937), vol. 1, pp. 7–11.

38. Gillis, *Youth and History,* pp. 16–18 and passim; Farber, *Guardians of Virtue,* pp. 199–200.

39. *The Life of Asa G. Sheldon, Wilmington Farmer* (Woburn, Mass., 1862), p. 16.

40. Ibid., p. 23.

41. Ibid., pp. 20–21.

42. Ibid., pp. 24–38.

43. Kendrick, *Life and Letters of Mrs. Emily C. Judson,* p. 21.

44. For a comparable pattern in Europe, see Gillis, *Youth and History,* pp. 9–14.

45. Porter, *The Jacksons and the Lees,* vol. 1, pp. 7–11; "Mr. Boyden's Reminiscences," *Proceedings of the Worcester Society of Antiquity, 1889* 9 (1890):65–66.

46. J. D. Van Slyck, ed., *New England Manufacturers and Manufactories,* 2 vols. (Boston, 1876).

47. Ibid., vol. 1, pp. 186–187.

48. Ibid., pp. 77–79; see also ibid., pp. 63–65, 238–239.

49. Ibid., vol. 2, pp. 700–701.

50. Ibid., pp. 468–471; ibid., vol. 1, pp. 182–184.

51. Lawrence W. Towner, "The Indentures of Boston's Poor Apprentices: 1734–1805," *Publications of the Colonial Society of Massachusetts* 43 (1956–1963):417–418; Margaret G. Davies, *The Enforcement of English Apprenticeship: A Study in Applied Mercantilism, 1563–1642* (Cambridge, Mass., 1956), p. 263.

52. Van Slyck, *Manufacturers,* vol. 1, pp. 210–212.

53. Ibid., pp. 391–393.

54. Ibid., vol. 2, pp. 633–634.

55. Ibid., pp. 597–598.

56. Ibid., vol. 1, pp. 172–173.

57. Ibid., vol. 2, pp. 495–499; ibid., vol. 1, pp. 213–214.

58. Ibid., vol. 2, pp. 450–451.

59. William Paret, *Reminiscences* (Philadelphia, 1911), pp. 15–20; W. J. Stillman, *The Autobiography of a Journalist* 2 vols. (London, 1901), vol. 1, pp. 14–15.

60. Gillis, *Youth and History,* pp. 16–18; Greven, *Four Generations,* chap. 4.

61. *Life of Asa G. Sheldon*, pp. 108–235; Jackson T. Main, *The Social Structure of Revolutionary America* (Princeton, 1965), pp. 17, 23, 27; James A. Henretta, "Economic Development and Social Structure in Colonial Boston," *William and Mary Quarterly* 22 (January 1965):75–92; Aubrey C. Land, "Economic Base and Social Structure: The Northern Chesapeake in the Eighteenth Century," *Journal of Economic History* 25 (December 1965):639–654; James T. Lemon and Gary B. Nash, "The Distribution of Wealth in Eighteenth-Century America: A Century of Change in Chester County, Pennsylvania, 1693–1802," *Journal of Social History* 2 (Fall 1968):1–24; Kenneth A. Lockridge, "Social Change and the Meaning of the American Revolution," *Journal of Social History* 6 (Summer 1973):403–439.

62. Richard D. Brown, "The Emergence of Urban Society in Rural Massachusetts, 1760–1820," *Journal of American History* 61 (June 1974):31–32.

63. Kendrick, *Life and Letters of Mrs. Emily C. Judson*, p. 17.

64. Daniel Scott Smith has indicated that parental control over marriage patterns weakened after the middle of the 18th century; see his "Parental Power and Marriage Patterns: An Analysis of Historical Trends in Hingham, Massachusetts," *Journal of Marriage and the Family* 35 (August 1973):419–428. See also Brown, "The Emergence of Urban Society," 49–50.

65. Charles Bell, *The Bench and Bar of New Hampshire* (Boston, 1894). Bell sought "to include the name of every member of the bar who has ever lived or practiced in New Hampshire, but not those practitioners who were never admitted to the bar; nor members of the bar who practiced here, but whose homes were out of New Hampshire; nor those admitted to the bar who never practiced, or who practiced elsewhere" (p. 5). I have based my conclusions concerning age of entry to practice on a sample of 500 (out of 780) of Bell's lawyers.

66. W. Scott Thomas, "Changes in the Age of College Graduation," *Report of the Commissioner of Education, 1902*, 2 vols. (Washington, D.C., 1903), vol. 2, pp. 2199–2206.

67. Daniel H. Calhoun, *Professional Lives in America: Structure and Aspiration, 1750–1850* (Cambridge, 1965), chap. 4. Calhoun relied on Henry A. Hazen, *Congregational and Presbyterian Ministry and Churches of New Hampshire* (Boston, 1875), and concluded that the typical New Hampshire minister was about 30 at ordination. For Massachusetts ministers of the same denominations, I have used *Contributions to the Ecclesiastical History of Essex County, Massachusetts* (Boston, 1865), pp. 57–219.

68. Calhoun, *Professional Lives*, p. 214, note 56.

69. Ibid., p. 111; David F. Allmendinger, Jr., *Paupers and Scholars: The Transformation of Student Life in Nineteenth-Century New England* (New York, 1975), chap. 1.

70. Calhoun notes that between the 18th and 19th centuries there was a rise of about three years in the age of ordination, and he doubts that the change was the result of the appearance of formal professional training for ministers; see Calhoun, *Professional Lives*, pp. 147–151.

71. Sidney Perley, "Alfred Poore," *NEHGR* 62 (January 1908):53.

72. William B. Atkinson, *Physicians and Surgeons of the United States* (Philadelphia, 1878). Atkinson included "all professors, hospital physicians and surgeons, officers of the more important medical societies, [and] authors, together with those who by length of service or success in the profession had become of eminence" (p. 3). My conclusions are based on a sample of 500 of the 2,700 physicians and surgeons in the directory.

73. Joseph F. Kett, *The Formation of the American Medical Profession: The Role of Institutions, 1780–1860* (New Haven, 1968), chaps. 1–3.

74. A work which bears comparison to Bell's collection of New Hampshire biographies is John B. O'Neall's *Sketches of the Bench and Bar of South Carolina*, 2 vols. (Charleston, 1859). More than two-thirds of the sixty-four lawyers in O'Neall's collection began to practice before the age of 25, with more than a quarter beginning between 18 and 21. Many of the late starters in South Carolina actually were raised in New England. Similarly, a sample of 400 antebellum lawyers drawn from the *Biographical Directory of the American Congress, 1774–1961* (Washington, D.C., 1961) reveals that congressmen who were born and admitted to the bar in the North were about twice as likely as their southern counterparts to have entered legal practice at late ages. Of the northerners, 52.7

percent were admitted to the bar between the ages of 18 and 24, 30.7 percent between 25 and 27, and 16.6 percent at 28 or over. Of the southerners (including natives of Maryland and Kentucky), 74.7 percent were admitted between 18 and 24, 17.3 percent between 25 and 27, and 8 percent at 28 or over.

75. Gillis, *Youth and History*, chap. 2.

76. Quoted in Thomas S. Perry, ed., *The Life and Letters of Francis Lieber* (Boston, 1882), p. 126.

Chapter 2

1. Warren S. Thompson and P. K. Whelpton, *Population Trends in the United States* (New York, 1933), chap. 4.

2. Charles G. Sommers, *Memoir of the Rev. John Stanford, D.D.* (New York, 1835), p. 80; Asa Cummings, *A Memoir of the Rev. Edward Payson, D.D., Late of Portland, Maine* (New York, 1830), p. 273.

3. Marcus Cunliffe, *Soldiers and Civilians: The Martial Spirit in America, 1775–1865* (Boston, 1968).

4. Mary R. Cabot, ed., *Annals of Brattleboro, 1681–1895*, 2 vols. (Brattleboro, 1921–1922), vol. 1, p. 325.

5. *The History of Warren County, Ohio* (Chicago, 1882), p. 342.

6. Cunliffe, *Soldiers and Civilians*, p. 238.

7. Ibid., p. 226.

8. On youthful enlistments in the Continental Army, see *Memorial of Mr. David L. Dodge, Consisting of an Autobiography, . . . With a Few Selections From His Writings* (Boston, 1854), pp. 19–20.

9. Susan R. Hull, *Boy Soldiers of the Confederacy* (New York, 1905); see also *Ages of U.S. Volunteer Soldiery* (New York, 1886), p. 6; "The Evils of Youthful Enlistments—and Nostalgia," *American Journal of Insanity* 19 (April 1863):476.

10. Levi W. Leonard and Joseph L. Seward, *History of Dublin, New Hampshire* (Dublin, 1920), p. 547.

11. Andrew D. White, *An Autobiography*, 2 vols. (New York, 1906), vol. 1, p. 14; *The Reminiscences of Neal Dow: Recollections of Eighty Years* (Portland, Me., 1898), p. 60; James M. Miller, *The Genesis of Western Culture: The Upper Ohio Valley, 1800–1825* (Columbus, Ohio, 1938), pp. 143–144, 153–154; John L. Thomas, *The Liberator: William Lloyd Garrison—A Biography* (Boston, 1963), pp. 28–30; John S. Stone, *A Memoir of the Life of James Milnor, D.D.* (New York, 1849), p. 17.

12. Carl Bode, *The American Lyceum: Town Meeting of the Mind* (New York, 1956), pp. 64, 73, 145, 151, 172, 196–200; Paul W. Stoddard, "The American Lyceum," Ph.D. thesis, history, Yale University (1947), p. 273.

13. *Catalogue of the Library of the Young Men's Association of the City of Milwaukee* (Milwaukee, 1861), pp. 12–14.

14. *Reminiscences of Neal Dow*, p. 60; *Life and Letters of Horace Bushnell* (New York, 1880), p. 19; Wilmer Atkinson, *An Autobiography* (Philadelphia, 1920), p. 61; John S. Stone, *A Memoir of the Life of James Milnor, D.D.*, p. 17.

15. Frank B. Kingsbury, *History of the Town of Surry, Cheshire County, New Hampshire* (Surry, 1925), p. 226. I have drawn a sample of 40 of the 65 members, using family registers in Kingsbury for dates of birth.

16. Charles H. Miller, "The Order of Cadets of Temperance," in *One Hundred Years of Temperance Work* (New York, 1886), p. 527.

17. Rena L. Vassar, ed., "The Life or Biography of Silas Felton, Written by Himself," *Proceedings of the American Antiquarian Society* 19, pt. 2 (October 21, 1959):127.

18. On the European origins of the tradition of youthful parody, see John R. Gillis, *Youth and History: Tradition and Change in European Age Relations, 1770–Present* (New

York, 1974), pp. 25–26; Barrett Wendell, *Cotton Mather: The Puritan Priest* (Cambridge, 1926), p. 241; Joseph Walker, *Hopewell Village: A Social and Economic History of an Iron-Making Community* (Philadelphia, 1966), pp. 386–387; Marion N. Rawson, *New Hampshire Borns a Town* (New York, 1942), pp. 244–245.

19. *The Autobiography of Brantley York* (Durham, N.C., 1910), p. 9.

20. *Journals of Hezekiah Prince, Jr., 1822–1828*, introduced by Walter M. Whitehill (New York, 1965), pp. viii–ix, 49, 311, 341.

21. William Stickney, ed., *Autobiography of Amos Kendall* (Boston, 1872), p. 3. The autobiography is written in the third person.

22. "Letters of the Four Beatty Brothers of the Continental Army, 1774–1794," *Pennsylvania Magazine of History and Biography* 44 (July 1920):225.

23. Ibid., 214.

24. *Journals of Hezekiah Prince, Jr.*, p. 49; John Frisch, "Youth Culture in America, 1790–1860" Ph.D. thesis, history, University of Missouri (1970), pt. 4.

25. Philander Stevens, *Recollections and Incidents of a Lifetime, or Men and Things I Have Seen* (Brooklyn, 1896), pp. 22–24; see also "Mrs. Ballard's Diary," in Charles E. Nash, *The History of Augusta* (Augusta, Me., 1904), p. 271.

26. I am indebted to Mr. William J. Gilmore for the timetable analogy.

27. Monte A. Calvert, "The Abolition Society of Delaware, 1801–1807," *Delaware History* 10 (October 1963):301, note 25.

28. Henry D. Dwight, *The Centennial History of the American Bible Society* (New York, 1916), pp. 93–94.

29. *Constitutions of the Order of the Sons of Temperance of North America* (Boston, 1865).

30. Wilson O. Clough, "A Journal of Village Life in Vermont in 1848," *New England Quarterly* 1 (January 1928):39.

31. J. C. Lovejoy, *Memoir of Rev. Charles T. Torrey* (Boston, 1847), p. 3; Zephaniah W. Pease, ed., *The Diary of Samuel Rodman: A New Bedford Chronicle of Thirty-Seven Years, 1821–1859* (New Bedford, 1927), pp. 170–171.

32. *Memoir of Samuel J. May* (Boston, 1873), p. 6.

33. Ibid.; Lewis O. Saum, "Death in the Popular Mind of Pre–Civil War America," *American Quarterly* 26 (December 1974):477–496.

34. Henry Ware, Jr., "Recollections of Jotham Anderson," in *The Works of Henry Ware, Jr., D.D.*, 4 vols. (Boston, 1846), vol. 1, p. 10.

35. On the estimates of physicians, see Edward H. Dixon, *Woman and Her Diseases From the Cradle to the Grave*, 10th ed.(Philadelphia, 1864), p. 19; Jonathan S. Wilson, *Woman's Home Book of Health: A Work for Mothers and for Families* (Philadelphia, 1860), pp. 5–9; James Copland, *A Dictionary of Practical Medicine*, 5 vols. (New York, 1847), vol. 5, pp. 959–960; ibid., vol. 4, p. 325. J. M. Tanner presented a series of estimates of the age of menarche in 19th-century Europe in "Sequence, Tempo, and Individual Variation in the Growth and Development of Boys and Girls Aged Twelve to Sixteen," *Daedalus* (Fall 1971):907–930. The age of menarche went as high as 18 in Scandinavia during the 19th century, but I have found no evidence in the comments of physicians that it was equally high in America. In 1900 the age of menarche was significantly lower in America than in Europe (ibid., p. 929). On attainment of height, see ibid., p. 928. As late as 1904, G. Stanley Hall was able to assemble evidence that Annapolis cadets and Amherst students did not attain final height until their mid-20s; see his *Adolescence: Its Psychology and Its Relations to Physiology, Anthropology, Sociology, Sex, Crime, Religion and Education*, 2 vols. (New York, 1905), vol. 1, pp. 26–28; William G. Simms, *Guy Rivers, a Tale of Georgia*, rev. ed. (New York, 1860), p. 16.

36. William C. Gannett, *Ezra Stiles Gannett, Unitarian Minister in Boston, 1824–1871* (Boston, 1875), p. 9.

37. Quoted in Charles W. Moore, *Timing a Century: History of the Waltham Watch Company* (Cambridge, 1945), p. 5.

38. James D. Phillips, "James Duncan of Haverhill," *Essex Institute Historical Collections* 88 (January 1952):2.

39. Jesse S. Myer, *Life and Letters of Dr. William Beaumont*, introduced by Sir William Osler (St. Louis, 1939), p. 18.

40. Alexis de Tocqueville, *Democracy in America*, Henry Reeve text, rev. Francis Bowen, ed. Phillips Bradley, 2 vols. (New York, 1945), vol. 2, pp. 202–208.

41. Ralph W. Emerson, "Education," in *Complete Works*, 12 vols. in 6 (New York, 1929), vol. 10, pp. 152–153.

42. George Moore, "Diaries," 4 vols. (Harvard College Library), vol. 1, January 1, 1829.

43. Joseph Lancaster, *The British System of Education, Being a Complete Epitome of the Improvements and Inventions Practised by Joseph Lancaster* (Washington, D.C., 1812); Warren H. Small, *Early New England Schools* (New York, 1969), p. 388; William S. Heywood, ed., *Autobiography of Adin Ballou* (Lowell, Mass., 1890), p. 22; Henry C. Wright, *A Human Life, Illustrated in My Individual Experience As a Child, a Youth, and a Man* (Boston, 1849), p. 50.

44. Philippe Ariès, *Centuries of Childhood: A Social History of Family Life*, trans. Robert Baldick (New York, 1962), pp. 92–99.

45. Augustus B. Longstreet, *Georgia Scenes, Character, Incidents, Etc., in the First Half Century of the Republic*, 2nd ed. (New York, 1850), pp. 75–80. For a similar narrative of a turn-out, see Hubert M. Skinner, ed., *The Schoolmaster in Literature*, introduced by Edward Eggleston (New York, 1882), pp. 553, 557–558; see also Joseph C. Guild, *Old Times in Tennessee* (Nashville, 1878), pp. 329–336; J. E. Godbey, *Lights and Shadows of Seventy Years* (St. Louis, 1913), pp. 10–11; "Account of the 'Barring-out' of President James Blair of the College of William and Mary," in Edgar W. Knight, ed., *A Documentary History of Education in the South before 1860*, 5 vols. (Chapel Hill, 1949–1953), vol. 1, pp. 474–476; Warren Burton, *The District School As It Was* (Boston, 1833), pp. 118–123.

46. R. C. Stone, *Life-Incidents of Home, School and Church* (St. Louis, 1874), pp. 121–125. Charles F. Moore described brutal fights between teachers and pupils at a school in Massachusetts in the 1840s in his *A Sketch of My Life* (Cambridge, 1927), p. 5; for Horace Mann's comments, see *Fourth Annual Report of the* [Massachusetts] *Board of Education, Together With the Fourth Annual Report of the Secretary of the Board* (Boston, 1841), pp. 86–88.

47. Some progressive ideas about school government were in the air by 1840, although progressives readily acknowledged that any attempts to upgrade the position of teachers or the quality of schools would meet resistance; see Alonzo Potter and George B. Emerson, *The School and Schoolmaster* (New York, 1842).

48. Edward H. Magill, *Sixty-Five Years in the Life of a Teacher* (Boston, 1907), p. 11.

49. Vassar, ed., "Silas Felton," 142.

50. Ibid.

51. Ibid.

52. Martin Duberman, *James Russell Lowell* (Boston, 1966), pp. 14–15.

53. *Memoir of Samuel J. May*, pp. 25–26.

54. Otis P. Lord, "Memoir of Asahel Huntington," *Historical Collections of the Essex Institute* 11 (July–October 1871):83.

55. It should be added that, during the antebellum era, even spokesmen for progressive ideals of education made the establishment of order in the classroom the first priority.

56. David F. Allmendinger, Jr., *Paupers and Scholars: The Transformation of Student Life in Nineteenth-Century New England* (New York, 1975), chaps. 3–5.

57. Philip Lindsley, *An Address Delivered at Nashville, January 12, 1825, at the Inauguration of the President of Cumberland College* (Nashville, 1825), p. 40.

58. Ibid.

59. "College Instruction and Discipline," *American Quarterly Review* 9 (June 1831):231.

60. Quoted in Knight, ed., *Documentary History*, vol. 3, p. 231.

61. George P. Schmidt, *The Old Time College President* (New York, 1930), p. 79; *Documentary History of Hamilton College* (Clinton, N.Y., 1922), pp. 136–154; "Harvard College Records, Part I," *Publications of the Colonial Society of Massachusetts* 15 (1925):187.

62. Charles E. Cunningham, *Timothy Dwight, 1752–1817: A Biography* (New York, 1942), p. 253.

63. Walter W. Jennings, *Transylvania: Pioneer University of the West* (New York, 1955), pp. 116–118.

64. Thomas J. Wertenbaker, *Princeton, 1746–1896* (Princeton, 1946), pp. 155–156; James H. Morgan, *Dickinson College: The History of One Hundred and Fifty Years, 1783–1933* (Carlisle, Pa., 1933), p. 296; Maximilian La Borde, *History of South Carolina College* (Charleston, 1874), p. 130; Walter C. Bronson, *The History of Brown University, 1746–1914* (Providence, 1914), p. 184.

65. Louis L. Tucker, *Puritan Protagonist: President Thomas Clap of Yale College* (Chapel Hill, 1962), pp. 232–261.

66. Bronson, *History of Brown University*, pp. 188–189.

67. Samuel E. Morison, *Three Centuries of Harvard, 1636–1936* (Cambridge, 1965), pp. 118, 133, 208–210, 211–212, 252–254.

68. Wertenbaker, *Princeton*, pp. 138–140; Philip A. Bruce, *History of the University of Virginia, 1819–1919: The Lengthened Shadow of One Man*, 5 vols. (New York, 1920–1922), vol. 2, pp. 306–311, 267–293.

69. "J. Marion Simms Reports a Duel in South Carolina College, 1833," in Knight, ed., *Documentary History*, vol. 3, p. 270.

70. Kemp P. Battle, *History of the University of North Carolina*, 2 vols. (Raleigh, 1907), vol. 1, p. 194.

71. Ibid., pp. 266–267.

72. Bruce, *History of the University of Virginia*, vol. 2, p. 293.

73. Battle, *History of the University of North Carolina*, vol. 1, p. 619.

74. Cornelius R. Shaw, *Davidson College* (New York, 1923), p. 77; Stickney, ed., *Autobiography of Amos Kendall*, p. 33.

75. Lindsley, *Address Delivered at Nashville*, p. 41.

76. David F. Allmendinger, Jr., "The Dangers of Ante-Bellum Student Life," *Journal of Social History* 7 (Fall 1973):75–83.

77. Ernest Earnest, *Academic Procession: An Informal History of the American College, 1636–1953* (Indianapolis, 1953), pp. 83–96; James McLachlan, "The Choice of Hercules: American Student Societies in the Early 19th-Century," in Laurence Stone, ed., *The University in Society*, 2 vols. (Princeton, 1975), vol. 1, pp. 449–494.

78. Earnest, *Academic Procession*, pp. 108–112.

79. Frederick Rudolph, *The American College and University: A History* (New York, 1962), pp. 98–99.

80. LaBorde, *History of South Carolina College*, p. 146.

81. Tucker, *Puritan Protagonist*, p. 238.

82. Frederick Rudolph, *The American College and University: A History*, pp. 218–219; Schmidt, *Old Time College President*, p. 87; Daniel W. Hollis, *University of South Carolina*, 2 vols. (Columbia, 1951), vol. 1, pp. 56–59.

83. Morison, *Three Centuries of Harvard*, pp. 253–254.

84. Charles Wall, "Students and Student Life at the University of Virginia, 1826–1860," Ph.D. thesis, history, University of Virginia (forthcoming), chap. 5.

85. Quoted in Battle, *History of the University of North Carolina*, vol. 1, p. 212; see also Wall, "Students and Student Life," chap. 5; Morison, *Three Centuries of Harvard*, pp. 118, 231, and passim.

86. Tucker, *Puritan Protagonist*, p. 79; Josiah Quincy, *History of Harvard University*, 2 vols. (Boston, 1840), vol. 2, p. 277.

87. "College Instruction and Discipline," 295.

88. Bronson, *History of Brown University*, p. 152.

89. Wall, "Students and Student Life," chap. 6.

90. Lewis S. Feuer, *The Conflict of Generations: The Character and Significance of Student Movements* (New York, 1969), chap. 7.

91. David J. Rothman, *The Discovery of the Asylum: Social Order and Disorder in the New Republic* (Boston, 1971), pp. 50–52.

Chapter 3

1. Edwin D. Starbuck, *The Psychology of Religion: An Empirical Study of the Growth of Religious Consciousness* (New York, 1906), p. 203; G. Stanley Hall, *Adolescence: Its Psychology and Its Relations to Physiology, Anthropology, Sociology, Sex, Crime, Religion and Education*, 2 vols. (New York, 1905), vol. 2, chap. 14.

2. Starbuck, *Psychology of Religion*, pp. 196, 203.

3. Norman Pettit, *The Heart Prepared: Grace and Conversion in Puritan Spiritual Life* (New Haven, 1966), p. 101.

4. C. C. Goen, *Revivalism and Separatism in New England, 1740–1800: Strict Congregationalists and Separate Baptists in the Great Awakening* (New Haven, 1962), pp. 12–13.

5. Alan Heimert and Perry Miller, eds., *The Great Awakening* (Indianapolis, 1967), pp. lii–liii.

6. To unravel Puritan attitudes toward the timing of conversion is admittedly difficult, mainly because of the gulf that often separated the assumptions which Puritans worked on from the official opinions which they expressed. Puritans often urged children to become religious, and praised the ones who did. For a very detailed account of this side of the Puritan mind, see Sandford Fleming, *Children and Puritanism: The Place of Children in the Life and Thought of New England Churches, 1620–1847* (New Haven, 1933). Those who follow Fleming in emphasizing the precocity of Puritan children are likely to point to the case of Phoebe Bartlett, the 4-year-old Northampton girl whose religious sentiments were so scrupulously recorded by Jonathan Edwards. But Edwards's own daughter did not think that Phoebe was at all typical of Puritan children; see Jeremiah E. Rankin, ed., *Esther Burr's Journal* (Washington, D.C., n.d.), pp. 9–10. Puritans thought that childhood was an inferior state, but they also believed that some children, under the influence of grace, could match the religious sentiments of adults.

7. On the age of church members in the 17th century, see Richard G. Pope, *The Half-Way Covenant* (Princeton, 1969), app. In the four churches studied by Pope, the median age for males "owning" the covenant (passing, that is, from halfway to full membership by public profession) went below 21 only twice. See also Philip J. Greven, Jr., "Youth, Maturity, and Religious Conversion: A Note on the Ages of Converts in Andover, Massachusetts, 1711–1746," *Essex Institute Historical Collections* 108 (April 1972):119–134.

8. John B. Boles, "The Religious Mind of the Old South: The Era of the Great Revival, 1787–1805," Ph.D. thesis, history, University of Virginia (1969), pp. 80–81; Elias Smith, *The Life, Conversion, Preaching, Travels and Sufferings of Elias Smith* (Boston, 1840), pp. 94, 99, 109.

9. Joshua Bradley, *Accounts of Religious Revivals in Many Parts of the United States from 1815 to 1818* (Albany, N.Y., 1819), p. 29; see also ibid., pp. 23, 25, 33, 39, 43, 61–62, 132–133; "The History of Revivals of Religion in Boston," *American Baptist Magazine* 13 (February 1833): 49–61; "Mr. Backus' Account of the Religious Revival in Somers, Connecticut, in the Year 1797," *Connecticut Evangelical Magazine* 1 (July 1800):19; "Revivals of Religion," *The Guardian* 4 (July 1822):248; Heman Humphrey, *Revival Sketches and Manual, in Two Parts* (New York, 1850), pp. 139, 145.

10. "Revivals," *The Congregationalist* (February 18, 1853):26.

11. Bennet Tyler, *New England Revivals, As They Existed at the Close of the Eighteenth, and the Beginning of the Nineteenth Centuries* (Boston, 1846).

12. Charles G. Finney, *Memoirs* (New York, 1876), p. 45.

13. Menzies Rayner, *A Dissertation Upon Extraordinary Awakenings, or Religious Stirs: Conversion, Regeneration, Renovation, and a Change of Heart* (New Haven, 1816), pp. 9–10, 44–45.

14. "The Visit," *Western New York Baptist Magazine* 2 (February 1817):154.

15. "Revivals of Religion in Rupert," *Connecticut Evangelical Magazine* 5 (September 1804):113; Bradley, *Accounts*, p. 25; "Revivals of Religion," *The Guardian* 3 (February 1821):67–68.

16. Jacob Abbott, *The Young Christian: A Familiar Illustration of the Principles of Christian Duty* (New York, 1832), p. 3.

17. On expectations about the timing of religious experience among Congregationalist youth, see Joseph Packard, *Recollections of a Long Life* (Washington, D.C., 1902), p. 48.

18. Ebenezer Porter, *Letters on the Religious Revivals which Prevailed about the Beginning of the Present Century* (Boston, 1858), pp. 5–6.

19. Rayner, *Dissertation*, pp. 7–8; "Revivals of Religion," *Evangelical Repository* 1 (January 5, 1828):149.

20. "Albert Gallatin Dow," in William R. Cutter, ed., *Genealogical and Family History of Western New York* 2 vols. (New York, 1912), vol. 2, p. 726.

21. "J. Q. A. Edgell," in *Contributions to the Ecclesiastical History of Essex County, Massachusetts* (Boston, 1865), p. 154; see also Henry B. Smith, *A Memorial of Anson G. Phelps* (New York, 1860), p. 20; Caroline C. Richards, *Village Life in America, 1852–1872, Including the Period of the American Civil War, As Told in the Diary of a School-Girl*, introduced by Margaret E. Sangster (London, 1912), p. 41; Mary M. Boardman, *Life and Labors of Rev. W. E. Boardman* (New York, 1887), p. 6.

22. Henry Wood, "Historical Sketch of Revivals of Religion in Dartmouth College, Hanover, N.H.," *American Quarterly Register* 10 (November 1836):177–182; on Sunday school conversions see "Early Conversions," [Conn.] *Sabbath School Herald* 3 (December 1831):415–419.

23. Philip Doddridge, *Sermons to Young People* (Charlottesville, Va., 1832), p. 185.

24. *Memoir of Micajah E. Way; A Young Christian Who Was Baptized at Twelve Years of Age and Died at Sixteen* (Philadelphia, 1848); Edward J. Young, *Christian Lessons and a Christian Life: Sermons of Samuel Abbot Smith* (Boston, 1866), p. xvii. A corollary of this widespread fear of early death was the belief, common among youthful diarists, that time was slipping away and that the opportunities and demands which life offered were not being utilized. Justin Edwards wrote in his diary in 1806: "I this day enter upon the twentieth year of my age. Nineteen years of my mortal life are gone, and how little of the great business of life has been performed." See William A. Hallock, *"Light and Love": A Sketch of the Life and Labors of the Rev. Justin Edwards, D.D.* (New York, 1855), p. 16.

25. Homesickness was, however, a powerful motive in some conversions; see "Francis V. Tenney," in *Contributions to the Ecclesiastical History of Essex County, Massachusetts*, p. 192.

26. Doddridge's *Rise and Progress* was originally published in London in 1745. A partial listing of the publication dates of its American editions would include 1794, 1804, 1806, 1833, 1841, 1843, and 1849. Matthew Mead's *The Almost Christian Discovered* appeared originally in 1661; the first American edition was in 1815. On the "steps" of conversion, see Edmund S. Morgan, *Visible Saints: The History of a Puritan Idea* (New York, 1963), pp. 66–68. See also "The Experiences and Death of Miss Margaret Anderson," *Methodist Magazine* 3 (August 1820):341.

27. Lyman Abbott, *Reminiscences* (Boston, 1915), p. 20.

28. Alvan Bond, *Memoir of Rev. Pliny Fisk, A.M., Late Missionary to Palestine* (Boston, 1828), pp. 13–15.

29. William A. Hallock, *Memoir of Harlan Page* (New York, 1835), p. 18. In the 18th century Jonathan Edwards observed that religious experience, at first a "confused chaos," was "insensibly strained to bring it to an exact conformity to the scheme established"; see "A Treatise Concerning Religious Affections," in *The Works of President Edwards*, 8 vols. (London, 1817), vol. 4, p. 70.

30. Elijah E. Hoss, *David Morton; A Biography* (Louisville, 1918), p. 32.

31. Alfred Lee, *A Life Hid With Christ in God: Being a Memoir of Susan Allibone, Compiled chiefly From Her Diary and Letters* (Philadelphia, 1855), p. 22.

32. Catharine E. Beecher, *The Religious Training of Children in the School, the Family, and the Church* (New York, 1864), p. 133; see also W. J. Stillman, *The Autobiography of a Journalist*, 2 vols. (London, 1901), vol. 1, p. 29.

33. Chauncy Hobart, *Recollections of My Life: Fifty Years of Itinerancy in the Northwest* (Red Wing, Minn., 1886), p. 19; William E. Hatcher, *Life of Jeremiah B. Jeter, D.D.* (Baltimore, 1887), p. 73; *The Life, Experience, and Travels of John Colby, Preacher of the Gospel, Written by Himself* (Lowell, Mass., 1838), pp. 5–10.

34. George Brown, *Recollections of an Itinerant Life, Including Early Reminiscences* (Cincinnati, 1866), p. 41.

35. Mary M. Boardman, *Life and Labours of the Rev. W. E. Boardman* (New York, 1887), pp. 17–19; E. G. Cogswell, *Memoir of the Rev. Samuel Hidden* (Boston, 1842), pp. 45–46.

36. Orestes A. Brownson, *The Convert, or, Leaves From My Experience* (New York, 1857), p. 9; Stillman, *Autobiography*, vol. 1, pp. 29–30.

37. *A Brief History of Joseph Smith, the Prophet, by Himself* (Salt Lake City, 1910), pp. 7–8.

38. George Rogers, *Memoranda of the Experience, Labors, and Travels of a Universalist Preacher* (Cincinnati, 1845), passim; Sylvanus Cobb, *A Memoir* (Boston, 1867), p. 39; Erasmus Manford, *Twenty-Five Years in the West* (Chicago, 1867), p. 12.

39. Carroll Smith Rosenberg, *Religion and the Rise of the American City: The New York City Mission Movement, 1812–1870* (Ithaca, 1971), pp. 64–65.

40. George M. Marsden, *The Evangelical Mind and the New School Presbyterian Experience* (New Haven, 1970), pp. 11–12; Martin Marty, *Righteous Empire: The Protestant Experience in America* (New York, 1970), p. 67. Marty describes evangelicalism as a national religion of sorts during the early 19th century.

41. David F. Allmendinger, Jr., *Paupers and Scholars: The Transformation of Student Life in Nineteenth-Century New England* (New York, 1975), chap. 1.

42. Clarence P. Shedd, *Two Centuries of Student Christian Movements: Their Origin and Intercollegiate Life* (New York, 1934), pp. 71–74, 122; James B. Reynolds, *Two Centuries of Christian Activity at Yale* (New York, 1901), passim. For an 18th-century young men's society, see "Articles of the Young Men's Association, August 18, 1741" (manuscript, at Massachusetts Historical Society).

43. Clifton J. Phillips, *American Protestantism and the Pagan World: The First Half Century of the American Board of Commissioners for the Foreign Missions, 1810–1860* (Cambridge, Mass., 1969), pp. 25–27.

44. Ibid.

45. Henry D. Sedgwick, *The Centennial History of the American Bible Society* (New York, 1916), pp. 7–15.

46. Quoted in ibid., p. 10.

47. Quoted in Charles Foster, *An Errand of Mercy: The Evangelical United Front, 1790–1837* (Chapel Hill, 1960), p. 164.

48. Quoted in Phillips, *American Protestantism and the Pagan World*, p. 9.

49. Ibid.; Foster, *Errand of Mercy*, p. 48.

50. Edward Judson, *The Life of Adoniram Judson* (New York, 1883), pp. 10–17.

51. Ibid., p. 18.

52. Hannah More, *Strictures on the Modern System of Female Education* (London, 1799).

53. Quoted in Judson, *Life of Adoniram Judson*, p. 15.

54. Phillips, *American Protestantism and the Pagan World*, pp. 26–27.

55. Gardiner Spring, *Memoir of Samuel J. Mills* (New York, 1820), p. 24.

56. Phillips, *American Protestantism and the Pagan World*, p. 30.

57. Spring, *Memoir of Samuel J. Mills*, pp. 15–16.

58. Lois W. Banner, "Religion and Reform in the Early Republic: The Role of Youth," *American Quarterly* 23 (December 1971):679.

59. Ibid., 679–688; Colin B. Goodykoontz, *Home Missions on the American Frontier, With Particular Reference to the American Home Missionary Society* (Caldwell, Idaho, 1939), p. 197.

60. Reynolds, *Two Centuries of Christian Activity at Yale*, pp. 315–316.

61. Banner, "Religion and Reform," pp. 688–695; Bertram Wyatt-Brown, "New Leftists and Abolitionists: A Comparison of American Radical Styles," *Wisconsin Magazine of History and Biography* 53 (Summer 1970):256–268.

62. Goodykoontz, *Home Missions*, p. 174; Banner, "Religion and Reform," p. 693, note 38.

63. "Address to Youth," *Panoplist* 12 (July 1816):294.

64. James D. Knowles, *Memoir of Mrs. Ann H. Judson, Late Missionary to Burmah* (Boston, 1829), p. 35; see also Edward Hooker, *Memoir of Mrs. Sarah L. Huntington, Late of the American Mission in Syria* 3rd. ed. (New York, 1846).

65. Knowles, *Memoir of Mrs. Ann H. Judson*, passim; see also George L. Prentiss, ed., *The Life and Letters of Elizabeth Prentiss* (New York, 1882), p. 4.

66. *Memoirs of Mrs. H. Newell, Wife of the Rev. S. Newell, American Missionary to India* (London, n.d.), p. 7.

67. Woods's sermon is reprinted in ibid., pp. 220–244.

68. Ibid., p. 28.

69. Ibid., p. 68.

70. Ibid., pp. 167–168.

71. Ibid., pp. 238–239.

72. Ibid., pp. 233–234.

73. For illustrations of the way in which conversions in youth led to activity in the field of Christian benevolence, see John A. Clark, *The Young Disciple; or A Memoir of Anzonetta R. Peters* (New York, n.d.), and Robert Baird, *Memoirs of Anna Jane Linnard* (Boston, 1835). Memoirs like these were often designed to encourage as well as inform readers; see also Joan I. Brumberg, "Bending at the Knee of Jesus," seminar paper, University of Virginia (1972).

74. William L. Burn, *The Age of Equipoise: A Study of the Mid-Victorian Generation* (London, 1964), p. 246.

75. Lydia H. Sigourney, *Letters to Mothers* (Hartford, 1838), p. 16; "Woman in America: Her Sphere, Duties, and Education," *Quarterly Review of the Methodist Episcopal Church, South* 13 (July 1859):401.

76. *The Mother's Manual, Containing Practical Hints by a Mother* (Boston, 1840), p. 10.

77. Moses M. Henkle, *The Life of Henry B. Bascom, D.D., LL.D.* (Louisville, 1854), chap. 3; William C. Richards, *Great in Goodness: A Memoir of George N. Briggs* (Boston, 1866), p. 32.

78. Starbuck, *Psychology of Religion*, p. 227.

79. Ibid., p. 214.

80. Erik H. Erikson, *Youth: Identity and Crisis* (New York, 1968), pp. 128–129.

81. Ibid., pp. 159–160.

82. William E. Hatcher, *Life of J. B. Jeter* (Baltimore, 1887), p. 90.

83. *Memoirs of the Life and Religious Experience of Ray Potter, Written by Himself* (Providence, 1829), pp. 27–31; William M. Wightman, *The Life of William Capers, D.D., . . . Including an Autobiography* (Nashville, 1858), p. 39.

84. Erikson, *Youth*, p. 132.

85. Greven, "Youth, Maturity, and Religious Conversion," 119–134.

86. Authors of books of advice addressed to young men living in the cities in the 1840–1860 period portrayed their audiences as indifferent if not hostile to religion; see, for example, J. B. Waterbury, *Considerations for Young Men* (New York, 1851), pp. 113, 132; Phillips, *American Protestantism and the Pagan World*, p. 30.

87. Daniel B. Shea, Jr., *Spiritual Autobiography in Early America* (Princeton, 1968), p. 106.

88. William S. Heywood, ed., *Autobiography of Adin Ballou, 1803–1890* (Lowell, Mass., 1890), p. 33.

89. Ibid., p. 34. For a statement of the psychology of radical change at conversion, see Reuben Smith, *Truth Without Controversy: A Series of Doctrinal Lectures Intended Principally for Young Professors of Religion* (Saratoga Springs, N.Y., 1824), p. 180; see also Hatcher, *Life of Jeter*, p. 82.

90. George W. Noyes, *Religious Experience of John Humphrey Noyes, Founder of the Oneida Community* (New York, 1923), pp. 9, 16.

91. Brownson, *The Convert*, p. 13; see also William J. Gilmore, "Orestes Brownson and New England Religious Culture, 1803–1827," Ph.D. thesis, history, University of Virginia (1971).

92. Catharine E. Beecher, *Common Sense Applied to Religion; or, the Bible and the People* (New York, 1857), pp. xv–xxxiv; Beecher, *Religious Training*, pp. 388–400.

93. Harriet B. Stowe, *Oldtown Folks and Sam Lawson's Oldtown Fireside Stories* 2 vols. (Boston, 1896), vol. 2, p. 83.

94. Henry C. Wright, *A Human Life: Illustrated in My Individual Experiences As a Child, a Youth, and a Man* (Boston, 1849), p. 146. The economist Richard T. Ely also resisted pressure for conversion in youth; see his *Ground Under Our Feet: An Autobiography* (New York, 1938), pp. 13–16.

95. Wright, *A Human Life*, pp. 9–10.

96. H. Shelton Smith, ed., *Horace Bushnell* (New York, 1964), pp. 22–23.

97. Horace Bushnell, *Christian Nurture*, introduced by Luther Weigle (New Haven, 1960), pts. 1–4.

Chapter 4

1. Sam B. Warner, Jr., *The Urban Wilderness: A History of the American City* (New York, 1972), p. 70.

2. Ibid., p. 73; see also Warner's *The Private City: Philadelphia in Three Periods of Its Growth* (Philadelphia, 1968), p. 17.

3. Warner, *Urban Wilderness*, p. 87.

4. James D. McCabe [Edward W. Martin, pseud.], *The Secrets of The Great City: A Work Descriptive of the Virtues and Vices, Miseries and Crimes of New York City* (Philadelphia, 1868), pp. 418–419.

5. George Ellington, *The Women of New York, or Social Life in the Great City* (New York, 1870), p. 70.

6. Henry Ward Beecher, *Lectures to Young Men* (New York, 1846), chap. 4.

7. Edwin H. Chapin, *Moral Aspects of City Life: A Series of Lectures* (New York, 1854), pp. 59–60.

8. Herbert Asbury, *The Gangs of New York: An Informal History of the Underworld* (New York, 1929), p. 175.

9. Herbert Asbury, *Sucker's Progress: An Informal History of Gambling in America From the Colonies to Canfield* (New York, 1938), p. 163.

10. Asbury, *Gangs of New York*, pp. 106–116.

11. McCabe, *Secrets of the Great City*, pp. 418–419.

12. J. T. Headley, *The Great Riots of New York, 1712–1873* (New York, 1873), p. 131.

13. Ibid., p. 89.

14. Asbury, *Gangs of New York*, p. 239.

15. Charles L. Brace, *The Dangerous Classes of New York and Twenty Years Work Among Them* (New York, 1872), passim.

16. Ibid., p. ii.

17. "Youthful Depravity—Home Influence," *Common School Journal* 4 (October 15, 1852):312.

18. On Five Points see Asbury, *Gangs of New York*, p. 9.

19. Daniel Calhoun, *The Intelligence of a People* (Princeton, 1973), pp. 112–114.

20. On overcrowding see Brace, *Dangerous Classes*, chap. 5. Very similar developments occurred in Europe in the mid-19th century; see John R. Gillis, *Youth and History: Tradition and Change in European Age Relations, 1770–Present* (New York, 1974), pp. 61–66.

21. Brace wrote: "It has been common since the recent terrible Communistic outbreak in Paris, to assume that France alone is exposed to such horrors; but, in the judgment of one who has been familiar with our 'dangerous classes' for twenty years, there are just the same explosive social elements beneath the surface of New York as of Paris" (*Dangerous Classes*, p. 29).

22. Leonard L. Richards, *Gentlemen of Property and Standing: Anti-Abolition Mobs in Jacksonian America* (New York, 1970).

23. Charles MacKay, *Life and Liberty in America; or, Sketches of a Tour in the United States and Canada in 1857–8* (New York, 1859), p. 35; George W. Sheldon, *The Story of the Volunteer Fire Department of the City of New York* (New York, 1882), pp. 365–368.

24. Sheldon, *Story of the Volunteer Fire Department*, pp. 393, 416, 410; *Our Firemen: A History of the New York Fire Departments* (New York, 1887), pp. 499, 506.

25. Sheldon, *Story of the Volunteer Fire Department*, p. 367; Gustavus Myers, *The History of Tammany Hall* (New York, 1917), pp. 131–132.

26. *Our Firemen*, p. 98; MacKay, *Life and Liberty in America*, p. 39.

27. Kathleen J. Kiefer, "Flying Sparks and Hooves: Prologue," *Cincinnati Historical Society Bulletin* 28 (Summer 1970):86–87.

28. Ibid., 105.

29. Marcus Cunliffe, *Soldiers and Civilians: The Martial Spirit in America, 1775–1865* (Boston, 1968), pp. 223–226.

30. Ibid., p. 236.

31. Ibid., pp. 25–26.

32. Daniel H. Calhoun, "The City As Teacher: Historical Problems," *History of Education Quarterly* 9 (Fall 1969):312–325.

33. Jack H. Nesson, "From Schoolhouse to Playhouse: Wilmington's Non-Professional Theatre, 1797–1872," *Delaware History* 8 (March 1959):271–272.

34. James Rees, *The Life of Edwin Forrest* (Philadelphia, 1874), pp. 46, 51.

35. Ibid.; Alice E. Smith, "Letters of Thomas Buchanan Read," *Ohio State Archaeological and Historical Quarterly* 46 (1937):68.

36. Asbury, *Gangs of New York*, pp. 104–106; Denis T. Lynch, *"Boss" Tweed: The Story of a Grim Generation* (New York, 1927), p. 35.

37. Douglass C. North, *The Economic Growth of the United States, 1790–1860* (Englewood Cliffs, N.J., 1961), pp. 46–51.

38. Samuel E. Morison, *Maritime History of Massachusetts, 1783–1860* (Boston, 1921), p. 125.

39. Warner, *Private City*, p. 7.

40. "Farming Life in New England," *Atlantic Monthly* 2 (August 1858):337.

41. Quoted in Percy W. Bidwell and John I. Faulconer, *History of Agriculture in the Northern United States, 1620–1860* (New York, 1941), p. 205; see also John Modell, "The People of a Working-Class Ward: Reading, Pennsylvania, 1850," *Journal of Social History* 5 (Fall 1971):71–95.

42. Thomas C. Atkeson and Mary W. Atkeson, *Pioneering in Agriculture* (New York, 1937), p. 68.

43. Eric Foner, *Free Soil, Free Labor, Free Men: The Ideology of the Republican Party Before the Civil War* (New York, 1970), pp. 12–13.

44. Ralph W. Emerson, "Greatness in Letters and Social Aims," *Complete Works of Ralph Waldo Emerson* 12 vols. (New York, 1929), vol. 8, p. 304.

45. Daniel Eddy, *The Young Man's Friend* (Philadelphia, 1865), p. 58. The first edition appeared ten years earlier.

46. Edward Hazen, *The Panorama of Professions and Trades; or Everyman's Book* (Philadelphia, 1839), p. vii.

47. Daniel Drake, *Pioneer Life in Kentucky, 1785–1800*, ed. Emmet F. Horine (New York, 1948), p. 22.

48. Carl Bode, *The Anatomy of American Popular Culture, 1840–1861* (Berkeley, 1959), p. 128.

49. Robert Phillip, *The Young Man's Closet Library*, 3rd ed., introduced by Albert Barnes (New York, 1857), p. 3.

50. Joel Hawes, *Lectures Addressed to the Young Men of Hartford and New-Haven* (Hartford, 1828), p. 15.

51. See Jared Waterbury, *Considerations for Young Men* (New York, 1851), p. 67; Daniel Wise, *The Young Man's Counsellor* (New York, 1853), p. 18; John A. James, *The Young Man From Home* (New York, 1850), p. 10. Authors of advice books used "youth" to signify both an age group and a quality. Joel Hawes, for example, followed his reference to a class of young men aged 15 to 25 with a reference to the "forming, fixing period" between 14 and 21. Others employed a variation on the theme, arguing that while young men were likely to leave home between the ages of 15 and 25, the "critical period" did not encompass the whole span of home-leaving ages but only the first few years out. Thus,

someone who left home at 15 might be over the critical stage at 18, while another who left at 25 would still be a "youth" at 27 or 28 if he had not yet settled down. See James, *The Young Man From Home*, p. 10; Waterbury, *Considerations for Young Men*, p. 10.

52. A comparable pattern existed during the 1930s in rural areas; see Robin M. Williams, "Rural Youth Studies in the United States," *Rural Sociology* 4 (June 1939):166–167. There is also some evidence that during the middle decades of the 19th century both native-born and immigrant urban girls left home earlier than their brothers. See Laurence A. Glasco, "The Life Cycles and Household Structure of American Ethnic Groups: Irish, Germans, and Native-born Whites in Buffalo, New York, 1855," *Journal of Urban History* 1 (May 1975):339–363.

53. "Farming Life in New England," 341.

54. A word of elaboration concerning my interest in the Sons of New Hampshire is necessary. Peter Knights of York University and I are cooperating on a full-scale study of the members of the organization which will seek to answer many questions not raised here. Data about the Sons presented below is drawn from the A–K part of the alphabet (last names), for which I am assuming responsibility.

55. *Festival of the Sons of New Hampshire with the Speeches, . . . Celebrated in Boston, November 7, 1849* (Boston, 1850), p. 17.

56. The words are Alphonso Taft's, applied to Vermont; see Ishbel Ross, *An American Family: The Tafts, 1678–1964* (Cleveland, 1964), p. 6.

57. *Second Festival of the Sons of New Hampshire, Celebrated in Boston, November 2, 1853* (Boston, 1854), p. 93.

58. Henry A. Blood, *The History of Temple, N.H.* (Boston, 1860), p. 88.

59. Using family registers in the various New Hampshire town histories, I have ascertained the age at first marriage of 92 of the Sons who signed the registry at the first festival in 1849. I concede, however, that such published registers might well contain a class bias. Hence, the following table is scarcely a definitive statement of marriage patterns among the Sons.

Age at First Marriage of 92 Sons of New Hampshire

AGE	19	20	21	22	23	24	25	26	27	28
Number	3	2	4	5	8	13	7	9	7	7
AGE	29	30	31	32	33	34	35>			
Number	6	4	9	2	0	0	6			

60. William Lawrence, *Extracts from the Diary and Correspondence of the Late Amos Lawrence, with a Brief Account of Some Incidents of His Life* (Boston, 1885), p. 40.

61. I have listed as similar rather than identical such designations as clerk-trader, merchant-grocer, clerk-merchant. Of course, in such cases the actual job performed might have been identical.

62. *Second Festival*, p. 117. Michael Anderson has noted the important role of kinship in migrations into 19th-century Lancashire; see his *Family Structure in Nineteenth-Century Lancashire* (Cambridge, England, 1971), pp. 53, 56–57. See also Robert E. Bieder, "Kinship as a Factor in Migration," *Journal of Marriage and the Family* 35 (August 1973):429–439.

63. In 1854, one-half of the Boston YMCA's 999 members were born in New England but outside of Boston; see William B. Whiteside, *The Boston Y.M.C.A. and Community Need: A Century's Evolution, 1851–1951* (Boston, 1951), p. 28.

64. Wise, *Young Man's Counsellor*, p. v.

65. Waterbury, *Consideration for Young Men*, p. 24.

66. Wise, *Young Man's Counsellor*, p. 151; [H. W. Longfellow], "Defence of Poetry," *North American Review* 34 (January 1832):76. On Byron's impact on American youth, see also [W. H. Prescott], "English Literature of the Nineteenth Century," *North American Review* 35 (July 1832):176–178; see also William E. Leonard, *Byron and Byronism in America* (Boston, 1905), pp. 112–161. For a typical rustic Byronist, see John T. Trowbridge, *My Own Story: With Recollections of Noted Persons* (Boston, 1903), p. 45.

67. Rufus Clark, *Lectures on the Formation of Character, Temptations, and Mission of Young Men* (New York, 1853), p. 92.

68. Wise, *Young Man's Counsellor*, p. 15.

69. Ibid., p. 17.

70. "Influence of Youth," *American Sunday School Magazine* 5 (April 1828):102.

71. "Hints to Young Ambition," *New-England Magazine* 2 (June 1832):513.

72. Ibid.; see also [Robert F. Walcott], "Review of *The Young Man's Aid*," *Christian Examiner* 3 ser. 7 (September 1838):43.

73. Waterbury, *Considerations for Young Men*, p. 106.

74. John M. Austin, *Golden Steps for Youth* (Auburn, N.Y., 1850), pp. 114–115.

75. Solomon Southwick, *Five Lessons for Young Men* (Albany, 1837), p. 88.

76. Charles J. Young, "Advice to Youth Literature in the Antebellum Period," seminar paper, University of Virginia (1972).

77. Sumner Ellis, *The Life of Edwin H. Chapin, D.D.* (Boston, 1882), p. 17.

78. Edwin H. Chapin, *Duties of Young Men*, 8th ed. (Boston, 1853).

79. John Foster, "On Decision of Character," in *Decision of Character and Other Essays* (New York, 1882), p. 101. Foster's essay had gone through nine editions by 1830. It was frequently presented to young people as a gift or prize book; see Fabian Franklin, *The Life of Daniel Coit Gilman* (New York, 1910), p. 6.

80. Foster, "On Decision of Character," p. 88.

81. Ibid., p. 89.

82. Ibid., p. 88.

83. Ben Barker-Benfield, "The Spermatic Economy: A Nineteenth Century View of Sexuality," in Michael Gordon, ed., *The American Family in Social Historical Perspective* (New York, 1973), pp. 336–372.

84. Foster, "On Decision of Character," p. 106.

85. Daniel Wise entitled a chapter in one of his books "Decision of Character," while youth was often explicitly associated with "indecision of character." See Wise, *The Path of Life* (New York, 1849), chap. 12; "Miscellany," *American Sunday School Magazine*, 1 (July, 1824).

86. Hawes, *Lectures to the Young Men of Hartford and New-Haven*, pp. 101, 17.

87. Wise, *Young Man's Counsellor*, p. 88.

88. Clark, *Lectures on the Formation of Character*, p. 44.

89. Edward A. Lawrence, *The Life of the Rev. Joel Hawes, D.D., Tenth Pastor of the First Church, Hartford, Conn.*, 2nd ed. (Boston, 1881), pp. 18–21, 106–120.

90. [Jared Waterbury], *Advice to a Young Christian on the Importance of Aiming at an Elevated Standard of Piety* (New York, 1832), p. iii.

91. Walter Houghton, *The Victorian Frame of Mind, 1830–1870* (New Haven, 1957), chaps. 3–7.

Chapter 5

1. Francis Wayland, *Thoughts on the Present Collegiate System of Education in the United States* (1842; reprint ed., New York, 1969), pp. 123–124.

2. James Walker, "Accidental Education," *American Institute of Instruction, Lectures, 1831*, (Boston, 1831), pp. 7–8.

3. Ibid.

4. Edwin C. Mack, *Public Schools and British Opinion, 1780–1860: An Examination of the Relationship Between Contemporary Ideas and the Evolution of an English Institution* (London, 1938), pp. 285–333.

5. John Locke, *Some Thoughts Concerning Education* (1690), in James L. Axtell, ed., *The Educational Writings of John Locke: A Critical Edition With Introduction and Notes* (Cambridge, England, 1968), p. 185; Philip Doddridge, *Sermons on the Religious Education of Children* (Philadelphia, 1793), p. 79; see also *The Family Instructor; or a Manual of the Duties of Domestic Life* (New York, 1840), p. 65.

6. Muriel Jaeger, *Before Victoria* (London, 1956), p. 107; for Mann on Maria Edgeworth see *Reply to the "Remarks of Thirty-One Boston Schoolmasters on the Seventh Annual Report of the Secretary of the Massachusetts Board of Education"* (Boston, 1844), p. 8.

7. Maria Edgeworth and Richard L. Edgeworth, *Practical Education*, 2 vols. in 1 (Boston, 1823), vol. 1, chap. 1.

8. Horace Bushnell, *Christian Nurture*, ed. Luther Weigle (New Haven, 1960).

9. Ibid., chap. 4.

10. Ibid.

11. Quoted in Mary E. Dewey, ed., *Life and Letters of Catharine M. Sedgwick* (New York, 1871), p. 41.

12. Bushnell, *Christian Nurture*, p. 76.

13. Ibid., p. 19.

14. Kathryn K. Sklar, *Catharine Beecher: A Study in American Domesticity* (New Haven, 1973), chap. 11.

15. Ibid.

16. *The Mother's Manual* 1 (January 1833):36; Anne L. Kuhn, *The Mother's Role in Childhood Education: New England Concepts, 1830–1860* (New Haven, 1947); Agatha Young, *The Women and the Crisis: Women of the North in the Civil War* (New York, 1959), p. 5.

17. The total fertility rate is "the average number of children per woman that would be born to a hypothetical group subject at each age to the childbearing rate experienced in the general population." See Ansley J. Coale and Melvin Zelnick, *New Estimates of Fertility and Population in the United States: A Study of Annual White Births from 1855 to 1960 and of Completeness of Enumeration in the Census from 1880 to 1960* (Princeton, 1963), pp. 36–37. See also Wilson H. Grabill, Clyde V. Kiser, and Pascal K. Whelpton, *The Fertility of American Women* (New York, 1958), p. 14. The decline in fertility was most pronounced in the Middle Atlantic states, New England, and the east north-central states. By its nature, fertility could be affected by changes in the marriage age for women. (If the latter went up significantly, fertility would decrease.) But the marriage age rose only slightly between the 18th and 19th centuries. See Robert V. Wells, "Demographic Change and the Life Cycle of American Families," *Journal of Interdisciplinary History* 2 (Autumn 1971):275.

18. On the idea of a family life-cycle, see Wells, "Demographic Change," 273–282.

19. Warren S. Thompson and P. K. Whelpton, *Population Trends in the United States* (New York, 1933), p. 131.

20. Samuel Phillips, *The Christian Home, As It Is in the Sphere of Nature and the Church* (Springfield, Mass., 1860), p. iii.

21. Bushnell, *Christian Nurture*, pp. 165–189; George Fredrickson, *The Inner Civil War: Northern Intellectuals and the Crisis of the Union* (New York, 1965), pp. 25–26.

22. Bushnell, *Christian Nurture*, pp. 165–189.

23. Kirk Jeffrey, "The Family as Utopian Retreat From the City," in Sallie TeSelle, ed., *The Family, Communes, and Utopian Societies* (New York, 1972), pp. 21–39.

24. On student discipline, see David F. Allmendinger, Jr., *Paupers and Scholars: The Transformation of Student Life in Nineteenth-Century New England* (New York, 1975), pp. 122–124; on biography, see Hugh A. Garland, *The Life of John Randolph of Roanoke* (New York, 1853), p. 9; John Ware, *Memoir of Henry Ware, Jr.* (Boston, 1846), p. 6.

25. Whitney Cross, *The Burnt-Over District* (New York, 1950), pp. 60–62.

26. Charles I. Foster, *An Errand of Mercy: The Evangelical United Front, 1790–1837* (Chapel Hill, 1960), p. 165; see also Frank G. Lankard, *A History of the American Sunday School Curriculum* (New York, 1927), pp. 61–65; Alfred Gregory, *Robert Raikes, Journalist and Philanthropist: A History of the Origin of Sunday Schools* (London, 1877), p. 48; Marianna C. Brown, *Sunday School Movements in America* (New York, 1901), pp. 22, 24, 26.

27. *American Sunday School Union Magazine* 1 (July 1824):6–7.

28. Quoted in George Stewart, *A History of Religious Education in Connecticut to the Middle of the Nineteenth Century* (New Haven, 1924), p. 320.

29. Ibid., p. 339; Henry C. Trumbull, *The Sunday-School: Its Origin, Mission, Methods, and Auxiliaries* (Philadelphia, 1888), pp. 130–131.

30. Ambrose Edson, "The Early Conversion of Children," *National Preacher* 5 (July 1830):23–24; "A Child's Idea of Thought," *American Sunday School Magazine* 1 (July

1824):19; Bennet Tyler, "Persuasives to Immediate Repentance," *National Preacher* 5 (November 1830):91.

31. Edward P. Hammond, *The Conversion of Children* (New York, 1882); P. C. Headley, ed., *The Harvest Work of the Holy Spirit, Illustrated by the Evangelistic Labors of Rev. Edward Payson Hammond* (Boston, 1862), p. 225.

32. G. Stanley Hall, *Adolescence: Its Psychology and Its Relations to Psychology, Anthropology, Sociology, Sex, Crime, Religion and Education,* 2 vols. (New York, 1905), vol. 2, p. 291 *n.*

33. James W. Cooper, "Child Nurture in the Church," *Andover Review* 2 (July–December, 1884):50.

34. Daniel Rice, "The Sunday School," *Independent* 27 (January 28, 1875):8.

35. *Sixth Annual Report of the Boston Young Men's Christian Association* (Boston, 1857), p. 14; Rufus Clark, *Lectures on the Formation of Character, Temptations, and Mission of Young Men* (Boston, 1853), p. 34; Thomas Clarkson, *A Portraiture of Quakerism,* 3 vols. (London, 1806), vol. 1, pp. 152–160; Lawrence Wylie, *Village in the Vaucluse* (New York, 1957), p. 103. Wylie notes that French villagers in the 1950s held onto the old belief that a young man must sow wild oats in youth before he can be presumed reliable.

36. Rice, "Sunday School," p. 8.

37. An illustration of the tendency toward earlier conversions can be found in the records of the Essex County North (Mass.) Ministerial Association, for its official history contains brief biographies and autobiographical conversion narratives of its candidates in the first half of the 19th century. The average age of conversion for candidates born between 1774 and 1798 was 19.5 years; for those born 1799–1812, 17.2 years; and for those born 1813–1833, 15.8 years. See *Contributions to the Ecclesiastical History of Essex County, Massachusetts* (Boston, 1865). The various volumes of *Virginia Baptist Ministers* edited by James B. and George B. Taylor provide an illustration of the same tendency. Of those ministers born prior to 1790, three-quarters were 22 or over at conversion; of those born between 1790 and 1834, 70 percent were 14 to 21 at conversion. See James B. Taylor, *Virginia Baptist Ministers. First Series* (New York, 1860); George B. Taylor, *Virginia Baptist Ministers. Third Series* (Lynchburg, 1912); Hall, *Adolescence,* vol. 2, chap. 14.

38. Mary A. Cheney, ed., *Life and Letters of Horace Bushnell* (New York, 1903), p. 607.

39. Henry W. Beecher, "Sudden Conversion," *New Star Papers; or, Views and Experiences of Religious Subjects* (New York, 1859), p. 175.

40. William L. Phelps, *Autobiography With Letters* (New York, 1939), p. 17.

41. For evidence on the degree of age grading by 1860, see Asylum Hill Sabbath School, "Records, 1860–1880," vols. 1, 4, Ms., Connecticut Historical Society; Christ Church, Ansonia, Conn., "Sunday School Register, 1871–1875," (manuscript, at Connecticut Historical Society).

42. Daniel P. Kidder, *The Sunday School Teacher's Guide* (New York, 1846); H. Clay Trumbull, *A Model Superintendent: A Sketch of the Life, Character, and Methods of Work of Henry P. Hazen* (New York, 1880).

43. George E. Peterson, *The New England College in the Age of the University* (Amherst, 1964), pp. 44–45.

44. Daniel Wise, *The Young Man's Counsellor* (New York, 1853), p. 152.

45. William D. Howells, *A Modern Instance* (New York, 1881), p. 27.

46. On the significance and application of terms like "laboring poor," see Jeffrey Kaplow, "The Culture of Poverty in Paris on the Eve of the Revolution," *International Review of Social History* 12 (1967):277–291.

47. Joseph Hawes, *Children in Urban Society: Juvenile Delinquency in the Nineteenth Century* (New York, 1971), chap. 2; Robert Mennel, *Thorns and Thistles: Juvenile Delinquents in the United States, 1825–1940* (Hanover, N.H., 1973), chap. 1; James McLachlan, *American Boarding Schools* (New York, 1970), p. 47.

48. *Annual Report of the Secretary of State on the Condition of the Common Schools, 1847* (Columbus, 1847), p. 12.

49. Ira Mayhew, *Popular Education for the Use of Parents, Teachers, and for Young Persons of Both Sexes* (New York, 1850), pp. 405–408.

50. "School Houses," *Connecticut Common School Journal* 3 (November 1, 1840):14–15; "Canterbury First School Society," *Connecticut Common School Journal* (December 15,

1840):51; William A. Alcott, "Prize Essay on the Construction of School Houses," *American Institute of Instruction, Lectures, 1832* (Boston, 1832), pp. 241–257.

51. *Report of the School Committee of Westfield, 1859–1860* (Westfield, Mass., 1860), p. 26; *Annual Report of the School Committee of the Town of Dedham, 1857* (Dedham, Mass., 1857), p. 20.

52. "Honor Due to Aged Teachers," *American Annals of Education* 7 (March 1837):118.

53. *Annual Report of the School Committee of the Town of Dedham, 1864* (Dedham, Mass., 1864), pp. 5–6; see also "Digest of Rules and Regulations of Public Schools in Cities," *American Journal of Education* 19 (1870):421–469.

54. James G. Carter, *Essays Upon Popular Education* (Boston, 1826), p. 37.

55. "Primary Schools," *Connecticut Common School Journal* 8 (September 1861):260.

56. Catharine E. Beecher, *The Evils Suffered by American Women and Children* (New York, 1846), p. 5. Between 1840 and 1865 the proportion of male teachers in Massachusetts schools declined from 61 percent to 14 percent; see Michael B. Katz, *The Irony of Early School Reform: Educational Innovation in Mid-Nineteenth Century Massachusetts* (Boston, 1968), p. 12. In 1856, Philadelphia had 862 female teachers and 78 males; see Edwin T. Freeley, *Philadelphia and Its Manufactures: A Handbook* (Philadelphia, 1859); see also Elizabeth H. Cawley, ed., *The American Diaries of Richard Cobden* (Princeton, 1952), p. 162.

57. Amariah Brigham, *Remarks on the Influence of Mental Cultivation Upon Health* (Hartford, 1832).

58. Ibid., p. 59.

59. Mayhew, *Popular Education*, pp. 134–135.

60. *Annual Report of the School Committee of the Town of North Andover, 1858–1859* (Lawrence, Mass., 1859), p. 6; *Annual Report of the School Committee of the Town of Dedham, 1861* (Dedham, Mass., 1861), p. 20.

61. Katz, *Irony of Early School Reform*, p. 56.

62. On the radical sources, see "The Second Split in the Party," in John R. Commons et al., *A Documentary History of American Industrial Society*, 10 vols. (Cleveland, 1910–1911), vol. 5, pp. 166–172.

63. "Moral and Educational Wants of Cities," *Connecticut Common School Journal* 4 (January 1, 1842):24; Jonathan Messerli, "Horace Mann: The Early Years, 1796–1837," 2 vols., Ph.D. thesis, education, Harvard University (1963), vol. 1, p. 530.

64. Walter Hardinge, ed., *Essays in Education (1830–1860) by Amos Bronson Alcott* (Gainesville, Fla., 1960), p. 199.

65. *Annual Report of the School Committee of the City of Salem, 1852* (Salem, Mass., 1852), p. 39; *Forty-First Annual Report of the Superintendent of Public Instruction of the State of Michigan, 1877* (Lansing, 1878), p. ix; *Thirty-Eighth Annual Report of the Superintendent of Public Instruction of the State of Michigan, 1874* (Lansing, 1875), p. xl.

66. Hardinge, ed., *Essays in Education (1830–1860) by Amos Bronson Alcott*, pp. 101, 209.

67. Taking ten-year intervals between 1810 and 1880, the percentage of students entering Phillips Exeter Academy between the ages of 13 and 19 (inclusive) was successively 57.7, 62.2, 77.4, 69.7, 86.7, 85.3, 87.3, and 90.4 percent. See *General Catalogue of the Officers and Students of Phillips Exeter Academy, 1783–1903* (Exeter, 1903).

68. W. Scott Thomas, "Changes in the Age of College Graduation," *Report of the Commissioner of Education, 1902*, 2 vols. (Washington, D.C., 1903), vol. 2, pp. 2199–2206.

69. Ibid.; *General Catalogue of Exeter*. Taking five-year periods at Exeter between 1810 and 1835, the percentage of students aged 12 and under in each entering class was successively 28.9, 27.3, 35.1, 13.5, 11.3, and 8.3 percent.

70. "The High School Policy of Massachusetts," *New-Englander and Yale Review* 16 (November 1858):872–873.

71. *Eleventh Annual Report of the School Committee of the City of Lawrence, 1857* (Lawrence, Mass., 1857), pp. 59–63.

72. Charles Hammond, "New England Academies and Classical Schools," *American Journal of Education* 16 (1866):425–427.

73. Calvin B. Hulbert, *The Academy: Demands for It and the Conditions for Its Success: An Address* (Boston, 1878), pp. 15–17.

74. Katz, *Irony of Early School Reform*, p. 61.

75. "French Views of American Schools," *Annual Report of the Board of Education of the State of Connecticut, 1879* (Hartford, 1879), p. 71.

76. David W. Hoyt, "Relation of the High School to the Community," *Education* 6 (March 1886):429–441.

77. In 1891 there were 85,219 male and 126,379 female students in public high schools; see *Report of the Commissioner of Education, 1890–1891*, 2 vols. (Washington, D.C., 1894), vol. 2, p. 792.

78. *Thirteenth Annual Report of the Public Schools of the City of Lawrence, 1859* (Lawrence, Mass., 1860), p. 29; *Report of the School Committee of the Town of Danvers, 1850–1851* (Salem, Mass., 1851), p. 13.

79. "Selections from the Report of the School Committee of Ware," *Common School Journal* 2 (September 1, 1840):278; *Report of the School Committee of the Town of Millbury, March 1, 1862* (Worcester, Mass., n.d.), p. 8.

80. W. B. Fowle, "Action and Reaction—School Discipline," *Common School Journal* 12 (July 1, 1850):196–198.

81. D. L. Leonard, "Women as Educators," *Chicago Schoolmaster* 5 (October 1872):276.

82. "The Proper School Age," *Pennsylvania School Journal* 12 (March 1864):268.

83. *Fifth Annual Report of the Superintendent of Public Instruction of the State of Illinois, 1863–1864* (Springfield, 1864), p. 7; Norman Ware, *The Industrial Worker, 1840–1860: The Reaction of American Industrial Society to the Advance of the Industrial Revolution* (Gloucester, Mass., 1960), pp. 12, 57; Emerson D. Fite, *Social and Industrial Conditions in the North During the Civil War* (New York, 1963), p. 188.

84. *Report of the School Committee of the Town of Millbury, March 1, 1863* (Worcester, Mass., n.d.), p. 5.

85. *Report of the School Committee of Marshfield, Read in Town Meeting, April 5, 1847* (Boston, 1847), p. 10.

86. "Second Annual Report of the Superintendent of Public Schools," in *Annual Report of the School Committee of the City of Boston, 1882* (Boston, 1882), pp. 25–28; John D. Philbrick, *City School Systems in the United States* (Washington, D.C., 1885), p. 154.

87. "Publications of the Massachusetts Sabbath School Union," *Spirit of the Pilgrims* 5 (June 1832):347.

88. E. C. Hewett, "How Shall We Keep the Boys?" *National Sunday School Teacher* 8 (October 1873):392–393.

89. Asa Bullard, *Fifty Years With the Sabbath School* (Boston, 1876), p. 193.

90. Hawes, *Children in Urban Society*, chap. 5.

91. Ibid., pp. 78–79; Charles L. Brace, *Home Life in Germany* (New York, 1853), p. 31.

92. *Thirteenth Annual Report of the Trustees of the State Reform School at Westborough, 1859* (Boston, 1859), p. 7.

93. *Eighteenth Annual Report of the Trustees and Officers of the State Industrial School for Girls, Oct. 1873* (Boston, 1874), p. 8; Susan E. Houston, "Victorian Origins of Juvenile Delinquency: A Canadian Experience," *History of Education Quarterly* 12 (February 1972):271–272.

94. *Eighteenth Annual Report . . . of the State Industrial School for Girls*, p. 8.

95. *Eighth Annual Report of the Trustees of the State Reform School at Westborough* (Boston, 1855), passim.

96. *Second Annual Report of the Trustees of the State Reform School at Cape Elizabeth, Together With the Annual Report of the Officers of the Institution* (Augusta, Me., 1856), p. 21.

97. *Thirteenth Annual Report of the Trustees of the State Reform School at Westborough, 1859*, p. 46.

98. Sanford J. Fox, "Juvenile Justice Reform: An Historical Perspective," *Stanford Law Review* 22 (June 1970):1187–1239. There is as yet no study of the actual treatment of juvenile offenders before the creation of a separate system of juvenile justice in America. Early 20th-century progressive reformers like Ben B. Lindsey argued that juvenile offenders had once been treated like adult offenders, and that prior to juvenile justice reform no distinction was made between juvenile and adult offenders. The reality was probably very different, however. A New York district attorney commented that prior to

the creation of the House of Refuge in the 1820s, lads of 14 or 15 "might have been arrested and tried four or five times for petty thefts, and it was hardly ever that a jury could convict" (quoted in "House of Refuge for Juvenile Delinquents," *Methodist Magazine* 11 [February 1826]:63).

99. Thomas Elyot, *The Boke Named the Governour* (London, 1907), bk. 1, chap. 14; Roger Ascham, *The Schoolmaster*, in J. A. Giles, ed., *The Whole Works of Roger Ascham*, 3 vols. (London, 1864), vol. 3, p. 123.

100. Philippe Ariès, *Centuries of Childhood: A Social History of Family Life*, trans. Robert Baldick (New York, 1962), p. 21; Charles Sayle, *The Ages of Man* (London, 1916), p. xv.

101. Pierre de La Primaudaye, *The French Academie*, trans. T. Bowes (London, 1618), pp. 231–232.

102. "The Stages of Human Life," *Boston Medical and Surgical Journal* 4 (June 14, 1831):289–291; E. G. Wheeler, "The Periods of Human Life," *Boston Medical and Surgical Journal* 22 (June 29, 1840):395–396.

103. *Sixth Annual Report of the* [Mass.] *Board of Education, Together With the Sixth Annual Report of the Secretary of the Board* (Boston, 1843), p. 150; Oliver W. Holmes, Sr., *Elsie Venner: A Romance of Destiny* (New York, 1886), pp. 334–335.

104. Jean-Jacques Rousseau, *Émile, or Education* (London, 1911), p. 172.

105. Philippe Hutin, *Manual of the Physiology of Man*, trans. Joseph Togno (Philadelphia, 1828), pp. 263–264; Robley Dunglison, *Human Physiology*, 2 vols. (Philadelphia, 1832), vol. 2, pp. 398–404.

106. Orson Fowler, *Sexual Science* (Philadelphia, 1870), pp. 100–102.

107. Ibid., p. 109.

108. Pliny Earle, "On the Causes of Insanity," *American Journal of Insanity* 4 (January 1848):200.

109. E. H. Hare, "Masturbatory Insanity: The History of an Idea," *Journal of Mental Science* 108 (1962):1–25; *An Hour's Conference With Fathers and Sons in Relation to a Common and Fatal Indulgence of Youth* (Boston, 1840); Samuel B. Woodward, *Hints for the Young, on a Subject Relating to the Health of Body and Mind* (Worcester, Mass., 1838); Charles Rosenberg, "Sexuality, Class and Role in 19th Century America," *American Quarterly* 25 (May 1973):137.

110. Orson Fowler, *Physiology, Animal and Mental: Applied to the Preservation and Restoration of Health of Body and Power of Mind*, 5th ed. (New York, 1848), p. 248; on Isaac Ray's views, see "The Proper Time for Sending Children to School," *Common School Journal* 13 (September 1, 1851):270.

111. Fowler, *Physiology*, p. 280; "The Proper Time for Sending Children to School," 270–271; "On the Causes of Insanity," 200.

112. "Educating Children to Death," *American Annals of Education* 7 (January 1837):15.

113. Andrew Combe, *The Principles of Physiology Applied to the Preservation of Health and to the Improvement of Physical and Mental Education* (New York, 1838), p. 203.

114. Rousseau, *Émile*, pp. 174–175.

115. Ibid., p. 177.

116. Elizabeth Blackwell, *The Laws of Life, With Special Reference to the Physical Education of Girls* (New York, 1852), pp. 134, 131–132.

117. J. Stainback Wilson, *Woman's Home Book of Health* (Philadelphia, 1860), p. 60.

118. Fowler, *Physiology*, p. 25.

119. Blackwell, *Laws of Life*, pp. 55, 146–147.

120. Martha Clark, *Victims of Amusement* (Philadelphia, 1849), pp. 57–58.

121. Sklar, *Catharine Beecher*, p. 123 and passim.

122. "Effects of Emulation," *American Annals of Education* 4 (August 1834):349–354; *Thirty-Ninth Annual Report of the Superintendent of Public Instruction of the State of Michigan, 1875* (Lansing, 1876), p. lxvi; Susanna Rowson, *Charlotte Temple: A Tale of Truth* (New York, 1905); James F. Beard, ed., *Tales for Fifteen (1823), by James Fenimore Cooper: A Facsimile Reproduction* (Gainesville, Fla., 1959); Holmes, *Elsie Venner*.

123. Eliza W. Farrar, *The Young Lady's Friend* (Boston, 1836); Lydia H. Sigourney, *Letters to Young Ladies*, 3rd. ed. (New York, 1837).

124. Emily Faithfull, *Three Visits to America* (Edinburgh, 1884), pp. 321–322; Paul Bourget, *Outre-Mer: Impressions of America* (New York, 1895), pp. 104–105; Katherine G. Busbey, *Home Life in America*, 2nd. ed. (New York, 1910), chap. 4; William Wasserstrom, *Heiress of All the Ages: Sex and Sentiment in the Genteel Tradition* (Minneapolis, 1959), pp. 5–7.

125. Joseph F. Kett, *The Formation of the American Medical Profession: The Role of Institutions, 1780–1860* (New Haven, 1968), chaps. 4, 5.

126. Thomas L. Nicolls, *Forty Years of American Life, 1821–1861* (New York, 1937), p. 206; William G. Sumner, "What Our Boys Are Reading," *Scribner's Monthly* 15 (March 1878):681–685; Matthew J. Bruccoli, ed., *The Profession of Authorship in America, 1800–1870: The Papers of William Charvat*, foreword by Howard M. Jones (Columbus, 1968), pp. 308–309; Mary Noel, *Villains Galore; The Hey-Day of the Popular Story Weekly* (New York, 1954).

127. Francis J. Grund, *The Americans in Their Moral, Social, and Political Relations*, 2 vols. in 1, introduced by Robert J. Berkhofer, Jr. (New York, 1968), p. 136; Richard Rapson, *Britons View America: Travel Commentary, 1860–1935* (Seattle, 1971), chap. 6.

128. David J. Rothman, *The Discovery of the Asylum: Social Order and Disorder in the New Republic* (Boston, 1971), p. 127.

129. Edward H. Dixon, *Woman and Her Diseases from the Cradle to the Grave*, 10th ed. (Philadelphia, 1864), p. 21.

130. E. H. Clarke, *Sex in Education; or, A Fair Chance for the Girls* (Boston, 1873); see also John S. Haller, Jr., "From Maidenhood to Menopause: Sex Education for Women in Victorian America," *Journal of Popular Culture* 6 (Summer 1972):49–70.

131. Clarke, *Sex in Education*, pp. 79–85.

132. Julia W. Howe, ed., *Sex and Education: A Reply to Dr. E. H. Clarke's Sex in Education* (Boston, 1874); Anna C. Brackett, ed., *The Education of American Girls, Considered in a Series of Essays* (New York, 1874); E. B. Duffey, *No Sex in Education; or An Equal Chance for Girls and Boys* (Philadelphia, 1874).

133. Anna C. Brackett, "Review of 'Sex in Education,' " in Brackett, ed., *Education of American Girls*, p. 375.

134. Mary E. Beedy, "Girls and Women in England and America," in ibid., pp. 227–228.

135. Howe, ed., *Sex and Education*, p. 89.

136. Ibid., p. 122; Brackett, ed., *Education of American Girls*, p. 101.

137. Sara A. Burstall, *The Education of Girls in the United States* (London, 1894), pp. 161, 163, 165.

138. Ibid., p. 55.

139. Peter M. Roget, *Thesaurus of English Words and Phrases* (Boston, 1854).

Chapter 6

1. Stanley Lebergott, *Manpower and Economic Growth: The American Record Since 1800* (New York, 1964), pp. 101–103.

2. Quoted in *Fourth Annual Report of the Bureau of Statistics of Labor of the State of New York, 1886* (Albany, 1886), p. 238.

3. Ibid., pp. 40–41, 44–47, 113, 141, 200.

4. *Massachusetts Bureau of Statistics of Labor, Annual Report for 1906* (Boston, 1906), pt. 1, pp. 6–85; Edward W. Bemis, "Relations of Trades Unions to Apprentices," *Quarterly Journal of Economics* 6 (October 1891):77; Paul H. Douglas, *American Apprenticeship and Industrial Education* (New York, 1922), chap. 1 and pp. 60–67, 74–75; for an English view, see Reginald C. Bray, *Boy Labour and Apprenticeship* (London, 1911), pp. 7–8.

5. *Ninth Annual Report of the* [Massachusetts] *Bureau of Statistics of Labor, 1878* (Boston, 1878), pt. 6.

6. *Fourth Annual Report of the Bureau of Statistics of Labor of the State of New York*, p. 112.

7. *Ninth Annual Report of the* [Massachusetts] *Bureau of Statistics of Labor,* pt. 6; *Massachusetts Bureau of Statistics of Labor, Annual Report for 1906,* pp. 6–85. In 1872 the lowest age for entering apprenticeships in Philadelphia was 16; see James S. Whitney, "Apprenticeship—And a Boy's Prospect of a Livelihood," *Pennsylvania Monthly* 3 (April 1872):200, 202.

8. *Seventh Annual Report of the Bureau of Statistics of Labor of the State of New York, 1889* (Albany, 1890), pp. 57–58; see also *Fifth Annual Report of the Bureau of Statistics of Labor of the State of New York, 1887* (Troy, 1888), pp. 45–46; *Fourth Biennial Report of the Bureau of Statistics of Labor of the State of Minnesota, 1893–1894* (St. Paul, 1895), p. 153.

9. Dixon Wecter, *When Johnny Comes Marching Home* (Cambridge, 1944), pp. 184–189; *Eighteenth Annual Report of the* [Massachusetts] *Bureau of Statistics of Labor, 1887* (Boston, 1887), p. 157.

10. Susan E. Bloomberg, "Industrialization and Skilled Workers: Newark, 1826–1860," Ph.D. thesis, history, University of Michigan (1974), chap. 3.

11. George E. Barnet, "The Printers: A Study in American Trade Unions," *American Economic Association Quarterly* 3 ser. 10 (October 1909):168–179; George E. Barnet, *Chapters on Machinery and Labor* (Cambridge, 1926), p. 67 and passim.

12. *Fourth Annual Report of the Bureau of Statistics of Labor of New York,* p. 40.

13. Bernard Bailyn, *Education in the Forming of American Society: Needs and Opportunities for Study* (Chapel Hill, 1960), pp. 29–36, 98–99; Robert F. Seybolt, *Apprenticeship and Apprenticeship Education in Colonial New England and New York,* Contributions to Education No. 85 (Teachers' College, Columbia University, New York, 1917), pp. 26, 30–31; James W. Alexander [Charles Quill, pseud.], *The Working Man* (Philadelphia, 1839), p. 115.

14. "Abuses of the System," in John R. Commons, et al., *A Documentary History of American Industrial Society,* 10 vols. (Cleveland, 1910–1911), vol. 5, p. 70.

15. *Working Man's Advocate,* April 20, 1844.

16. Norman Ware, *The Industrial Worker, 1840–1860: The Reaction of American Industrial Society to the Advance of the Industrial Revolution* (Gloucester, Mass., 1959), pp. 12, 57; Emerson D. Fite, *Social and Industrial Conditions in the North During the Civil War* (New York, 1963), p. 188; [James D. Burn] *Three Years Among the Working Classes in the United States During the War* (London, 1865), pp. 188–189.

17. James M. Motley, *Apprenticeship in American Trade Unions* (Baltimore, 1907), pp. 22–24.

18. Blanche Hazard, *The Organization of the Boot and Shoe Industry in Massachusetts Before 1875* (Cambridge, 1921), p. 144; ibid., pp. 146, 144.

19. Monte Calvert, *The Mechanical Engineer in America, 1830–1910; Professional Cultures in Conflict* (Baltimore, 1967), pp. 6–8, 29.

20. Motley, *Apprenticeship in American Trade Unions,* p. 21.

21. Harold F. Williamson, *Winchester: The Gun That Won the West* (Washington, D.C., 1952), pp. 86–87.

22. Ibid., chap. 7.

23. Francis A. Walker, *The Wages Question: A Treatise on Wages and the Wages Class* (New York, 1968), p. 195; see also David A. Wells, *Recent Economic Change* (New York, 1889), p. 61.

24. *Report of the* [Massachusetts] *Commission on Industrial and Technical Education* (Boston, 1906), pp. 31–125, 55–56, 84; see also *Twenty-Fifth Annual Report of the Commissioner of Labor* (Washington, D.C., 1911), p. 96.

25. Evan B. Alderfer, *Earnings of Skilled Workers in a Manufacturing Enterprise, 1878–1930* (Philadelphia, 1935).

26. Theodore Marburg, "Domestic Trade and Marketing," in Harold F. Williamson, ed., *The Growth of the American Economy* (Englewood Cliffs, N.J., 1951), pp. 521–530.

27. C. Wright Mills, *White Collar: The American Middle Classes* (New York, 1951), p. 72.

28. *Fourth Annual Report of the* [Massachusetts] *Bureau of Statistics of Labor, 1873* (Boston, 1873), pp. 383–394. For a general discussion of the problem of native American youth in manual trades, see Emile Levasseur, *The American Workman,* trans. Thomas S. Adams,

ed. Theodore Marbury (Baltimore, 1900), pp. 152–167. For a general discussion of job opportunities for youth in this period, see Oscar Handlin and Mary F. Handlin, *Facing Life: Youth and the Family in American History* (Boston, 1971), pp. 145–147.

29. Between 1890 and 1900, public secondary school enrollments rose from 202,963 to 519,251; see U.S. Bureau of the Census, *Historical Statistics of the United States: Colonial Times to 1957* (Washington, D.C., 1960), p. 207; on the problems faced by the dropout, see *Report of the* [Massachusetts] *Commission on Industrial and Technical Education*, pp. 31–125.

30. James P. Wickersham, *School Economy: A Treatise on Preparation, Organization, Employment, Government, and Authorities of School* (Philadelphia, 1867); see also "Digest of Rules and Regulations of Public Schools in Cities," *American Journal of Education* 19 (1870):421–464.

31. Calvert, *Mechanical Engineer*, pp. 6–8, 13–14, 70–71; Berenice M. Fisher, "Public Education and 'Special Interest': An Example From the History of Mechanical Engineering," *History of Education Quarterly* 6 (Spring 1966):31–40.

32. James R. Parsons, "Professional Education," in Nicholas M. Butler, *Education in the United States: A Series of Monographs* (New York, 1910), pp. 469, 471, 477, 467.

33. Ibid., pp. 523–525.

34. Park Benjamin, *The United States Naval Academy* (New York, 1900), pp. 152–156, 177–181, 192.

35. Ibid., pp. 152–156.

36. Abraham Flexner, *Medical Education in the United States and Canada: A Report to the Carnegie Foundation for the Advancement of Learning* (New York, 1910).

37. Calvert, *Mechanical Engineer*, p. 105.

38. Edmund J. James, "Commercial Education," in Butler, *Education in the United States*, pp. 658–660.

39. Quoted in ibid., p. 663.

40. Ibid., p. 661.

41. Ibid., p. 662.

42. Ibid.

43. Ibid., p. 665.

44. Calvert, *Mechanical Engineer*, pp. 69–70.

45. Cheesman A. Herrick, *Meaning and Practice of Commercial Education* (New York, 1904), pp. 195–196, 199–200.

46. *Historical Statistics of the United States*, pp. 203, 210; Theodore R. Sizer, *Secondary Schools at the Turn of the Century* (New Haven, 1964), p. 199.

47. Frederic B. Crossley, *The Courts and Lawyers of Illinois*, 3 vols. (Chicago, 1916); *The Bench and Bar of Chicago* (Chicago, n.d.); Edmund Q. Keasbey, *The Courts and Lawyers of New Jersey, 1667–1912*, 3 vols. (New York, 1912). I have used vols. 2 and 3 of Crossley and vol. 3 of Keasbey, eliminating in each case lawyers born outside the United States and those whose admission to the bar was delayed by service during the Civil War. Had the latter been included, the difference in the age of entrance to legal practice between those born before and after 1860 would have been even more pronounced.

48. Randolph S. Bourne, "The Two Generations," *Atlantic Monthly* 107 (May 1911): 594–596.

49. Richard Weiss, *The American Myth of Success: From Horatio Alger to Norman Vincent Peale* (New York, 1969), p. 128.

50. Randolph S. Bourne, *Youth and Life* (New York, 1913), p. 40.

51. Eugene R. Whitmore, *Keeping Young After Forty* (New York, 1928), p. vii.

52. Warren S. Thompson and P. K. Whelpton, *Population Trends in the United States* (New York, 1933), pp. 128–138.

53. "The Real Awkward Age," *Nation* 93 (December 14, 1911):571; see also "On Being Middle Aged," *Atlantic Monthly* 101 (January 1908):140–141; Florence Bell, "On Some Difficulties Incidental to Middle Age," *Living Age* 225 (April 14, 1900):98–107. The only precedent for this concern about middle age lay in the tradition of books on ways to prolong life; see, for example, Christopher W. Hufeland, *The Art of Prolonging Life*, 2 vols. (Orig. German ed., 1796; English ed., London, 1796). But books of this kind concerned ways to ward off senility rather than to cope with middle age.

54. Daniel Eddy, *The Young Man's Friend* (Philadelphia, 1865).

55. Ibid., p. 52.

56. Ibid., p. 27.

57. Ibid., p. 28.

58. Ibid., p. 36.

59. William Mathews, *Getting on in the World, or, Hints on Success in Life* (Chicago, 1874), chap. 10.

60. Kenneth H. Wayne, *Building the Young Man* (Chicago, 1912).

61. R. Richard Wohl, "The 'Country Boy' Myth and Its Place in American Urban Culture: The Nineteenth-Century Contribution," ed. by Moses Rischin, *Perspectives in American History* 3 (1969):104–105.

62. *Annual Report of the Board of Education of the State of Connecticut, 1869* (New Haven, 1869), p. 97.

63. Ray Stombaugh, *A Survey of the Movement Culminating in Industrial Arts Education in Secondary Schools*, Contributions to Education no. 670 (Teachers College, Columbia University, New York, 1936), pp. 59, 168–169, 15.

64. Ibid., p. 15.

65. John H. Kellogg, *Man, the Masterpiece, or Plain Truths Plainly Told, About Boyhood, Youth and Manhood* (1886; Battle Creek, Mich., 1894).

66. Ibid., pp. 445–453.

67. Ibid., p. 385.

68. C. Cuthbert Hall, "Personal Purity," in William W. Wolf, ed., *Some Things That Trouble Young Manhood* (New York, 1899), pp. 18–19.

69. John d'Entremont, "John Harvey Kellogg and the Cult of Sexual Purity," seminar paper, University of Virginia (1974).

70. Frank C. Haddock, *Power of Will* (Meriden, Conn., 1916); Haddock, *Business Power* (Meriden, Conn., 1918).

71. John G. Cawelti, *Apostles of the Self-Made Man* (Chicago, 1965), p. 176.

72. Weiss, *American Myth of Success*, chap. 7; Donald Meyer, *The Positive Thinkers: A Study of the American Quest for Health, Wealth and Personal Power from Mary Baker Eddy to Norman Vincent Peale* (Garden City, N.Y., 1965), chap. 13.

73. Orison S. Marden, *The Young Man Entering Business* (New York, 1907) chaps. 9, 10; Marden, *Choosing a Career* (New York, 1905), pp. 17, 68.

74. Whitelaw Reid et al., *Careers for the Coming Men of America* (Akron, Ohio, 1904), p. 7; Charles F. Wingate, *What Shall Our Boys Do for a Living?* (New York, 1898).

75. Orison S. Marden, *Architects of Fate* (Boston, 1895), p. 7.

76. Orison S. Marden, *Making Life a Masterpiece* (New York, 1916), pp. 168–169.

77. James I. Vance, *A Young Man's Make-Up* (New York, 1904), p. 10.

78. Cunningham Gieke, *Entering on Life: A Book for Young Men* (New York, 1897); Orison S. Marden, *Pushing to the Front; or Success Under Difficulties* (New York, 1894), p. 183; William Drysdale, *Helps for Ambitious Boys* (New York, 1899), pp. 2, 5–6.

79. Bourne, *Youth and Life*, pp. 233, 228–232.

80. Ibid., pp. 233, 238.

81. As Bourne himself recognized; see ibid., pp. 4, 25–26.

82. John R. Gillis, "Conformity and Rebellion: Contrasting Styles of English and American Youth, 1900–1933," *History of Education Quarterly* 13 (Fall 1973):249–260.

83. Walter Z. Laqueur, *Young Germany: A History of the German Youth Movement*, introduced by R. H. S. Crossman (New York, 1962).

84. *Sixth Annual Report of the* [Massachusetts] *Bureau of Statistics of Labor, 1875* (Boston, 1875), pp. 363–364, 370–371. Data from working-class budgets indicate that the average earnings of young people rose sharply after age 14 and that the number of young people contributing to their parents' support dropped sharply at age 19.

85. Susan E. Bloomberg et al., "A Census Probe Into Nineteenth-Century Family History: Southern Michigan, 1850–1880," *Journal of Social History* 5 (Fall 1971):34; Michael B. Katz, *The People of Hamilton, Canada West: Family and Class in a Mid-Nineteenth Century City* (Cambridge, Mass., 1975), p. 276; John R. Gillis, *Youth and History: Tradition and Change in European Age Relations, 1770–Present* (New York, 1974), pp. 56–61, 122–128.

86. For a description of street-corner society, see Robert A. Woods, ed., *The City Wilderness: A Settlement Study by the Residents and Associates of the South End House* (Boston, 1898), pp. 114–120, passim.

87. For a delightful account of some of Baden-Powell's ideas about sex, see Norman Mackenzie, "Sweating It Out With B-P," *New Statesman* 70 (October 15, 1965):555. See also Francis E. Clark, *The Great Secret: Health, Beauty, Happiness, Friend-Making, Common Sense, Success* (Boston, 1897), and his *Danger Signals: The Enemies of Youth from the Business Man's Standpoint* (Boston, 1885); Michael V. O.'Shea and John H. Kellogg, *The Body in Health* (New York, 1915). On Kellogg and the WCTU, see Mary Earhart, *Frances Willard: From Prayers to Politics* (Chicago, 1944), pp. 306–307. See also Edwin Markham, ed., *The Foundation Stones of Success*, 10 vols. (Chicago, 1917).

Chapter 7

1. Andrew Ten Broeck, *American State Universities: Their Origin and Progress* (Cincinnati, 1871), pp. 5, 23.

2. Abraham Flexner, *The American College: A Criticism* (New York, 1908), p. 57.

3. Henry D. Sheldon, *Student Life and Customs* (New York, 1901), p. 206; Henry S. Canby, *College Sons and College Fathers* (New York, 1915), pp. 13–14; David F. Allmendinger, Jr., *Paupers and Scholars: The Transformation of Student Life in Nineteenth-Century New England* (New York, 1975), p. 124.

4. Laurence R. Veysey, *The Emergence of the American University* (Chicago, 1965), pp. 277, 280.

5. Henry S. Canby, *Alma Mater: The Gothic Age of the American College* (New York, 1936); Veysey, *The Emergence of the American University*, pp. 280–282.

6. *The Education of Henry Adams: An Autobiography* (Boston, 1927), pp. 305–306.

7. Canby, *Alma Mater*, p. 36.

8. Ibid., p. 34.

9. For a portrait of late Victorian family life, see Henry S. Canby, *The Age of Confidence: Life in the Nineties* (New York, 1934).

10. Cornelius H. Patton and Walter H. Field, *Eight O'Clock Chapel: A Study of New England College Life in the Eighties* (Boston, 1927), p. 188.

11. Francis L. Patton, *Religion in College* (Princeton, 1889), p. 6.

12. LeBaron R. Briggs, *Routine and Ideals* (Boston, 1906), p. 30; Robert F. Leavens and Arthur H. Lord, *Dr. Tucker's Dartmouth* (Hanover, N.H., 1965), p. 48; Eugene R. Richards, "College Athletics," *Popular Science Monthly* 23 (February 1884):446.

13. Andrew D. White, "College Fraternities," *Forum* 3 (May 1887):243–253.

14. Sheldon, *Student Life and Customs*, pp. 180–192.

15. Ibid., p. 206.

16. Ibid., pp. 246–247.

17. Patton and Field, *Eight O'Clock Chapel*, p. 185.

18. William De Witt Hyde, *The Evolution of a College Student* (New York, 1898).

19. Ibid., p. 36.

20. William De Witt Hyde, *The College Man and the College Woman* (Boston, 1906), p. 3.

21. On the decline of the revival, see Veysey, *The Emergence of the American University*, p. 280.

22. Arthur W. Comey, "Growth of Colleges in the United States," *Educational Review* 3 (February 1892):120–121.

23. Sheldon noted that the class survived as a moral unit in the small colleges rather than in the large ones; see *Student Life and Customs*, p. 197.

24. "Stenographic Report: Discussion of 'The Actual and Proper Lines of Distinction between College and University,'" in *Association of American Universities, Fifth Annual Conference, 1904* (1904), pp. 36–37.

25. Ibid., p. 35.

26. Ibid., pp. 37–38.

27. Ibid.

28. Ibid., p. 42.

29. Joseph A. Scoville [Walter Barrett, pseud.], *The Old Merchants of New York City*, 4 vols. (New York: 1863–1866), vol. 2, p. 102.

30. R. T. Crane, *Utility of All Kinds of Higher Schooling: An Investigation* (Chicago, 1909), pp. 54–76; for a reply to Crane, see David S. Jordan, "Business Men's Criticisms of the College," *Independent* 54 (August 14, 1902):1932–1935.

31. Numerous studies sought to demonstrate the cash value of college education; see "Earning Power of College Men," *Literary Digest* 44 (February 3, 1912):212–213; "What Princeton Men Earn," *Literary Digest* 45 (July 20, 1912):105–106; Ernest G. Draper, "The College Man in Business," *Outlook* 106 (January 3, 1914):27–29.

32. Orison S. Marden, *Pushing to the Front; or, Success under Difficulties* (New York, 1894), p. v.

33. Quoted in Charles Thwing, "College Training and the Business Man," *North American Review* 177 (October 1903):597.

34. J. F. Shigley, "To Be Marked a 'Youth of Promise': Uplift and the Changing Motivations in the Late 19th-Century College Student," M.A. thesis, University of Virginia (1973), p. 114.

35. "Should Your Boy Go To College?" *Munsey's Magazine* 13 (August 1895):464.

36. Quoted in *Report of the Commissioner of Education, 1889–1890*, 2 vols. (Washington, D.C., 1893), vol. 2, p. 1142.

37. Walter D. Scott, *Influencing Men in Business: The Psychology of Argument and Suggestion*, 2nd. ed. (New York, 1919), pp. 11–12; see also Charles Lanier, "The Working of a Bank," *Scribner's Magazine* 21 (May 1897):586.

38. Quoted in Robert M. La Follette, ed., *The Making of America*, 10 vols. (Philadelphia, 1905), vol. 1, p. 224.

39. Henry D. Sedgwick, "American Colleges," in *The New American Type and Other Essays* (Boston, 1908), p. 170; see also Thomas Davidson, "The Ideal Training of an American Boy," *Forum* 17 (July 1894):571–581.

40. Canby, *Alma Mater*, p. 235.

41. John E. Bradley, *Work and Play: Talks With Students* (Boston, 1900), pp. 142, 151; see also Hugo Munsterberg, *The Americans*, trans. Edward Holt (New York, 1904), pp. 405–406.

42. Noah Porter, *The American Colleges and the American Public* (New Haven, 1870), pp. 179–183; Clayton S. Cooper, *Why Go to College?* (New York, 1910); George E. Peterson, *The New England College in the Age of the University* (Amherst, 1964), p. 44.

43. Cooper, *Why Go to College?* p. 132.

44. Charles Thwing, *The American College in American Life* (New York, 1897), p. 272.

45. Sheldon, *Student Life and Customs*, p. 299.

46. Bertha L. Gardner, "Debating in the High School," *School Review* 19 (October 1911):534–535.

47. Joel H. Spring, *Education and the Rise of the Corporate State* (Boston, 1972), p. 111.

48. Ella F. Young, "The Public High School," *School Review* 18 (February 1910):77.

49. Webster Cook, "Deportment in the High School," *School Review* 10 (October 1902):629.

50. Ibid., 633, 629–630.

51. Florence Milner, "School Management from the Side of Social Life," *School Review* 8 (September 1900):218.

52. William B. Owen, "Social Education Through the School," *School Review* 15 (January 1907):16.

53. Franklin W. Johnson, "The Social Organization of the High School," *School Review* 17 (December 1909):670, 677, 679.

54. John A. Porter, "The Secret Society System of Yale College," *New Englander* 53 (May 1884):377–393; Porter, "College Fraternities," *Century* 36 (September 1888):749–760; P. E. Piper, "College Fraternities," *Cosmopolitan* 22 (April 1897):641–648; Henry E. Howland, "Undergraduate Life at Yale," *Scribner's Magazine* 22 (July 1897):3–29.

55. Isaac Sharpless, "What Is the Present Consensus of Opinion as to the Most Im-

portant Problems in Preparatory and Collegiate Education," *School Review* 6 (March 1898):151; C. P. Cary, "Proposed Changes in the Accrediting of High Schools," *Proceedings of the National Education Association* 47 (1909):211.

56. On the lower-middle-class origins of normal school graduates, see Sheldon, *Student Life and Customs*, p. 292.

57. Cited in Edward A. Krug, *The Shaping of the American High School* (New York, 1964), pp. 290–291.

58. William T. Foster, "The Elective System in Public High Schools," *School Review* 13 (March 1905):243–262.

59. "The Washington Decision in the High-School Fraternity Question," *School Review* 14 (December 1906):739–743; William B. Owen, "The Problem of the High School Fraternity," *School Review* 14 (September 1906):492–504.

60. J. G. Masters, "High-School Fraternities," *School Review* 25 (June 1917):432.

61. Sheldon, *Student Life and Customs*, pp. 255–271.

62. Spring, *Education and the Rise of the Corporate State*, p. 77.

63. Seymour J. Mandelbaum, *Boss Tweed's New York* (New York, 1965), p. 155.

64. Ibid.

65. John Corbin, *An American at Oxford* (Boston, 1902), pp. 271–272.

66. Frances M. Morehouse, *The Discipline of the School* (Boston, 1914), pp. 6, 38.

67. Albert Shaw, "The School City," *Review of Reviews* 20 (1899):693.

68. Mandelbaum, *Boss Tweed's New York*, p. 67; Denis T. Lynch, *"Boss" Tweed: The Story of a Grim Generation* (New York, 1927), p. 35.

69. Robert A. Woods, ed., *The City Wilderness: A Settlement Study by Residents and Associates of the South End House* (Boston, 1898), pp. 118–120.

70. Charles H. Levermore, *Samuel Train Dutton: A Biography* (New York, 1922), pp. 12–13, 22–23, and passim.

71. Hiram Orcutt, *The Teacher's Manual* (Boston, 1871), pp. 59, 62.

72. Morehouse, *The Discipline of the School*, p. 159.

73. Ibid.

74. Nathaniel Butler, "Parents' Associations," *School Review* 16 (January 1908):78–88.

75. John H. Vincent, "The Coming Church," *Independent* 44 (July 7, 1892):1; John T. Beckly, "Young People's Movement No Menace to the Church," ibid., 7; "The Epworth League," ibid., 4.

76. Leonard W. Bacon and Charles A. Northrop, *Young People's Societies* (New York, 1900), pp. 51–52, 45, 47; M. G. Kyle, "The United Presbyterian Young People's Christian Union," *Independent* 44 (July 7, 1892):7; Gerald Jenny, *The Young People's Movement in the American Lutheran Church: A Review and an Estimate* (Minneapolis, 1927); Frank O. Erb, *The Development of the Young People's Movement* (Chicago, 1917). Other branches included the Luther League, the Brotherhood of St. Paul (Methodist), the Baptist Young People's Union, the Young People's Christian Union of the Universalist Church (est. 1889), the Brotherhood of St. Andrew (P.E., est. 1886), and the Daughters of the King (P. E., est. 1885). The Boys' Brigade was imported from Britain.

77. George Stewart, Jr., *A History of Religious Education in Connecticut to the Middle of the Nineteenth Century* (New Haven, 1926), p. 81.

78. Hervey Wilbur, *A Discourse on the Religious Education of Youth, Delivered at Homer* [N.Y.] (Boston, 1814).

79. Wade C. Barclay, *The Methodist Episcopal Church*, vol. 3 of *The History of Methodist Missions*, 3 vols. (New York, 1949–1957), pp. 196–198.

80. Ibid., p. 217.

81. Daniel Dorchester, *Christianity in the United States From the First Settlement Down to the Present Time*, rev. ed. (New York, 1895), p. 693; Addie G. Wardle, *History of the Sunday School Movement in the Methodist Episcopal Church* (New York, 1918), pp. 92–93, 101.

82. Winthrop S. Hudson, *Religion in America* (New York, 1965), p. 273.

83. Newell L. Sims, *A Hoosier Village: A Sociological Study With Special Reference to Causation*, Columbia University Studies in History, Economics, and Public Law, no. 117 (New York, 1912), pp. 113–115; see also H. N. Morse and Edmund deS. Brunner, *The*

Town and Country Church in the United States (New York, 1923), pp. 162–163. Although the theological impulse behind the young people's movement was mildly progressive, young people's societies emerged in some conservative denominations; see Herbert Asbury, *Up From Methodism* (New York, 1926), p. 31.

84. Richard Jensen, *The Winning of the Midwest: Social and Political Conflict, 1888–1896* (Chicago, 1971), chap. 7. Jensen provides ample evidence of the middle-class nature of evangelical Protestantism in the Midwest at the end of the 19th century. See also Gregory H. Singleton, "Essay Review: 'Mere Middle-Class Institutions': Urban Protestantism in Nineteenth-Century America," *Journal of Social History* 6 (Summer 1973):489–502.

85. Mary Earhart, *Frances Willard: From Prayers to Politics* (Chicago, 1944), p. 287; J. J. Ashley, *History of the Georgia Women's Christian Temperance Union From Its Organization, 1883 to 1907* (Columbus, Ga., 1914), p. 71; C. L. Pearson and J. Edwin Hendricks, *Liquor and Anti-Liquor in Virginia, 1619–1919* (Durham, N.C., 1967), p. 197; James R. Jackson, *History of Littleton, New Hampshire*, 3 vols. (Cambridge, Mass., 1905), vol. 2, p. 414.

86. Hugh A. Orchard, *Fifty Years of Chautauqua* (Cedar Rapids, Iowa, 1923); John H. Vincent, *The Chautauqua Movement* (Boston, 1886), p. 39; Rebecca Richmond, *Chautauqua: An American Place* (New York, 1943).

87. Richmond, *Chautauqua*, p. 65.

88. Orchard, *Fifty Years*, pp. 64–65, 78–79.

89. Richmond, *Chautauqua*, p. 103.

90. Ibid., p. 101.

91. Francis E. Clark, *Training the Church of the Future* (New York, 1902), pp. 91–92.

92. Cotton Mather, *Religious Societies: Proposals for the Revival of Dying Religion by Well-Ordered Societies for That Purpose* (Boston, 1724).

93. Clark, *Training the Church of the Future*, p. 114.

94. Amos R. Wells, "The Christian Endeavor Movement: II. A New Religious Force," *New England Magazine*, n.s. 6 (June 1892):524.

95. William B. Forbush, "The Conditions and Needs of Young People's Societies," *Proceedings of the Second Annual Convention of the Religious Education Association, 1904* (Philadelphia, 1904), pp. 380–381.

96. Ibid., p. 381.

97. Beckly, "Young People's Movement No Menace to the Church," 7; Wayland Hoyt, "The Power of the Pledge," *Independent* 44 (July 7, 1892):3.

98. Olive Anderson, "The Growth of Christian Militarism in Mid-Victorian Britain," *English Historical Review*, 86 (January 1971):72, 46–52, 66–69; John W. Jones, *Christ in the Camp; or, Religion in Lee's Army* (Richmond, 1888), p. 15; Edward P. Smith, *Incidents of the United States Christian Commission* (Philadelphia, 1871). My generalization about military schools is based on data which I have worked up from Robert D. Cole, *Private Secondary Education for Boys in the United States* (Philadelphia, 1928). Of 926 non-Catholic private schools admitting boys, 47.8 percent were founded between 1870 and 1909. Of the 110 military schools in this group, 49.9 percent were founded during this period. Cole listed only schools still in existence in 1926. Of course, thousands of academies established between 1800 and 1850 had disappeared by then. Since very few academies had been military in character, the above percentages sharply understate the proportionate popularity of military schools between 1870 and 1909.

99. Anderson, "Growth of Christian Militarism," 70.

100. John Foster, *The Glory of the Age: An Essay on the Spirit of Missions, Being the Substance of a Discourse Delivered Before the Baptist Missionary Society. Bristol, England* (Boston, 1833), p. 13.

101. Beckly, "Young People's Movement No Menace to the Church," 7.

102. "Address of Rev. R. L. Greene," *Minutes of the Ninth Annual Conference of the Young People's Society for Christian Endeavor, 1890.*

103. Theodore Cuyler, *Newly Enlisted: A Series of Talks With Young Converts* (New York, 1888).

104. J. Ross Stevenson, "The Purpose of the Student Missionary Gathering," in *Student Missionary Appeal* (New York, 1898), p. 25.

105. John R. Mott, "What of the War?" in ibid., p. 274.

106. James Vance, "The Minister's Essential Relation to the Success of the Foreign Missionary Campaign," in *Students and the Modern Missionary Crusade* (New York, 1906), p. 40.

107. Luther Wright, *Education: An Address delivered at Leicester, Dec. 25, 1833* (Leicester, 1834), p. 9.

108. "Capt. Alden Partridge's Argument for Military Education, 1825," in Edgar S. Knight, ed., *A Documentary History of Education in the South Before 1860*, 5 vols. (Chapel Hill, 1949–1953), vol. 4, pp. 156–157.

109. Wells, "Christian Endeavor Movement: II," 524.

110. Bacon and Northrop, *Young People's Societies*, pp. 35–70.

111. "Boyish" might not be the right word to describe the infantile techniques of an organization like the Knights of King Arthur, whose watchwords were "adult-leadership" and "hero-worship." To graduate from "page" to "esquire" in the Knights, the youth had to accumulate 1,000 points, a slow process inasmuch as only one-eighth of a point was granted for every page read in a book about some hero. But there was a compensating feature, for the youth who read three books on Lincoln could go around calling himself Sir Abraham Lincoln, although still several hundred points short of esquire status. Oddly, this particular society was organized in a college; see Frank Masseck, "Knights of King Arthur," in Edgar M. Robinson et al., *Reaching the Boys of an Entire Community* (New York, 1909), pp. 175–189.

112. Quoted in Laurence L. Doggett, *Life of Robert McBurney* (Cleveland, 1902), p. 28.

113. Edgar M. Robinson, *The Early Years: The Beginnings of Work With Boys in the Young Men's Christian Association* (New York, 1950), p. 6.

114. C. Howard Hopkins, *History of the Y.M.C.A. in North America* (New York, 1951), pp. 200–202; "Save the Boys," *The Watchman*, November 1, 1879.

115. Richard C. Morse, *My Life With Young Men: Fifty Years in the Young Men's Christian Association* (New York, 1918), p. 88.

116. *The Watchman*, April 15, 1882; see also Robinson, *The Early Years*, p. 66.

117. Hopkins, *History of the Y.M.C.A.*, pp. 239–240.

118. Robinson, *The Early Years*, pp. 41–42, 76.

119. Ibid., p. 18.

120. Ibid., p. 76.

121. Henry Drummond, *The Natural Law in the Spiritual World* (New York, 1884).

122. For a critique of Drummond, see George A. Smith, *The Life of Henry Drummond* (New York, 1898), p. 155.

123. Ibid., p. 138.

124. Ibid., pp. 368–369; see also Clarence P. Shedd, *Two Centuries of Student Christian Movements: Their Origin and Intercollegiate Life* (New York, 1934), pp. 279–286.

125. Quoted in Smith, *Life of Drummond*, p. 384.

126. Henry Drummond, *The New Evangelism and Other Addresses* (New York, 1899), pp. 26–27.

127. Quoted in Smith, *Life of Drummond*, p. 489.

128. Luther H. Gulick, "Psychological, Pedagogical, and Religious Aspects of Group Games," *Pedagogical Seminary* 6 (March 1899):148. On Gulick's life, see Ethel J. Dorgan, *Luther Halsey Gulick, 1865–1918*, Teachers College, Columbia University, Contributions to Education no. 635 (New York, 1934).

129. Gulick, "Psychological, Pedagogical, and Religious Aspects of Group Games," 145.

130. On muscular Christianity, see David Newsome, *Godliness and Good Learning: Four Studies on a Victorian Ideal* (London, 1961), pp. 197–198, 36–37; Thomas Hughes, *The Manliness of Christ* (New York, 1880).

131. G. Stanley Hall, "The Moral and Religious Training of Children," *Princeton Review* 10 (January 1882):26–48.

132. Arthur H. Daniels, "The New Life: A Study in Regeneration," *American Journal of Psychology* 6 (October 1893):61–103; James H. Leuba, "A Study in the Psychology of Religious Phenomena," *American Journal of Psychology* 7 (April 1896):309–385.

133. Edwin D. Starbuck, *The Psychology of Religion:An Empirical Study of the Growth

of Religious Consciousness (London, 1906), p. xii. George Coe's major works were *The Spiritual Life: Studies in the Science of Religion* (New York, 1900), *The Religion of a Mature Mind* (Chicago, 1902), and *A Social Theory of Religious Education* (New York, 1917).

134. Dorothy Ross, *G. Stanley Hall: The Psychologist As Prophet* (Chicago, 1972), pp. 334–335, 416, 418.

135. Leuba, "A Study in the Psychology of Religious Phenomena," 310–311.

136. Coe, *The Religion of a Mature Mind*, pp. 60–61.

137. Ibid., p. 64.

138. Leuba, "A Study in the Psychology of Religious Phenomena," 311.

139. Ibid., 313, 315, 321.

140. Discussing the findings of professional religious psychologists, a veteran minister commented with respect to the age of conversion that the facts were "indisputable." He went on to say that this had "all my life and long before, been a sort of commonplace truth among wise and successful ministers of the gospel, and has determined the direction of many of their most earnest efforts." See Daniel W. Fisher, *A Human Life: An Autobiography With Excursions* (New York, 1909), p. 58.

141. Starbuck, *Psychology of Religion*, p. 7. Yet James utilized Starbuck's material in *The Varieties of Religious Experience* (London, 1907).

142. G. Stanley Hall, *Adolescence: Its Psychology and Its Relations to Anthropology, Sociology, Sex, Crime, Religion and Education,* 2 vols. (New York, 1905), vol. 2, p. 292.

143. Ibid., 302.

144. Ibid., 345; see also Coe, *The Spiritual Life*, p. 71.

145. Hall, *Adolescence,* vol. 2, pp. 429, 343. Bacon and Northrop came closer to the truth when they observed that the young people's movement was marked by an excessive reaction to "unwholesome introspection and self-analysis which has prevailed like an epidemic in earlier generations and down to a recent time"; see their *Young People's Societies,* p. 67.

146. B. W. Spiller et al, *The New Convention Normal Manual for Sunday School Workers* (Nashville, 1907).

147. Dorgan, *Gulick,* p. 148.

148. George Stewart, Jr., *The Life of Henry B. Wright* (New York, 1925), p. 108.

149. G. Douglas, "Social Purity," *Official Report of the Twelfth International Christian Endeavor Convention* (New York, 1900), p. 254.

150. Coe, *Spiritual Life*, pp. 6–7.

151. E. G. Lancaster, "The Psychology and Pedagogy of Adolescence," *Pedagogical Seminary* 5 (July 1897):127.

152. Norman E. Richardson and Ormond E. Loomis, *The Boy Scout Movement Applied by the Church* (New York, 1915), p. 65. Richardson and Loomis estimated that over 90 percent of all Boy Scout troops were connected with local churches and Sunday schools and that nearly 80 percent of all Boy Scouts were Protestants; see ibid., p. 57.

Chapter 8

1. Gillis notes a similar pattern of attempted democratization of adolescence in Europe after 1900; see John R. Gillis, *Youth and History: Tradition and Change in European Age Relations, 1770–Present* (New York, 1974), pp. 133–134.

2. Ibid., pp. 145–146.

3. Ibid., p. 118; Warren S. Thompson and P. K. Whelpton, *Population Trends in the United States* (New York, 1933), chap. 8.

4. Susan E. Bloomberg et al, "A Census Probe into Nineteenth-Century Family History: Southern Michigan, 1850–1880," *Journal of Social History* 5 (Fall 1971):38.

5. Thompson and Whelpton, *Population Trends in the United States*, p. 141.

6. John R. Gillis, "Conformity and Rebellion: Contrasting Styles of English and German Youth, 1900–1933," *History of Education Quarterly* 13 (Fall 1973):249–260.

7. G. Stanley Hall, *Adolescence: Its Psychology and Its Relations to Anthropology, Sociology, Sex, Crime, Religion and Education,* 2 vols. (New York, 1905); George Partridge, *Genetic Psychology of Education: An Epitome of the Published Educational Writings of President G. Stanley Hall of Clark University* (New York, 1912).

8. Hall, *Adolescence,* vol. 1, chaps. 4–6.

9. Dorothy Ross, *G. Stanley Hall: The Psychologist as Prophet* (Chicago, 1972), pts. 3–4.

10. Partridge's *Genetic Psychology of Education* contains a more complete statement of Hall's recapitulation theory than does *Adolescence.* On the philosophical origins of recapitulation, see Charles Strickland, "The Child and the Race: The Doctrine of Recapitulation and Culture Epochs in the Rise of the Child-Centered Ideal in American Educational Thought, 1870–1900," Ph.D. thesis, education, University of Wisconsin (1963). Long before Hall there were references to the idea that the child recapitulated the history of the race. See, for example, John W. Dodge, "Boys and Civilization," *Pennsylvania School Journal* 20 (December 1871):176.

11. G. Stanley Hall, *Educational Problems,* 2 vols. (New York, 1911), vol. 1, p. 67.

12. Ibid., pp. 103–104, 86–88.

13. Hall, *Adolescence,* vol. 1, p. 173.

14. Ibid.

15. Ibid.

16. Hall, *Educational Problems,* vol. 1, p. 643.

17. Ibid.; see also Hall's *Morale: The Supreme Standard of Life and Conduct* (New York, 1920).

18. G. Stanley Hall, *Aspects of German Culture* (Boston, 1881), p. 306.

19. G. Stanley Hall, *Life and Confessions of a Psychologist* (New York, 1923), pp. 148–149, 131, 133.

20. John Higham, "The Reorientation of American Culture in the 1890s," in John Weiss, ed., *The Origins of Modern Consciousness* (Detroit, 1965), pp. 25–48.

21. Leta S. Hollingworth, *The Psychology of the Adolescent* (New York, 1929), p. 17.

22. Nathan I. Huggins, *Protestants Against Poverty: Boston's Charities, 1870–1900* (Westport, Conn., 1971), pp. 93–94, 101–102; William E. Hall, *100 Years and Millions of Boys* (New York, 1961), chap. 1; Jacob Riis, *The Children of the Poor* (New York, 1961), chap. 13; Anthony M. Platt, *The Child Savers: The Invention of Delinquency* (Chicago, 1969).

23. William B. Forbush, *The Boy Problem: A Study in Social Pedagogy,* introduced by G. Stanley Hall (Philadelphia, 1902); William A. McKeever, *Training the Boy* (New York, 1913).

24. Alvan F. Sanborn, "About Boys and Boys' Clubs," *North American Review* 167 (August 1898):254–256; George W. Fiske, *Boy Life and Self-Government* (New York, 1912), p. 163.

25. *The Boy Problem* went through eight editions between 1902 and 1913.

26. J. Adams Puffer, *The Boy and His Gang,* introduced by G. Stanley Hall (Boston, 1912).

27. Ibid., p. 141.

28. William D. Murray, *The History of the Boy Scouts of America* (New York, 1937); J. O. Springhall, "The Boy Scouts, Class and Militarism in Relation to British Youth Movements, 1908–1930," *International Review of Social History* 16 (1971):125–158.

29. On William R. George, see Jack M. Holl, *Juvenile Reform in the Progressive Era: William R. George and the Junior Republic Movement* (Ithaca, N.Y., 1971).

30. Brian Morris, "Ernest Thompson Seton and the Origins of the Woodcraft Movement," *Journal of Contemporary History* 5 (1970):183–194; "The Boy Scout Movement: To Perpetuate Docility, Stupidity, and Brutality," *The Masses* 1 (February 1911):17.

31. David Snedden, "Some Pedagogical Interpretations and Applications of the Methods of Boy Scout Education," *Association Boys* 18 (January 1917):2.

32. Edgar M. Robinson, "Boys as Savages," *Association Boys* 1 (August 1902):129.

33. Puffer,*The Boy and His Gang,* p. 7.

34. H. W. Gibson, *Boyology, or Boy Analysis* (New York, 1922).

35. Henry S. Curtis, "The Boy Scouts and the Salvation of the Village Boy," *Pedagogical Seminary* 20 (March 1913):82.

36. Henry S. Curtis, "The Normal Course in Play," *Playground* 3 (October 1909):22; K. Gerald Marsden, "Philanthropy and the Boston Playground Movement, 1885–1902," *Social Service Review* 35 (March 1961): 48–58.

37. Joseph Lee, *Play in Education* (New York, 1915), p. 234. Lee was primarily interested in reaching teenagers rather than small children through playgrounds.

38. Henry S. Curtis, "The Proper Relation of Organized Sports on Public Playgrounds and in Public Service," *Playground* 3 (September 1909):14.

39. Lorna H. Leland, "The Proper Relation of Organized Sports on Public Playgrounds and in Public Schools," ibid., 14.

40. Lee, *Play in Education*, p. 436.

41. Jane Addams, *The Spirit of Youth and the City Streets* (1909; reprinted, New York, 1916).

42. Ibid., pp. 75–76.

43. Ibid., p. 13.

44. See James's review in the *American Journal of Sociology* 15 (January 1910):533.

45. Louise deKoven Bowen, *Safeguards for City Youth at Work and at Play* (New York, 1914).

46. Edward J. Ward, "Playground and Social Center Work in Rochester, New York," *Playground* 4 (June 1912):103; Henry S. Curtis, *The Practical Conduct of Play* (New York, 1915), p. 245.

47. On Louise deKoven Bowen, see Anthony M. Platt, *The Child Savers: The Invention of Delinquency* (Chicago, 1969), pp. 83–92.

48. Joseph Lee, "What Substitutes for War," *Survey* 33 (October 1914):31–32; Lee, "The Community: Maker of Men," *Proceedings; National Conference on Social Work*, 48th sess. (1921), p. 49.

49. Arthur Holmes. "Moral Aspects of Physical Education," *Proceedings, National Education Association* (hereinafter *PNEA*) 59 (1921):519; Benjamin C. Gruenberg, "The Relation of Physical Education to Social Hygiene," *PNEA* 60 (1922):1091–1094; Colin A. Scott, *Social Education* (Boston, 1908); Milton E. Potter, "Social Organization in the High School," *PNEA* 50 (1912):181–187.

50. Jay B. Nash, "The Relation of Public Playgrounds and Recreation Centers to Our National Ideals of Democracy," *PNEA* 59 (1921):521.

51. Hall, *Educational Problems*, vol. 1, p. 109.

52. Robert A. Woods, ed., *The City Wilderness: A Settlement Study by Residents and Associates of the South End House* (Boston, 1898), pp. 148–149; Josephine Goldmark, ed., *Boyhood and Lawlessness*, pt. 1, vol. 1 of *West Side Studies* (2 vols., New York, 1914), chap. 4.

53. Forbush, *The Boy Problem*, p. 56; Edgar M. Robinson et al., *Reaching the Boys of an Entire Community* (New York, 1909), passim

54. Boys-workers often claimed that boys were instinctive hero worshipers; see M. Jane Reaney, "The Psychology of the Boy Scout Movement," *Pedagogical Seminary* 21 (September 1914):410.

55. Ross, *G. Stanley Hall*, chap. 15; William Kessen, *The Child* (New York, 1965), pp. ix, 4–6; Sara E. Wiltse, "A Preliminary Sketch of the History of Child Study for the Year Ending September, 1896," *Pedagogical Seminary* 4 (October 1896):116, 118. For various reports on the progress of child study, see *PNEA* 33 (1894):1001–1002 and *PNEA* 36 (1897):859, 865. See also Ernest Belden, "A History of the Child Study Movement in the United States, 1870–1920," Ed.D. thesis, University of California at Berkeley (1965); Wilbur Dutton, "The Child Study Movement in America, 1880–1920" Ph.D. thesis, Stanford University (1945).

56. William James, *Talks to Teachers on Psychology; and to Students on Some of Life's Ideals* (London, 1905), p. 13; John Dewey, "Criticisms Wise and Unwise on Modern Child Study," *PNEA* 36 (1897):867–868.

57. Mrs. Theodore W. Birney, "Sympathetic Parenthood," in Mary H. Weeks, ed., *Parents and Their Problems: Child Welfare in Home, School, Church, and State*, 8 vols. (Washington, D.C., 1914), vol. 8, p. 157; Mary H. Weeks, "Hannah Kent Schoff," in ibid., pp. 45–50.

58. On the linkage of the National Congress of Mothers to purity reform, see David J. Pivar, *Purity Crusade: Sexual Morality and Social Control, 1868–1900* (Westport, Conn., 1973), pp. 228–229. Mrs. Birney's conversion to purity reform came, appropriately, in Kellogg Hall at Chautauqua, so named because it had been built with money donated by John H. Kellogg and his wife.

59. Mrs. Theodore W. Birney, "The Need for Organization," in *Parents and Their Problems*, vol. 8, p. 32; "The Congress of Mothers," *Woman's Journal* 33 (January 4, 1902):84.

60. Ross, *G. Stanley Hall*, chap. 16.

61. O'Shea's papers are in the Wisconsin State Historical Society, Madison, Wisconsin.

62. Irving King, *The High School Age* (Indianapolis, 1914); C. Ward Crampton, *Anatomical and Physiological Age* (New York, 1908); William Healy, *Honesty: A Study of the Causes and Treatment of Dishonesty Among Children* (Indianapolis, 1915).

63. King, *The High School Age*, p. 117.

64. Dorothy C. Fisher, *Self-Reliance: A Practical and Informal Discussion of Methods of Teaching Self-Reliance, Initiative, and Responsibility to Modern Children* (Indianapolis, 1916).

65. Ibid., p. 51.

66. Ibid., p. 5.

67. For examples of the conservative and traditional nature of much of the advice purveyed to parents by child study, see Kate G. Wells, "The Futility of a Lie," *Childhood* 1 (February 1893):86–88; Sherman R. Davis, "Growth and Education of the Child," *Kindergarten Magazine* 14 (April 1902):489.

68. James R. Miller, *Young People's Problems* (New York, 1898).

69. Michael Anderson, *Family Structure in Nineteenth-Century Lancashire* (Cambridge, England, 1971), pp. 62, 90–91. Historians of the family often distinguish between family and household structure. During the last two centuries, household structure has probably changed more noticeably than family structure, mainly because of the sharp decline in the proportion of households containing lodgers. Proponents of middle-class family ideals in the early 1900s often claimed that the presence of lodgers was inconsistent with privacy and purity. Yet the sharp decline in lodging began only after 1920. The decline is better viewed as an effect rather than a cause of the family ideology described in the text; see John Modell and Tamara K. Hareven, "Urbanization and the Malleable Household: An Examination of Boarding and Lodging in American Families," *Journal of Marriage and the Family* 35 (August 1973):467–479.

70. Eliza W. Farrar, *The Young Lady's Friend* (Boston, 1836).

71. Daniel Bell, *The Coming of Post-Industrial Society: A Venture in Social Forecasting* (New York, 1973), pp. 69–70.

72. May W. Sewall, "Woman's Work in Education," *PNEA* 23 (1884):153–157.

73. Charles H. Thurber, "Child Study in Its Effects Upon the Teacher," *Child-Study Monthly* 1 (February 1896):247.

74. Corinne Harrison, "What Makes—What Mars the Teacher," *PNEA* 33 (1894):141; Zella R. Nicholson, "Child Study in the Kindergarten," *Child-Study Monthly* 2 (April 1897):682.

75. Quoted in Thomas P. Bailey, "Child Study in the Tompkins Observatory School, II," *PNEA* 35 (1896):853.

76. Many of Hall's students found positions in normal schools and represented his views at conventions. School principals, on the other hand, were often hostile to child study. See "Report from Various Sections of the National Association for Child Study," *PNEA* 33 (1894):1002.

77. National Education Association, Commission on the Reorganization of Secondary Education, *Cardinal Principles of Secondary Education*, U.S. Bureau of Education Bulletin no. 35 (Washington, D.C., 1918).

78. Forest C. Ensign, *Compulsory School Attendance and Child Labor* (Iowa City, 1921), pp. 183, 153.

79. *Forty-Ninth Annual Report of the Public Schools of the City of Fall River, 1914* (Fall River, Mass., 1914), p. 29.

80. For a study of various movements in secondary education in this period, see Edward A. Krug, *The Shaping of the American High School* (New York, 1964).

81. Charles E. Chadsey, "The Relation of the High School to the Community and to the College," *PNEA* 47 (1909):203–207; David Snedden, "Discussion," *PNEA* 46 (1908):590.

82. Franklin W. Johnson, "The Social Organization of the High School," *School Review* 17 (December 1909):670–679.

83. George Creel, "Wyoming's Answer to Militarism," *Everybody's Magazine* 34 (February 1916):150–159.

84. "Report of the Committee on Military Training in the Public Schools," *PNEA* 55 (1917):780.

85. Calvin O. Davis, *Junior High School Education* (Yonkers, N.Y., 1924), pp. 38–39; G. Stanley Hall, "Needs and Methods of Educating Young People in the Hygiene of Sex," *Pedagogical Seminary* 15 (March 1908):82–91; Bryan Strong, "Ideas of the Early Sex Education Movement in America, 1890–1920," *History of Education Quarterly* 12 (Summer 1972):129–161.

86. Joseph K. Hart, *A Social Interpretation of Education* (New York, 1929), p. 362.

87. E. L. Thorndike, "Magnitude and Rate of Alleged Changes at Adolescence," *Educational Review* 54 (September 1917):140–147.

88. *Cardinal Principles of Secondary Education*, p. 9.

89. J. Crosby Chapman and George S. Counts, *Principles of Secondary Education* (Boston, 1924), chaps. 20, 29; Ralph W. Pringle, *Adolescence and High School Problems* (Boston, 1922), p. 166.

90. Arthur C. Perry, *Discipline As a School Problem* (Boston, 1915), p. 248.

91. Frank Parsons, *Choosing a Vocation* (Boston, 1909), chap. 2.

92. William A. McKeever, *Training the Boy* (New York, 1913), p. 226.

93. Katherine Blackford, *The Job, the Man, and the Boss* (New York, 1914); Robert Hoxie, *Scientific Management and Labor* (New York, 1920), p. 157.

94. Randolph Bourne, *Education for Living* (New York, 1917), pp. 199–205.

95. Owen Lovejoy, "Vocational Guidance and Child Labor," in *Vocational Guidance*, U.S. Bureau of Education Bulletin no. 14 (Washington, D.C., 1914), p. 12; George S. Counts, *School and Society in Chicago* (New York, 1928), p. 173.

96. John M. Brewer, "The Recent Progress in Vocational Guidance," in Frederick J. Allen, ed., *Principles and Problems of Vocational Guidance: A Book of Readings* (New York, 1927), p. 45.

97. Ernest R. Henderson, "The Industrial Factor in Education," in Meyer H. Bloomfield, *Readings in Vocational Guidance* (Cambridge, Mass., 1924), p. 66.

98. E. L. Thorndike, "The Permanence of Interests in Their Relations to Abilities," *Popular Science Monthly* 81 (November 1912), 449–456.

99. Frank M. Leavitt, "The School Phases of Vocational Guidance," *School Review* 23 (December 1915):696.

100. [B. B. Breese], "Vocational Guidance," *Unpopular Review* 4 (1915):354.

101. Frank Watts, "The Outlook for Vocational Psychology," *British Journal of Psychology* 11 (January 1921):197–198; Donald G. Paterson, "The Vocational Testing Movement," *Journal of Personnel Research* 1 (October–November, 1922):297; Harry D. Kitson, *The Psychology of Vocational Guidance* (Philadelphia, 1923), pp. 234–235.

102. Max Freyd, "Measurement in Vocational Selection: An Outline of Research Procedures," *Journal of Personnel Research* 2 (October 1923):215.

103. Benjamin Stolberg, "Vocational Guidance: A Study in the Predicament of Public Education," *Nation* 114 (June 7, 1922):717.

104. Edgar Z. Friedenberg, *The Vanishing Adolescent* (Boston, 1959); Elizabeth Douvan and Joseph Adelson, *The Adolescent Experience* (New York, 1966), pp. 351–354. See also Friedenberg's *Coming of Age in America: Growth and Acquiescence* (New York, 1963).

Chapter 9

1. August de B. Hollingshead, *Elmtown's Youth: The Impact of Social Class on Adolescents* (New York, 1949), pp. 272, 298.
2. John B. Stephenson, *Shiloh: A Mountain Community* (Lexington, Ky., 1968), p. 61.
3. Robin M. Williams, "Rural Youth Studies in the United States," *Rural Sociology* 4 (June 1939):166–178.
4. Carl Withers [James West, pseud.], *Plainville, U.S.A.* (New York, 1945).
5. Ibid., pp. 107–110.
6. Ibid., p. 194.
7. Aaron G. Knebel, *Four Decades With Men and Boys* (New York, 1936), p. 23.
8. Withers, *Plainville*, pp. 198, 107–110.
9. Liberty H. Bailey, *The Country Life Movement in the United States* (New York, 1911); Parris T. Farwell, *Village Improvement* (New York, 1918), pp. 278–279; Walter Terpenning, *Village and Open-Country Neighborhoods* (New York, 1931), p. 58.
10. John M. Gillette, "The Socialization of Rural Minds," *Journal of Social Forces* 1 (March 1923):290–292.
11. Farwell, *Village Improvement*, pp. 278–279; Constance D. MacKay, "Suggestions for Country Plays and Pageants," *Rural Manhood* 11 (February 1920):51–52.
12. W. J. Campbell, "The Whole Country Side in the Awakening," *Rural Manhood* 5 (April 1914):162.
13. Dell C. Vandercook, "Rural Delinquency," *Rural Manhood* 4 (May 1913):150–152.
14. " 'We Need a Place' and What Happened," *Rural Manhood* 6 (March 1915):118.
15. J. H. Kolb and Edmund deS. Brunner, *A Study of Rural Sociology* (Boston, 1935), p. 530.
16. Edmund deS. Brunner et al., *American Agricultural Villages* (New York, 1927), pp. 157–159; Brunner, *Churches of Distinction in Town and Country* (New York, 1923), p. 47; R. Richard Wohl, "The 'Country Boy' Myth and Its Place in American Urban Culture: The Nineteenth-Century Contribution," ed. Moses Rischin, *Perspectives in American History* 3 (1969):150–153.
17. William H. Kendrick, *The 4-H Trail* (Boston, 1926), pp. 2–6.
18. Ibid., p. 6.
19. Jesse Steiner, *The American Community in Action: Case Studies of American Communities* (New York, 1928), p. 150.
20. On adult-sponsored youth organizations in a metropolis, see Nettie P. McGill and Ellen N. Mathews, *The Youth of New York City* (New York, 1940), chap. 13.
21. William B. Forbush, *The Boy Problem: A Study in Social Pedagogy*, introduced by G. Stanley Hall (Philadelphia, 1902), p. 73.
22. *Thirty-Third Annual Report of the Boy Scouts of America, 1942*, 78th Cong., 1st sess., House Doc. no. 17, p. 16.
23. In 1924 the percentage of scoutmasters who were clergymen was half of what it had been in 1919, 11.02 percent rather than 22.2 percent. In 1924, 37.08 percent of scoutmasters had "mercantile" occupations; see *Fifteenth Annual Report of the Boy Scouts of America, 1924*, 69th Cong. 1st sess., House Doc. no. 109, pp. 142, 149.
24. Robert S. Lynd and Helen M. Lynd, *Middletown: A Study in Contemporary American Culture* (New York, 1929), p. 211.
25. Hollingshead, *Elmtown's Youth*, p. 90.
26. Ibid., passim; Gordon W. Lovejoy, *Paths to Maturity: Findings of the North Carolina Youth Survey, 1938–1940* (n.p., 1940), p. 148. A few attempts have been made to launch working-class alternatives to scouting, the most notable being the establishment in 1924 of Pioneer Youth for Democracy under the influence of the American Federation of Labor. Pioneer Youth bore some resemblance to the Kibbo Kift Kindred, founded in Britain in 1924 as a working-class rival to the primitive nationalism and paramilitary organization of the early scouting movement. See "A New Education for Labor," *New Republic* 43 (June 10, 1925):60–62; Leslie Paul, *The Republic of Children: A Handbook for Teachers of Working-Class Children* (London, 1938), pp. 27–31.

27. Hollingshead, *Elmtown's Youth*, p. 252.
28. Ibid., p. 246.
29. Ibid., p. 149.
30. Ibid., pp. 150–151.
31. Ibid., p. 169.
32. Ibid., pp. 389–390.
33. David Matza, *Delinquency and Drift* (New York, 1964), pp. 12–21; Arthur E. Fink, *Causes of Crime: Biological Theories in the United States, 1800–1915* (Philadelphia, 1938). For an illustration of the positivist mentality, see V. C. Branham, "The Classification and Treatment of the Defective Delinquent," *Journal of the American Institute of Criminal Law and Criminology* 17 (August 1926): 183–217. For a contemporary critique of positivism, see W. Beran Wolfe, "The Psychopathology of the Juvenile Delinquent," *Journal of Delinquency* 11 (September 1927): 159. On the Chicago school, see James F. Short's introduction to Clifford R. Shaw and Henry D. McKay, *Juvenile Delinquency and Urban Areas*, rev. ed. (Chicago, 1969), pp. xxv–liv.
34. G. Stanley Hall, *Adolescence: Its Psychology and Its Relations to Anthropology, Sociology, Sex, Crime, Religion and Education*, 2 vols. (New York, 1905), vol. 1, chap. 5.
35. Ben B. Lindsey and Wainwright Evans, *The Revolt of Modern Youth* (New York, 1925), pp. 81–83.
36. Ibid., pp. 82–83.
37. Frederic Thrasher, *The Gang: A Study of 1313 Gangs in Chicago* (Chicago, 1929), chap. 20.
38. William Healy and Augusta F. Bronner, *Delinquents and Criminals; Their Making and Unmaking: Studies in Two American Cities* (New York, 1926), p. 216; on rates of recidivism, see ibid, pp. 117–120.
39. Harry M. Shulman, *Juvenile Delinquency in American Society* (New York, 1961), pp. 19–20; Paul Lerman, *Juvenile Delinquency and Social Policy* (New York, 1970), pp. 24–25.
40. Shaw and McKay, *Juvenile Delinquency and Urban Areas*, p. 43. Interestingly, Shaw and McKay rejected an even looser definition of delinquency proposed by the 1930 White House Conference on Children and Youth: "any such juvenile misconduct as might be dealt with under the law" (in other words, whether or not it was dealt with).
41. Arthur W. Towne, "Shall the Age Jurisdiction of Juvenile Courts Be Increased?" *Journal of the American Institute of Criminal Law and Criminology* 10 (February 1920): 493–502. By 1912, twenty-two states had enacted separate juvenile court laws; by 1932 every state but two had a juvenile court system organized under separate law. In 1914 the Chicago Boys' Court extended juvenile court procedure to those aged 16 to 21. As of 1927 a juvenile could be tried as a minor under his 18th birthday in fourteen states, 16th birthday in thirteen states, 19th birthday in one state, and 20th birthday in one state. Even in 1970 there were wide variations among states, although the age range affected by the juvenile court was never lower than 16 or higher than 21. See Robert Bremner et al., eds., *Children and Youth in America: A Documentary History*, 3 vols., (Cambridge, Mass. 1971), vol. 2, pp. 440–441; H. H. Lou, *Juvenile Courts in the United States* (Chapel Hill, 1927), pp. 47–48; Lerman, *Juvenile Delinquency and Social Policy*, p. 22. Although the concept of adolescence was used to justify the upward extension of the age jurisdiction of juvenile courts, the real impulse might have been administrative rather than psychological. That is, upward extension of age jurisdiction might have appealed to legislators because it made it easier to place juvenile offenders on probation and thus helped to relieve the overcrowding of reform schools.
42. Gerald D. Suttles, *The Social Order of the Slum: Ethnicity and Territory in the Inner City* (preface by Morris Janowitz, Chicago, 1968), p. 169, note 5.
43. Edmund W. Vaz, ed., *Middle-Class Juvenile Delinquency* (New York, 1967).
44. Thrasher, *The Gang*, pp. 191–220.
45. Suttles, *The Social Order of the Slum*, pp. 166–167, 170.
46. Walter F. Whyte, *Street Corner Society: The Social Structure of an Italian Slum* (Chicago, 1955), pp. 354–356; Harold P. Levy, *Building a Popular Movement: A Case Study of the Public Relations of the Boy Scouts of America* (New York, 1956), p. 87.

47. Thrasher, *The Gang*, pp. 288–289.

48. Goodwin Watson, *Youth After Conflict* (New York, 1947), p. 49. By 1926 there were twenty times as many articles on the conduct of youth indexed in the *Reader's Guide to Periodical Literature* as there had been in 1918.

49. George A. Coe, *What Ails Our Youth?* (New York, 1924). Ben B. Lindsey described the juvenile court as "a moral hospital"; see Lindsey and Evans, *The Revolt of Modern Youth*, p. 75.

50. Miriam Van Waters, "The Juvenile Court as a Social Laboratory," *Journal of Applied Sociology* 7 (1923):318.

51. W. I. Thomas, *The Unadjusted Girl, With Cases and Standpoint for Behavior Analysis* (Boston, 1923), p. 71.

52. Miriam Van Waters, *Youth in Conflict* (New York, 1925), p. 117.

53. Margaret Mead, "Adolescence in Primitive and Modern Society," in V. F. Calverton and Samuel D. Schmalhausen, *The New Generation: The Intimate Problems of Modern Parents and Children* (New York, 1930), pp. 173, 174.

54. Lynd and Lynd, *Middletown*, chap. 21; Hollingshead, *Elmtown's Youth*, p. 6.

55. A Professor, "The Young Person," *Atlantic Monthly* 135 (February 1925), 217.

56. Lindsey and Evans, *The Revolt of Modern Youth*, p. 81.

57. Lynd and Lynd, *Middletown*, pp. 137–138.

58. Albert Blumenthal, *A Sociological Study of a Small Town* (Chicago, 1933), p. 246.

59. U. S. Bureau of the Census, *Historical Statistics of the United States: Colonial Times to 1957* (Washington, D.C., 1960), pp. 211–212.

60. Quoted in Phyllis Blanchard and Carolyn Manasses, *New Girls for Old* (New York, 1930), p. 1; Ernest Earnest, *Academic Procession: An Informal History of the American College, 1636–1953* (Indianapolis, 1953), pp. 268–272; Calvin B. T. Lee, *The Campus Scene, 1900–1970: Changing Styles in Undergraduate Life* (New York, 1970), pp. 34–35. For fraternities and sororities, I have counted the number of chapters established per decade, 1900 to 1939, using as a source Harold J. Baily, ed., *Baird's Manual of American College Fraternities*, 15th ed. (Menasha, Wis., 1949), pp. 83–444. For social fraternities, 366 chapters were established between 1900 and 1909; 363, 1910–1919; 761, 1920–1929; and 349, 1930–1939. For social sororities the comparable figures are 203 in 1900–1909; 380, 1910–1919; 658, 1920–1929; and 337, 1930–1939.

61. Lewis M. Terman et al., *Psychological Factors in Marital Happiness* (New York, 1938), p. 321.

62. On Kinsey, see Daniel Scott Smith, "The Dating of the American Sexual Revolution: Evidence and Interpretation," in Michael Gordon, ed., *The American Family in Social-Historical Perspective* (New York, 1973), pp. 328–329.

63. Terman, *Psychological Factors*, p. 43. In Terman's sample, 47.8 percent of the husbands and 38.1 percent of the wives were college graduates. The mean age of the husbands was 38.84 years; of the wives, 35.7 (ibid., p. 44). Hence, a preponderance of Terman's subjects would have graduated from college around 1920, when only 8.09 percent of the population aged 18–21 was enrolled in college. On the biases of Kinsey's sample, see Smith, "The Dating of the American Sexual Revolution," p. 328.

64. Ibid. The rate of premarital pregnancy can be calculated from the number of births that occur within nine months of marriage. This has obvious limitations as a measure of changing standards of sexual and moral conduct; a fair degree of tolerance has long been extended to premarital intercourse between an engaged couple. See also Theodore Newcomb, "Recent Changes in Attitudes Toward Sex and Marriage," *American Sociological Review* 2 (October, 1937):664. On the sexual mores of lower-class youth in the 1920s, see Thrasher, *The Gang*, pp. 236–238, 243.

65. James R. McGovern, "The American Woman's Pre–World War I Freedom in Manners and Morals," *Journal of American History* 55 (September 1968): 315–333; Henry F. May, *The End of American Innocence: A Study of the First Years of Our Own Time, 1912–1917* (New York, 1959); David M. Kennedy, *Birth Control in America: The Career of Margaret Sanger* (New Haven, 1970); Earnest, *Academic Procession*, p. 249.

66. Michael Gordon, "From an Unfortunate Necessity to a Cult of Mutual Orgasm: Sex in American Marital Education Literature, 1830–1940," in James Henslin, ed., *Studies in the Sociology of Sex* (New York, 1971), pp. 61–62, 64–73.

67. Gertrude Atherton, *Black Oxen* (New York, 1923), esp. pp. 135–146; Paul Kammerer, *Rejuvenation and the Prolongation of Human Efficiency: Experiments with the Steinach Operation on Man and Animals* (New York, 1923).

68. Mark Schorer, *Sinclair Lewis: An American Life* (Toronto, 1961), p. 3. For changes in the novel of youth, contrast Herman Melville's *Redburn: His First Voyage* (New York, 1849) and Benét's *The Beginning of Wisdom* (New York, 1921). See also J. F. Carter, " 'These Wild Young People,' By One of Them," *Atlantic Monthly* 126 (September 1920):301–304; Ellen W. Page, "A Flapper's Appeal to Parents," *Outlook* 132 (December 6, 1922):607.

69. On Julius Langbehn, see Fritz Stern, *The Politics of Cultural Despair: A Study in the Rise of German Ideology* (Berkeley, 1961), pp. 166–169. On youth polls, see Lee, *The Campus Scene*, pp. 34–35; William I. Engle, "Some Undangerous Ages," *Outlook* 130 (March 8, 1922):380; Blanchard and Manasses, *New Girls for Old*, pp. 263–264; Watson, *Youth After Conflict*, pp. 74–80. On Berger, see Gary Schwartz and Dan Merten, "The Language of Adolescence," *American Journal of Sociology* 72 (March 1967):454, note 2. On the idea of adolescent culture as a myth, see Frederick A. Elkin and William A. Westley, "The Myth of Adolescent Culture," *American Sociological Review* 20 (December 1955):680–684. For a strong statement of the oppositional nature of the adolescent subculture, see James S. Coleman, *The Adolescent Society: The Social Life of the Teenager and Its Impact on Education* (New York, 1961). But see also Coleman's reassessment of his position in his foreword to Denise B. Kandel and Gerald S. Lesser, *Youth in Two Worlds* (San Francisco, 1972), pp. xiii–xiv.

70. Matza, *Delinquency and Drift*, p. 28.

71. Ibid., p. 26; Lynd and Lynd, *Middletown*, pp. 138–139.

72. Samuel H. Adams [Warner Fabian, pseud.], *Flaming Youth* (New York, 1923); *Boston Transcript*, March 3, 1923, p. 3.

73. Anne Temple, "Reaping the Whirlwind," *Forum* 76 (July 1926):22.

74. Edward A. Krug, *The Shaping of the American High School. Vol. 2:1920–1941* (Madison, 1972), pp. 218–219, 311.

75. *Thirty-Third Annual Report of the Boy Scouts of America, 1942*, 78th Cong., 1st sess. no. 17, p. 16.

76. Wellington G. Pierce, *Youth Comes of Age* (New York, 1948), opposite frontispiece.

77. "Crazy Kids with Cars," *Newsweek* 53 (March 2, 1959):26–30; Jesse Bernard, "Teen-Age Culture: An Overview," in Vaz, ed., *Middle-Class Juvenile Delinquency*, p. 38. On the age of menarche, see J. M. Tanner, "Sequence, Tempo, and Individual Variation in the Growth and Development of Boys and Girls Aged Twelve to Sixteen," *Daedalus* 100 (Fall 1971):929. Tanner's data is for Western Europe. On the age of marriage, see Ben J. Wattenberg, in collaboration with Richard M. Scammon, *This U.S.A.: An Unexpected Family Portrait of 194,067,296 Americans Drawn From the Census* (Garden City, N.Y., 1965), p. 35.

78. Grace Hechinger and Fred M. Hechinger, *Teen-Age Tyranny* (Greenwich, Conn., 1964), pp. 132–133, 141–142; Dwight Macdonald, "A Caste, A Culture, A Market," *New Yorker* 34 (November 22, 1958):57–94; ibid. (Nov. 29, 1958):57–107.

79. Lewis Yablonsky, *The Violent Gang* (New York, 1962), p. 147; George Paloczi-Horvath, *Youth up in Arms: A Political and Social World Survey, 1955–1970* (London, 1971), pp. 84–86, 91–92; Hunter S. Thompson, *Hell's Angels: The Strange and Terrible Saga of the Outlaw Motorcycle Gang* (New York, 1967).

80. These statements are derived from the following *Annual Reports* of the Boy Scouts of America (by public law submitted to Congress): *15th* (1924), 69th Congr, 1st sess., House Doc. no. 109, pp. 147–149; *40th* (1949), 81st Cong., 2nd sess., House Doc. no. 534, pp. 5–11; *49th* (1958), 86th Cong., 1st sess., House Doc. no. 101, pp. 5–6; *57th* (1966), 90th Cong., 1st sess., House Doc. no. 87, p. 209; *58th* (1967), 90th Cong., 2nd sess., House Doc. no. 287, pp. 119–121; *Girl Scouts of the United States of America, Annual Report, 1953*, 83rd Cong., 2nd sess., House Doc. no. 359, p. 3.

81. "Youth in College," *Fortune* 13 (June 1936):99–102, 157–158, 162.

82. Earnest, *Academic Procession*, pp. 298–303.

83. Bernard, "Teen-Age Culture," pp. 36–37. On left-wing student politics in the 1930s, see Lewis S. Feuer, *The Conflict of Generations: The Character and Significance of Student Movements* (New York, 1969), pp. 341–353.

84. Richard Flacks, "The Liberated Generation: An Exploration of the Roots of Student Protest," in Anthony M. Orum, ed., *The Seeds of Politics: Youth and Politics in America* (Englewood Cliffs, N.J., 1972), pp. 353–364; Jeanne H. Block et al., "Socialization Correlates of Student Activism," in ibid., pp. 215–231.

85. On the growth of the new middle class, see Lewis Corey, *The Crisis of the Middle Class* (New York, 1935), p. 142; Daniel Bell, *The Coming of Post-Industrial Society: A Venture in Social Forecasting* (New York, 1973), pp. 129–136. On changes in child socialization, see Garry C. Myers, *The Modern Parent: A Practical Guide to Everyday Problems*, introduced by Michael V. O'Shea (New York, 1931), chap. 1; Daniel H. Calhoun, *The Intelligence of a People* (Princeton, 1973), pp. 25–27. One major exception to the tendency noted in the text was the popularity, particularly in the 1920s and 1930s, of rigid scheduling in infancy, an offshoot of Watsonian behaviorism.

86. John R. Seeley, R. Alexander Sim, and Elizabeth W. Loosely, *Crestwood Heights: A Study of the Culture of Suburban Life* (New York, 1956), pp. 99, 304.

87. Herbert J. Gans, *The Levittowners: Ways of Life and Politics in a New Suburban Community* (New York, 1967), p. 30.

88. Daniel R. Miller and Guy E. Swanson, *The Changing American Parent: A Study in the Detroit Area* (New York, 1958), chap. 4; Coleman, *Adolescent Society*, p. 292. Some investigators have found that the fundamental cleavage in child socialization patterns is between middle and working class rather than between the bureaucratic and entrepreneurial middle classes; see Allison Davis, "American Status System and the Socialization of the Child," *American Sociological Review* 6 (June 1941): 345–356.

89. Gans, *The Levittowners*, p. 30. This mixture of child orientation and child-centeredness pervaded much of the post-1920 literature on how parents could be "pals" with their children. See, for example, H. C. Fulcher, "My Son and I Go Fishing," *Parents Magazine* 5 (May 1930):32–33; J. P. Warbasse, "Fathers as Pals," *Parents Magazine* 11 (August 1936):74.

90. Coleman, *Adolescent Society;* Schwartz and Merten, "The Language of Adolescence," pp. 457–459.

91. Kenneth Keniston, *Young Radicals: Notes on Committed Youth* (New York, 1968), pp. 273, 279. In Keniston's view, these qualities were shared both by political activists and cultural dissenters in the 1960s.

92. On the mediocratizing tendencies of the adolescent subculture, see Matilda W. Riley and Samuel H. Flowerman, "Group Relations As a Variable in Communications Research," *American Sociological Review* 16 (April 1951):174–180; Ralph Turner, *The Social Context of Ambition: A Study of High-School Seniors in Los Angeles* (San Franscisco, 1964), pp. 164–170.

93. Willard Waller, "The Rating and Dating Complex," *American Sociological Review* 2 (October 1937):727–734; President's Science Advisory Committee, Panel on Youth, *Youth: Transition to Adulthood* (Washington, D.C., 1973), pp. 115–116.

94. Theodore Roszak, *The Making of a Counter Culture* (New York, 1969); Charles Reich, *The Greening of America* (New York, 1970); Richard King, *The Party of Eros: Radical Social Thought and the Realm of Freedom* (Chapel Hill, 1972), pp. 178–204.

95. Albert Parry, *Garrets and Pretenders: A History of Bohemianism in America* (New York, 1933). For a suggestive analysis of the relationship between youth culture during the 1960s and class cultures, see Herbert J. Gans, *Popular Culture and High Culture* (New York, 1974), pp. 94–100.

96. Carol B. Stack, *All Our Kin: Strategies for Survival in a Black Community* (New York, 1974), chap. 5.

INDEX

Index

Female influence, 112; in churches, 192; in
infancy, 14–16
Fertility rate, 115
Feuer, Lewis S., 59
Fights, 53–54, 91, 92
Fine system in colonial colleges, 56, 57
Finney, Charles G., 64
Fire companies: professionalization of,
91–92; volunteer, 40, 90–93
Fisher, Dorothy Canfield, 231–234, 236
Fisk, Ezra, 71
Fisk, Pliny, 67
Five Points district (New York City), 89
Flaming Youth (Adams), 264
Fleming, Sandford, 281n
Flexner, Abraham, 156, 174
Flushing Institute, 122
Foot, Samuel A., 16
Forbush, William B., 195, 223, 252
Forrest, Edwin, 93
Forrester, Charles, 91
Fortune (magazine), 267
Forty Little Thieves, 89
Foster, John, 105–107, 163
Foundation Stones of Success, The (Markham,
ed.), 171
4-H, 250
4-H Trail, The (Kendrick), 250, 251
Fowler, Orson, 134–136, 139, 140
Fox, David, 100
Fox, Edward, 100
France, 16
Fraternities, 176, 177, 185–186, 260
Freedom, 38, 41, 42; of college students, 52,
56, 57; semidependence and, 29, 42, 60;
social class and, 29
Freyd, Max, 242
Frothingham, Octavius B., 18
Fundamentalist Protestants, 251

Gambling, 88
Gangs, 88–93, 187, 254, 256–258, 263–266
Gannett, Ezra Stiles, 17
Gans, Herbert J., 168
Garrison, William Lloyd, 74
Geary, John W., 39
General Assembly of the Presbyterian
Church, 69
Generational conflict, 75, 263–264
George, William R., 223
Georgia Scenes (Longstreet), 47
Germany, 216
Getting on in the World (Mathews), 163
Gibson, H. W., 224
Gilbert, Eugene, 265
Gilmore, William G., 278n

Girls: boys-workers' views of, 224; in cities,
95–96; conduct-of-life books for, 138, 233;
education of, 20–21, 129, 138, 141, 142;
homeleaving of, 95–96, 247; in 19th cen-
tury, 137–142; puberty and, 44, 134, 141;
religious conversion of, 65, 75–79; *See also*
Children
"Going steady," 270–271
Graduate education, 179, 270
Great Awakening (1740s and 1750s), 63, 64,
76
Greele, Samuel, 101
Greene, Nathanael, 11
Greven, Philip J., Jr., 81, 274n
Griffen, Capt., 47
Griscom, John, 122
Griswold, Samuel C., 95
Groton School, 122
Group membership vs. individual success,
236
Growth, physical, 44–45
Gulick, Luther Halsey, 171, 201, 203–204,
208

Haddock, Frank C., 166
Hall, Rev. C. Cuthbert, 165
Hall, G. Stanley, 6, 62–63, 66–67, 71, 79–81,
118, 119, 171, 204–207, 216–229, 234–239,
243, 244, 262; adolescent psychology of,
218, 220–223; child study movement and,
228–229; on delinquency, 255; on educa-
tion, 219; on military training, 219–220;
personal life of, 217–218, 220; on recapitu-
lation, 218–219, 224; social educators and,
236–237
Hamilton College laws (1802), 52
Hammond, Charles, 128
Hammond, Edward Payson, 118
Harrison (Professor), 54
Harvard Divinity School, 71
Harvard University, 53, 55–57, 178
Hasseltine, Ann, 72, 75
Haverhill Academy, 275n
Hawes, Joel, 95, 107
Hazard, Blanche, 149
Hazen, Edward, 94
Hazen, Henry A., 276n
Hazing, 58, 178
Headley, J. T., 89
Healy, William, 230, 256
Height of youth, 44
Henderson, Ernest R., 241
Heroin use, 188
Hewett, E. C., 131
Hierarchy: in colleges, 58, 59; in families,
45–46; in schools, 50; in the South, 35

conversion of, 65, 75–79; sexual behavior of, study of, 261, 262; teachers, 123–125, 129–130, 234; *See also* Motherhood; Mothers; *and entries starting with* Female

Women of New York, or Social Life in the Great City (Ellington), 88

Women's Christian Temperance Union, 171, 192, 193

Wood, Fernando, 93

Woods, Leonard, 76–78

Worcester Free Institute, 156, 157

Work, *see* Labor of children

Work ethic, 246

Working-class families, 169, 170

Working-class youth, 151, 171

Working Man's Advocate (New York), 148

Wright, Carroll, 146

Wright, Henry B., 208

Wright, Henry Clarke, 83–84

Wylie, Lawrence, 290*n*

Yale Moral Society, 70

Yale University, 52, 53, 55, 56, 74, 175

YMCA, *see* Young Men's Christian Association

York, Brantley, 41

Young, Ella Flagg, 183

Young Christian, The (Abbott), 65

Young Man Entering Business, The (Marden), 166

Young Man's Friend, The (Eddy), 95, 162–163

Young Man's Guide, The (Alcott), 95

"Young men," use of phrase, 11, 13, 44

Young Men's Association of the City of Milwaukee, 40

Young Men's Christian Association, 40, 73, 102, 199–201, 203, 204, 207, 248–250

Young Men's Missionary Society of New York, 75

Young Men's New York Bible Society, 43

"Young people," usage of term, 11, 13, 65, 247

Young people's societies, *see* Societies

Young People's Society for Christian Endeavor, 13

"Young People's Total Abstinence Society," 39

"Young Riflemen," 39

Youth: brotherhood of, in modern youth movements, 74; censure of, 103; childhood and adulthood distinguished from, 12–13; counselors' view of (1800s), 102–103; defined, in conduct-of-life books, 95; as difficult time, 81; early 20th-century views of, 243–244; mid-19th-century view of, 118–119; prolongation of, 167–168; as time of indecision, 36, 37; as time of preparation, 167; usage of word, 11–13, 44, 248; *See also* Adolescence

Youth and Life (Bourne), 168, 262

Youth counselors, 95, 102–108, 112, 133, 163, 167, 168; *See also* Success writers

Youth culture: lower-class, 87, 90, 93; postadolescent, 269, 270; postmodern, 270, 271

Youth organizations: adult-sponsored, *see* Adult-sponsored youth organizations; *See also* Societies

Youth subculture, middle-class, 258, 262–266, 269

Youth workers, 61; *See also* Boys-work

Youthfulness, 167, 168, 198

327